Organizational Communication and Technology in the Time of Coronavirus

Larry D. Browning
Jan-Oddvar Sørnes • Peer Jacob Svenkerud
Editors

Organizational Communication and Technology in the Time of Coronavirus

Ethnographies from the First Year of the Pandemic

palgrave
macmillan

Editors
Larry D. Browning
Business School
Nord University
Bodø, Norway

Jan-Oddvar Sørnes
Business School
Nord University
Bodø, Norway

Peer Jacob Svenkerud
Inland Norway University of
Applied Science
Elverum, Norway

ISBN 978-3-030-94813-9 ISBN 978-3-030-94814-6 (eBook)
https://doi.org/10.1007/978-3-030-94814-6

This Palgrave Macmillan imprint is published by the registered company Springer Nature Switzerland AG.
The registered company address is: Gewerbestrasse 11, 6330 Cham, Switzerland

Preface

Let us first lay out our rationale for this collection of ethnographies of organizational communication during the first eight months of the COVID-19 pandemic beginning in 2020. Given the pandemic's historic importance, we thought it useful (1) to collect, for future study, the personal and professional impact of it on a broad subset of communication scholars, and (2) to have them relate those experiences narratively.

In brief, what was the story of organizational communication and technology (OCT) in the early months of the virus?

Ahead, you will hear from a collection of scholars explain how they grappled with the coronavirus, typically both in their workplace and at home. For them, as for all of us, the challenges proved life-changing. Indeed, since its beginning in late January 2020 and its official recognition as a pandemic on March 11, 2020, when the World Health Organization (WHO) declared the coronavirus an official pandemic, this virus has turned everyone's world upside down.

Bodø, Norway — Larry D. Browning, Jan-Oddvar Sørnes

Elverum, Norway — Peer Jacob Svenkerud

Acknowledgments

We thank Nord University and Inland Norway University of Applied Sciences for the grant support to edit this book. A special thanks goes to John Trimble, Distinguished Teaching Professor of English Emeritus, University of Texas at Austin for editing the introduction and conclusion to this book. To Victoria who does art with spirit and to Wencke who looks like a princess on her way to the castle, we thank you from the bottom of our hearts.

Contents

Notes on Contributors

Ana M. Aquilar is a doctoral candidate in organizational communication and technology at The University of Texas at Austin. Her research centers around the topics of resilience, trauma, and time in various contexts. She is a program research analyst with The David and Lucile Packard Foundation.

Karen Lee Ashcraft, PhD, is Professor of Organizational Communication at the University of Colorado Boulder, USA. She studies gender as it intersects with other relations of difference to constitute various scenes of labor. Her work draws on communication theories of culture, identity, and affect toward the goal of greater diversity, dignity, and equity in work and organizational life.

Brianna L. Avalos (MA, San Diego State University) is a doctoral candidate in the Hugh Downs School of Human Communication at Arizona State University. She is interested in researching strong-tied dyads, social support, and organizational stress.

Bjørn Tallak Bakken (PhD, BI Norwegian Business School) is Associate Professor of Crisis Management at the Department of Organization, Leadership and Management, Inland Norway School of Business. He is the head of the BA program in crisis management, and specializes in strategic and operational decision making applied to crisis management.

Dawna I. Ballard, PhD, is Associate Professor of Organizational Communication and Technology at the University of Texas at Austin and an expert in chronemics—the study of time as it is bound to human communication. She researches what drives our pace of life and its impact on the communication practices and long-term vitality of organizations, communities, and individuals.

Jean M. Bartunek is the Robert A. and Evelyn J. Ferris Chair and Professor of Management and Organization at Boston College. She is a past president of the Academy of Management and past dean of the Fellows of the Academy of Management. Her primary research interests have to do with organizational change and academic-practitioner relationships.

Larry D. Browning (PhD, Ohio State University) is Professor Emeritus, William P. Hobby Centennial Professor of Communication, Department of Communication Studies, University of Texas at Austin, Moody College of Communication, and Adjunct Professor of Management, Nord University Business School, Bodø, Norway.

Barry Brummett is the Charles Sapp Centennial Professor of Communication in the Communication Studies Department of the University of Texas at Austin. He received his PhD from the University of Minnesota in 1978. Brummett studies the rhetoric of popular culture. He has previously held faculty positions at Purdue University and at the University of Wisconsin at Milwaukee, and has a Concurrent Faculty Appointment, Zhengzhou University, P.R.C., and is Honorary Director, Rhetorical Criticism Research Center of Shanghai University, P.R.C.

Barbara Czarniawska is Senior Professor of Management Studies at Gothenburg Research Institute, University of Gothenburg, Sweden. She takes a feminist and processual perspective on organizing, recently exploring connections between popular culture and practice of management, the future of the welfare state, and the robotization of work. She is interested in techniques of fieldwork and in the application of narratology to social science studies.

Stephanie L. Dailey (PhD, The University of Texas at Austin) is an associate professor in the Department of Communication Studies at Texas State University. Her research explores the processes of organizational socialization and identification—how people learn about and feel part of organizations.

June Borge Doornich, PhD, is Associate Professor of Strategy and Control, and the Vice Dean of Education at the Business School, Nord University. She is an expert in management of international business and has a strong passion and curiosity for how mindfulness promotes extraordinary leadership qualities and capabilities.

Luke A. Dye (MA, Texas State University) is a PhD student in the Department of Communication at Cornell University. His research approaches communication in dyadic, group, and organizational contexts, and focuses on how communication can help people feel supported, included, and valued. Much of his work explores specific populations, like US military servicemembers, veterans, and their families.

Åse Storhaug Hole (Cand Scient., Norwegian School of Sports), MPA, University of Karlstad, is Professor of Organization and Management at the Department of Organization, Leadership and Management, Inland Norway School of Business. Research interests are crises management, leadership, and whistleblowing.

Sheryl Johnson-Fambro obtained her MA from Wayne State University and works full-time in corporate communications.

Kerk Fong Kee (PhD, The University of Texas at Austin) is Associate Professor of Media and Communication at Texas Tech University and his research focuses on the diffusion of innovations—the study of how a new technology, behavior, idea, and/or social movement, and so on spread in social systems over time. He investigates diffusion in organizational, science, health, environmental, and societal contexts.

Prosper Ameh Kwei-Narh, PhD, is Associate Professor of Work and Organizational Psychology at the Inland Norway University of Applied Sciences. He researches on team performance, talent management, and team communication.

Shelby Lasky is an MA student of public relations and organizational communication at Wayne State University.

Allison Lucas, MPA, is a PhD student of Communication at Wayne State University and NSF-funded trainee in the Transformative Research in Urban Sustainability Training (T-RUST) program. Her research focuses on the intersections of urban sustainability and entrepreneurship.

Jens Petter Madsbu, PhD is an associate professor at Inland School of Business and Social Sciences, Norway. He is the head of the Department of Organization, Leadership and Management. He researches on digitalization, qualitative methods, public sector reforms, and management.

Laura Martinez (MA, California State University, Fullerton) is a doctoral candidate in the Hugh Downs School of Human Communication at Arizona State University. Her research interests include identity work, organizational and group-level identification, resilience in the face of trauma, sensemaking, socialization, and qualitative methods.

Rahul Mitra, PhD, is Associate Professor of Organizational Communication at Wayne State University and he examines how communicative practices enable resilience in a variety of organizations and communities. His scholarship focuses on environmental organizing, corporate social responsibility (CSR), grassroots entrepreneurship, and meaningful work.

Martin N. Ndlela, PhD, is Professor of Communication at Inland School of Business and Social Sciences, Norway, and research associate at the Department of Strategic Communication, University of Johannesburg in South Africa. He researches on crisis communication, social media, digital communication, and organizational communication.

Josef Pallas is a professor at the Department of Business Studies, Uppsala University, Uppsala, Sweden. His research focuses on organization and governance of public sector organizations in general, and universities, governmental agencies, and municipalities in particular. He is interested in dynamics, consequences, and interplay of governing ideas connected to public appraisal and evaluation, media and news production, communication, as well as the issues associated with professionalism and collegiality.

Sarah A. Parker is the social media manager for MURAL and brings to that position years of experience in content marketing for various tech companies, as well as years of freelance writing work, speaking, and guest lecturing. All of this is supported by an unfortunate dedication to being Extremely Online.

Elena Raviola is Torsten and Wanja Söderberg Professor of Design Management at the Academy of Art and Design, University of Gothenburg. She is also director of the Business and Design Lab, a research center between the Faculty of Arts and the School of Business, Economics and Law at the University of Gothenburg. Her research explores how digitalization and automation transform the organization of professional work, especially in the cultural and creative industries.

Rebecca M. Rice (PhD, University of Colorado Boulder) is an assistant professor in the Department of Communication Studies at University of Nevada, Las Vegas. Her research focuses on interorganizational collaboration and risk and crisis organizing using ethnographic methods.

Leif Rydstedt, PhD, is Senior Professor of Work and Organizational Psychology at the Inland Norway University of Applied Sciences. His major research themes are consequences of job strain, recovery from work-related strain, and the role of the environment in the recovery process, as well as working conditions for elderly workers.

Frode Soelberg (PhD, University of Nordland) is Associate Professor of Entrepreneurial Marketing at Nord University Business School and an expert in small business management and marketing in new ventures.

Jan-Oddvar Sørnes (PhD, NTNU) is Professor of Organizational Communication at Nord University Business School and adjunct professor at Inland Norway University of Applied Science.

B. Liahnna Stanley (MA, University of South Florida) is a doctoral student in the Hugh Downs School of Human Communication at Arizona State University, an institution located on the unceded homelands of the Tohono O'odham, Akimel O'otham, and Pee-posh Peoples.

Keri K. Stephens (PhD, The University of Texas at Austin) is Professor of Organizational Communication Technology, a Distinguished Teaching Professor, and Co-Director of TIPI in the Moody College of Communication at The University of Texas at Austin. Her research program examines the role of technology in organizational practices and organizing processes, especially in contexts of crisis, disaster, and health.

Peer Jacob Svenkerud (PhD, Ohio University) is professor and rector at Inland Norway University of Applied Science, Norway, and adjunct professor at Nord University Business School, Bodø Norway.

Susan Szmania (PhD, The University of Texas at Austin) is an independent scholar and expert in countering violent extremism. She has held multiple academic and government positions at the US Department of Homeland Security and the US State Department, where she served abroad in Sweden, Spain, and Jordan. Szmania earned her doctorate in Communication Studies from the University of Texas at Austin.

Sophia Town (PhD, Arizona State University) is Assistant Professor of Organizational Behavior at the Gabelli School of Business, Fordham University. Her research centers around leadership, mindfulness, and human flourishing in an increasingly complex world.

Sarah J. Tracy (PhD, University of Colorado) is Professor of Organizational Communication and Qualitative Methodology and Interim Director of the Hugh Downs School of Human Communication at Arizona State University. Her teaching and research focus on emotion, leadership, and human flourishing.

Claire Van Raaphorst is a marketing and communications professional, who obtained her MA from Wayne State University.

Tine Viveka Westerberg is Assistant Professor of Maritime Management at the University of South-Eastern Norway and is an expert on maritime competence. She researches the potential and the challenges of maritime industry and university cooperation, focusing on the development of maritime competence for the future.

Alaina C. Zanin (PhD, University of Oklahoma) is Assistant Professor of Organizational and Health Communication in the Hugh Downs School of Human Communication at Arizona State University. Her research interests include structuration and sensemaking theories as well as organizing issues related to identity, power, and resistance.

List of Figures

List of Tables

CHAPTER 1

Organizational Communication and Technology in the Time of Coronavirus: Ethnographies from the First Year of the Pandemic

Larry D. Browning, Jan-Oddvar Sørnes, and Peer Jacob Svenkerud

Focus of the Book

We want to analyze the communication conditions at the beginning of the pandemic by writing ethnographically about the event as it unfolded over time. Our chief research question was: How do we make sense of our work life via the way we communicate in this new and dangerous coronavirus

L. D. Browning (✉) • J.-O. Sørnes
Business School, Nord University, Bodø, Norway
e-mail: lbrowning@austin.utexas.edu; lbrowning@mail.utexas.edu; Jan-Oddvar.Sornes@nord.no

P. J. Svenkerud
Inland Norway University of Applied Science, Elverum, Norway
e-mail: peer.svenkerud@inn.no

L. D. Browning et al. (eds.), *Organizational Communication and Technology in the Time of Coronavirus*,
https://doi.org/10.1007/978-3-030-94814-6_1

world? Also, how do our lives change? This pandemic may not only be an elongated emergency; it may in fact mark that rare moment in time when everything is forever different. It may indeed be the new normal. But how did people experience its outset—that crazy transitional period?

The stories told in this book are by, and about, people who make their living communicating to an array of audiences and stakeholders who form a part of their professional life.

We offer here three types of ethnographies of communication. One type takes the form of pure autoethnographies written from a personal perspective (Bochner & Ellis, 2002). Others are ethnographic reports on analytic subjects, including university students, frontline emergency workers, and medical-school students. Still others are techno-ethnographies, which are social-scientific analyses of subcultures, without much attention to the emotion and personal orientation typical of ethnographies. We include all three types here, as all three offer valuable perspectives on that early period of the pandemic.

These ethnographies can be viewed as stories. Stories are structured through a sequence of non-random past events connected to each other in a way that schematizes the meaning for the listener or reader (Ricoeur, 1984). Narrative's structure allows us to analyze functions both within and across narratives (Dailey & Browning, 2014). The most compelling way to represent experience, we believe, is through a story.

Our chapter writers were asked to ponder 21 questions before constructing their narratives:

1. How did coronavirus change your work life?
2. What did you stop doing that you dearly miss?
3. What did you start doing that brings you no joy?
4. What, if anything, has grown in importance?
5. What value, or commitment, has dropped away?
6. What is your professional vista? (Elaborate on ten important professional events of your past and ten important professional events in your future; see El Sawy et al., 1988.)
7. Construct a 2 × 2 matrix with you identifying the competing points that make it orthogonal. Where are you on this 2 × 2? Others? What difference does your and their placements make?
8. What has happened to your looking-glass self in the time of coronavirus?
9. How do others experience you?

10. To what extent have you adapted your communication persona as a result of your interactions in 2020?
11. What is your "presentation of self" under these conditions?
12. How do you want others to perceive you?
13. What presentation of yourself are you "giving off"?
14. What is your energy like? What drains you? What replenishes you?
15. What have you said publicly in a meeting or email that you now regret?
16. How has your technological-self changed?
17. What programs, if any, do you now use that are new to you?
18. What old knowledge, if any, did you rely on with success?
19. What have been the costs of the changes?
20. What have been the rewards?
21. How would others assess your communication competence?

When suggesting directions for authors in our previous edited books (Soelberg et al., 2019; Sørnes et al., 2015), we found that writers find leading questions like these both teasingly intriguing and useful. Their natural tendency, though, is to select one or more of them as points of departure and go from there. The accounts within the chapters are made distinctive by the writers' natural tendency to discover, and share, what's important in their own story. The resulting self-directed chapters are likely to produce a kind of *emergent complexity*—many answers to the 21 questions in many forms (Furholt et al., 2020).

Section I: Theorizing the Present: This Is How to See It Now

Our first three chapters open the book because they set into place larger, theoretical positions on how to view present circumstances. Czarniawska and her colleagues offer us a neologism—"pandemicracy"—to account for contemporary organizing in Sweden. Brummet, meanwhile, addresses the question: How do we bring this narrative into control for our benefit? And Ashcraft joins the theoretical fray as she punctuates the ivory tower with its middle-class whiteness.

We'll let each of them preview their own stories for you now.

Chapter 2: "Pandemicracy and Organizing in Unsettling Times" by Barbara Czarniawska, Josef Pallas, and Elena Raviola

In recent years, the public sectors in many countries have been reformed many times, due to cycles of centralization and decentralization and many other restructurings. Several studies have shown an overall trend of increased managerialization of public administration, which has subjected public employees to complicated systems of measurements and reporting. Even when such changes were justified by the disruptiveness of external transformations like digitization, they have by no means been comparable in timing and scope to those caused by the recent COVID-19 pandemic. Over the past 70 years, no events have so broadly challenged—and in many respects reformed—the functionality and sustainability of the organization of professional work at the core of our welfare infrastructures. The effects of the COVID-19 pandemic are visible far beyond the public health sector. Employees within social services, family counseling, therapy, culture, education, migration, business support, research, and many other public services are experiencing dramatic, previously almost unthinkable challenges (Mazzucato & Kattel, 2020). Media reporting and the first research reports (Banks et al., 2020; Lemieux et al., 2020; López-Cabarcos et al., 2020) describe major adjustments and challenges that governments, public-sector organizations, and welfare occupations and professions have undergone to deal with the effects and consequences of the pandemic.

Chapter 3: "The Mysteries of Iconic Leadership on Zoom" by Barry Brummett

Institutional reactions to the Covid pandemic brought about a great many changes in work life. One important, complex change was in how people see each other and see leaders in organizations. This change was influenced by the rapid and widespread use of Zoom as a way to communicate. In particular, the appearance of (usually) small icons on a screen both created strangeness and mystery among organizational agents, and gave limited access to knowledge of others, especially leaders, in organizations. This chapter turns to some theories of the American scholar Kenneth Burke to explain how Zoom creates a push-pull of mystery yet attraction. Communication balances on the knife's edge between strangeness and scanty knowledge, on the one hand, and access to the means, if limited, of achieving identification within organizations, on the other hand. This balance is ancient and comes down to us from an origin in religious symbolism.

Chapter 4: "Organizational Communication in Crisis: Beyond Academic Civility" by Karen Lee Ashcraft

Organizational communication, as field and practice, was arguably in crisis before the COVID-19 pandemic. Work intensification streaming from the neoliberal university ("Neoliberal U") was already colliding with racial intensification in the communication discipline, evident in growing calls to break the unyielding grip of whiteness on the field's professional apparatus ("Whitewashing U"). The year 2020 saw this collision come to a head, issuing a renewed imperative to address the racist foundations and continuing inequities of higher education and academic disciplines. This chapter dwells on one element of that system: "academic civility," the primary mode of professional communication that constitutes scholarly relations. I argue that academic civility connects and sustains Neoliberal U and Whitewashing U. I use my own experience to illustrate how this is so, playing on the recently popularized notion of "Karen" as a composite of racist habits associated with white women. Accordingly, I call for a shift in professional communication, from immaculate politeness (or moralizing perpetual composure) to imperfect presence (or assuming flawed engagement). My goal is to suggest how white faculty in particular can take meaningful action on the 2020 racial imperative and, in so doing, improve the quality of their work lives too.

Section II: Self-Organization a Response: Beyond Academic Civility

The four chapters in this next section invoke the concept of self-organization emphasizing basic concepts of an order that (1) has no hierarchical designer or director, (2) emerges from equivocal conditions that produce networks and interaction, and (3) scales from micro to macro, including the individual, team, and organizational levels, up to larger subsets of culture. The first two authors in this section self-organize by writing ethnographic declarations in which they now scan their environment, select their personal responses, and position themselves in power in organizations in which they could easily have become dependent. Keri Stephens accounts for a domestic environment where each family member self-organizes his/her own space. She combines the smell of the roses and the coffee, and imagines ambitious research plans that extend far beyond the backyard in which she is standing. Tine Viveka Westerberg marvels at her own identity shock to discover that, even in a pandemic, she could perform well beyond what she expected of herself by delivering at work while also home-schooling her own children. Sarah Parker's self-organization occurs in the face of a corporate buy-out, in which her organization is taken over by, and becomes dependent on, the direction of almost completely new leadership—a team that tries to establish authority and credibility under conditions of stress, distance, and scarcity. Finally, to account for the organization of the logistics of personal protective equipment (PPE) in Norway, Frode Soelberg analyzes the chaos of the distribution.

Chapter 5: "The COVID-19 Pandemic: Self-organizing at the Edges of Chaos and Stability" by Keri K. Stephens

A cosmology event—a severe disruption where people no longer understand the universe to be rational—is my best way to describe the COVID-19 pandemic. Being quarantined during those early months actually helped me create new structures to cope. Going outdoors, for example, became a highly treasured break, and since my office had no doors, I created a façade that helped me feel more privacy as I fashioned an acceptable background for my new way of meeting: Zoom! I turned my illusion of control into reality by focusing on research and teaching and beginning five new research studies. Yet I also overworked incessantly and dealt with family health issues that had me question whether I could be a good mother. I existed in a zone of emergent complexity: the space between the edge of chaos and the edge of stability, a sweet spot where innovation occurs. Living in this zone forced me to bounce back and forth between these edges of chaos and stability, sometimes slipping, even if briefly, into full chaos. Yet from this constant motion, I also know I must keep moving forward.

Chapter 6: "Digital Teaching During COVID" by Tine Viveka Westerberg

Even when the world is not plagued by a pandemic, those of us who work in the maritime industry must prepare for the unexpected, and it's my job as a maritime lecturer in Norway to prepare students for a career in this volatile industry. Having barely dangled my feet in teaching online, the pandemic threw me right overboard into a new professional setting as a digital teacher. I had not only just returned from a round-the-world trip with my boys, but also now found myself stuck at home without the social and academic aspects of being on campus. Slowly I adjusted to, then embraced, the challenge of becoming a competent user of both the digital tools available and digital pedagogical methods. Both of them eventually proved fun. This is a beginner's story about the practice of teaching digitally during the pandemic.

Chapter 7: "Through the Looking Glass in a Pandemic: Inside of a Global Comms Corporation, Navigating COVID-19 on Top of Structural Change" by Sarah A. Parker

This chapter explores one marketer's perspective inside a large global corporation in the communication software market, during the time of COVID-19 when the challenges of the novel coronavirus were compounded by organizational changes made by new leadership installed by the venture-capital company that acquired ours prior to the pandemic. The new leadership was strictly interim leadership. It works by acquiring companies, using their contracted leadership in hopes of making them more efficient while also then replacing themselves with yet another team of new leadership, ultimately moving on to the next acquisition project. With this known model in place, staffing changes—and cuts—were expected prior to COVID-19, but were felt far more deeply by the impact of a non-existent job market in a growing global depression and the low morale associated with it. Interim leadership was further challenged by being virtually unknown, forced to build relationships remotely, and countering resentment from staffing cuts, restructuring, and clashing office cultures from various acquisitions.

Chapter 8: "Chaos: International Sourcing of PPE and the Covid-19 Pandemic" by Frode Soelberg

Resilience is a major issue in Supply Chain literature. In practice, however, global supply chains are cut so lean that one tiny hiccup can cause cascading failure. This chapter elaborates on the hectic months of March and April 2020, viewed through the lens of a Senior Executive at an international sourcing company in Bodø, Norway. The whole structure of an international business broke down, all the way from international politics, tariffs, and terms of trade, to business ethics and the norms of cooperation and competition, to micro strategic management, to organizing the sourcing operation, quality controls, and risk management. The experiences and solutions to these challenges carry implications for international sourcing in general and "just in time management" in particular.

Section III: Communication Philosophy: Apprehending Opportunity in Time of Crisis

These next four chapters are written from the perspective of positional roles and responsibilities. What to do in times of crisis? Each chapter recounts someone's editing or leadership responsibilities during the early months of the pandemic. Jean Bartunek reports on her quandary of what to emphasize: Do I give voice to the infamous Ed Schein's rant on the current lack of trust, community, and cooperation? Do I honor Camus' *The Plague*, which obligates us to account for life in a crisis? Or do I emphasize my role in organizing scholarship about this eventful period? June Borge Doornich describes her effort to manage a university department and the difficulty of persuading people to follow the science. Sarah J. Tracy and her colleagues, meanwhile, tackle their experience in a graduate methods class—one accustomed to face-to-face contact, but that must now find a way of developing community under stress, from a distance. In the final chapter of this section, Susan Szmania accounts for her staff role at the US Embassy in Amman, Jordan, amidst stark changes in the embassy's normal practices—including converting from an emphasis on personal contact to diplomacy via Zoom.

Chapter 9: "The Fellows and a Book: Unexpected Opportunities for Practice and Theory" by Jean M. Bartunek

A good deal of my scholarship addresses academic-practitioner relationships and tensions. The pandemic provided me with unexpected opportunities to explore this relationship and its tensions through my own experience. In this chapter I describe two sets of unforeseen events that I experienced during the pandemic. One, during the summer of 2020, had to do with the unplanned need to carry out activities associated with the

Deanship of the Fellows of the Academy of Management that I had previously delegated to others and/or needed to create in a new form. The other, which began in April 2020, arose from my sudden urge to edit a book dealing with how social scientists can contribute to responses to serious crises. That book, which came to be named *Social Scientists Confronting Global Crises*, was published at the end of 2021. I explore both events through the lens of tensions between academia and practice.

Chapter 10: "Mindful Management of the (Un)Expected" by June Borge Doornich

Managing and making sense of (un)expected unfolding events during the pandemic has required a balance between change and stability while remaining vigilant and defensive. With no experience in crisis management, my approach to ensure "business as usual" in education at the Business School, Nord University, was colored by "learning by doing" based on the terms given by the corona virus. I was managing faculty and students in the digital space from my home kitchen table. I brought my private mindful practice into my management, enhancing my capacity for attention and awareness to the multifaceted consequences of the pandemic in the many aspects of our educational activities. Mindfulness also enhanced my capacity for resilience to deal with the many surprises and high stress level over a long period of time. But resilience is not inexhaustible, and defeat can be triggered by small insignificant trifle. Exactly one year after the Norwegian government first enforced a national lockdown on us to curb the COVID-19 pandemic, the government overrode its own infection control initiatives in the Bodø municipality and enforced yet another lockdown because of a new spike. Making me lapse from a mindful mental state to a mindless management of the crisis.

Chapter 11: "Compassion, Burnout, and Self-care During COVID-19: On the Collective Impact of Self-soothing Super Highways" by Sarah J. Tracy, Brianna L. Avalos, Laura Martinez, B. Liahnna Stanley, Sophia Town, and Alaina C. Zanin

This is a story of six researchers who came together to make sense of the tumult triggered by the COVID-19 pandemic. Our team centered emotion and affectivity, letting the pandemic guide everything—our research design, our team meetings and the ways we related with interviewees and each other. The project also prompted us to critically examine our habits and realize the relatively privileged ways our own strategies of self-soothing tactics could have problematic repercussions on the collective. As such, centering compassion and emotion not only served as a method of individual coping but also served to critically reveal how we as academics are also enmeshed in systems that bring trauma to bear. Our chapter closes with several ideas about how we might engage in research methods during and about times of collective suffering that move beyond individual emotional release and may prompt relational work toward communal catharsis and systematic change.

Chapter 12: "Improvisation in Public Diplomacy During the COVID-19 Pandemic" by Susan Szmania

This chapter examines my personal and professional experiences as an academic turned diplomat in Amman, Jordan, as I navigated the early days of the COVID-19 pandemic. I describe how government-imposed lockdowns changed the very nature of my job, including allowing telework from home and a loss of the ability to interact with people in face-to-face settings. Drawing on the seminal work by Mary Catherine Bateson, I examine how the concept of improvisation informed my approach to developing new work routines amid uncertainty. I conclude with observations on how the pandemic may reshape official diplomatic work in the future.

Section IV: Techno-Ethnography: Using Social Science Methods to Study the Virus

Section IV showcases techno-ethnographies, which are distinct from another sub-branch, technographies, that use "technology to do ethnography" (Kien, 2008, p. 1102). These chapters are techno-ethnographies that examine subcultures with social-science axioms about organizational communication technology in the pandemic. They are written about organizational communication in a pandemic and the larger structures that influence local behavior in the same way that Ricoeur (2004) modeled selecting our history to match our conception of ourselves. In Chap. 13, Ndlela and Madsbu track the practices of a single department head in Norway as he turns to emails to manage the crisis. Next, in Chap. 14,

Storhaug Hole and Bakken describe the requirements of the culture at Inland Norway University College during the lockdown. In Chap. 15, Prosper and Rydstedt examine the Norwegian Institute of Public Health (NIPH) communication, public perception of the institute's trustworthiness, and its general reputation.

Chapter 13: "Internal Communications During the Pandemic: Challenges and Implications" by Martin N. Ndlela and Jens Petter Madsbu

The Covid-19 pandemic exerted enormous stress on organizations across the world, setting dampers on business operations, effectiveness, and viability. It negatively impacted both an organization's internal and external environments. The immediate implication of the lockdown measures imposed during the Covid-19 was that non-essential organizations had to shut down their premises or reduce the number of employees in any physical spaces. Changes in the way most workplaces function during the pandemic put internal communication practices into the fore. Employee communication is considered the lifeblood of any organization. The crisis compelled organizations to respond to, and adapt to, sudden disruptions in their communication order. This chapter examines the internal communication challenges experienced by universities during the pandemic, as well as how institutions responded to these disruptions and the new dispersed communication environment. It captures the experiences of a department head in the aftermath of the lockdown and how that department navigated the turbulent situation.

Chapter 14: "The Impact of Trust in the Time of Covid-19: Trust in Crisis Management and Crisis Communication in Inland Norway University College" by Åse Storhaug Hole and Bjørn Tallak Bakken

Inland Norway University College suddenly locked down on March 12, 2020. The Norwegian government had just announced a national lockdown, with large consequences for working-life and everyday life. Our students and employees got little preparation time and we were ordered to leave campus and our offices at 1800 on that day, and to take our computers, headsets, devices, and books with us. Within days, most of us teachers had changed our teaching methods, from classroom meetings to communicating and teaching digitally. Academics accustomed to autonomy found themselves thrown into a situation where a central emergency management group directed everybody. This chapter examines trust in crisis management and crisis communication during the Covid-19 crisis. Overall, we found a high degree of satisfaction with the crisis management at the institutional level. At the lower levels, the results were more mixed. Trust in crisis management seems to be strong under three conditions: (1) one's expectations of being taken care of are met, (2) information arrives on time and is precise, and (3) self-managed work during the crisis is appreciated by colleagues and management. Trust declines when expectations are violated, consciously or unconsciously.

Chapter 15: "The Role of Communication, Institutional Trust and Reputation to Health Advice Adherence: Lessons from a Case Study of the Norwegian Institute of Public Health During the COVID-19 Pandemic" by Prosper Ameh Kwei-Narh and Leif Rydstedt

Globally, the COVID-19 pandemic has caused untold financial, health, and social problems. Collaborations among governments, state institutions, and the media to encourage people to adhere to COVID-19 health-oriented interventions, such as social distancing and regular handwashing, have mitigated these negative impacts. To better understand adherence behaviors within a convenient sample of Norwegian respondents, we used a case-study method involving data triangulation to examine the Norwegian Institute of Public Health (NIPH) communication, public perception of NIPH's trustworthiness, and the reputation of the NIPH. We obtained data on NIPH's reputation from a secondary source, the Ipsos annual organization reputation survey. These sources enabled us to develop a comprehensive account of COVID-19 crisis management, situating our discussion within situational crisis communication theory and the creeping crisis framework to create a narrative of crisis management during the COVID-19 pandemic. In doing so, we highlight our contribution to theory and to future crisis-management practice.

Section V: Understanding the People at Risk

Many of the previous chapters reflect the very particular experience of professional people with minimal job insecurity but confronting a change in how their security gets enacted. Most people, of course, have not experienced the pandemic in this way; they've suffered job loss in the tens of millions or, perhaps just as frighteningly, have had to work essential-service jobs so that those of us who have the privilege to hunker down at home still get our supplies of toilet paper. And, of course, the effects of the pandemic on working-class black and brown bodies have far outweighed the effects on middle/upper-middle-class white bodies. Our next five chapters focus on field research about that very particular experience of professional people with no job insecurity, but simply a change in the ways that their security gets enacted. They include Rahul Mitra's chapter on BIPOC (Black, Indigenous, and Person of Color) entrepreneurs, Aquilar and Ballard's analysis of medical doctors-in-training, Rice's crisis responders on a county emergency management team, Dye and Dailey's at-home organizational members who discover that being at home and away from the physical workplace results in their feeling less identity with the organization, and Kee's struggles and strategies with his Asian identity in West Texas.

Chapter 16: "A Mosaic of Researcher 'Back-Stories' and Oral History 'Front-Stories': COVID-19 and Metro Detroit BIPOC Entrepreneurs' Resilience" by Rahul Mitra, Allison Lucas, Sheryl Johnson-Fambro, Claire Van Raaphorst, and Shelby Lasky

This chapter draws on an ongoing oral history project with Black, Indigenous, and Person of Color (BIPOC) entrepreneurs in Metro Detroit navigating the personal and professional trauma of the COVID-19 pandemic. Our chapter blends narrative strands from these oral histories with our own researcher "back-stories" to demonstrate the intersecting themes of lived experience that connect us. As faculty and students at a Detroit-based urban research university, our lives intersect with these narrators. Some of us are BIPOC entrepreneurs or their long-term customers or are married/related to small-business owners; while others have tested positive for the coronavirus, or we know friends/family who have fallen sick or passed away from COVID; while still others are completely new to the area and thus must traverse a difficult space as "outsiders" peering in, as we engage in this project together. By connecting the "back-stories" of our multiracial research team with the "front-stories" of the entrepreneurs, we co-create a pluri-vocal mosaic of resilience storytelling amid this pandemic.

Chapter 17: "Even Heroes Need Help: The Impact of COVID-19 on Physicians Already at Risk for Burnout" by Ana M. Aquilar and Dawna I. Ballard

We begin this story in the same year that the COVID-19 pandemic emerged, by focusing on a medical crisis: the Association of American Medical Colleges estimated that, by 2032, the United States will have a deficit of physicians (from 46,900 to 122,000) across all specialties. A rapidly aging population, a stagnant rate of new physicians, and an alarming rate of turnover have all contributed to a serious problem that has been compounded in light of COVID-19. Amidst a backdrop of stark deficiencies in resources—for example, a lack of PPE (personal protective equipment) and ventilators—physicians have largely been offered symbolic (rather than material- or policy-based) support. In this chapter, we interrogate the public celebrations of their sacrifice and active framing of physicians as "heroes" in light of ongoing threats to their work quality and personal wellbeing. Rather than supernatural beings (as is suggested by the hero frame), physicians are employees who—under normal circumstances—attempt to manage despite limited resources. In framing healthcare workers as heroes, their institutions and the general public place additional, moral-based expectations on a system already teetering on failure.

Chapter 18: "Applied Scholarship in Extreme Contexts: Emotion, Meaning, and Risk in Pandemic Response" by Rebecca M. Rice

The COVID-19 pandemic impacted my identity as an early career scholar and created a bifurcation between my professor life and my researcher life. I embarked on an ethnographic project related to COVID community response teams and took on the role of a volunteer who participated virtually in daily meetings about the pandemic. The organization I observed, Community Emergency Team, was made up of various city and county organizations that worked together to create crisis communication messages and determine county policy about social distancing, testing, and vaccine distribution. After offering to join as a researcher, I took on a role in the "situational awareness" unit of the organization, where I created and shared daily meeting notes, helped facilitate daily Zoom meetings, and kept updated numbers of COVID cases for the county. This role as a volunteer-ethnographer meant that I was now a researcher and participant; as such, I experienced a changing relationship with research methods, technology, and a new understanding of my research area of emergency and crisis organizations. I embraced autoethnography and used technology to facilitate reflections on my experiences.

Chapter 19: "Identity Interruptions: Organizational and Occupational Identification During a Global Health Pandemic" by Luke A. Dye and Stephanie L. Dailey

Previous studies have demonstrated various factors that influence identification, a construct that explains employees' sense of belongingness to their work. This project extends identification research by exploring how the COVID-19 pandemic changed workers' organizational and occupational identification. Using personal interviews with various types of workers, including (non-)essential and (non-)remote employees, we show how identifications waxed and waned throughout the pandemic. Stories from the field provide insight into the role of personal identity, perceived organizational support, and team communication in the attachment process. Through these ethnographic accounts, we encourage future research to consider factors outside of management's purview which may impact workers' identifications, and we provide a rationale for why convenient samples may help scholars better understand the complex and communicative underpinnings of identification in marginalized and underrepresented communities.

Chapter 20: "The Perpetually Conditional Citizen" by Kerk Fong Kee

According to StopAAPIHate.org, in the single year between March 2020 and March 2021, there were almost 4000 anti-Asian hate crimes documented by its website. In this chapter, I tell the story of the Chinese Faculty and Staff Association (CFSA) at Texas Tech University over an approximately 12-month period, and how they put together the LOVE (Lubbock cOVid-19 rElief) Projects in Spring 2020, which included multiple community service and funding activities. Behind the public messages and community service was the fear of becoming the victims of anti-Asian hate crimes. This ethnography documented how (a) an Asian association organized community-service events that branded Chinese as good citizens (impression management), but in private also (b) built relationships with the police department (alliance building), (c) created a "Lubbock Chinese Friends of Guns Group" on WeChat (self-reliance), and (d) met weekly on Friday for 30 minutes on Zoom for what they called the "CFSA Weekend Square" to maintain an active informal network (ongoing conversations). This ethnography reveals that CFSA members (sub)consciously realized that their belonging to the local community and the United States is perpetually conditional (and alienated) due to their race and ethnicity.

Chapter 21: "Review: A Grounded Theory of Organizational Communication and Technology (OCT) of COVID-19 Before Delta and the Vaccine" by Larry D. Browning, Jan-Oddvar Sørnes and Peer Jacob Svenkerud

The final chapter is a grounded theory analysis of the 19 content chapters of this book. Our analysis produces an 18-category sorting of the chapters that condenses further down to 3 grand concepts: uncertainty, structure, and the future. We elaborate the narrative features of these grand concepts to conclude the book.

References

Banks, S., Cai, T., De Jonge, E., Shears, J., Shum, M., Sobočan, A. M., ... & Weinberg, M. (2020). Practising ethically during COVID-19: Social work challenges and responses. *International Social Work, 63*(5), 569–583.

Bochner, Arthur P., & Ellis, Carolyn (Eds.). (2002). *Ethnographically speaking: Autoethnography, literature, and aesthetics* (Vol. 9). Rowman Altamira.

Dailey, S., & Browning, L. D. (2014). Retelling stories in organizations: Understanding the functions of narrative repetition. *Academy of Management Review, 39*(1), 22–43.

El Sawy, O. A., Clark, J. W., & Hall, B. (1988). *Temporal biases in strategic attention.* Working Paper DS-88-11, University of Southern California.

Furholt, Martin, Grier, Colin, Spriggs, Matthew, & Earle, Timothy. (2020). Political economy in the archaeology of emergent complexity: A synthesis of bottom-up and top-down approaches. *Journal of Archaeological Method and Theory, 27*(2), 157–191.

Kien, Grant. (2008). Technography = technology + ethnography: An introduction. *Qualitative Inquiry, 14*(7), 1101–1109.

Lemieux, T., Milligan, K., Schirle, T., & Skuterud, M. (2020). Initial impacts of the COVID-19 pandemic on the Canadian labour market. *Canadian Public Policy, 46*(S1), S55–S65.

López-Cabarcos, M. Á., Ribeiro-Soriano, D., & Piñeiro-Chousa, J. (2020). All that glitters is not gold. The rise of gaming in the COVID-19 pandemic. *Journal of Innovation & Knowledge, 5*(4), 289–296.

Mazzucato, M., & Kattel, R. (2020). COVID-19 and public-sector capacity. *Oxford Review of Economic Policy, 36*(Supplement_1), S256–S269.

Ricoeur, P. (1984). *Time and Narrative*, translated by K. McLaughlin and D. Pellauer. Chicago, University of Chicago Press, 8, 16.

Ricoeur, P. (2004). *Memory, History, Forgetting*. (trans Blamey and Pellauer). Chicago: University of Chicago Press.

Soelberg, Frode, Browning, Larry, & Sørnes, Jan O. (Eds.). (2019). *High north stories in a time of transition: Gutsy narratives and wild observations*. Routledge.

Sørnes, Jan O., Browning, Larry, & Henricksen, Jan T. (2015). *Culture, development and petroleum: An ethnography of the high north*. Routledge.

SECTION I

Theorizing the Present: This Is How to See It Now

CHAPTER 2

Pandemicracy and Organizing in Unsettling Times

Barbara Czarniawska, Josef Pallas, and Elena Raviola

In short, the everyday work conditions of thousands of public sector employees have been challenged, and in some cases even redefined—in practice and/or in documents outlining job descriptions. Expectations and demands of the continuous and expanded provision of public goods and services have made the tasks of many public sector organizations and their employees grow, both in relative and absolute terms. Emotional and at times desperate responses to the increased intensity, uncertainty, unpredictability, emotional stress, discomfort, and even life-threatening working conditions are not uncommon in stories from various societal sectors (Lee, 2021).

Most of testimonies and stories that have been gathered in popular and academic texts and studies focus, however, on work performed by people

B. Czarniawska (✉) • E. Raviola
Gothenburg Research Institute, University of Gothenburg, Gothenburg, Sweden
e-mail: barbara.czarniawska@gri.gu.se; elena.raviola@gu.se

J. Pallas
Department of Business Studies, Uppsala University, Uppsala, Sweden
e-mail: Josef.Pallas@fek.uu.se

L. D. Browning et al. (eds.), *Organizational Communication and Technology in the Time of Coronavirus*,
https://doi.org/10.1007/978-3-030-94814-6_2

in *front-line* professions and occupations—nurses, physicians, and other healthcare professionals within primary and elderly care. What has happened to working conditions in occupations and professions that operate in other parts of the public sector is less well known. How are social workers, preschool personnel, teachers, immigration officers, cultural workers, urban planners, public sector managers, and administrators dealing with such pandemic-related challenges as social distancing, hygiene routines, facial masks, and sick leaves?

In this chapter we describe a Swedish variation of the phenomenon we call "pandemicracy"—various governance efforts to control the pandemic and public sector employees' reactions to it. Inspired and motivated by an expanding vocabulary of the working ethos of public sector organizations, which now includes such words as sacrifice, solidarity, dejection, and determination, we have collected stories from people working in various parts of the Swedish public sector. These stories describe daily work in times of turmoil within a country that has been internationally deemed to be an exception for the ways in which the pandemic has been managed. Indeed, Swedish officials decided not to introduce a general lockdown, even if many other constricting measures have been taken. But in Sweden, as in all other countries, there are medical, societal, and economic effects of the pandemic that may set a hallmark for the future organization and governance of public sector organizations.

Our Study

At the end of March 2020, we placed a following post (in Swedish) on our Facebook accounts and on the Gothenburg Research Institute website:

> To: Nurses, physicians, police officers, administrators, social workers, investigators, teachers, cultural workers, communicators, researchers and epidemiologists – all public employees who face challenges from the COVID-19 epidemic on a daily basis and who would like to share their thoughts and reflections on what is happening in their organizations. If you – despite your incredible workload – have the strength and desire to participate (completely anonymously of course), we would like to ask you to write as often as possible a few lines about the challenges you face in your workplaces, the thoughts and feelings they raise, and, in general, how your organization adapts to the spread of the virus. Tell us what you feel is most important, most difficult and most challenging, but also what lifts you up, helps and

> facilitates. We are then planning to write a book about how "public Sweden" has faced a crisis like this.
>
> If you are interested in sharing your experiences, please write to us at [e-mail addresses] and we will tell you more about what our study looks like, how to cancel your participation at any time, how we handle information from you, and much more!

To those who contacted us, we sent a following letter:

> Thank you so much for wanting to join us! We think it is important to document everyday life in the crisis with stories from people, and not only with public documents. We are very interested in your work and your workplace, as well as the thoughts and feelings you have when you handle the changes and adaptations that your organization makes in connection with the spread of the virus. [...]
>
> You can write in the form that suits you best. You can send what you wrote or recorded to any of us via email, SMS, WhatsApp, or in any other way – choose it yourself! We will save all material in an anonymous manner according to the Swedish Research Council's ethical principles, and you can stop contacting us whenever you wish.

We received some answers, but not as many as we hoped for. (At the time, we probably didn't realize how busy and overworked our potential interlocutors were.) Thus, we completed the study by interviewing people we knew, including some university colleagues. And thanks to the dog that one of us had to walk regularly, we also gained stories from dog owners who worked in the public sector and who were kind enough to join our efforts. In this way, we received 37 accounts from people employed at healthcare organizations, schools (from preschool[1] to university), and municipal and state units involved in or influenced by COVID-19 counter efforts. When quoting their utterances, we call them "N+number", N standing for narrator.

We have divided our analysis in four periods of 2020:

- March–April, when the first attempts to counteract the pandemic began;
- May–June, when responses to the pandemic were truly developed and established and when people are starting to realize that their work was likely to be different for foreseeable future;

- July–August, when handling the pandemic was becoming routinized, and when people had started to reflect on the previous six months; and
- September–October, when the pandemic in Sweden became somewhat of a "new normality", with people leaving the "crisis mode".

Here are the stories and our readings of them.

March–April 2020

The first confirmed case of COVID-19 in Sweden was in Jönköping on January 31, 2020, but it was on March 10 that the Swedish Public Health Agency changed the risk level of virus spread in society from moderate to very high. The first reactions were—as to be expected—uncertainty and confusion.

In a home for persons with certain functional impairments, many personnel reported sick, while those who remained often worked from 1.5 to 2 days without a break. They started wearing visors, but their boss told them that this gear was frightening the residents, who were called "users" in such units. Some users moved home to their parents. The personnel explained that, in fact, both the users and their parents were afraid—not of visors, but of the virus—but received no reply. In order to obtain some response, they had to send their letter three levels up, to the Chief Safety Representative.

> Our Chief Safety Representative immediately took up the issue – apparently, we were not the only ones who had contacted him for this reason. He contacted the Division Manager, who gave him the same response we had received. Our boss questioned the idea that this would be perceived as offensive by our patients. Many of our users who can speak for themselves had requested that the personnel wear protective equipment. Could it be that it was perceived as offensive if the personnel did NOT wear protective equipment? Could it be that many [users] actually felt unsafe in their residence? He also wondered if anyone from management had talked with our users and asked them how they felt? Obviously not… (N1, assistant nurse)

A similar situation has been observed in other places. Typically, it was managers in positions distant from line work who felt confused or were not well informed and therefore failed to inform their subordinates. In some places, the subordinates felt that their bosses were close to panic (N3, Swedish Armed Forces). One of several reasons for their panic was the fact that even people with light colds were supposed to stay at home, which meant that fewer and fewer persons were left to fulfill the growing number of tasks. Line managers who were closer to the actual operations started preparing risk assessments and collecting medical information, even before the state agency rang the alarm bell (N1, municipal environment inspector).

The impact of the pandemic obviously varied from workplace to workplace. The uncertainty was a heavy burden for people working in social emergency services (SES):

> Our work requires emergency assessments and decisions – evenings, nights and weekends – assessments and decisions that cannot wait until the next day, such as acute child protection in cases of child abuse, parents' mental or physical illness, parental abuse. There are persons (mostly women) who may need protection after being victims of violence, addicts who may need immediate care, homeless people who need accommodation for the night, and other people who have experienced dramatic events. We are contacted by private citizens, but also police, healthcare units, social services.... After 2 AM we are on standby from home (...). In other words, my colleagues and I have experienced a thing or two in our job, and usually remain quite calm, even when horrible things happen. COVID-19, however, even if we have all begun to get used to it, is a different challenge, as our own health is threatened, and we are in need of support and protective equipment to be able to do our jobs. (N10, SES district secretary)

The uncertainty in this case concerned their services—what should they do? Visit people in troubled homes? The visitors were no longer allowed to enter the office unless absolutely necessary. Otherwise, one was forced to conduct the conversation through a glass door. On April 4, the personnel received protective equipment: visors, respiratory protection, protective aprons, and gloves.

> It feels good to know that the protections are here. We may not have to use them, but their presence is comforting. I worked during the Estonia disaster and the tsunami. The difference is that there my own health was not at risk. Still, now I want to give emergency support to children who may have been abused or in other ways victimized and to other persons who may need emergency interventions. (N10, SES district secretary)

At a preschool, the uncertainty and confusion were often felt in contacts with the parents. In the beginning, personnel received many detailed directives from above, yet a careful reading soon revealed that many of these directives were impossible to follow. The personnel did their best, but sometimes had problems explaining to the children why certain things must be done differently. The directives suggested that as many children as possible should stay at home, but few did. Scenes like this preschool teacher described were typical:

> In the afternoon, one of the children sneezes, and we have to wipe away slimy snot. We know the parents, and we know they will be reluctant to keep the child at home. It is snack time and the child is sneezing again. We take pictures to have evidence and send them to the parents. One of the staff goes to warn the principal in case a parent comes by to talk. The parent comes and asks if the child really needs to stay at home. We refer to the directives from the Public Health Agency. (…)
>
> Another child is coughing. We send a message to a parent who promises to come but needs about an hour to travel from work.
>
> A child in the class next door is coughing too. The parents don't speak Swedish. We use an app on our iPad to translate a message into the parents' mother tongue. We explain that the child is coughing, and that children showing the slightest symptom of cold need to stay at home. We hope we got it right and the parents accept it. (…) The children cough, sneeze or have running noses every day, however, and normally we would not even have reacted to such things. But the situation now is different, and these children need to stay home. (N6, preschool teacher)

In many public services, the schedule and tasks of many workers were changed to address the emergency, and these changes generated different worries—for infection in the case of healthcare front-liners and for unexpected consequences of the pandemic-containment measures. At the special surgery section, all planned surgeries were stopped to create room for COVID-19 patients in need of intensive care. It seemed to be a certain relief for the personnel, but at the same time, the fear of infection reached its peak, while the protective means were not yet delivered in adequate volumes:

> We were running low on working material, as it was rarely refilled, while many people became desperate to get hand sanitizers for their homes, rather than remembering that good hand sanitizer lasts a long time, and that in

> general it should be prioritized for hospitals. So, we could be missing several containers of hand sanitizers in our changing rooms when we were leaving for home. (N7, nurse at a special surgery section)

At an elementary school, the teaching scheme was constantly changed, and classes were combined. Teaching took place half in the class, half digitally. Teachers worried about contagion, as it was difficult to follow all the restrictions and recommendations in the case of children:

> It's not like children excel in keeping their distance, not picking their noses, or not touching everything and everyone. It goes against being a child. Then the teenagers do each other's makeup, hang together in groups and sit in each other's laps and cuddle. (…)
>
> One student who is moving to a new foster care home in another city had his last day yesterday – a student with taped glasses and dirty clothing… I hugged him at least ten times that day, despite the directives. (N5, elementary school teacher)

Apart from the infection, teachers worried about other consequences of the restrictions: after all, teenagers who don't go to school can be enlisted by gangs, and their recruitment begins when they are as young as 12. Then there are children who get real food only at school and those whose parents are drug addicts. Many children started crying in class. But N5 promised herself to become more positive: "I have started to draw a dot on my hand with a permanent marker every time I complain about something, because I have become so tired of my own complaining. I will try to get my act together."

Many public employees felt anxiety, and managers needed to calm them down. The coordinator at the municipal social services contracted COVID-19, but continued to work; Zoom meetings continued from 8.30 to 17.00, some in parallel:

> We need to manage a lot of worries, but there is also a lot of information that comes almost daily from the Care Coordination, from the Institute of Infectious Disease Control, from the Public Health Agency. (…) Our personnel feel strong anxiety, but it can be reduced with facts. (N11)

Anxiety was felt even at universities, but perhaps a different type of anxiety that was dealt with differently: distance teaching, hand washing and extra-emergency meetings—tiresome, but necessary. But then a university administrator went out to buy some lunch and experienced something similar to what the elementary school teacher had experienced:

> Suddenly a young girl falls head down on the concrete floor. I rush over and lift her head onto my lap to make contact with her. I talk close to her face, and pat her lightly on the cheek to keep her conscious as I yell at the staff to call 112. The whole situation gets resolved when the ambulance arrives. I go and buy a sandwich wrapped in plastic, but then realize that I cannot eat it until I have returned to the office, washed my hands and used hand sanitizer. It strikes me, that right then and there, when the girl fell, I didn't think one bit about COVID-19 or the spread of the infection. (N12, university administrator)

University teachers get tired, but they are used to distant teaching:

> I have become a Zoombie, this living-dead creature who, with hollow eyes, sits cowardly, hour after hour staring at the screen – at other living-dead screen workers. In the beginning, it was a bit like with people in the beginning of the 20th century using a telephone for the first time: You talk with the loudest voice possible to be heard across the digital expanses. Now, after a few zoom meetings and lectures, I am a zoom veteran and have found the feature that adds a beautifying filter over my hollow eyes. (…) But gods help us if we have to teach zoom in the fall too. It is difficult to keep eye contact with a screen camera. A computer has neither a heartbeat nor humor. It doesn't laugh politely at my jokes. (N9, social sciences lecturer)

There are also other worries to consider: "I dread the day when schools and preschools close. I dread that my parenting will not be able to handle it" (N9).

Art schools, like museums and theaters, had more problems with the restrictions and distancing. Cultural organizations are closed; most cultural events have been cancelled. As reported in the media, the pandemic has meant loss of contracts and severe economic difficulties for many cultural workers. An art-school teacher told us: "I received a message sent to me on Instagram, it said: 'Online Art School is Not Art School'. I agree" (N8).

Cultural workers who had part-time jobs lose them; COVID-19 is definitely an enemy of precariat (N2, doctoral student).

And, last but not least, what did politicians do?

During the first weeks, I had abrasions on my ear from the phone's earpiece and even bigger ones in my head from all the communication apps, each with its own double security code that I still haven't managed to memorize. I constantly have voices in my ear, but rarely a person nearby.

The meetings that are most important for me as an elected representative are canceled – I cannot meet with sick, frail or dying people now. I absolutely do not want to disturb the employees in healthcare or care units. They have enough to do anyway. At the same time, it is impossible to do a good job without being able to listen to the people potentially affected by my suggestions and decisions.

Sometimes I have problems falling asleep at night after having heard stories about protective equipment that chafes wounds in the face, or the hours of helplessness behind misty visors, or the sadness in the voices of isolated people, sometimes couples who have loved each other for sixty years who have not met for weeks. After hearing about such things, I believe my life is almost as usual. (N18, MP)

"Almost as usual" was practically the motto of the next period.

May–June 2020

After the initial shock and anxiety of March and April, the following couple of months saw a more thoughtful reorganizing of life and work for many units of the public sector and their employees. Life became almost as usual, and when it could not be so, as in the case of people in the so-called risk group—70+, chronic diseases—it could be reorganized:

As soon as I heard about the virus, I went home and sat in quarantine. I have chronic heart failure after a small heart attack, asthma that gets worse with pollen, and impaired lung function. I am lucky to have a job that I can do from home, three children who live nearby and who can help me with shopping and such. I sometimes meet my children and grandchildren outdoors – keeping our distance, of course. I also sometimes meet friends, go for walks and talk. (N14, social services, also a politician)

In many situations, even "the usual" needed to be reorganized somewhat:

Then we have the situation caused by COVID-19 when you suddenly have consumed a whole annual consumption of a product in one week instead of one year. Then, the whole system collapses. After all, everything is based on how we usually do things, and this is not a "how-we-usually-do", when the

> deliveries fail, then the transportation fails, and so on. Such situations reveal that our "usual ways of doing things" are based on standard situations that rarely exist. (N19, hospital administrator)

There are routines for practically everything, but they had to be adapted now:

> We are falling behind a mountain of work that is in front of us, and much of it is surgeries, because they have staff that can be moved to intensive care units. Thus, by opening more intensive care units, the surgery capacity is cut down. These patients whose surgery is delayed are assumed to be stable and not getting worse during the waiting period, but in the end you never know. If the waiting time changed from three months to nine, how much has their condition changed? If nothing else, such waiting time has been painful and difficult for the person awaiting surgery. (N19, hospital administrator)

The reorganization of routines also sharpens existing tensions between administrators and front-line medical staff:

> The common story is that the healthcare staff are the heroes, and the others are just rubbish; they just sit and complain. And anyone who is not in direct contact with patients is an administrator. Yet a nurse can also act as an administrator if he/she is sitting and planning care visits, but that is not how they see themselves; they are as something else. And then it is often the case that the nurse who administrates care visits may not do this efficiently. Instead, it should be some administratively trained person who would do this more efficiently. (N19, hospital administrator)

Nevertheless, everybody gets used to how things are:

> It has become normal life. I do not believe anyone knows how this will end; right now, it is how it is. I get the feeling that the healthcare professionals will continue to do the same for many, many years, while non-healthcare workers probably believe that in December everything will be normal again. I thought at first that in the worst-case scenario, we would have to deal with this for three years – which felt so insanely long, so one was ready to give up already. Then I came to grips with it, and time goes on. It works! Even if it does not work very well. (N19, hospital administrator)

For many persons, it wasn't unusual that the old problems met new problems, as in the case of a culture organization that has been reorganized and renovated, and was about to be re-opened when COVID-19 came. No wonder some of cultural workers felt somewhat overburdened:

> The old usual Atlas syndrome begins; the world rests on my shoulders. (Talk about hubris; I'm just annoying.) My hands are shaking, my hereditary tremor has gotten an extra boost, the coffee spills. I feel sick. (N13, art teacher, who also made a few drawings to illustrate this situation)

Not only did old problems meet new problems, but there were also various conflicts within the hierarchy—almost as usual, but somewhat different. Screen instructions from the top of the hierarchy became a daily event, but they were barely helpful:

> The Municipal Culture Director tells us from the screen to go home to our families, not to be alone (as if it were a cancer diagnosis), and if we have any questions, we should turn to our manager. Turn to our manager means turn to the person who has made a career (during less than one year serving as manager) of not answering emails, not visiting the facilities, not attending meetings, and by conducting reprimanding conversations with staff who were made to sign loyalty contracts and promise never to miss the bus or leave the children in preschool never again … The Cultural Director should take part in these reprimanding meetings that leave staff anxious and confused. Yet the Cultural Director says, "talk to your manager".... (N13, art teacher)

Conflicts and dysfunctional relations among different levels in the hierarchy are common in organizations, but the pandemic seems to have made them increasingly visible. As one schoolteacher told us:

> All of a sudden there came a directive from the Swedish National Agency for Education, saying that all pupils who are at home must return to school; otherwise, their absence would be reported to the Compulsory School Unit. They would then need to submit a medical certificate showing that they have relatives or people they live with in the same house who are in a risk group.
>
> The tragicomic thing about this is that the two families that I know are in risk groups responded immediately. I wrote to tell them that they must

> obtain a medical certificate, because of course the pupils should stay at home. They thanked me very much. Then they returned saying that they contacted a physician who told them that there were no such certificates. (…) What could I do? I could keep one child in a single room as much as possible, which I did. I made sure that the other child went to lunch break with me five minutes earlier to avoid the queues and could finish school five minutes earlier to go alone to the cloakroom. (N17, elementary schoolteacher)

Nevertheless, the teacher added, "The pupils themselves gradually adapted, some directly, and others after a while (…) The school must adapt in such a way that parents can send their children to school without being too worried about them acquiring infection."

There were many risk assessments being done and to convince pupils to maintain distance, one looked for attractive metaphors: "keep a distance of a small elk"—or maybe a large elk? Hand sanitizer was at every entrance, and meetings were held outside—if it didn't snow.

New and highly controversial was the extreme media attention paid to COVID-19, and not only by journalists. Researchers, especially epidemiologists and virologists, received a great deal of attention in the media, both through their own articles and through interviews conducted by journalists. The announcements made regularly by the Public Health Agency of Sweden and its main epidemiologist, Anders Tegnell, constituted the center of the agitated debate, which continues as we write this text. The reactions differed.

Interviewer: What is your feeling about the decisions made by the Public Health Agency? How have they been received within your research circle?

N15: It varies. Some think they were great. (…) I would say that the reactions in our circle were quite close to opinions in the general public. Researchers and physicians are not more or less critical, but, like everybody else, they feel the psychological effect of the crisis. The common reaction is that you join up behind a strong leader, and the Public Health Agency has given a calm and trustworthy impression in the beginning. The general feeling was that you should join them rather than add to the anxiety.

> Now I do not know. Now maybe people are starting to think that being calm and passive is not right. Now they might want someone who says: "This is what we should do to get rid of this shitty virus." But many still think "Let the experts decide. They know this stuff; we should not question it…". (N15, medical researcher)

Another person (N16, researcher in medicine) has had a decisively negative view of this matter:

> I think the media has handled this quite badly, especially TV. They insist that they are meticulous because they really want to give society an answer to important questions. In my case, I tried, time after time, to say that there is no answer, and it wouldn't be very smart of me to guess, because then people will think that I really know. So instead of informing people that we actually do not know, they asked the poor experts who were invited the same questions time and time again. X felt quite exposed when they cut down her statement and placed it in opposition to the person who was there the night before (…) as if they had some kind of debate, when they really were two people who did not know, either of them. They just have slightly different views.

The mediatization of their expertise exposed researchers to hate messages from social media:

> X received a load of hate emails after her appearance on TV. "Another bloody expert who says she does not know. That's how it is with women in academia. They don't have to work hard, those gender quota idiots!" Well, obviously people become emotional when they watch this program… (N16)

> A colleague whom I greatly admire started writing personal attacks against PHA's critic, and I said that what you are writing is wrong. And that it's weird to hang someone out like that on social media. A long discussion then began in which that person slightly changed the text but still maintained the same position. I said that I hope we can respect each other's opinions, even if we think differently (…) Then my colleague answered: "No! I save my respect for those who work hard at the Public Health Agency! Not for their critics. I have no respect for them". (N15)

Yet universities experienced also some positive developments. In an unusually short time, new international networks have been created, and they keep working with a shared data base (N15). A well-known Swedish foundation donated a large sum for COVID-19 research, and in three days 280 applications arrived (N16). N16 was also of the opinion that the crisis helped the very organization of the university:

> One thing that I hope will last is that we now can see what works and what does not work within the academy. For example, the leadership election was in progress at my university. (…) It turned out that during the days we were to vote for the vice-principal [a large] conference was on, so it was impossible to vote via link. The problem has been resolved by removing various outdated nonsense. This also applies to the course descriptions and other things that have had to be simplified. Everything does not necessarily get worse.

It is possible, however, that universities have better opportunities to solve problems and introduce new and better methods than do other organizations. An employee at the Immigration Authority was not enthusiastic about the new rule according to which people applying for asylum had to be interviewed via video.

> On the first day the system works poorly, and I suffer from a real surge in my stress level. The translation via telephone is slow, and I often need to repeat myself. The applicant does not see me well enough to understand whether or not I am satisfied with the answer. After three hours of that, I go home and have to sleep for two hours.
>
> This way of interviewing continues for two weeks until the technology is improved. We then get separate screens for protocols and video. The interpreters continue to maintain an uneven quality. Approximately every other interview must be canceled due to poor translations. About half the applicants do not come to their asylum interview, referring to cold-like symptoms. (N18)

Although changes in technology were common in all organizations, Immigration Authority employees experienced a dramatic change that had an enormous impact on their work: closed borders.

> It is a strange feeling to work at a migration agency when the national borders are closed. Asylum seekers are rapidly changing from new arrivals to people who speak decent Swedish, and who have lost their jobs due to the pandemic. As they did not have a work permit, they worked "a little here and there" as they say. I get the feeling that this is the end of open borders

> and that I am holding the last asylum interviews of my life – perhaps the last in the whole world. I'm wondering what the Swedish Immigration Authority will do when no one is able to travel either in or out – perhaps start verifying people in the country like the Swedish Public Employment Service does? No, this will probably rather be the new role of the border police (...) Several of my colleagues are now transferring to the police. What should I do? I like my job. (...) I push that question away and keep on working. (...)
>
> I have little to do at work right now, and my motivation has plummeted quickly. The few asylum interviews that can actually be carried out are far from enough to keep me busy. I take unnecessary and complicated courses on how certain EU directives correlate with certain sections of the European Convention. I read the Aliens Act with comments. I read several hours a day but long to work quickly like I did before. The competition with myself seems to be over now. How to find the motivation that will last until this crisis is over? (N18)

One has to hope that the immigration employee got in a better mood during summer holidays (if able to enjoy them). Many employees in public sector organizations worked during the summer, but the virus was less aggressive then, and there was more time for reflection. Also, many persons got themselves "corona dogs" (N16, N24, and one of us) and could spend more time outside walking them. The better weather helped too:

> Today I sat on the balcony and first watched our press conference and then the Public Health Agency's press conference. Am happy with my balcony. (N15, university press officer)

July–August 2020

Reflections often lead to divided conclusions: on the one hand, but on the other hand. And apparently so it was even in summer 2020: on the one hand, most public sector employees became used to the new state of affairs, but on the other hand, they speculated about whether things will change or remain the same after COVID-19 disappears. Obviously, the main hopes and fears concerned just that: they hoped it would disappear, but they were aware that another wave was expected.

As to their daily practices, the digital meetings became shorter and more effective, but there were so many of them that people felt tired. And practically all our respondents complained about lack of physical contact, both in the sense of missing observations of body language and in the sense of touch in the form of hand shaking and embraces. Yet they realized that constant hand washing and physical distancing may prevent the spread of viruses and bacteria in the future, which would be beneficial for health-care units and schools, and even for society in general.

Family adjustments also took place. On the one hand, work and life were completely mixed together; on the other hand, parents could spend more time with their children. Some people felt crowded in their flats, others felt lonely; yet better weather (and corona dogs) permitted more time outside, in the fresh air, in parks, and in nature.

Two developments did not have a silver lining: the sorrow of those who lost family members, and the isolation of the elderly who lived in homes. Here, our respondents were in the same situation as everybody else in the country.

A university teacher in the social sciences suggested that the wave of COVID-19-related death "dehumanized" death itself:

> When we got the outbreak of the pandemic, there was also some kind of dehumanizing of those who died. People started saying that it is "only" the elderly and sick that die. What do they mean by only? It was the whole society that built the welfare state taking care of the elderly, and then suddenly we exclude them. This is where the first (…) exclusion happened, at these press conferences where they listed the death tolls: Today 115 have died, today 14 have died, we can see a trend, and so on. It became a kind of death raffle somehow. (N21)

Over the summer, many tensions within the hierarchy seemed to calm down, but the contrast between that which was recommended and that which was possible continued, not the least in the Swedish Armed Forces:

> My experience is that the Swedish Armed Forces has classified itself as carrying a vital societal function, which means that some of the Public Health Agency's recommendations have not been implemented. I am thinking mainly of the recommendation that employees should work from home as much as possible, which has not been observed, with the exception of employees that have had special cause; but even in such cases it has been the unit manager's decision. The reason for this, I believe, is a combination of the fact that Armed Forces is a vital societal organization, but also that our IT systems are not built for working from home and that insurance is not valid when working from home. (N20)

Even if the IT system works well in some jobs—that of family counsellors,[2] for example—secrecy obligation excludes the use of digital meetings and contacts. They check their own and their clients' health, keep their distance and continue with their work. It was only family counsellors who noted quite a few surprising and even paradoxical reactions. For some, COVID-19 meant less rather than more stress.

> It has reduced stress enormously, especially for families with small children. I have heard parents say "Hallelujah! Thanks! We are not allowed to visit my parents-in-law, hooray!"
>
> It's a bit provoking, because otherwise the media has stayed mostly with "more crises, more divorces", etc. But then I looked at the statistics, and, yes, there were a few more couples who applied for divorce in July, but was it statistically significant? Perhaps they would have divorced earlier but postponed it because now it's COVID-19 times, more leisure, so they did it in droves. But the focus is usually on what is worse because of the pandemic. Yet there are quite a few persons who come here and say "Good, there is less stress, we work at home, we have coffee together as if we were co-workers, you can joke a bit more." More time with the kids. More excursions. I have not met anyone who says shit towards the Corona – no, not a single one. I think that is a bit strange considering the media. But we are not supposed to say anything. (N23)

Even the lack of physical contact has become normal, but family counsellors would prefer to go back to it:

> Yes, you can work normally without shaking people's hands. It is possible to make people feel welcomed anyway, just in a different way. You look people in the eye. You look a little kinder and so on. Everyone knows how to reach out.
>
> But I think that having closeness and physical contact is important. That if someone breaks down, it would be quite nice if I could lean over and just pat him or her. I don't do that now; I discreetly hand the person a tissue instead. I do it differently, but I miss being more personal – personal, not private. The new directives raise a barrier; though perhaps it does not matter with the new contacts. But I have to explain that I am not shaking hands every time I meet somebody in these new times. These will soon be old times; in a few months, this will be "how we have always done it". Our visitors would be shocked now if we shook hands. (N23)

Family counsellors were almost amazed at their own and other people's capacities to adapt:

> There was a period, before K and I fell ill, when everyone was extra introspective and afraid. We all thought "Wow, it will be here soon!" And personally, I was quite scared. I had cancer before, have quite sensitive lungs, and am in my 60s. So it was a period when we were all a bit hypochondriac. But by now we are used to it.
>
> I think it has been surprisingly easy to adapt. Everyone else had to do it, so we must do the same. It is an amazing ability that we humans have: We adapt! It feels a little strange at first, but then it is not too strange. I find that fascinating. (N23)

Even after more than half a year since the pandemic came to Sweden, the counsellors, to their surprise, kept noticing several positive effects:

> I think there is something good in it: People have become healthier. I was ill, but it was probably because I handed that sick kid into the pram. No stomach aches, because we have become cleaner, or because we keep our distance. That's unbelievable.
>
> … and there is a concern about how you are doing. Ask, check with neighbors, those who have been ill. "How are you? Can I do your shopping for you…?" People have become kinder, and it is a different pace when you are out shopping. (…) People wait, are not stressed, keep their distance. And even if somebody does not do this, you ask them to, and no one gets angry about it.
>
> Some have received calls even if they are not 70+. People asked "How are you? Should we grocery shop for you?" This is caring! You have to help each other. It was a lot like that in the beginning, but now it has ebbed out. But people are still hovering over their circle of acquaintances: If someone is ill, you call and check, send a text. I think there is much more caring. (N23)

But how was it in the center of things—at hospitals where COVD-19 patients were treated? In August, we were able to interview a nurse who had joined a newly created COVID-19 section in April. In the beginning, it was like in all other places: nobody knew much.

> All of a sudden, I ended up in this department. We were simply thrown in: different nurses and assistant nurses and infection physicians. All of a sudden, we were in a department where they told us "Just like you, we know

> nothing. This is completely new to us, too. We haven't a clue what is to come. We do think this equipment will be great." So that was what we focused on. We were familiar with the department and knew how to put on and take off the equipment we needed. Then it was just a matter of receiving patients. (N22)

Were they trained? Were there things they were supposed to learn first—new routines, new devices? Or should they just start working?

> No, we just went for it. We have [a platform], with updates that come almost daily, and so you learn that "you may not need to have those gloves when you have this kind of contact with the patient, but when it comes to bodily fluids, always wear them". (…) You try to stay updated via email where there are usually links, while the managers usually make updates on the bulletin board: "Follow this link!" "Check this out! A physician has now made a video about new things we should think about!" (N22)

Healthcare workers became more and more used to their new job, where it soon became clear that, in order to be effective, everybody must be prepared to do everything—not least in order to save the protective equipment:

> As a nurse with COVID-19 patients, you need to save the equipment so that it doesn't run out, so you should try to take on as many tasks as possible before you go into the ward, to avoid going out again. (…) Sometimes we do the assistant nurse's job as well. It's great fun when perhaps the physicians are sitting there, and you say "… as you're already in there, can't you take the blood sugar level as well? Can you bring the pills for these patients?"
>
> But the physicians still have to go in and talk to the patient daily, describe the situation and so on. And it's funny because they have to do everything, be both nurses and assistant nurses. (…) This has always been the case, I think, throughout the hospital. I have been to another department to see if I wanted to work there. Then the manager came and told me that "Today I'm an assistant nurse, we'll talk later!" She was just giving a shower to a patient. You are like a jack-of-all-trades, or you turn into one. (N22)

But in this new section of the hospital, death was much more common than in the other sections. How does one deal with that?

> You definitely become more thick-skinned. My changing room is next to the cold storage where the bodies end up. I'm starting an evening shift, and on

> the way to my dressing room there is a bed, and I see that a bit of a bumpy surface outlining a face. It's a body lying underneath, but you think "Oh, I'll just go by and get changed!" And then you think, "What or who did I just pass by? Should I just continue my day?" It feels unreal. And we have had many situations where the restrictions did not allow relatives to come and say goodbye to their loved ones, to their father, to their grandfather… (N22)

How do other people react when they learn that you work in a COVID-19 section?

> They retreat. Every time I tell them that I work in a COVID-19 department, I notice they often say, "Well, is that so…". Then you feel a little like the plague. I received a text message today from a friend who had a baby: "I don't think we should meet, because you are still working in that department." But there is a greater risk for me to be infected in a grocery store, in the gym, and in other hospital departments, but people don't know that, and how can they know? They hear only that I work with COVID-19 patients. It's quite funny how people get so damn afraid. In my world, it's fine to be seeing each other as long as you keep your distance, maintain good hygiene, don't hug and don't shake hands.
>
> Yes, one feels like a bit of a plague, especially in the beginning. I thought then that I could not meet anyone, not even my family. Now I know that I can do it as long as we are outdoors. (N22)

So, you are not treated as a hero?

> Not at all. I just do my job. I try to remember that patients are persons. I am not here to give them pills and run out of here, but to make them know that even Aunt Agda must be well cared for.[3] Then you get to hear a lot from them too, when they can forget that they are sick, and instead feel that they are persons, and that they can talk to you about anything. Otherwise, they feel very lonely there, as they are not allowed to meet anyone, and they haven't met anyone since Easter. Then you hear some nice things: "You are an angel!" "Well, thank you!" (N22)

And in such a mix of positive and negative feelings and experiences, Sweden entered the new wave of COVID-19.

September–October 2020

We have received only three accounts from this period, which was another support for our conclusion that a "new normal" has been established. Furthermore, all three respondents, whom we interviewed, offered us a story of adaptations to COVID-19 from the first to the second wave of the pandemics, emphasizing the changes that took place.

N25, a vice-director of a regional medical clinic, estimated that 80% of the vice-director's role was dedicated to issues related to COVID-19 in March, whereas in September it was only 25%.

As digital skills continued to improve, new fora were created. At a state-owned company educating people with disabilities (N24), there are Teams meetings every morning at 08.30: "good for the psyche!" The medical clinic created a special forum that meets once a week and includes all public and private primary caregivers in the region, together with regional hospitals and representatives of relevant state agencies. Many questions are being asked about general guidelines, but also quite a few about protective equipment, which was scarce at the beginning, but well provided later.

> In my experience, it has been difficult to provide information that will reach all 800 managers. You can follow the waterfall principle, but we know that it is not secure. And so now we started a "Team Channel", which contains information, and where one can ask questions and see what the latest guidelines are. They say that out of 800 managers, 797 have read the information, which indicates commitment and involvement. Previously, we might have reached 400: That's a big difference! (N24)

> Overall, I think that [digital meetings] work very well. No matter if it is two people who meet, like now or if they are larger meetings. We had a meeting with 100 people. In the beginning, it was awkward: People forgot to unmute and there was a hassle, but everybody has become great at this now. And these meetings are much more efficient, though shorter. I think that in the future, we shouldn't have full-day management team meetings. (…) You could halve the time of all meetings. But I do not believe in digital only; it's good to meet in person, to have some small talk in the coffee room. I think somewhere in between would be good. (N25, vice-director at a regional medical clinic)

Apart from nostalgia for IRL (in real life) contacts with colleagues, there are also certain tasks that are difficult to perform digitally—recruitment, for example:

> I have been recruiting, and it's not much fun to begin with (…) It is an even bigger challenge doing it digitally. If you have interviews or meetings via Teams, you have to stay even more present than if you had sat in a physical meeting. Maybe not during an [in-person] interview, when you have to stay alert, but at regular meetings, where you can be more relaxed. Digitally you have to be constantly aware of what is happening and think through your approach very carefully, because if you talk for too long, you will lose people's attention. (N24, employee working with people with disabilities)

Although new leadership challenges may be even exciting, the reasons for their emergence have been somewhat frightening:

> At first, it was a bit exciting to be a part of this from a leadership perspective. Then it was mixed with horror after seeing that there are a lot of people in intensive care, and people dying. What should we do? How can we contribute to reducing the spread of infection? But from a leadership perspective, it was still cool to see that, all of a sudden, our decision-making route became much shorter. We made quicker decisions that could have the disadvantage of not everyone being involved, but faster, direct decisions.
>
> For me personally, it was extremely hard work. I've never worked so much. (…). I came home at eight o'clock every night and I worked every weekend. At first it was also exciting, but when I went on holiday for Midsummer, I felt that I wanted to go to the summer cottage and be alone, putter around in the garden… No bastard to ask me anything because I did not want to answer any more questions. I did not want to make any more decisions! It has been a very intense and tough time. (N25, vice-director at a regional medical clinic)

It needs to be added that one of the most dramatic developments in Sweden was the number of deaths at homes for the elderly. Since the 1992 reform, the homes were under municipal responsibility, but it was social workers, not physicians, who decided how they should be run. Yet, it was the medical clinic that had to take care of persons who became infected.

> I felt great responsibility when I sat with these municipal managers responsible for social services. From my perspective – that is, a physician's perspective – they were way too late in the game. I thought, "We have to segregate!

> We must separate infected people from healthy ones." They thought that these people live there, it is their residence, many of them are demented, and we have no right to coerce them. So we had very different worldviews. I felt "Help! We must do something!" They thought we were going overboard and didn't understand their perspective. I thought that social workers did not have the proper medical skills (…), and that there should be not only nurses, but also physicians in the homes.
>
> It was truly frustrating. I got a report from our specialists: "This is not possible; they are letting them die!". They may have thought that some of the things we said were provocative, but quite a lot of changes were needed. (…). When I look back, I understand that it was very tough for them. They had almost no equipment, as it was prioritized to the regions, not to municipalities. There are a lot of part time staff, and new staff who lack training. Now I can see their perspective as well. (N25)

In the end, there was a greater understanding of challenges met at different levels and different places—an understanding that hopefully will remain. Also, our respondents understood the relative advantage of the fact that they were working in public sector organizations and were not threatened, therefore, by redundancies and firings.

One noteworthy observation was that managing—planning, coordinating and monitoring subordinates' work—seems to be based more on trust:

> The largest change is working based on trust (…) My subordinates and I do more or less the same things, but as the opportunity for dialogue is not great, an email will do: "Can you look at this issue, please?" (…) We know that email is not a good communication channel, so we try to shorten messages, highlight what is central, and base our work on that. And then we have to solve the problem and get back if they need support. (N32, manager at Immigration Authority)

All our interlocutors missed social contacts, not least because such contacts are the best way of handling anxiety, which unavoidable in a pandemic situation. They were also convinced that the border between work and home has been erased for good and predicted that there will be much less need for office spaces. People will travel less in the future, and there will be no further need for "digital education". Hopefully, "corona dogs" will remain and will be well taken care of!

Short Summary

As described by our respondents, the changes caused by the pandemic in public sector organizations began with a period of uncertainty, great confusion and miscommunications among hierarchical levels. Some directives were impossible to follow, whereas some necessary requirements remained unanswered.

In the next stage, the old routines were adapted, and new routines were introduced. Digitalization of communication, among the employees and externally, achieved levels never reached before. And while the internal conflicts practically ceased, the public and the social media dramatized their news, creating as many conflicts as possible.

During the summer, COVID-19 slowed down a bit; some people were able to take holidays, and there was much time and opportunity to reflect over what had happened and what will happen in the future. Accounts of positive and negative developments could be made.

As the next wave of the pandemic came in the autumn, public sector organizations were much better prepared for it, so the situation could be seen as the "new normal".

Were those developments typical for Sweden? The international media were not behind the national media, working together at creating dramatic contrasts between "the Swedish strategy" and that of its neighbors. Although this dramatization continues, we have no similar field material from other countries to compare with ours, although we do hope to receive them from Norway.

Pandemicracy at Work

The stories in this chapter illustrate how various governance efforts related to the pandemic influenced public sector employees' thoughts, feelings and actions. The pandemicratic practices were transformed between March and October 2020 from an anxiety-generating emergency to a new normal, with a debated projection of the future between a longing for IRL and the unimaginable possibility to get back to a pre-COVID19 world. A specific pandemicratic ethos is detectable in the stories presented here, an ethos relying on personal sacrifice, flexibility, sympathy, and work/life blurring—in spite of the background of frustration, social isolation and the temporary feeling of meaninglessness.

Despite old and new problems, our interlocutors, whether writing or talking, have testified to the efforts and capacity of the public sector to deal with the pandemic by adjusting existing ways of working and by inventing and accepting novel routines, working conditions and spatial arrangements. We highlight here two ways in which the pandemicracy has been performed: the professional response and the organizational response. These responses have had different timing and at times conflicted with one another, as witnessed by our narrators.

The professional response to the pandemic has built on previously acquired expertise, and the professionals' abilities and autonomy of judgment based on that expertise. Outside the healthcare sector, the expertise of teachers, social workers, cultural workers, and others provided the basis on which they could quickly transform and expand their professional conduct. This was especially visible in the first months of the pandemic and seemed to be crucial in shaping the resilience of the public sector. Paradoxically, necessary changes in practices guaranteed continuity of the welfare infrastructure, despite the disruptions caused by new restrictions and recommendations. It was due to these disruptions that in the first, critical period, many public employees perceived organizational responses to the pandemic more as an obstacle to their professional work than a support.

From the summer of 2020 onward, public sector organizations seemed to catch up with the changes introduced by the professionals, and the sharp controversies between professions and management typical of the spring gave way to a more balanced relationship. The professional resilience of teachers, nurses, physicians, social workers, administrators, researchers, and other professionals were often in our stories, presented in contrast to the administrative burdens and expectations of adherence to various management trends and bureaucratic practices. But the post-summer "new normal" revealed many a compromise (e.g., Hendrikx & Van Gestel, 2017).

One could actually distinguish different phases of organizational adaptation to the pandemic:

Initial paralysis: unpreparedness, malpractice, decoupling, poor protection;

Obstruction: counteracting, cancelling, delaying, sticking to formal procedures, inertia, feeling diminished by the "heroic" professionals;

Recognition: acceptance of necessary changes, temporal adjustments, simplification, delegation, and realization that such changes may last.

One could claim that the pandemic has had a revealing effect on what constitutes the core of public activities. The stories we collected testify to the role of professional knowledge and skills for the resilience of the public sector, visible especially at the outset of the pandemic, and to the shifting relationships between professional and organizational responses over time. In normal times, governing public sector organizations is typified by significant efforts and resources linked to formal coordination, policies and rules within and between organizations. Yet, in crisis, it was not this type of effort and resources that guaranteed the continuity of public services, but the professional expertise of public servants (see also Christensen & Lægreid, 2017).

In conclusion, our study of Swedish pandemicracy at work demonstrates the need for a better understanding of the tensions between professional and organizational knowledge, and of the different effects of bureaucratization and managerialism at different times (Ahlbäck Öberg & Bringselius, 2014). Many studies of the public sector indicate that modern rationalization makes contemporary public sector organizations and their governance increasingly complex, bureaucratized, and de-professionalized (e.g., Lindberg et al., 2015; Wällstedt & Almqvist, 2015). At the same time, opinions of the users clearly indicate that it is the professionality of the public sector servants that is most valued and expected (e.g., Solli et al., 2020). Developments during the pandemic show that the reduced autonomy of professionals is neither necessary nor positive.

Notes

1. "Daycare" (*daghemmet*) is now called "preschool" in Sweden.
2. We interviewed two of them at the same time, and they spoke as one voice.
3. Aunt Agda is character from books by Hungarian-Swedish writer Adam Gönczi, symbolizing an older person living in the countryside with no digital skills.

References

Ahlbäck Öberg, Shirin, & Bringselius, Louise. (2014). Professionalism and organizational performance in the wake of new managerialism. *European Political Science Review, 7*(4), 499–523.

Banks, Sarah, Cai, Tian, de Jonge, Ed, Shears, Jane, Shum, Michelle, Sobočan, Ana M., Strom, Kim, Truell, Rory, Úriz, Maria Jesùs, & Weinberg, Merlinda. (2020). Practising ethically during COVID-19: Social work challenges and responses. *International Social Work, 63*(5), 569–583.

Christensen, Tom, & Lægreid, Per. (2017). *Transcending new public management* (2nd ed.). Routledge.

Hendrikx, Wiljan, & Van Gestel, Nicolette. (2017). The emergence of hybrid professional roles: GPs and secondary school teachers in a context of public sector reform. *Public Management Review, 19*(8), 1105–1123.

Lee, Helena. (2021). Changes in workplace practices during the COVID-19 pandemic: The roles of emotion, psychological safety and organisation support. *Journal of Organizational Effectiveness: People and Performance, 8.* Advanced online publication.

Lemieux, Thomas, Milligan, Kevin, Schirle, Tammy, & Skuterud, Mikal. (2020). Initial impacts of the COVID-19 pandemic on the Canadian labour market. *Canadian Public Policy, 46*(S1), 55–65.

Lindberg, Kajsa, Czarniawska, Barbara, & Solli, Rolf. (2015). After NPM? *Scandinavian Journal of Public Administration, 19*(2), 3–6.

López-Cabarcos, M. Àngeles, López-Carballeira, Analia, & Ferro-Soto, Carlos. (2020). New ways of working and public healthcare professionals' well-being: The response to face the COVID-19 pandemic. *Sustainability, 12*(19), 80–87.

Mazzucato, Mariana, & Kattel, Rainer. (2020). COVID-19 and public-sector capacity. *Oxford Review of Economic Policy, 36*(1), 256–269.

Power, Michael. (1999). *The audit society: Rituals of verification.* Oxford University Press.

Solli, Rolf, Czarniawska, Barbara, Demediuk, Peter, & Anderson, Dennis. (2020). *Searching for the new welfare models.* Palgrave Macmillan.

Wällstedt, Niklas, & Almqvist, Roland. (2015). From 'either or' to 'both and': Organisational management in the aftermath of NPM. *Scandinavian Journal of Public Administration, 19*(2), 7–25.

CHAPTER 3

The Mysteries of Iconic Leadership on Zoom

Barry Brummett

The Mysteries of Iconic Leadership on Zoom

In the spring semester of 2020, I was Chair of a large academic department. The pandemic arrived on my watch, and I was centrally involved in the planning and preparation for how to adjust to new realities. I stepped down as Chair in the summer. This changed world paralleled the start of the role of Chair in August 2001, just days before another series of events occurred that would "change everything": 9/11. So I came in and went out in crisis. But the pandemic brought some technological changes to how leaders were publicly presented in that we all became, from time to time, pictures on Zoom or other media platforms.

As for the pandemic, I think all of us shared the sentiment so often expressed in popular media, that the world had changed, especially the world of work and organizing, and would never be the same. Popular outlets issued declarations such as "An altered future seems inevitable. Just over half of those polled in September by the Pew Research Center said they expect their lives will remain changed in major ways after the

B. Brummett (✉)
The University of Texas at Austin, Austin, TX, USA
e-mail: brummett@austin.utexas.edu

L. D. Browning et al. (eds.), *Organizational Communication and Technology in the Time of Coronavirus*,
https://doi.org/10.1007/978-3-030-94814-6_3

pandemic" (della Cava, 2020, p. 1). "The Pandemic Changed Everything," trumpeted one headline (Shuey, 2020, p. 1), and another announced, "How the Coronavirus Changed Everything" (Bridges, 2020, p. 1), while another declared, "COVID-19 pandemic changed everything this year—including how I prepared to have a baby" (Lips, 2020, p. 1).

One change was that online education, previously so widely scorned as a vehicle of substandard, second-rate, and mail-in diploma mills, had suddenly become the way that teaching and learning happened across the academy. For most of the academy as well as business in general, work life went online. I was struck by how quickly my university went from strict prohibitions against staff working from home to strict prohibitions against staff coming in to work. We went from decades of "this work cannot be done from home" to "this work must be done from home." My Dean wisely forbade all but the most essential staff from coming to our buildings, even if, as he said, we were suffering from cabin fever. In fact, I cannot recall the last time I saw my Dean in person. I have new colleagues whom I have never met in person. Most of my students I have never seen. Across the nation, public schools toggle back and forth between in person and completely mediated interactions. Implications across organizations have been striking. Would workers ever congregate together physically again? What would happen to real estate prices and rents if office spaces stayed empty? How can a cohesive organization be maintained online? How can business be conducted under such conditions?

Likewise, families and friendships shifted away from immediate personal contact to mediated interaction. One dared not see the grandchildren, for what if little Grizelda or Boldegard had been exposed to the virus at school? Simple friendly handshakes were replaced by Covid fistbumps, if that, and more often by completely mediated interaction. I well recall a visit in person with family members who were awaiting test results (eventually, negative) and the children were sternly warned by parents to keep their distance due to my age and certain risk factors. Since then we often have "reunions" online.

It quickly became apparent that the main vehicle for this shift of interaction was the software program Zoom. "While gathering considerable popularity and coming to run profitably in the following years, Zoom truly entered the public consciousness during the coronavirus pandemic of 2020. It was to Zoom that users across the world turned to stay in touch during the lockdown effected to stop the spread of the virus" (Iqbal, 2021, p. 1). Workers, teachers, students, and administrators scrambled to learn its intricacies. Zoom became a staple of business operations. Most, if not all, instruction from first grade through graduate school became grounded in Canvas, Blackboard, and so forth, with which many were unfamiliar. Even these online teaching platforms such as Canvas were supplemented by Zoom lectures, office hours, and one-on-one meetings. Senior staff and instructors scrambled to learn the ropes. My College assembled teams of experts to render advice, to assemble FAQs, and to establish hotlines for help with newly adopted technologies of interaction. It was not a matter of learning Zoom for the fun of it. Rather, it became integrated into other technologies, into the deep organization of groups and institutions. New folk maladies were declared such as Zoom fatigue. War stories were shared among those who had to leave one Zoom meeting to go attend another, perhaps for the fifth time that day. Knowing how to set up a Zoom meeting became an essential skill. A technology that few knew of in 2019 became central to shared life.

Unfamiliarity and anxiety with online technology seemed to afflict senior staff and faculty the most. The running joke for those who were puzzled was, go ask a thirteen-year-old. This befuddlement fell especially hard on those like me, who have gradually seen technology slip away from us. I have been a fairly constant user of technology in my personal and professional life, but on both fronts I see it outrunning me (see Fig. 3.1). As I approach retirement, I yearn for when I might just go sit in an easy chair with a book. Now, if I need to use Zoom with others, I ask them to initiate it, as even that skill is floating away from me. Zoom and these other technologies of interaction are increasingly mysterious to me.

Given the novel centrality of Zoom to mediated work and personal lives during the pandemic, it is important to understand its dynamics, how it shapes those who use it, and how those who use it must adapt to Zoom. The centrality of Zoom makes it not just a technology to master but a way to interact with others, to manifest ourselves in public, to organize work, and to conduct human affairs. There are many attempts to explain and understand this new Zoom-ified world (Hu, 2019; Morris, 2020; Wiederhold, 2020), but I want to offer a rhetorical, aesthetic explanation of what Zoom is doing to us and how it works cognitively. As a basis for this explanation, I turn to the twentieth-century American theorist Kenneth Burke (1969, 1970).

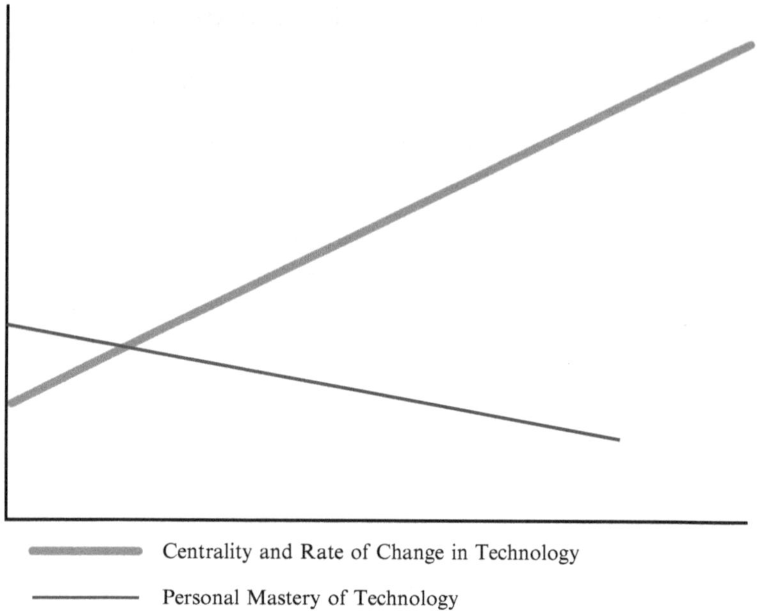

Fig. 3.1 Personal mastery of technology

Identification and Mystery in Human Affairs

Kenneth Burke has been described as a "Yankee crank." Born as the twentieth century was arriving, his youth was spent in Pittsburgh. He studied briefly at The Ohio State University, but never earned a college degree. He was a literary and music critic in the Greenwich Village, New York City, intellectual and cultural scene, and made a living doing reviews and writing critical articles. Later he was a visiting faculty at several universities, most notably Bennington. He made his home in a New Jersey farmhouse that lacked electricity for decades. He died at the end of the twentieth century.

A key concept for Burke (1969) is *identification*. I think most people who have read very little Burke will know that concept and be able to give a simple but accurate account of it. Burke sees the long history of rhetorical theory and action as essentially *agonistic*, that is to say, based on a sense of conflict and struggle as key to human life. Rhetoric, in this tradition, is the practice and rationale of winning the war of words, of getting one over on the other fellow, of gaining the upper hand. But Burke proposes a new perspective for our times. He does not deny the importance of what he calls The Barnyard Scrabble (Burke, 1969, p. 20), but he identifies a competing motive which he sees as of increasing importance in our era of potential mass destruction, genocide, and ongoing war. That motive is identification.

Burke argues that a central human motive, easily as strong as competition and conquest, is that of identification. Identification occurs when people share, perceive that they share, or can successfully claim to share common interests: "A is not identical with his colleague, B. But insofar as their interests are joined, A is *identified* with B. Yet at the same time he remains unique, an individual locus of motives. Or he may *identify himself* with B even if their interests are not joined. Thus he is both joined and separate, at once a distinct substance and consubstantial with the other" (Burke, 1969, p. 20). He observes that identification is compensatory to the divisions and differences among people, and that in fact identification is sought precisely because there is division: "Identification is affirmed with earnestness precisely because there is division. Identification is compensatory to division" (Burke, 1969, p. 22). We are all of us different from others, and to that extent we are *mysteries* to each other (Blankenship, 1988). Mystery can be threatening, and so it is that we seek out identification to counter mystery. Persuasion, social influence, thus arises in the tension between mystery and identification, for if there were no differences one would have no motive to persuade, nor would one persuade if there were nothing but differences, for then there would be no shared interest in the other to latch on to.

Identification can be found in the politician who goes into rural areas and declares, "I'm a farm boy myself," or who addresses union workers by declaring that her family worked in the automobile factories and were members of the United Auto Workers (UAW) from long back. Leaders and candidates who mine their own histories for stories of family struggle are likely seeking to show people with family struggles that they share interests. All the while, such persuasive attempts occur in the shadow of mystery. The "farm boy" may be a Catholic addressing a rural audience of Protestants, the one with UAW family members may be White addressing a Black audience. Identification never banishes difference but seeks sufficient connection in the face of difference to ground shared action and organization.

People establish identification through what Burke (1969) calls hierarchies, social arrangements that cluster and organize around shared interests in a context of mystery (Duncan, 2017). This is what organizations do. People who are different establish identification through the structure of General Motors, the local Baptist Church, the Rotary Club, or a motorcycle gang. Professors and students come to a classroom on the first day of each semester just as strange as they can be to each other, but they are bound together in the hierarchy of that class, of a department and major, of a college.

Yet division among people, or mystery, strangeness, always gnaws at the borders of hierarchies and organizations, for several reasons (Tompkins et al., 1975). One is that it is usually impossible to meet all the principles of identification that draw a hierarchy together, all of the time. It is hard if not impossible to follow the rules that hold hierarchies together. We are simply going to cheat and fail from time to time. Also, the different hierarchies we are enrolled in make conflicting demands on us, and so one may have to miss a son's dance recital (bruising the family hierarchy) so as to align with a supervisor's request to stay late after work (reaffirming the employment hierarchy). And as soon as hierarchies form, the fact that they inevitably situate their members in different roles and statuses causes mystery. Students and professors identify through the hierarchy of the class, but that very structure then makes them different from and mysteries to one another, for they take on different roles and responsibilities in the hierarchy. In a business, someone "has to" be boss and someone employee and subordinate. That artifact of organizing introduces difference and mystery. Duncan (2017) explains, "Mystery springs from difference and strangeness. … Men and women become mysteries simply through differences they uphold, and even accentuate." (p. 117).

But behold! Burke (1969) shows us another mystery, for while difference and division is threatening to many, it also is the *only* ground for the pleasure which comes from finding common ground and coming together. An absence of division, or mystery, is boring and not motivating. "In pure identification there would be no strife. Likewise, there would be no strife in absolute separateness … But put identification and division ambiguously together so that you cannot know for certain where one ends and the other begins, and you have the characteristic invitation to rhetoric" (Burke, 1969, p. 25). If there is even a little joy in overcoming mystery, then mystery has its own attractions even if at times repellent. This truth has been observed by other theorists in different terms and different language. The critical scholar bell hooks (2014) describes the pleasures of "Eating the Other," obtained from association (identification) with different others, precisely because of the difference. Her focal example is Whites who pursue social or even sexual linkages, identifications, with other races just because of the pleasurable frisson offered by overcoming mystery even as, precisely because, mystery endures: "the point is to be transformed by the convergence of pleasure and Otherness" (hooks, 2014, p. 24). Travel abroad, consuming the cuisines of different cultures, decorating one's home with artifacts of the mysterious Other, may all participate in the attractions of mystery. Similarly, the cultural scholar Virgina Postrel (2013) describes "glamor" as an attractive strangeness. Those who are glamorous are perforce different from the general public. Those differences are likely to be carefully curated and maintained by the glamorous or by their agents. The thrill that so many in the public feel at finding a celebrity in the bookstore or restaurant comes precisely from that tension between identification and mystery ("We were right there at the same bar, can you believe it?"). Note that the glamorous cannot tip over into the grotesque or abhorrent and remain attractive. Strangeness can be alluring, but too much strangeness, with little to offer to overcome it, is to be feared or avoided. Different motivations arise for our following news stories of sophisticated uptown cannibals. But unless one wants to share in a little bit of eating someone's liver, here we have mysteries that cannot be overcome.

Anyone can be mysterious and thus attractive in the right context. As a baby, I was taken by my parents to the Philippines where they were missionaries. As the only white child most Filipinos had seen, I was a mystery and a wonder. Imagine what kind of mystery I was to American children when we returned in my fifth year and took up residence briefly in New England. I had no idea how to be an American child, and everyone knew it. And I think continuing throughout my youth to be the son of a local minister added to my mystery for many. Actually, both my parents were ordained and thus I was that rare and mysterious creature, a "dual PK," or Preacher's Kid, and so even more mysterious.

For another example of my mysteriousness, I was once walking around a small town in Norway when I came across The Big Horn restaurant, featuring an enormous representation of Bevo, the University of Texas longhorn steer which is our logo, and thus a sign of Texas. I realized that there I was exotic. Also, I travel regularly to China to teach and lecture. There I am exotic at the very least for being White. The last time I went I took with me a teaching colleague who is from Uganda, and at the same time I had let my beard grow to an unusually long length. Between the two of us, we were exotic mysteries, yet attractive to the locals. We were gently mobbed in public by those seeking photos with us.

Icons and Mystery

Let me now turn toward an important and ancient cultural practice that I think brings us closer to how Zoom works. And I intend to connect this to mystery and its attractions. I refer to the use of *icons* in religious practice. An icon in this context is a visual image intended to call to mind—not necessarily represent—some saint or deity, and to give a focal point for attention. This practice is central to religion, and studies have successfully identified the influence of religious forms and patterns upon cultural, even seemingly secular, practices (Brummett, 2019). An important purpose, perhaps the main purpose, of the centuries-old and globally distributed practice of religious icons is to strike an appealing balance between mystery and identification (Cormack, 2007). Icons are in use in religious practices even when not, as they are in the Orthodox traditions, actually called icons. Any image of Christ in a Baptist church is an icon. The Sistine Chapel is covered in icons. Statues of the Buddha found in profusion in Buddhist temples are icons. Statues of Hindu gods are icons.

When it comes to the saints and so forth of any religion, icons manifest the saint so that the faithful may have a point of reference—or shall we say identification?—and at the same time that everyone (usually) understands that they hide access to the "real" historical, holy saint, who thus remains a mystery (Cormack, 2007). We understand that nobody knows what Saint Mary looked like, and so she is a mystery, but we are given images, icons, of Saint Mary as a focal point of adoration—or shall we say identification? Icons allow the paradox of identifying with a mystery. Cormack notes that the purpose of icons in the Christian faith from its beginnings was to allow believers to see God even when they could not see God: "Although one can never see the form of God, Christians have been enabled to draw a likeness of him, enveloped in human form. Christ is the image of the invisible God, but he is not identical to the archetype" (Cormack, 2007, p. 28). We are given an image of Christ for identification, knowing that the image gestures toward a mystery.

Much as some academic leaders would like it to be true, their images on Zoom are not of saints. They nevertheless function as secular icons on some important dimensions. Werner Binder notes that "Secular icons, as the name already indicates, are no longer religious in the strict sense of the term. Nevertheless, they have structural similarities to religious icons" (Binder, 2012, p. 102). Large, complex organizations likewise have icons, although they would rarely call them such. How many General Electric employees have actually met their CEO in the flesh, yet company literature, web sites, and so forth will likely manifest him or her through a photo or through videos, motivational speeches, and the like. Proportionate to the population, very few Americans have encountered the President in person enough to establish any direct connection, but that official's image is all over the news, public commentary, propaganda, and the like. So when we refer to icons, the meaning and practice of them may be grounded in ancient religions, but we find them represented, manifested, in images all the time. We all know these images to be ways to make some connection (identification) with them at the same time we understand that the image is denying us full contact with a reality that remains distant and different.

The way that Zoom works is precisely to remake the real, the immediate, the physically experienced into something mediated. That does not mean these become unimportant, but I think we can understand how Zoom works by thinking in terms of how icons work. Anyone on Zoom becomes an icon, leaders especially so. We all of us are icons and gaze at the faithful from within our little frames, and they at us. People who are not leaders are also transformed. The last Zoom I experienced, I saw our new undergraduate work study student on the screen for the first time. I don't know that I have ever seen him in the flesh. In the context of our department, the context for that Zoom, he is useful but hardly a leader. Nevertheless, he became an icon. I have, of course, encountered genuine leaders on Zoom: my Dean, Directors of majors, centers, special programs, and so forth. I used to hang out with these good people in person. Now they have become icons. Since the start of the pandemic, I have stepped down as Chair of my department, but on Zoom I have become an icon, and perhaps to new faculty and staff I am the mysterious Grey Eminence they might have heard about. They shudder and despair.

Leadership outside of Zoom tends to take at least two forms: the distant, impersonal, and often bloodless form of the organizational memo, on the one hand, and the immediate contact with a leader in person, on the other hand. This latter has been called "leading by walking around," and may also be seen in ordinary meetings. But in Zoom, the leader becomes a mediated image. The thin signification of the memo is replaced by a signification full of meaning. We know there is a real person at the end of the chain of technology, but we do not encounter that person in the flesh. But on the other hand, neither are we distanced from that person by the memo. The leader on Zoom occupies a space in between, a space toggling between mystery and identification.

How can we understand the appeal of this mediated leader by seeing it in the ways we use and encounter icons? I want to look at three means by which Zoom images, especially of leaders, are made iconic mysteries: the association of objects and attributed with the image, the icon performs a direct visual address and invites one in return, and the technical quality of the image is poorer than need be.

One recurring characteristic of religious icons is that the saint is usually depicted with some kind of object or attribute that serves to identify the icon (Cornwell & Cornwell, 2009). These are signs and representations of something that really, or in legend, was associated with the saint. Nobody has any idea what Saint Mark actually looked like, but an icon that depicts the saint with a lion will be recognized by the faithful as representing (even as it hides) Saint Mark. Holding a palm branch usually indicates that the saint suffered martyrdom. Often the icon will also include a sign of the means of that martyrdom. Saint Lawrence is recognized by the inclusion of a gridiron, a representation of the instrument of torture on which the good Saint was roasted to death. These attributes attest to the hidden mystery of the saint. Now, there are hundreds, if not thousands, of sacred figures who might be presented in icons, and not even the most devout observer will remember the signs of all of them. But the saints to whom one is most devoted, who are most central to one's faith, one will likely recognize and remember these.

So it is for the icons we encounter on Zoom. It is just a personal impression based on my experience, but I think that the higher the leader, the more predictable the identifying signs attached to her. More junior staff may vary their virtual backgrounds often and creatively. One meeting someone might be "on a beach," the next meeting floating in outer space. One mid-level faculty in my department is known for owning a huge variety of hats, many of them whimsical, and for changing hats in the middle of a meeting. I suppose the fantastic hat itself may be a sign of this person. But I think for the most part that higher leaders such as the Dean tend to be stable in the signs they gather around them. We can recognize the Dean's home office in most of his Zoom meetings, for instance. The mysteries of how this Dean lives his home life are thus teasingly revealed to a small extent. We expect to see an extensive set of book shelves in the backdrop of a former Dean's Zoom self. So in a manner parallel to the way in which Saint Denis is always manifested to us with his head tucked under his arm, we may expect this leader always to display the book cases, the office, and so forth.

A second characteristic of the icon is that for the most part, although not entirely, the saint is depicted as staring at the viewer, confronting the viewer directly. Group scenes of icons, relatively rare, may vary this rule, but most icons show the saint in direct and solitary engagement with the viewer. You will never see a statue of the Buddha playing poker with some minor deities around a celestial table. He is facing in your direction and has your attention, and you have his. An encounter with an icon is therefore never trivial or fleeting. One is invited to stare back. Icons in the Orthodox traditions will very often have enlarged eyes that facilitate this very stance of engagement. One is addressed directly and response is therefore invited, even demanded. It is difficult to ignore this visual hook.

A parallel characteristic of the icons on Zoom is that for the most part we are "talking heads," images depicting the face or face and upper torso at the most. A running joke has been that one may show up in underwear below the waist so long as there is business attire from the waist up, because the latter is what will be seen. We are situated mainly in the physical, visual stance of the icon when on Zoom. We are also in the place of Bentham's (2017) Panopticon, the imaginary prison in which a central vantage point allows jailers to observe prison cells arranged in a circle all around, without a given prisoner knowing when or that s/he is being observed. The logic of real or possible visual engagement reigns supreme. Even if one is in a meeting of fifty on Zoom, you dare not pick your nose just in case someone sees it. The awareness of real or potential observation on Zoom helps to make of us and others icons, just as the icons in an Orthodox church are solemnly observing you. In an actual physical meeting one can slouch, whisper to a neighbor, let the attention wander, and so forth, with only minimal awareness of being observed. Certainly, in person, one will only have passing moments of awareness that one is observed focally. But the peculiar position of a Zoom icon is that one sees everything, and every other icon can closely observe you; you just don't know if they are or not. The phenomenon of "Zoom fatigue" mentioned earlier may be at least in part attributable to this phenomenon. In this dynamic, appointed leaders are in a stance to observe more than others. They usually control who may enter the meeting. They are usually on constant watch among the icons of attendees to see who may have posted a Chat comment or who may be asking to make a comment. While we are all icons on Zoom, some are more powerful, more far-seeing, than others. These are the powers of committee gods, presented yet also hidden by icons.

I will note one final parallel between the religious icon and Zoom, although there may be many more. With the religious icon, accurate and realistic representation is hardly ever a standard. Nobody could possibly think that most religious icons depict the saint as s/he actually was. It's clear that was not a goal of the artist. Most of the Orthodox icons show the long head and huge eyes that we associate with fictitious representations of space aliens. This is true of ancient icons but also those being painted now, as many are. The deliberate refusal of realistic representation adds to the logic of the Mystery. The icon *could* have been painted realistically so that we might see that the saint resembles people we see on the street. Instead, the icon is exotic and, well, mysterious. The icon points to but does not represent, thus hiding its mystery.

Secular icons on Zoom are not of course meant to be accurate representations, for the quality is low. Some people choose to appear on Zoom as avatars, and then all pretense of accurate representation is abandoned. Mainly what one sees is a small screen within one's own computer screen. If more than a few are attending a meeting, the small icons are even smaller, details harder to see, faces lost in a sea of icons. This replicates the feel of Bentham's (2017) Panopticon, in which a sea of small images might be accessible from the central tower. One can click on one of these small icons and see a larger image, but then others are excluded from view, and the image is still not as highly detailed as it would be of someone in person. These facts are inevitable consequences of a technology making use of the relatively small computer screen.

What lies ahead? I began this chapter with widespread observations that everything has changed. Organizations may well begin to wonder why they should invest in brick and mortar campuses when it's become clear that work can get done online. Conferences and conventions across the world of work may be a thing of the past. The travel industry may shrink as the virtual experience industry expands.

If it seems clear that the practice of Zoom is the practice of the religious icon, then the ascendance of Zoom in organizations must have important implications for who people think they are, for their identity, for what is called elsewhere here the looking glass self. If we Zoom, then we participate in organizations not with a sense of who we are "really" but with a sense of ourselves as balanced in the push-pull between mystery and identification, *because we have become icons*. This chapter has almost entirely considered the question of who or what people think icons are. But you see, now I turn it to invite consideration of who icons think people are. Who are these others who access us and yet do not? What is the future of organizing and interacting if there is less of walking into the office next door for a chat and more of the pulling of levers, making lightning flash and smoke bombs belch, as we become mysterious icons? Distinct from the logics of interpersonal relationships that have been asserted for direct, flesh, and blood organizational contacts, what new patterns of interaction will be put in place as the reality of iconic identity comes to define us all?

The Author's Professional Vista

1973: Graduated from undergraduate school and began taking courses and teaching in graduate school.
1975: MA earned, University of Minnesota. Just a bump in the road. Got my first article published.
1976: Published an article in *Philosophy and Rhetoric* that really launched my career.
1978: PhD earned, University of Minnesota. Began full-time career at Purdue University.
1984: Promoted to Associate Professor at Purdue.
1985: Moved to University of Wisconsin-Milwaukee as Visiting Associate Professor, appointed as tenured Associate Professor the following year.
Early to mid-1990s, first began engaging computers, word processing, dual floppy disks, the whole thing, with some skepticism, but I grew addicted especially to email.
1990–1993: Chair of the Department at UW-Milwaukee.
1991: Promoted to Professor, UW Milwaukee.
2001–present: Professor, University of Texas at Austin.

References

Bentham, Jeremy. (2017). *Panopticon: The inspection house*. CreateSpace.
Binder, Werner. (2012). The emergence of iconic death: Secular icons in a contemporary perspective. In Jeffery C. Alexander, Dominik Bartmanski, & Bernhard Gieson (Eds.), *Iconic power: Materiality and meaning in social life* (pp. 101–116). Palgrave Macmillan.

Blankenship, Jane. (1988). 'Magic' and 'mystery' the works of Kenneth Burke. In Herbert W. Simons & Trevor Melia (Eds.), *The legacy of Kenneth Burke* (pp. 128–155). University of Wisconsin Press.

Bridges, John. (2020, December 27). How the coronavirus changed everything. *Austin American-Statesman*, A1.

Brummett, Barry. (2019). My 600 pound pilgrimage: Ritual and rhetorical homology. *Journal of Communication and Religion, 42*(2), 5–20.

Burke, Kenneth. (1969). *A grammar of motives*. University of California Press.

Burke, Kenneth. (1970). *Rhetoric of religion*. University of California Press.

Cormack, Robin. (2007). *Icons*. Harvard University Press.

Cornwell, Hillarie, & Cornwell, James. (2009). *Saint, signs, and symbols: The symbolic language of Christian art*. Morehouse Publishing.

della Cava, Marco. (2020, December 26). What could post-vaccine cities look like? *Austin American-Statesman*, A4.

Duncan, Hugh D. (2017). *Communication and social order*. Routledge.

hooks, bell. (2014). *Race and representation*. Routledge.

Hu, Jingchen. (2019, May 22). *Teaching a shared/hybrid/online course using Zoom* [Workshop]. Blended Learning in the Liberal Arts Conference, Bryn Mawr College, Bryn Mawr, PA. https://repository.brynmawr.edu/blended_learning/2019/2019/9/

Iqbal, Mansoor. (2021, September 2). *Zoom revenue and usage statistics*. Business of Apps. https://www.businessofapps.com/data/zoom-statistics/

Lips, Karin A. (2020, December 25). COVID-19 pandemic changed everything this year—Including how I prepare to have a baby. *USA Today*. https://www.usatoday.com/story/opinion/voices/2020/12/25/birth-baby-pandemic-advice-maternity-care-column/3993851001/

Morris, Betsy. (2020, May 29). Why does Zoom exhaust you? Science has an answer. *Wall Street Journal*. https://www.wsj.com/articles/why-does-zoom-exhaust-you-science-has-an-answer-11590600269

Postrel, Virginia. (2013). *The power of glamour: Longing and the art of visual persuasion*. Simon and Schuster.

Shuey, Mickey. (2020, December 24). 2020 year in review: The pandemic changed everything—Business, sports, travel—In 2020. *Indiana Business Journal*. https://www.ibj.com/articles/how-we-got-here

Tompkins, Phillip K., Fisher, Jeanne Y., Infante, Dominic A., & Tompkins, Elaine L. (1975). Kenneth Burke and the inherent characteristics of formal organizations: A field study. *Communications Monographs, 42*(2), 135–142. https://doi.org/10.1080/03637757509375887

Wiederhold, Brenda K. (2020). Connecting through technology during the coronavirus disease 2019 pandemic: Avoiding "Zoom fatigue". *Cyberpsychology, Behavior and Social Networking, 23*(7), 437–438. https://doi.org/10.1089/cyber.2020.29188.bkw

CHAPTER 4

Organizational Communication in Crisis: Beyond Academic Civility

Karen Lee Ashcraft

The Scene: Work and Race Relations Intensify in the Academy

Long before the pandemic, we were in crisis.

"Who's we?" you might ask. Good question, and do keep asking, to keep me honest. *We* in higher education, though I can only speak with any confidence about faculty. Those of us reeling from the latest whims of upper administration yet still sheltered by tenure (or its promise) from the growing precarious class. *We* the overwhelmingly white professoriate at predominantly white institutions (PWI) in the US. *We* employed in state universities beholden to legislators on a perpetual spree to squeeze budgets. *We* organizational communication scholars who study this stuff and purport to know better.

K. L. Ashcraft (✉)
Department of Communication, University of Colorado Boulder, Boulder, CO, USA
e-mail: Karen.ashcraft@colorado.edu

L. D. Browning et al. (eds.), *Organizational Communication and Technology in the Time of Coronavirus*,
https://doi.org/10.1007/978-3-030-94814-6_4

We had been charged to "do more with less!" for so many years that the ever-constricting belt became a badge on the uniform. So we kept right on going—sprinting, wheezing, and medicating, whetting our cynical tongues—through individualized workloads that spiraled out of control. Here and there, we'd check out for a spell, or check in with a colleague: "You too?" Work intensification, this was called, a trend happening in cases eerily familiar, yet often comfortably removed, from ours (e.g., Pérez-Zapata et al., 2016). Few critics dared to write about work intensification in academia (e.g., Gill, 2009). But it's time to press on now, shall we? Dust yourself off; suck it up. Set that upper lip, and you'll look no worse for wear. You know the treadmill picks up speed when you take time out. Welcome to Neoliberal You. Oops, I meant Neoliberal U (Ashcraft, 2017).

Which is Whitewashing U as well. *We* had all the warning in the world that a racial reckoning was on its way. Alerts echoed around the academy, and if our too-busy, sand-buried heads didn't catch those alarm bells, they were sounding close to home as well. #CommunicationSoWhite (Chakravartty et al., 2018) and the 2019 National Communication Association (NCA) Distinguished Scholar uproar told us outright. Scholars of color had been saying for years that socialization into faculty life was a whitening process, which entails learning to perform a strain of professionalism that tries to swallow you whole (Allen, 1996, 2000; Allen et al., 1999; Cruz, 2018; Gist-Mackey, 2020). The same professionalism that breeds stoic compliance with Neoliberal U, by the way. But I get ahead of myself.

We sustained our frantic pace amid institutional and societal fields racked with white supremacy. Rising tensions were bubbling over, and we had no excuse not to know it. I was serving on a department committee devoted to confronting anti-Black racism in our community. I was the Associate Dean for Diversity, Equity, and Inclusion (DEI) in our college. I had studied difference, power, and organization my whole career. So I could hardly claim surprise when the SMS texts started rolling in as my train rolled out.

The first one read, "Whoa, major debacle at the top paper panel!" Moments later, from another colleague, "Looks like it's finally our turn." Leaving Baltimore early for a family gathering, I had just missed the Organizational Communication Division's top paper session at the 2019 NCA. I knew that two of the papers addressed whiteness, however, so my imagination ran on ahead. Organizational Communication was known as a particularly white club, friendly if you could flash the credentials and connections of sameness, tough to navigate belonging if not. Finally, the reckoning had caught up to *us*.

Let me put it this way: Before COVID hit, work intensification and racial intensification were already on a collision course. The pandemic just put a point on their relation.

The Claim: Academic Civility Maintains the Status Quo, Inhibits Justice

In 2020, these mounting work and race crises reached an inflection point in the wake of two bombshells. First was the COVID-19 pandemic, which upended basic organizational communication practices and set off acute budget challenges, both of which stand to permanently alter higher ed. The second was a succession of widely circulated anti-Black murders, most at the hands of police, which summoned everyone to confront anew how Black Lives Matter. Put bluntly, in the span of about three months—March to June 2020—Neoliberal U and Whitewashing U became newly untenable, thanks to the merging of COVID-19 and the Black Lives Matter uprising in response to increasingly public racial injustice. Together, these developments issue a 2020 imperative for higher ed: As the academy remakes itself in response to the pandemic, it must also come to terms with its colonizing and white supremacist history and present, *continuing* legacies that pose a daunting matrix of racial inequities to confront.

In this short piece, I focus on one small but significant thread in the tangle of inequities: the main mode of organizational communication that constitutes scholarly relations, often referred to as *academic civility*. My goal is to suggest how white faculty—particularly the *we* described earlier—can take meaningful action on the imperative of 2020 and, in so doing, improve the quality of our work lives too.

I contend that **academic civility is *the* communicative practice of white professionalism that connects and sustains Neoliberal U and Whitewashing U**. This practice preserves the surface order of intellectual decorum at the cost of acknowledging and resisting organizational inequities. Even as organizational communication scholars express concern for inequities, *we* tend to look away when they riddle our own work communities and experiences (Ashcraft, 2018; Ashcraft & Allen, 2009). Academic civility is a primary accomplice in averting our eyes. It is an instrument of whiteness—a variant on an old white supremacist tool, in fact (Bramen,

2017)—that suppresses all faculty, albeit some far more than others. It harms even those who appear to profit from its reign in comfort, status, and other "rewards." I thus suggest that it is in the interests of all faculty to rework our dominant mode of interaction. By doing so, we can build shared capacity to resist Neoliberal/Whitewashing U at once.

Specifically, I call for a **turn from immaculate politeness to imperfect presence**. As elaborated below, this means shifting from professional habits of *moralizing perpetual composure* (i.e., assuring atomized individuals that they become "right/good" through calm neutrality) to *assuming flawed engagement* (i.e., showing up "for real" in relationship). Navigating this turn is especially, though not exclusively, incumbent on white PWI faculty. All the more so on those in organizational communication, where communicative practices are the very focus of study, *and* a local racial reckoning is underway.

We could seize this opportunity to answer calls for white folks to rework their relation to whiteness. Many have begun to articulate the hard work necessary in order for white people to cultivate "cultural gifts" (MacMullan, 2009), navigate "critical self-love" (Sullivan, 2014), and develop racial literacy in encounter (Stevenson, 2014). I hasten to underscore that such calls reject white pride and any "lite" (or deceptively defanged) version thereof. In other words, they are not about rehabilitating positive white identities that sidestep the unavoidable intimacy of whiteness and white supremacy. Rather, they seek to challenge white supremacy by undermining its manifestation in the mundane habits of "good white people," among whom I suspect most white faculty would count themselves.

These calls for white racial work do entail positive—as in (re)constructive—action, or replacing old habits with new practices more conducive to justice. A good example is Robin DiAngelo's (2018) effort to dismantle "white fragility" and build in its place white stamina for the relational work of racial justice. This is the spirit in which I hope to approach academic civility: at once de- and re-constructive, aware that we are steeped in the practice we seek to change and, thus, making ample space for *un*learning (Harris, 2019), mistakes, repair, and growth.

At the very least, striving to rework academic civility is more productive than wallowing in white defensiveness, guilt, or helplessness. It is one tangible and promising answer to the ubiquitous white question "But what can I possibly do about systemic racism…?" and its COVID addendum "…from my home office?"

Interestingly, the remote work necessitated by the pandemic has already begun to unsettle academic civility, at least in part, by dragging private lives onscreen. Spotless composure is next to impossible when babies and furry friends are crawling around. Grooming lags, backgrounds reveal, wireless fails, and all of this opens portals to imperfection and authenticity. Academic civility is disrupted right now. Thanks to COVID, the veneer is cracked, and the shine is off. The moment is ripe to mess with scholarly professionalism.

One more caveat before we dive in: If you find yourself thinking, "Beyond civility? *In*civility is the real threat!"—I beg you to suspend judgment. The breed of academic civility described here is about maintaining the appearance of a benign surface for intellectual banter by sweeping all manner of harms under the rug. It is shrouded in a shell of niceness but is not nice, as in relationally mindful or generous. Faculty could collaborate to infuse all sorts of good feeling into scholarly work, and to foster genuine community, but *we* must let go of academic civility as we know it for this to become possible. That is the world I seek here.

The Concepts: Whiteness by Politeness, Academic Civility, and *Karen*

Many, many people of color have brought white politeness—and its place in norms of professional conduct—to attention (e.g., Ross, 2013). *We* owe gratitude for their powerful insights, thanks to which the notion needs little explanation. Basically, it entails doing one's part, in tandem with others, to uphold the hygienic surface of interaction. *Clean* here may be synonymous with decorous, gracious, tactful, courteous, civil, nice, genial, diplomatic, emotionally composed, appropriate, respectful of rules and boundaries, avoiding ripples or ruptures, and so forth. Key to white politeness is the *stress* (in both senses: emphasis and pressure) on *surface*. Appearances and optics, or how things seem, rather than how they are. *Dirt*—which includes any "uglier" truths and impulses, like the flip side of the descriptors above—belongs hidden, underneath, under wraps, behind a smile or standard procedure, above all deniable.

If I were pressed to condense the feeling profile of white politeness into one word, it would be *tight*: constricted, taut, stiff, strict, severe, stingy, disciplined, regulated, or restrained. I say this because white politeness operates along an intricate yet implicit code, which *we* will be loath to tell you about even if you violate it. That would be *im*polite. But you will be made to feel the stretch, the strain—"the discomfort you have caused"—nonetheless, until those narrow parameters start to feel like second skin.

To those most intimate with its practice, white politeness need not feel tight at all. Once the hot shame of childhood violations fade, *we* may even get off on the (also gendered) pleasures of feeling self-possessed, unflappable; cool, calm, and collected; charming and likeable; playful or aggressive within limits. But that is only because the code became skin, and "Others" are expected to wear it as such too. A clear moral overtone guides this imperative. Nice, proper, *good* people are polite. "White fragility" follows precisely this: perceived violations of requisite politeness by "mean," "bad-faith"—in a word, *bad*—actors (DiAngelo, 2018).

There is more than one code, of course. Class norms also spill from the description above, suggesting the ways white politeness intensifies as you climb class hierarchy. The specific form that concerns me here is that of professorial professionalism, but even that slice corrals multitudes. Scholarly norms vary by discipline, region, and institution, to name a few. Return to the opening *we* for the limited scope of my claims: professionalism among white, US-based, organizational communication faculty at PWI and, specifically, state schools.

I draw these lines not simply because I know them by heart but also because they frame what I experience as a **distinctive code of academic civility**: a vaguely US Midwestern Protestant middle-class sensibility merged with the norms of intellectual industry. This version blurs the usual finer-grained distinctions one might make—for example, between civility as adherence to formalized decorum and niceness as informal friendliness (Bramen, 2018)—into a hybrid politeness that conflates intellectual poise with being nice. It is quite different from the norms I've encountered, for example, in US business schools or management departments in Scandinavia or the UK. Readers beyond the *we* invoked here can consider to what extent my account resonates with and differs from their own setting. Such comparisons could prove enormously helpful in tracking the shape-shifting operations of whiteness through professorial professionalism.

As a vector of power, whiteness can operate through many bodies with manifold racial identities. Racially unmarked (usually white) as well as racialized (usually brown and black) folk can carry the force of whiteness along, though the former have far more "possessive investment" in doing so (Lipsitz, 1998). A useful parallel here is a woman who performs masculinity and perpetrates sexism (as I have done countless times). This is the nature of hegemonies: They offer nearly everyone at least a bite of carrot to entice participation.

If the fact that a diverse range of bodies can enact and enforce academic civility leads you to question what it has to do with whiteness, you might enjoy a nuanced historical analysis like Carrie Tirado Bramen's (2017) *American Niceness: A Cultural History*. She traces how a new kind of polite sociability, contrasted with "British snobbery," arose in the formative years of the US and reverberates to this day. This unique affability—fashioned around gendered images of friendly, open, cheerful, likeable, optimistic, "plucky" white settlers—quickly became, and remains, a cleansing device for the cruelties of nation-building through colonization and white supremacy. In essence, American politeness individualizes social relations and directs traffic toward the interpersonal rather than collective or systemic level. From that personal place, it then simultaneously denies and absolves racist violence ("Who, me? But I'm an agreeable—read: *good*—person!"). Niceness of this sort works like a soap or disinfectant, a means to wash your hands of contamination in 20 seconds. Ah yes, a metaphor made for COVID times.

This is why I depicted white politeness in terms of a *hygienic* surface, emphasizing clean appearances with the dirt swept underneath. American niceness has long performed a sanitizing function, and *our* academic civility follows in this tradition. In stronger terms, academic civility is not a tic that "somehow" came to be associated with white scholars. Whiteness aligned with politeness not by accident, but because the latter is an original, founding, and persisting instrument of American racial injustice. This time-honored politeness is the very hand-sanitizing tool that creates a condition of innocence around the question framing the previous paragraph: Is academic civility *really* about whiteness?

Thus far, I have referred to academic civility as the dominant "mode of organizational communication," and as a "communicative practice." With these terms, I am deliberately trying to resist the way white politeness points to the individual and interpersonal as the main terrain that matters. Academic civility certainly plays out there, yes. But it is also thoroughly systemic, a relational practice that constitutes scholars and their working sensibilities all the way down. It is a shared, compulsory disposition to intellectual interaction, long-rehearsed, regularly practiced, and routinely policed. In this sense, it traverses what we often think of as levels of analysis (like individual, dyad, group, organization) or experience (physiology, discourse, norm, policy, structure). Academic civility shows up in our physical reflexes, self-presentation, conversational practices, styles of writing and leadership, institutional policies and statements, funding priorities—you name it. It is a constitutive relational practice in this, and not merely the interpersonal, sense.

This conception also helps to frame the snippets of personal narrative offered below. I do not regard "my story" as personal in a purely subjective or idiosyncratic sense, but also in a systemic way. The recently popularized notion of "a Karen" helps to put this in shorthand (e.g., Wong, 2020). Essentially, *Karen* is a pejorative term for white women who wield racial entitlement to get their way ("I demand to speak with the manager!"). It is also my given name. Karen thus affords me a creative way to acknowledge at once both the experience of a particular person ("Karen A") *and* the structuring relation, or institutional nodal point, to which I have access (always potentially "a Karen" of higher ed). For a twist, let's put it this way: It would be just like Karen to center her story. One way I can try to retune that impulse is to narrate academic civility from the simultaneous vantage point of "Karen A" *and* "a Karen."

A Karen occupies a uniquely split position, in higher ed as elsewhere. Generally speaking, she is marginalized from the centers of power by gender, concentrated in staff positions or at the lower end of intellectual hierarchies. If she has managed a higher ascent, you can bet there aren't many like her. Theoretically, she may seem like a probable candidate to join forces in resistance to oppression. I say theoretically because, on the other hand, she has plenty of reason to maintain the current system. She can brandish white privilege, for example, especially in heteronormative ways that catch the attention and support of (more powerful white) men colleagues. In brief, Karen is the white woman scholar who tears up in antiracist workshops, claims to feel "attacked," makes it all about her, avoids conflict, is pleasant to your face but goes behind your back, throws you under the bus like a casual hair toss, and squeezes venom into a smile. Hers is the gendering of white politeness that *American Niceness* historicizes (Bramen, 2017).

What the current conversation about Karen rarely grasps is how this emotional performance is part of, and actually integral to, her gender subordination, which only makes it more complex (and, conceivably, could give her motive to stop playing it). Countless scholars of color rightfully experience Karen as a fearsome, duplicitous figure engaged in a powerful, even lethal wielding of whiteness. Think of the murder of Emmett Till, or of white women calling the police on Black people going about living. Her investment in white bonding, however, tends to pay dividends that boost her relative sense of sway (via race) without ever empowering her (via gender).

Indeed, Karen's conspicuously absent white man counterpart—let's call him "Ken" (Berical, 2021)—effectively uses her, hides behind her, even beams blamelessly against her foil. His directness, for example, appears refreshing in contrast with her two-faced racism. And yet, his assertiveness and her passive aggression, her cries for help and his "heroic" protection, enact not only heteronormative white bonding but also the very gender inequity between them. Most importantly for my aim here, Ken counts on Karen to be the arbiter of academic civility, an emotional thermostat that maintains the racist status quo *and* lightens his load as a bad guy.

What might be learned from *Karen* "coming clean" about academic civility? Not as in cleansing her hands of it but, rather, exploring her role in its racial injustice.

The Evidence: Karen's Vignettes

#1: Her reflex to restore comfort. It is early December 2019, and interested department members are gathered to talk about the recent NCA top paper panel. Technically, I called the meeting as part of my "org comm colloquium coordinator" role this year, which also makes me one of the facilitators. An impulse I have honored for years begins to turn sour: When things start to "get real"—turn awkward, silent, tense, risky, uncertain, or otherwise "perilously" electric—I tend to crack a joke. You know, some lightly humorous, playful, or self-deprecating observation. In the chuckles that follow, you can watch the group exhale. Bodies relax—relieved, perhaps appreciative. Oxygen returns to the room, which is another way of saying, *I* feel better, maybe *we* feel better. But our ease is beside the point of this meeting. No, wait, the fact that I/we need this security is precisely the point, or at least one of them: Conversations like this are forever pitched on the terms of *our* comfort (Okun, n.d.).

I am a thermostat for academic civility. This may (or may not) be an endearing and effective practice in certain cases, but it is surely a roadblock here. Karen is working to defuse discomfort at exactly the moment *we* need to dwell in its misery.

#2: Her fear of appearing imperfect and, thus, bad (when she knows damn well she is). Lockdown is less than two weeks away, but few are taking the prospect seriously. I am sitting in a riveting workshop on challenging anti-Black racism, and I am sad. Looking around the room, I can't help but regard my white colleagues—including myself—with something akin to a tired, affectionate sigh. Many of us are stiff in rapt observation. Some are tongue-tied, searching for the correct word. Some weigh in with poised proof of their relative rightness, while others look down or away. Several white women wear a pleasant smile, adjacent to white men with arms crossed tight in front of them. The Black scholar-facilitator is 110% crushing it. Despite their disarming, inviting style, I can feel the air crackling among the white folks. Monitoring, ever monitoring. Individuals *we* are, bound by a whiteness that pits us against each other even in this: wanting to be good, to be right, smarter, *perfect*, preferably in the light of another white colleague's regrettable slip.

Many have noted the "good/bad binary" that halts productive race talk with white people. As DiAngelo (2018, p. 72) describes it,

> Within this paradigm, to suggest that I am racist is to deliver a deep moral blow—a kind of character assassination. Having received this blow, I must defend my character, and that is where all my energy will go—to deflecting the charge, rather than reflecting on my behavior.

Shannon Sullivan (2014) casts this white, middle-class habit of moral polarization as residue of a protestant ethic that presents earnestness as proof of goodness. My sense is that these binary proclivities are "dialed up to 11" in higher ed, where the sort of perfectionism Tema Okun (n.d.) aligns with white supremacy culture runs rampant. *We* value highly individualized achievement, intellectual heft, and continuous equanimity—the unflustered capacity to give and take critique, defined as constant flaw-finding. I am ever-ready to defend my rightness against your wrongness with nice neutrality, objectively polite. Insecurity, mistakes, not knowing, "haven't read that," "I'm sorry," failure—in a word, vulnerability—belong backstage. Everyone feels it (hence, academic impostor syndrome). But to wear it openly as part of scholarly being and relating? Not just scary: bad.

We must get over this, I think in the workshop. How could I be a better model of dropping habitual defenses and embracing imperfection? As I grapple with this question and the heavy operations of whiteness, a lump forms in my throat. The very next thought is: OMG, YOU CANNOT CRY! No matter what the emotion responds to, you simply cannot look like *that* white woman. Tears are a classic, cardinal Karen sin (e.g., Patton, 2014)! People will see you are flawed, *bad*. And there it is again, just as I was straining to resist it.

Meanwhile, a colleague who was obliged to learn, and truly excels at, academic civility is trembling. They are taking the microphone, and a very real risk, to reveal what it feels like to be coded Black in this place. To a room full of white folks like me, worrying over their goodness that never was.

#3: No time to fight anti-Black racism. Lockdown went into effect the week a college workshop on decolonizing pedagogy was scheduled. As Associate Dean of DEI, I postponed it while the generous facilitator retooled it for Zoom. Still skeptical of whether it would work in this medium, we forged ahead, and the results were stunning. Zoom was temporarily rendered an intimate and vulnerable space to question and rework the colonial logics of time, body, and spirit that govern academic practice. In a breakout "room," I was tasked to simply look into a colleague's eyes on screen without saying a word for 90 tellingly unbearable seconds. A classic sensitivity training exercise assumed new life and power on the screen. For me, time was powerfully inverted in this session. I could feel the ticking of the clock, a ceaseless *lack* of time, as a clenching knot in my chest. Then, I swiftly cut off an amazing interaction and ended the workshop because—you guessed it—we ran out of time. Some kind of cable news anchor transition fell from my mouth, "OK, we're gonna have to leave it there," as I panted my way to the next Zoom meeting.

Two months later, I listened more carefully to the way I asked college administrators to participate in the online curriculum generously assembled by Academics for Black Survival and Wellness (http://www.academics4blacklives.com). In effect, I handed my mostly white colleagues a way out. I started by acknowledging that *we* are already too strained with work; thanks to Neoliberal U, none of *us* have time. If you could just give one day, one hour, that would be great. I did not point out, or even grasp in the moment, how this chronic time crunch is caught up in whiteness. Specifically, academic civility has come to accommodate work intensification by "respecting" the inevitability that everyone is strapped for time. This fuels what Tema Okun (n.d.) identifies as an eternal sense of individualized urgency, which constantly defers collective work toward racial justice. Neoliberalized academic civility ensures there is no time to think too hard or do too much about Whitewashing U. Other than let it wash over you.

#4: Sanitizing white supremacy, in the most polite way. In early June, it was part of my job to compose a college statement against anti-Black racism (College of Media, 2020, June 5). It seemed that every university, even unit, was obliged to post their own declaration of outrage at violations to *our* DEI values. The mincing of words in most of these statements was chilling. For example, the university personnel tasked to review such things objected to our use of the term racialized "murder" to describe the deaths of Breonna Taylor, Ahmaud Arbery, George Floyd, and many others. When pressed, they put their foot down and offered "killing" as the strongest permissible substitute. We went ahead with our original phrasing, and a high-level administrator at the system level used the same term the following day.

That retaining this one word felt like any kind of victory is testament to the racist "even-handedness"—the sanitization of white supremacy—required by academic civility. In the act of writing "reasonable" statements against racism, *we* are doing what we profess to rail against (Ashcraft & Allen, 2020). *We* minimize and disinfect white supremacy, wielding and defending one of its cherished tools: the white right to characterize race relations more "objectively," dispassionately. As if *we* could ever be disinterested. Our judgment on the matter is the least impartial and most untrustworthy.

To be clear, this is what it took to keep "murder" in the statement: five hours on the phone and Zoom, plus a meeting and vote of all college chairs and directors. Over a single word. That ticking clock be damned; turns out, Neoliberal U will make ample time to address anti-Black racism, as long as that means strategizing how to sweep it back under the rug.

#5: Gendered relational work and the tacit white contract. Nearly 20 years had passed since Brenda J. Allen and I wrote "The Racial Foundation of Organizational Communication" (Ashcraft & Allen, 2003). Still, when I heard of the upset at the 2019 NCA top paper panel,[1] I felt a familiar shiver. What struck me were reports that the respondent chided the "tone" of a presentation critical of white supremacy in the field, even as that presentation—moments before—identified "tone-policing" as a classic move of racism. Memories began to flood. The initial presentation of Dr. Allen and my paper, at NCA in 2001, remains to this day the most nerve-wracking talk I have given. Our paper analyzed how several organizational communication textbooks in wide use at the time normalized whiteness through subtle yet pervasive messages. These textbooks were authored by influential figures in the field—white folks who had shown me generosity, some of whom had helped to advance my early career. I felt as if I were betraying them, or someone close to me. So much so that I took the time and energy to seek out each one before we went public. I let them know of our project, invited feedback, and assured them we meant no disrespect with our critique; on the contrary, our choice of texts was a compliment to their impact on the field. I think my hope was to soften any perceived blow. All were gracious in response, and most thanked me for reaching out. I relaxed somewhat. I was still a *good* girl (diminutive intended); I had not frayed the bonds.

Dr. Allen seemed both supportive of and puzzled by all this extra effort. Surely these scholars would take our case in stride like any other. Did I do this every time I critiqued someone's work? Did I want her to join me in these entreaties? No, I replied. It's just that I'm a junior scholar, and this feels potentially scary. Or maybe I'm not used to rocking the boat. She asked if or how she might help to shield me from the risk I perceived. I repeat: *She* offered to shield *me*. From what I realized, years later, was a fear of what might happen if I broke the white bonds of academic civility. I must have had an inkling even then, because I refused Dr. Allen's help with a clarity that this was my relational work to do, not hers. I also contemplated asking another young white scholar, who was writing about race too, if she experienced similar misgivings, and if we could process together the racial dynamics involved. The vulnerability of that gesture gave me pause: What exactly was I feeling, anyway? Should I expose it, and should white folks be talking about it? So I kept it to myself and diplomatically smiled on.

You could've heard a pin drop during our presentation. I was unusually sweaty, uncomfortable. The paper was met with customary applause, and I don't recall any questions. In fact, that I know of, no one has *ever* asked a critical question or engaged us in debate of the arguments. But over the years, the paper accumulated a heap of citations, most of which invoke the piece as proof that *we* do address race, after all. Even though it expressly says the opposite.

My short read of the 2019 top paper panel, to be taken with a grain of salt since I wasn't there: Some presenters didn't genuflect to academic civility, and the bonds were broken. Of course things got ugly. As one white colleague later described their sense of the room, "You could almost smell the rot rising to the surface..." Sure, the awkwardness, distress, and ire continue, but you know what else does too? Actual, spirited, and, potentially, *sustainable* engagement with racial injustice in our midst. This is more than "The Racial Foundation" accomplished. I think the paper gave some hope to marginalized scholars who encountered it, but I would not say it disturbed the fabric of whiteness. I fear its chances were stunted, in part, by all that gender-race work I did ahead of time to preserve academic civility.

The thermostat needs to fail, *Karen*. Let it go.

Conclusion: *We* Can Do This

This chapter suggests one modest but meaningful change in response to the 2020 imperative. *We*—at least white, US-, and PWI-based organizational communication faculty, and maybe more—can reject and rework academic civility, the communicative practice of white professionalism that supports Neoliberal/Whitewashing U.

It is worth pausing to further refract the subtitle here. **We *can* do this.** Changing up academic civility does not require structural change elsewhere first. It is already within our purview, which is not to say that our purview is limited to individual and interpersonal arenas. Academic civility both operates within and transcends these domains. It is a structuring practice that constitutes scholarly selves and relations across so-called levels. To transform it in our midst is to begin to change "the system." In this light, there is nowhere else to cast accountability. Also, **we can *do* this.** We need not wait; we can start nourishing new modes of interaction immediately. Now is the time, because the iron is hot. Thanks to COVID, norms of academic civility are already interrupted and reshuffling. Finally, surely **we can do *this*,** as in—this is the very least we can do, a beginning. The start of what else, exactly, necessarily remains unclear, but this much we know: Willingness and capacity to rupture *our* comfort is necessary to dismantle racial injustice. It is also integral to improving the quality of academic labor.

I have argued that academic civility maintains the neoliberal racist status quo and inhibits justice. Specifically, academic civility is usefully read as a "for-profit" code of **immaculate politeness** (Bramen, 2018). As demonstrated above, this code constrains challenges to racism by isolating individuals on a redemption-by-perfection quest and requiring a "respectful" surface for their interaction. By this same means, it also hinders resistance to neoliberalization among a collective actor—tenured professors—who could still exert powerful influence were they not deflated by radical individualization (Ashcraft, 2017). Academic civility has become a primary instrument of that disempowerment.

Not only does academic civility detach individuals, it commends them for looking away from the systemic inequities they inhabit. In the 25-year span of my career, this code has come to accommodate neoliberal encroachments by normalizing work and time intensification, valorizing extreme productivity, and invoking such mandates to perpetually deflect and delay serious attention to institutionalized oppression. In this sense, academic civility is derivative of white politeness: It covers white supremacy and related systems of power in a cloak of personal goodness proved through interpersonal style. It moralizes perpetual composure, assuring atomized scholars that they are made "right" through constant poise, including a posture of racial "correctness."

Admittedly, this chapter has not developed a detailed alternative to academic civility. I lack the space, ability, and—most importantly—prerogative to pursue that endeavor alone. It is not an "individualize-able" task.[2] The change proposed here can only be enacted by individuals to the extent that *we* come to know ourselves in and through relation. Refusing the mandatory separation of immaculate politeness, and committing to stay in and grow through relationship, is a vital first step. This calls to mind Bramen's (2018) contrast between "for-profit" and "nonmarket" niceness. The latter supplants the composed individualism of the former with shared concerns and hopes for justice. Nonmarket relations, in other words, convert interpersonal courtesy into a relational infrastructure that supports rather than isolates.

This is why, at the outset, I called for a turn from immaculate politeness toward **imperfect presence**. Such a communicative practice would entail doing our best to show up (presence) as we are (imperfect), or "keeping it real" even as we stay engaged, acknowledging our mutual yet varied impact and susceptibility. This is a code that assumes flaws but imbues them with new meaning. Vulnerability becomes the baseline. Mistakes are not sins to be purged; they are relational insights that fuel collective awareness and growth. Flaw-finding serves up a different pleasure than it does in the mode of immaculate politeness: neither trump card nor personal moral victory or failure but, rather, a precious fact of life that keeps delivering occasions to build group stamina for fighting inequity. Like this, imperfect presence is necessarily aspirational. Not an achievable outcome, it is a communicative practice that welcomes an ongoing, incomplete effort to enact a dream in common. To embrace imperfection, it must be so.

This aspirational spirit returns full circle to my earlier request of those who fear that the end of academic civility necessarily brings *in*civility. I asked you to withhold judgment as I tried to make a case that this need not be the case. Now, I ask you to consider how longing for a return to civility circulates nostalgia for an academic community that never really existed. Or I should say, whatever community *we* felt was premised on constitutive racialized othering and exclusion. *Karen* knows/says this from the unique position of a gendered outside and a racial inside, a structural role vividly demonstrated by my behavior as co-author of "The Racial Foundation." I recognize the nostalgic calls I hear now—in response to racial intensification in the field—because they echo calls I once heard with regard to the "good old days," when professors enjoyed real authority and discretion and, "coincidentally," mingled in a club for men only. My point is that we do not face a choice between preserving civility and devolving into incivility. Instead, the opportunity before us is to evolve toward actual community.

All hands are needed on this deck. *Karen* has much work ahead and looks forward to doing it. But no one can do it alone. What part will you play in unraveling and refashioning academic civility? C'mon, "Ken," and the rest of *our* associates, as yet unnamed. We can, and must, do this together.

Notes

1. For a fuller description of the 2019 NCA Top Papers in Organizational Communication panel and surrounding events, composed by those who were present, see the "Critical Intervention Forum" in the Summer 2020 volume of *Departures in Critical Qualitative Research* (Chawla, 2020).
2. This is *not* to say that individuals can do nothing on their own. Indeed, they can engage right away with essential preparatory work, such as that delineated in Saad's (2020) guide, *Me and White Supremacy.*

References

Allen, Brenda J. (1996). Feminist standpoint theory: A black woman's (re)view of organizational socialization. *Communication Studies, 47*, 257–271.

Allen, Brenda J. (2000). "Learning the ropes": A black feminist standpoint analysis. In Patrice M. Buzzanell (Ed.), *Rethinking organizational and managerial communication from feminist perspectives* (pp. 177–208). Sage.

Allen, Brenda J., Orbe, Mark P., & Olivas, Margarita Refugia. (1999). The complexity of our tears: Dis/enchantment and (in)difference in the academy. *Communication Theory, 9*(4), 402–429.

Ashcraft, Karen Lee. (2017). 'Submission' to the rule of excellence: Ordinary affect and precarious resistance in the labour of organization and management studies. *Organization, 24*(1), 36–58. https://doi.org/10.1177/1350508416668188

Ashcraft, Karen Lee. (2018). Critical complicity: The feel of difference at work in home and field. *Management Learning, 49*(5), 613–623.

Ashcraft, Karen Lee, & Allen, Brenda J. (2003). The racial foundation of organizational communication. *Communication Theory, 13*, 5–38.

Ashcraft, Karen Lee, & Allen, Brenda J. (2009). Politics even closer to home: Repositioning CME from the standpoint of communication studies. *Management Learning, 40*(1), 11–30.

Ashcraft, Karen Lee, & Allen, Brenda J. (2020). How words come to matter: A statement on statements. *Management Communication Quarterly, 34*(4), 597–603.

Berical, Matt. (2021). What is the male version of a Karen? *Fatherly*. https://www.fatherly.com/love-money/male-version-of-karen-meme/

Bramen, Carrie Tirado. (2017). *American niceness: A cultural history*. Harvard University Press.

Bramen, Carrie Tirado. (2018). Niceness in a neoliberal age. *Public Culture, 30*(2), 329–350.

Chakravartty, Paula, Kuo, Rachel, Grubbs, Victoria, & McIlwain, Charlton. (2018). #CommunicationSoWhite. *Journal of Communication, 68*(2), 254–266. https://doi.org/10.1093/joc/jqy003

Chawla, Devika. (2020). An extra-ordinary critical intervention forum. *Departures in Critical Qualitative Research, 9*(2), 120–121.

College of Media, Communication and Information. (2020, June 5). *CMCI statement on anti-black racism and the pursuit of racial justice*. Retrieved from https://www.colorado.edu/cmci/2020/06/05/cmci-statement-anti-black-racism-and-pursuit-racial-justice

Cruz, Joëlle M. (2018). Brown body of knowledge: A tale of erasure. *Cultural Studies ↔ Critical Methodologies, 18*(5), 363–365.

DiAngelo, Robin. (2018). *White fragility: Why it's so hard for white people to talk about racism*. Beacon Press.

Gill, Rosalind. (2009). Breaking the silence: The hidden injuries of the neoliberal university. In Róisín Ryan-Flood & Rosalind Gill (Eds.), *Secrecy and silence in the research process: Feminist reflections* (pp. 228–244). Routledge.

Gist-Mackey, Angela N. (2020). The pain of performative professionalism: Emotionally embodying business as usual. *Departures in Critical Qualitative Research, 9*(2), 140–143.

Harris, Kate Lockwood. (2019). *Unlearning border defensiveness, undermining white supremacist violence: Renewing the case for interdisciplinary inquiry in organizational communication studies.* Paper presented at the National Communication Association Conference, Baltimore, MD.

Lipsitz, George. (1998). *The possessive investment in whiteness: How white people profit from identity politics.* Temple University Press.

MacMullan, Terrance. (2009). *Habits of whiteness: A pragmatist reconstruction.* Indiana University Press.

Okun, Tema. (n.d.). *White supremacy culture.* dRWORKS. https://www.dismantlingracism.org/uploads/4/3/5/7/43579015/okun_-_white_sup_culture.pdf

Patton, Stacey. (2014). White women, please don't expect me to wipe away your tears. *Dame.* https://www.damemagazine.com/2014/12/15/white-women-please-dont-expect-me-wipe-away-your-tears/

Pérez-Zapata, Oscar, Pascual, Amparo Serrano, Álvarez-Hernández, Gloria, & Collado, Cecilia Castaño. (2016). Knowledge work intensification and self-management: The autonomy paradox. *Work Organisation, Labour & Globalisation, 10*(2), 27–49. https://doi.org/10.13169/workorgalaboglob.10.2.0027

Ross, Sabrina N. (2013). The politics of politeness: Theorizing race, gender, and education in White Southern space. In W. M. Reynolds (Ed.), *A curriculum of place: Understandings emerging from the southern mist* (pp. 143–159). Peter Lang.

Saad, Layla. (2020). *Me and white supremacy: Combat racism, change the world, and become a good ancestor.* Sourcebooks.

Stevenson, Howard C. (2014). *Promoting racial literacy in schools: Differences that make a difference.* Teachers College Press.

Sullivan, Shannon. (2014). *Good white people: The problem with middle-class white anti-racism.* SUNY Press.

Wong, Julia Carrie. (2020). The year of Karen: How a meme changed the way Americans talk about racism. *The Guardian.* https://www.theguardian.com/world/2020/dec/27/karen-race-white-women-black-americans-racism

SECTION II

Self-Organization a Response: Beyond Academic Civility

CHAPTER 5

The COVID-19 Pandemic: Self-organizing at the Edges of Chaos and Stability

Keri K. Stephens

Finishing an insightful two-hour Zoom interview as part of my National Science Foundation (NSF) grant, I glanced left at my mobile phone sitting easily within reach. Thirteen text messages from my husband, and the last one said he urgently needed my son's insurance information because they were at the emergency room! I didn't look at the other messages, but immediately called, only to hear, "I'll call you in a few, Keri. We are with the doctor." I frantically paced and looked through the cryptic texts, quite confused. Thirty minutes later, my son walked in the door and said, "Eight stiches. They sewed my little toe back on."

When I asked what had happened, my husband looked stunned. "You didn't hear all the commotion as we unsuccessfully tried to stop the bleeding? We walked right behind your computer and told you we had to go the emergency room fast. Your son wasn't wearing shoes and dropped a paint scraper on his foot and practically severed his small toe."

K. K. Stephens (✉)
Communication Studies | Moody College of Communication, The University of Texas at Austin, Austin, TX, USA
e-mail: keri.stephens@austin.utexas.edu

L. D. Browning et al. (eds.), *Organizational Communication and Technology in the Time of Coronavirus*,
https://doi.org/10.1007/978-3-030-94814-6_5

I was in complete disbelief. I even watched the video interview I had recorded through Zoom to hear them shout at me in the background. They were not exaggerating! I was so focused on conducting the interview, I had completely missed the accident, and since my make-shift COVID-19 home office had no doors, and I never wear a headset, the emergency had happened right behind me.

I spent the next several weeks pondering how I could have missed my son's screams and my husband's frantic attempts to stop the bleeding. I felt incredibly guilty because I'm a mom, and moms don't miss something like this! But I had, and now, four months later, I have a clearer understanding of how my self-organizing practices led to this laser focus.

Acknowledging My Privilege

Before I rewind this story and explain how my own self-organizing led to this laser focus, I need to pause and reflect on the incredible privileges I had during the pandemic. While the isolation was hard on my family and me, I feel guilty because I know my path has been so much easier than many other people. I live in a reasonable-sized home where everyone can have a separate place to work. My husband and I kept our jobs, my children are fairly independent at 17 and 21, and my son's small high school transitioned fully online with minimal disruption. I am well educated, and in addition to being a social scientist, I have a bachelor's degree in biochemistry, so I have a baseline knowledge of how pandemics happen, and how to clean surfaces with isopropyl alcohol (rubbing alcohol) when all the stores have sold out of hand sanitizer. My husband is helpful and regularly takes care of our children so I can have uninterrupted time to work. I was in a good position to handle the explosive equivocality around the emerging pandemic.

I Knew It Was Coming

February 18, 2020, my colleague, Bo Xie, emailed me with the opportunity to participate in a collaborative opinion paper on what the field of information can learn from the COVID-19 Epidemic (as it was called at the time). The day before I had been waiting for an elevator and a colleague asked me what I knew. His wife was from China and he whispered under his breath, "I'm hearing very scary things from her family in China. I don't think we are hearing the whole story in the U.S." One of Bo's collaborators was located in Wuhan, China, and as I joined the writing effort with them, we framed the opinion piece around the health information crisis happening in other parts of the world (Xie et al., 2020). But while writing this chapter, the team of authors were constantly discussing the likelihood that this virus would spread to the U.S. And I kept remembering the conversation I had participating in while waiting for the elevator.

The weekend before that, February 7–9, 2020, I had been in Bend, Oregon, at my son's National Climbing Competition, and I had only read a small bit about the coronavirus that was so contagious that Wuhan, China, was on lockdown. During our three-hour layover in the San Francisco, California airport, I sat in the food court and watched as many people walked by with masks covering their faces. I remember thinking, "are this many people sick?" While I had seen pictures of people in China wearing masks to protect their lungs from pollution, and I'd read about their cultural, collective values of protecting others when they go into public while they are sick, I still felt very uncomfortable and confused. These seemingly healthy people were scurrying past us donning face masks. I asked my son to wash his hands really well and to avoid touching his face; he sighed and gave me that son-to-mother look. I had not heard any of these recommendations being uttered in the U.S., but something told me this was serious.

Over the next three weeks, between February 10th and March 1st, there was much more talk in the U.S. about this coronavirus. People told us to wash our hands and sing the song Happy Birthday twice, to be sure we washed for a full 20 seconds. So, we joyfully stood elbow-to-elbow in our building bathrooms washing our hands and singing songs. I decided to cut my nails short; something that had not happened for over 25 years. I needed to be sure I could keep my hands as clean as possible, but still we had no talk of recommendations for covering our noses and mouths.

Hand sanitizer and toilet paper were sold out everywhere in Austin, and I was really concerned about boarding a plane on March 6, 2020, and flying to El Paso, but my son made it to State in Lincoln Douglas Debate and I was accompanying him to judge. Thinking back now, participating in this event was probably the worst possible activity: high school students speaking passionately, with words spewing for an hour at a time, trying to win the debate, and we were all within a 10–20-foot area. I decided I would wait between rounds by sitting alone at an eight-seater folding table, and carefully wiped down all the surfaces I touched with alcohol wipes. It was a lonely three days, and I was the only person wiping down my table, so I felt a bit foolish. Yet before leaving El Paso, I found a CVS (a US-wide store that contains a pharmacy) that still stocked rubbing alcohol, and I purchased some to take back to Austin.

On Monday, March 9, my colleague who shared a wall with me heard me coughing and asked if I was OK. I assured her it was not coronavirus because my allergies had been causing my cough for over a month. I do not believe it was COVID-19, but looking back, I am worried that my cough scared her, and I wish I had taken more care to avoid people.

The following week I had meetings with graduate student committees and other organizations all over campus since we were trying to wrap up activities before our week of Spring Break. While there was hand sanitizer at every event, I found myself trying to sit a few seats away from others; a practice that made me worry I was being overly paranoid. I took a photo of my graduate students, happily collaborating during class on Tuesday, March 10th, in our Communication Studies building. I told them then at that meeting that I was concerned this might be our last time physically together for the semester. It was. I made the decision that Wednesday would be my last day on campus before Spring Break; I just felt unsafe around other people. I phoned into a meeting on Friday and learned three days later that the Dean who led that meeting had tested positive for COVID-19. He was the second person on our campus diagnosed.

My daughter arrived home from college on Friday, March 13th. On Saturday morning, we ate breakfast—outside, away from other people at my request—at a local restaurant called *Juan in a Million*. Before anyone sat down, I grabbed my rag with alcohol on it and wiped down the table, chairs, and menus. I apologized to the waitress, told her I was being paranoid, and that my behavior was not meant to insult the cleanliness of their restaurant. My family was embarrassed, and I'm pretty sure they were talking about me behind my back for being so overly cautious.

Every few hours for the next several days, my employer made announcements through email. We were to avoid campus during Spring Break. The students got an extra week of Spring Break so professors could transition their course online. Administrators and their family members were diagnosed with COVID-19. And finally, we were going on lockdown and not returning to campus.

So for me, this cosmology event—such a severe disruption that people no longer understood the universe to be rational (Weick, 1993)—the shut-down of our country and almost entire world, was not a complete shock. My months of paranoid feelings were protecting me and preparing me for a dramatic shift in how to live life in a pandemic.

A Spring Break at Home, Kinda

Once I learned that our administration expected the faculty to transition our courses fully online in less than two weeks, I knew Spring Break was not going to be a break. I was completely torn because my daughter was home from college and my son was out of school, so I wanted to spend time with them. But I knew I would have to learn new technology-teaching tools, specifically Zoom, to be able to have meaningful discussions in a three-hour graduate course online. I also knew I needed more than a week to re-work both of my courses and figure out how to manage my research projects while working from home with my entire family.

In between reading about how to use Zoom breakout rooms, I had a bit of time to enjoy my family. Two days before my daughter was scheduled to fly back to Chicago, we cancelled her plane ticket. I could not stand the thought of having her be in a crowded airport, a crowded airplane, and then on crowded Chicago public transportation. Her car from high school was old and we were afraid it would not make it to Chicago, so we bought her a new car. She had always wanted a Ford Transit Connect. This is not the typical car a young adult asks for, but my daughter is not a typical young adult. This vehicle is like a small van, and since she is an architecture and construction management student, she dreamed of transporting long two-by-four pieces of wood and large sheets of plywood back to her dorm so she and her friends could build amazing projects for their studio classes. She loaded up her new car, drove back to Chicago, and I started worrying around the clock: she is resident advisor in the dorm at school, so not only does she live with 100 other students, but she is the one they turn to for help.

Self-organizing to Work from Home

Since I started re-designing my courses to be fully online during Spring Break, I did not have access to any experts at my university, The University of Texas at Austin (UT) to help me. Everyone was supposedly on Spring Break, but in reality, most of us were frantically working from home trying to figure out how we would pull this off. These events made the radical shift of working full time from our homes even more isolating. No one in our administration provided clear guidance, so there was an absence of a hierarchical designer, a driver in the need for me to self-organize (Kurtz & Snowden, 2003). I had to chart my own path, make decisions rapidly, and know that I had limited resources to help.

Since I had studied workplace technologies for over 15 years, I had more expertise than many people on our campus. For example, I had an entire teaching unit in one of my courses on "Webconferencing," and for the past 12 years I taught my students how to conduct and participate in videoconferences, teleconferences, and how to use the interactive tools inside webconferencing platforms. While I had never used Zoom before, and that was the platform our university chose, I found myself quickly diving into the more advanced features like breakout rooms. I watched online tutorials, looked back through research articles, and realized some important things to make breakout rooms work. Specifically, I knew that students, even graduate students, working independently in private breakout rooms would need structure. I created more detailed class agendas, encouraged students to use shared documents to collaborate, and had deliverables due by the end of each class. This is when I first created what I called "interactive lesson plans," that not only outlined the content I covered for each class but also designated forms of interactivity I would use during class to engage my students.

I also knew how to make a work environment conducive for desktop videoconferencing. For years I had shown my students inexpensive ways to raise their laptops to eye level so the camera would not be set for the unattractive sight of looking up their noses. You simply use books you have laying around and put the laptop on a stack of them. I taught them to place a yellow sticky note next to their camera with the word "smile" on it, to remind them to maintain eye contact. I also understood the importance of natural lighting on the face because I do photography.

But there was a problem I faced that was new for me: my office location at home had no doors since I converted my formal dining room into my office. This was not a problem when my children attended school outside the home and my husband worked at an office, but with all of us at home, I had no privacy. I played around with various ideas and realized I could move bookshelves behind my desk into the middle of the room, add a plant, and include an easel with flip chart paper, and it gave me a boundary and looked like I was in a real office.

At this point, I had created a home office ready for teaching through Zoom and spent no money to construct it. Unlike some corporations who provided employees stipends to help them set up home offices (Nova, 2020), our university provided no monetary resources. We had to make do, and that is what I did for a while. Eventually I did purchase a desk lamp for extra light for my face and a new external camera because the one on my laptop was quite fuzzy, but these were considered personal expenses and not reimbursed by my employer. This is another example of how I used self-organizing practices and my own resources to create my home office.

After receiving many questions about my home office setup, I decided to make a behind-the-scenes video to show others how to be scrappy and pull together what they have to make the best of working from home. The University-wide online teaching effort learned of my use of Zoom Breakouts and the tips I shared concerning webconferencing, so they asked me to make some videos to be used by faculty as they transitioned to working fully from home. These videos are available at these links: https://youtu.be/lWjGGWe3u-w, https://youtu.be/WKf-GifILOE

A Material Girl (Not in the Madonna[1] Sense)

Yes, I must confess: materiality guides both my work style and collaboration practices. I still use a pen and paper calendar, print out articles and write all over them, and store papers in physical binders organized by major project. When beginning to work on a project, I ritualistically open that specific binder, and when I complete my work for the day, I close the binder and place it back on the shelf. I have a clean desk at the end of the day.

Historically, my collaboration practices also have reflected my need to engage with material objects, including meeting with others in person. I love the spontaneity of bouncing ideas around, physically engaging large whiteboards, and taking breaks by walking across the street with my collaborators and getting a cup of coffee or a diet coke. Ask anyone who has worked with me and they will tell you, "Keri is a meet-in-person type of collaborator!"

While the pandemic has not changed the materiality of my individual work style, it abruptly put an end to all physical collaborating. Booking a conference room for an afternoon and working collaboratively on whiteboards while covering all the walls with sticky note pad sheets—my favorite way of working—has not happened since March 8, 2020. The options for the present are scheduling a Zoom meeting or using the telephone to communicate synchronously.

In March and April of 2020, this lack of accessibility helped me increase my productivity; the only forms of interruption were self-interruptions and family requests. It wasn't easy to stop by a colleague's office and ask a question; that spontaneous act now required planning: sending an email, figuring out a time to meet, scheduling a meeting, and then talking. Talk about unfulfilling for a material collaborator like me! It was a lot of effort, and I know that I sidelined many projects that required creativity and interacting with others. Missing that spontaneity also forced me to ponder how many times, when we were in physical offices on campus, I bothered my colleagues just to satisfy my need to feel their energy and get the spark I needed to continue working.

My Rising Stress and the Cycle of Overworking

As soon as my daughter returned to Chicago, her classes were converted to being online. More people were dying every day, and I was scared to death she would get COVID-19 and I could not travel to be with her if she needed help recovering. I was working as many hours as I could to keep my mind off my concern for my daughter. She started calling regularly and I could hear in her voice that she was literally scared for her life and for the lives of those around her. She didn't leave her dorm room except when absolutely necessary, and she was getting more and more lonely. I helped her craft an email to her boss asking if she could return to Texas and perform her RA duties remotely; in early April, she got permission.

We had a glorious week when she returned because I finally slept, and I felt like I could be a mom if something happened to her. Then, she walked into my bedroom one night and said, "Mom, I'm pretty sure I have a kidney stone and it really hurts." This is something she has dealt with for four years now, so we decided to have her wait it out (she had pain pills left over from her last kidney stone). After a day and half of her writhing in pain on the bathroom floor, I told her we really needed to go to the hospital.

We were both so reluctant to go to the hospital because it was mid-April and we had heard that the hospitals were filled with COVID-19 patients. I posted a note on Facebook asking if anyone could share advice on which hospital had the fewest COVID-19 patients and within 5 minutes one of my Facebook friends, who I've only met a few times, said she knew the chief nurse at one of the hospitals and they were not accepting patients who were suspected of having COVID-19. This is where we would go. But before we left, I knew we were both taking a huge risk and exposing ourselves. I packed our overnight bags, and before we left, I prepared lectures, recorded talks, and made sure everything was in order. I contacted two different colleagues who agreed to take over my courses if I got COVID-19. I was ready to accompany my daughter to the hospital and help her get out of pain. I was going to see her through this.

We arrived at St. David's Hospital and immediately the young woman stationed at the door took my daughter's temperature. Whew, no fever so they would let her enter their emergency room. I told her I would park the car and be in shortly when the young woman said, "I'm so sorry ma'am, but no visitors are allowed in the emergency room or hospital. We are too concerned about COVID-19 and we can't take that risk." My daughter had already entered the ER, so I asked the young woman to let her know to call me when she could. So the hospital was self-organized in its own way, and I was set apart from that structure before I knew it.

Several hours went by, and for once I kept my phone next to me everywhere I went. My family gives me a hard time because I don't carry my phone with me, and I do everything I can to create boundaries so my mobile phone doesn't rule my life. But now it was different. Finally she called. They had her on morphine, but it was more serious than in the past and they would be doing a surgery as soon as the surgeon arrived. There was an infection that complicated things. Now we are facing major emergency surgery in the upswing of the pandemic. I, the person who likes to plan, organize, and control situations, was completely isolated from the problem.

There was nothing I could do. I started journaling to document my feelings because I felt like I was forced to abandon her in the hospital, and that is not what moms do! That helped a bit, but I still felt useless. I tried to work, but I couldn't. I can barely remember what I did during that time, but I'm certain I didn't sleep.

The nurse called me five hours later to say she was out of surgery, and the surgeon called shortly after to give me an update and provide a list of things I needed to do. I remember being confused because I couldn't understand the technical medical terms the doctor used. He said something about elective surgeries being postponed due to COVID and that all he could do was get her to a stable condition, which seemed like a fairly low-level forecast. Yet, the following day I picked her up as the hospital discharged her; she had tested negative for COVID-19, but due to possible exposure at the hospital we both had to quarantine for 14 days. Thankfully, neither of us became sick, but it was a full three weeks before my daughter was allowed to return to the hospital to have her final surgery, to complete the work needed to allow full recovery.

Retreat to Nature

Life on Zoom quickly became all consuming and I found myself seriously overworking. I lost track of time, forgot to get up to fix dinner for my family, and I justified this by telling myself I had nowhere to go, and if I quit working, I'd be tempted to leave the house. I've always been prone to overworking because I like what I do, but deep down I knew this was not sustainable. My family was frustrated that I worked all the time, so one day I realized that I needed to create a ritual to end my day, and my retreat to the backyard began as a daily ritual.

At the end of my work day, I began going into the kitchen and getting a large glass of sparkling water with lime. It is beautiful in April in Austin and we have a small hot tub in the backyard. I put on my swimsuit, grabbed my sparkling water, invited my cat, Rock, to go outside with me, and I hopped into the hot tub. Sitting out there every evening helped me escape and, being surrounded by nature, opened my eyes to things I had forgotten. I had the time to look carefully at my flowers and notice which ones were about to bloom. I watched the squirrels chase each other through the trees and across the roofs. A green lizard had such personality, and for four straight months he visited me as I got into the hot tub. He had a favorite branch where he sat and I talked to him like I did to my cats. One day I realized we were in a routine, and that seeing him helped me escape fully into the nature of my yard and out of my world of Zoom. Before I started this coping ritual, the last time I had taken the time to truly appreciate nature had been when my son was young. As a young boy, he would point out flowers, notice the lizards, and try to protect pill bugs from being stepped on.

Rise of New Collaboration Structures

For someone with a strong preference for in-person collaborations, it was hard for me to learn how to make on-line collaborations work. Since all collaboration had to occur through computer-mediated channels, it did not matter if I collaborated with people in my own organization, or those geographically dispersed. By mid-April our daughter had recovered and I had healthy children, our family members were taking turns cooking, and I had my afternoon backyard retreats into nature. Earlier, while I had been coping with the pandemic by overworking, I had applied for several research grants, and now I decided I wanted to apply for a National Science Foundation (NSF) RAPID grant. I turned to group of scholars and practitioners I had met at a conference who lived in Utah, Washington, DC, and Virginia. I told them I had an idea for a proposal if they wanted to join me. A month later, we received that NSF grant.

Our project focused on community emergency response team (CERT) volunteers who were working with my CoPI, Hemant Purohit's, machine learning system called Citizen Helper. The effort was located in the Washington DC area of the U.S. and these 20 volunteers on the CERT team were asked to examine Twitter data and label the Tweets that described COVID-19 risky or prevention behaviors. While this labeling is a well-established practice in the emergency response community, our team logged onto the Citizen Helper system and interviewed the CERT volunteers as they labeled these tweets. Our interview schedule contained questions to better understand the decisions they made as well as their opinions around working with artificial intelligence. We called this *human-AI teaming*, and we named ourselves the HAT Team, which stood for Human-AI Teaming. Over the next three months we conducted 61 interviews all through Zoom. We learned so much about computer-mediated qualitative research that our first publication from this project is a roadmap for conducting this type of research (Stephens et al., 2021). What is most meaningful in this paper is our transparency in having to learn new software, new ways to collaborate, and how to build trust when there is a video screen separating us from our study participants.

On May 8, 2020, at 6 pm CST we assembled the HAT team and jumped on a Zoom call to celebrate our success at securing the funds to be able to do the NSF RAPID project. One essential member of our team was our community partner, and he did his community work in the evenings because eight-to-five pm was reserved for his government job. This meant that our first task was figuring out how to manage his needs to meet after hours with the rest of our teams needs to maintain a sense of a more standard work day. Fortunately, he lived in the Eastern time zone, so if we met at 5 pm his time, it was 4 pm CST and 3 pm MST. These time differences were very important for our project because we had to find collaboration tools that would help us manage this time zone difference. For example, we used a tool called Calendly that automatically accounted for our different time zones.

I approached one of my graduate students and asked her to be the lead Graduate Research Assistant (GRA) since she had also been involved in the frantic writing of the NSF proposal. She was at the ideal time in her program to learn about writing these proposals since she had just completed coursework that included my grant-writing course. In retrospect, the choosing her was one of the best decisions I made during the early months of the pandemic. She was organized, loved creating structures to collaborate online, and our working relationship become mutually beneficial in a profound way.

Despite having my GRA institute some meaningful collaboration tools, there was time in May when I told my husband I refused to learn another piece of software; I craved stability! For the transition to online teaching I learned Zoom, expanded my knowledge of Canvas, and learned how to record and edit my own videos using Photoshop, YouTube, and Camtasia. For my collaborations, my life was much more complicated. I used Microsoft Teams for my NSF team, Slack for a COVID-19 research group, WebEx for new grant I had received, and Zoom for most other meetings. I used Outlook for my email and calendar, and I learned that all of my graduate students were using Google Calendar, so they wanted me on that system. Then we added Calendly, Doodle Poll, and Need to Meet to help us coordinate and schedule meetings. For file storage we used our official UT Box site for most projects, but my students wanted to use Google products, and my external collaborators wanted me to use DropBox. I could go on, but hopefully you already empathize with me a bit. Setting up collaboration structures when everyone is working online is complex!

My friend and colleague, Kerk Kee (see Chap. 20 in this book), studies cyberinfrastructure and remote teams, and I've read his work, so I know the infrastructure for remote research teams can be challenging (Kee et al., 2016). Team members have different preferences, levels of access, and there are so many options people can become overloaded very quickly. Furthermore, collaborations among researchers at different institutions can be particularly chaotic since academic institutions are less likely to prescribe specific technologies rather than stock technologies that are used by industry organizations. Remote collaboration online necessitates self-organizing if teams are to share documents, meet online, and communicate effectively. Everyone has to learn it and do it themselves. It must be self-initiated.

Rise of a New Collaborative Coping Structure: OPTIC Lab

In addition to collaboration tools, we also had to learn how to cope during the pandemic. Graduate students provide one another a pivotal amount of social support during graduate school. While teaching my graduate course, I realized they were already missing one another and struggling to cope. When summer arrived, and they had no regular graduate classes, this issue mushroomed. My lead GRA and I decided we would schedule research lab meetings twice a month, and we would not limit attendance. During our first lab meeting, I told them we needed a name, and OPTIC Lab (Organizing Practices through Information and Communication) was born. The meetings were 100% optional, but throughout the summer everyone we invited attended! We had a new structure that continued to thrive during the Fall of 2020 and is currently still going strong.

How did a research lab meeting help us collaboratively cope? I believe the magic was in our structure, and my GRA gets a lot of credit for its success. For example, we listened to the needs of the graduate students. One meeting was just a series of breakout rooms where they shared their struggles and put links to helpful articles in the chat. The students had to learn many new things with no direction. Organizing and sharing literature online was one challenge they shared, so we hosted a librarian who taught us how to use a free tool called Zotero. We made time during every lab meeting for us to share our struggles. One time, I allowed myself to sit and cry in the group for 5 minutes after telling everyone how scared I was for my daughter. We made it a safe place to collectively cope with the most equivocality and uncertainty we had ever experienced in our lives. Others expressed emotions as well. We all knew this was hard for everyone and we acknowledged that.

Chaos, Stability, and Laser Focus

I imagine my own work-from-home innovations happened because I was forced to exist in a zone of emergent complexity (Carlisle & McMillan, 2006). Tapsell and Woods (2010) describe this zone as being the space that exists between the edge of stability and the edge of chaos, and it is the sweet spot where innovation occurs. Living in this zone almost constantly for a year, I feel like I have been continuously bouncing back and forth between these edges, and sometimes slipping, even if briefly, into full chaos. As a former biochemist, this reminds me of the motion of molecules. If you look under the microscope, they are in constant motion, much like a person who is nodding their head up and down rapidly. I think my body and mind have felt this rapid oscillation constantly during the COVID-19 Pandemic, and this has given me the energy to operate between stability and chaos and be more innovative. Everything is moving and I am too.

While the new collaboration and collaborative coping structures are clear evidence of how I innovated through self-organizing practices, my laser focus is another, less conscious, innovation. I set up my office in a deliberative manner, and the layout provided me a clear transition between my home and my work. When I walked into my formal dining room/make-shift home office, there was a small entry between the edge of my desk and the large floor plant. I turned sideways to enter and immediately sat down in my chair. I was at work. Even though I was in a room with no doors, and my family complained daily that they could hear everything I said, my tiny area provided me the structures I needed to tune out the world around me and have laser focus.

Sensemaking into the Future

As a scholar who has studied work technologies and remote work since the start of my academic career (e.g., Browning et al., 2008; Stephens, 2020; Stephens & Kee, 2019; Stephens & Powers, 2020), I regularly contemplate the future of work. I have watched how difficult it is for essential workers, families, and people without adequate internet services to function during this pandemic, and their suffering has helped me realize how privileged I am. Much of the prior research on what was originally called telework was written around people who chose that way of working. They teleworked only part of the week (Scott & Timmerman, 1999), had adequate child care, could fulfill their interaction needs through travel and meeting with friends, and had the technology resources provided by their organizations to help them do their work (Stephens et al., 2020). This is not what happened during the pandemic. For the fortunate workers who could work from their homes and keep their jobs, many of them were not set up for success—they were forced to self-organize.

College students in their final years of undergraduate education working part time for experience—called interns—were one group of workers who often suffered through work that was fully remote. I taught an internship class in fall of 2020, and in a roundtable discussion one of my students commented that she never wanted another remote job because she was so lonely and was left to figure everything out herself. I explained to this group of students that what they have experienced is not typical remote work. They smiled politely, ignored my comments, and all chimed in saying they could not wait to get their full-time jobs where they can have a *real* work experience in a physical office. As I now reflect on their comments, it worries me. Will we have a generation that is resistant to remote work because of their COVID-19 work experiences that have been 100% remote? What consequences will surface from a large portion of the workforce having managers who had little to no knowledge of how to manage remote workers?

I also worry that managers who have experienced personal positive outcomes of full-time remote work, like no commute, will not be able to see past their own privilege when they plan their teams' future at work. They may assume that employees do not need dedicated physical office space because they *should* be able to work from home without training or additional material resources. They have not seen the private suffering of their employees who have hidden their physical and mental challenges by trying to be productive while poorly managing a crumbling personal life. While there is considerable talk about having empathy and understanding, families with members engaged in front line work and people who have needed to provide care to others have faced extreme hardships. Will organizations actually create structures that do not punish people who were disadvantaged during the pandemic? If they do create structures, will they take the form of some family policies in the U.S. where the policy exists, but employees cannot use them because they fear judgment and retaliation (Kirby & Krone, 2011)? A host of organizational concerns await us that we will immediately face once it is possible to return to physical offices.

There will also be people, like myself, who have developed some useful practices that will change how they want to work. Reflecting on my experiences, I realize how important it is to prepare people for unexpected disasters because they will experience less shock when they have more time to contemplate what will be an *ecological change*, an event that forces people to make new sense of ecological processes and material landscapes (Weick, 1979). My new collaboration and collaborative coping structures have challenged my beliefs and helped me develop confidence in trusting others. But please realize, my systems are far from perfect. Every day I have to fight my tendencies to overwork, and I have to force myself to slow down and listen to the needs of others to create useful collaborative structures that work for everyone on our teams. Sustaining the positive practices takes work, and I worry that hierarchical systems will try to re-exert their control and wipe away some of what my forced self-organizing has accomplished.

In writing this narrative, I have been able to *sensemake* (Weick, 1995) and to cobble together experiences and emotions around my early journey through what certainly will be one of the most marked cosmology events (Weick, 1993) of my life. Browning and Boudes (2005) explain that characters in a narrative "are most interesting when they make, or struggle with, independent choices" (p. 37). I hope I openly communicated my own struggles in ways that help you make sense around your COVID-19 pandemic experiences. I also hope you can see that we all have a responsibility to participate in the major challenges we face around the future of work. While we have incredible opportunities to create new, productive, and meaningful structures born by being forced to bounce between the edges of chaos and stability (Tapsell & Woods, 2010), this constant motion has been incredibly hard for many people. We have a responsibility to be truly empathetic through our actions, and not simply pay lip service to the work-life struggles of so many of our friends, family, and colleagues. Even though the COVID-19 Pandemic has impacted everyone, we will all have different journeys into the future of work.

On any given week, I may begin by believing that ICTs are very useful, and I'm not feeling overloaded much at all. But over time, people ask me to communicate over Zoom, Microsoft Teams, WebEx, Google Hangouts, Slack, Confluence, LaTeX, and Google Docs—sometimes in a single day—and my ICT overload takes over my belief that ICTs are useful (see Fig. 5.1 for a visual representation of my sensemaking around ICTs). I fight these conflicting feelings every day, and the patterns are not uniform: they depend on others' expectations. Sometimes, I'm only slightly overloaded, and other times, that perception takes control of me. Then, I have to re-set myself, find new coping mechanisms, and begin working again. By graphing my technology beliefs over time, I better understand why I wrote a paper on communication overload (Stephens et al., 2017). Overload is not a constant state; it varies with different interactions over time. I also better understand how I was able to be so productive early during the pandemic. Even though parts of my personal life were pulling me in many directions, I wasn't interacting with very many different types of people. My predominant ICTs for work were Zoom and email. Spending two months without feeling overloaded with ICTs meant I could be more productive (Table 5.1).

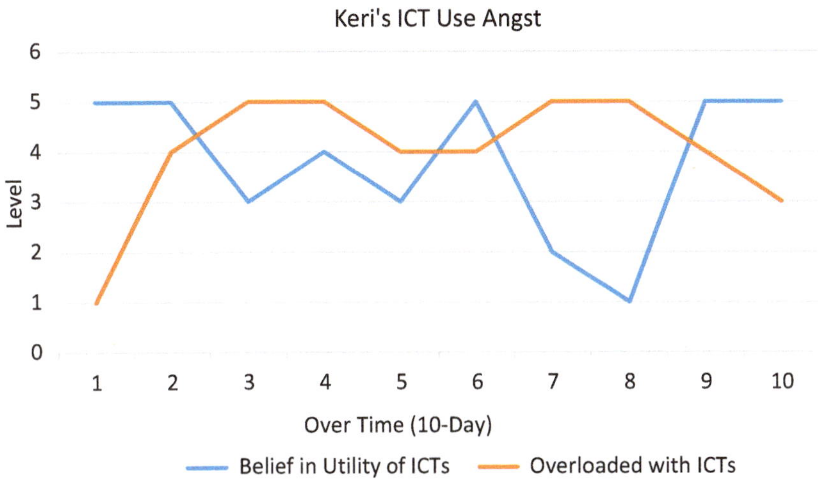

Fig. 5.1 Keri's ICT use angst

Table 5.1 Keri Stephens' professional vista

Date	*Event*	*Importance*
Past		
May 1990	Graduated with my BS in Biochemistry	This degree helped me get my first job with Hewlett Packard, a company that used cutting-edge mobile and computing technologies
1990s	Used bag cell phones, pagers, and flip phones	I used cell phones before most people knew what they were. I oscillated between being a power user and giving them up because they intruded on my life
June 2003	First trip to Norway with my husband, daughter, and 6-month-old son	Having conversations about organizational technologies with people from around the world opened my eyes to the fact that the U.S. was behind many other countries, including Norway
Aug. 2005	Graduated with my Ph.D. from UTexas	I had spent 6 years getting my MA and Ph.D. focused on organizational communication and technology
Sept. 2007	Began tenure-track position at UTexas	I spent two years at Texas State on faculty and learned so much, but now, the pressure was on for me to produce top-quality scholarship
2008	First co-authored book published	Co-authored a book with Browning, Sætre, and Sørnes, on narratives and organizational technology

(*continued*)

Table 5.1 (continued)

Date	*Event*	*Importance*
2013	Received tenure and Associate Professor	I picked my head up long enough to set new goals, but I continued producing quality scholarship and teaching
2018	Book with Oxford University Press won two national awards	The hardest project I had ever done was write *Negotiating Control: Organizations and Mobile Communication*. It contained over two decades of data about using technology at work
2019	Edited book with Routledge won a national award	*New Media in Times of Crisis* was the most enjoyable, collaborative project I've ever done. It showed me how much I value collaborative work
2020	Became a Full Professor and earned five grants	I had been trying to get NSF grants for over 10 years, and this was the year I demonstrated I could be the PI on grants with engineers and computer scientists
Future		
2021	Additional grant funding	I am using my grant funding to help me become known as a scholar whose work (technology and disasters) makes a direct difference in communities
2022–2025	Receive funding for my Communicating for Disaster Resilience Center	I leverage my relationships and experiences to find a funder willing to support a large interdisciplinary initiative that supports students and communities
2023–2024	#Calls for Help is published	My next monograph about rescue communication is published with a top press
2024–2027	Recognition for disaster resilience	The Center has done so much good to help communities we are recognized nationally
2024–2030	Time for me to volunteer and give back	I find an opportunity to volunteer in a disaster-related organization where my expertise is helpful
2024–2030	My popular press book is successful	I finally write the technology-related popular press book I've been contemplating for decades
2024–2030	My organizational technology textbook is in print	I finally write a textbook focused on organizational technology that engages undergraduates and helps them think inspirationally about new media

(*continued*)

Table 5.1 (continued)

Date	*Event*	*Importance*
2030	My advisees have been recognized in meaningful ways	I've always been committed to helping others be successful, but this is the point I look back and admire the amazing, diverse forms of their success
2030–2040	I travel giving talks	I get invited to interesting locations around the globe to speak about the power of organizing and using technologies at work and for disaster resiliency
2040–2060	I'm an Emeritus Professor	I still hang around UT, occasionally teach, help disaster, volunteer organizations, accomplish meaningful things, and spend time with my family

Note

1. Madonna was a pop star in the 1980s and 1990s who had a song called Material Girl.

References

Browning, Larry D., & Boudes, Thierry. (2005). The use of narrative theory to understand and respond to complexity: A comparative analysis of the Cynefin and Weickian models. *Emergence: Complexity & Organization, 7*(3&4), 32–39.

Browning, Larry D., Sætre, Alf-Steinar S., Stephens, Keri K., & Sørnes, Jan-Oddvar. (2008). *Information & communication technologies in action: Linking theory and narratives of practice.* Routledge.

Carlisle, Ysanne, & Mcmillan, Elizabeth. (2006). Innovation in organizations from a complex adaptive systems perspective. *Emergence: Complexity & Organization, 8*(1), 2–9.

Kee, Kerk F., Sleiman, Mona, Williams, Michelle, & Stewart, Dominique. (2016). The 10 attributes that drive adoption and diffusion of computational tools in e-science. In P. Navrátil, M. Dahan, D. Hart, A. Romanella, & N. Sukhija (Eds.), *Proceedings of the 2016 XSEDE (Extreme Science & Engineering Discovery Environmental) conference.* ACM. https://doi.org/10.1145/2949550.2949649

Kirby, Erika, & Krone, Kathy. (2011). "The policy exists but you can't really use it": Communication and the structuration of work-family policies. *Journal of Applied Communication Research, 30*(1), 50–77. https://doi.org/10.1080/00909880216577

Kurtz, Cynthia, & Snowden, David. (2003). The new dynamics of strategy sense-making in a complex-complicated world. *IBM Systems Journal, 42*(3), 462–483. https://doi.org/10.1147/sj.423.0462

Nova, Annie. (2020, June 3). Working from home? You might be able to expense a new desk. *CNBC*. https://www.cnbc.com/2020/06/03/companies-are-paying-for-their-workers-home-offices.html

Scott, Craig R., & Timmerman, C. Eric. (1999). Communication technology use and multiple workplace identifications among organizational teleworkers with varied degrees of virtuality. *IEEE Transactions on Professional Communication, 42*(4), 240–260. https://doi.org/10.1109/47.807961

Stephens, Keri K. (2020). The complexities of using mobiles at work. In R. Ling, L. Fortunati, G. Goggin, S. S. Lim, & Y. Li (Eds.), *Oxford handbook of mobile communication, culture, and information*. Oxford University Press. https://www.oxfordhandbooks.com/view/10.1093/oxfordhb/9780190864385.001.0001/oxfordhb-9780190864385-e-23

Stephens, Keri K., Jahn, Jody, Fox, Stephanie, Charoensap-Kelly, Piyawan, Mitra, Rahul, Sutton, Jeannette, Waters, Eric D., Xie, Bo, & Meisenbach, Rebecca J. (2020). Collective Sensemaking around COVID-19: Experiences, concerns, and agendas for our rapidly changing organizational lives. *Management Communication Quarterly, 34*(3), 426–457. https://doi.org/10.1177/0893318920934890

Stephens, Keri K., & Kee, Kerk F. (2019). Technology and organizational communication. In A. Nicotera (Ed.), *Organizational communication: A comprehensive introduction* (pp. 370–389). Taylor and Francis.

Stephens, Keri K., Mandhana, Dron, Kim, Ji Hye, Li, Xiaoqian, Glowacki, Elizabeth, & Cruz, Ignacio. (2017). Reconceptualizing communication overload and building a theoretical foundation. *Communication Theory, 27*(3/4), 269–289. https://doi.org/10.1111/comt.12116

Stephens, Keri K., Nader, Karim, Harris, Anastazja G., Montagnolo, Caroline, Hughes, Amanda L., Jarvis, S. Ashley, Senarath, Yasas, & Purohit, Hemant. (2021). Online-computer-mediated interviews and observations: Overcoming challenges and establishing best practices in a human-AI teaming context. In T. Bui (Ed.), *Proceedings of the 54rd annual Hawaii international conference on social systems* (pp. 2896–2905). Computer Society Press. http://hdl.handle.net/10125/70967

Stephens, Keri K., & Powers, Courtney J. (2020). Communication technology and organizational life. In H. D. O'Hair & M. J. O'Hair (Eds.), *Handbook of applied communication research* (pp. 251–265). Wiley.

Tapsell, Paul, & Woods, Christine. (2010). Social entrepreneurship and innovation: Self-organization in an indigenous context. *Entrepreneurship & Regional Development, 22*(6), 535–556. https://doi.org/10.1080/08985626.2010.488403

Weick, Karl E. (1979). *The social psychology of organizing*. Addison–Wesley.
Weick, Karl E. (1993). The collapse of sensemaking in organizations: The Mann Gulch disaster. *Administrative Science Quarterly, 38*(4), 628–652. https://doi.org/10.2307/2393339
Weick, Karl E. (1995). *Sensemaking in organizations*. Sage.
Xie, Bo, He, Daging, Mercer, Tim, Wang, Youfa, Wu, Dan, Fleischmann, Ken R., Zhang, Yan, Yoder, Linda H., Stephens, Keri K., Mackert, Mike, & Lee, Min Kyung. (2020). Global health crises are also information crises: A call to action. *Journal of the Association for Information Science and Technology (JASIST)*. https://doi.org/10.1002/asi.24357

CHAPTER 6

Digital Teaching During COVID

Tine Viveka Westerberg

I am an assistant professor in the Department of Maritime Operations at the University of South-Eastern Norway. Over the past decade, I've taught a variety of topics, but my academic background is within international relations, management and leadership. My domain is the maritime industry.

The maritime industry is defined as all enterprises that own, operate, design, build, supply equipment or specialized services to all types of ships and other floating units (Jacobsen & Espelien, 2011). The industry consists of a number of different types of business such as shipping companies, maritime service providers, shipyards and equipment producers. It is an industry that incorporates massive contrasts: from tiny family owned companies to huge global enterprises. From companies working in the smallest places on the coast of Norway to companies with offices in hundreds of countries, the maritime industry transports 80% of the world's shipping, which makes it the center of world trade. It is also part of the national infrastructure in many countries with ferries and catamarans, in addition

T. V. Westerberg (✉)
Department of Maritime Operations, University of South-Eastern Norway, Kongsberg, Norway
e-mail: TVW@usn.no

L. D. Browning et al. (eds.), *Organizational Communication and Technology in the Time of Coronavirus*,
https://doi.org/10.1007/978-3-030-94814-6_6

to the cruise segment. Maritime operations within oil and gas, offshore fish farming, offshore mining and offshore wind are also a big part of the maritime industry. While conservative in many respects, the maritime industry is one of the most innovative and progressive industries, developing green technology and digitalizing both business models and operations to cut emissions to reach the climate goal of zero emission by 2050. Even when the World is not plagued by a pandemic, those who work in shipping must prepare for the unexpected. In addition to the challenges of being at sea, such as sea and weather conditions, it is an extremely volatile industry with high-risk investments and markets that are heavily affected by both politics and economics. One example of the volatility of the markets is the daily rates to contract one ship to participate in a rig move. For example, the anchor handler *Havila Jupiter* has been under different contracts with day rates ranging from USD 7500 per day to USD 180,000 per day since she was launched in 2010.

The unexpected at sea challenges the principle of experience (Torgersen & Sæverot, 2015, p. 21). Normally both people and organizations learn from experience, but sometimes there is not a lot of history to learn from. It had been a hundred years since the earth experienced a worldwide pandemic and none of the previous viruses changed our practices in a significant way, and unlike a war or disaster at sea, there was no lasting image to capture meaning.

An Industry Sailing in Tailwind

The Norwegian maritime cluster is the world's most complete maritime cluster, including shipowners, yards, equipment producers and service providers (Maritimt Forum, 2021). A cluster is a "concentration of interconnected companies and institutions in a particular field" (Porter, 1998, p. 78). Companies that belong to strong clusters have higher value creation and more innovation power than stand-alone companies (Porter, 1998). Companies within a cluster will benefit from a joint knowledge base and labor market, and from economies of scale with regard to infrastructure and logistics. Knowledge sharing and joint research and development projects within the cluster increase innovation. Clusters enable a closer cooperation between industry, academia and public administration. The Norwegian maritime cluster holds a position as the world's leading maritime cluster for both green technology, automation and digitalization (Maritimt Forum, 2021).

In January 2020 the Norwegian maritime industry published their annual report on the value creation of the maritime industry (Maritimt Forum, 2020). The size of an industry can be measured in different ways, and a good way is to use value creation. Value creation is the company's turnover minus purchased goods and services. This means that the company's value creation corresponds to the sum of labor costs and profit before depreciation and amortization. The value creation of the maritime industry is thus the sum of wage costs and earnings before interest, taxes, depreciation and amortization (EBITDA) in all the maritime companies in Norway. The annual report painted a picture of an industry that was looking forward to a decade of tailwind. There was a reason for optimism for the value creation, and the accompanying employment numbers, both pointing in the right direction. Norwegian shipowners own and operates almost 3000 ships, making Norway, a small country of 5.3 million people, the fourth largest shipping nation in the World measured in value. It employs more than 50,000 seafarers and offshore workers worldwide and has a total of 80,000 employees onshore and at sea. This makes the maritime industry the second largest in Norway, only beaten by the oil and gas industry. The industry was on an updrift and slowly recovering from the challenges it had faced following the oil crisis in 2014.

The Norwegian maritime cluster was expected to blossom due to the possibilities of the decarbonization of the shipping industry. The projections were that the Norwegian maritime industry's 5000 companies and subdivisions were forecasted to reach a value creation of USD 20 billion during 2020. The Norwegian maritime cluster is uniquely positioned in the World with regard to green technology and has worked on making the maritime industry more environmentally friendly since the 1990s. As a result, the Norwegian maritime industry has established itself as the world leader in green technology including LNG, batteries, hydrogen and ammonia. The Norwegian ferry *Glutra* was launched in 2000 as the World's first LNG fueled ferry. In 2020 Norway had 61 of the World's ships fueled by LNG (DNV, 2021). In 2015 the launch of the world's first fully electrified ferry, *Ampere*, marked the beginning of the battery revolution in the maritime sector. By 2020 almost half of Norway's 200 ferries are hybrid or fully electrical and nearly half of these are built in Norwegian shipyards. By 2030 the entire ferry fleet is set to be low or zero emission. Late 2019 the world's largest plug-in hybrid ferry, *Color Hybrid*, with the capacity of 500 cars and 2000 passengers was launched to sail from Sandefjord Norway to Strømstad Sweden crossing the Oslo fjord twice a day. In addition, more than 20 offshore supply vessels have gone through retrofitting with battery packages or are in the process to do so. The next step in making the maritime a greener and cleaner industry is currently being developed and *Viking Energy* will be the first zero emission offshore supply vessel with a fuel cell run on ammonia installed in 2023. Another Norwegian vessel, *Yara Birkeland,* will be the world's first fully electrical and autonomous container ship. The research and innovation put into the development of these great ships have placed Norway in the position as one of the most innovative maritime clusters in the World.

Sailing into a Headwind

On March 12, 2020, about one month after the annual report was published, the maritime industry was facing the first consequences of the pandemic. The Norwegian government stated that they were to implement the "most invasive measures in peace time." This included closing down our borders, schools, workplaces, public transportation and most of the rest of society. We were sent home to home-school our children, work in our home offices and practice social distancing.

Most industrial production was closed down due to these restrictions, and the maritime industry faced both a supply and a demand challenge. When production closed down, both the companies and the employees lost income. A natural consequence in times of insecurity is to start saving, which created a decreased demand for goods and services. The decrease in demand was further escalated by the lack of possibilities to use money in a lockdown. The decrease in demand for goods hits the shipping industry hard because, as stated earlier, 80% of the world trade is transported by ship. By the end of March, the maritime industry was projecting that the consequences for the industry would be severe no matter how long the crisis lasted. The prediction was that the feeling of insecurity and increased vulnerability would affect the global economic growth long term. The drop in demand would lead to investments being stopped or postponed, leading to lower growth and higher unemployment. The projections were that 20,000 would become unemployed and the industry would lose USD 6 billion over the next three years if the pandemic did not end shortly (Eksportkreditt, 2020).

Rough Seas

In the beginning of 2021 the annual report of *Maritimt Forum*, the Norwegian maritime industry's interest organization, claimed that the financial consequences of the pandemic, combined with the fall in oil prices, has created the deepest crisis in the maritime industry in modern times. The value creation has decreased by 9% in 2020 and the number of employees in the maritime industry has decreased with 6%, leaving close to 6000 unemployed, a number which will probably be even higher when the government's layoff policy changes back to normal and the companies are forced to terminate the employment contracts, rather than having their staff temporarily laid off.

Travel bans and closed boarders throughout the world has restricted crew changes and led to crew immobility. Worldwide, some 400,000 seafarers are unable to disembark, leaving them stranded onboard for very long periods. Some have been onboard for close to two years now. This means that others are left unemployed waiting to embark. For the industrial workplaces onshore in Norway, this is critical as well. A lot of the skilled workers in the shipyards are from other countries, and with the current travel restrictions there are not enough employees, leading to reduced production. This means that production is delayed, leaving the yards and equipment producers with not only reduced income but also fines for being in breach of contract.

The cruise industry, especially the expedition cruise segment which sailed to exotic places like the Arctic and the Antarctic, was growing steadily until the pandemic hit. This had positive ripple effects for the Norwegian yards and equipment producers due to the restructuring from building offshore service vessels (Maritimt Forum, 2021). The many new vessels ordered before the pandemic are currently being launched, but there is no demand for them. This increase in the fleet, combined with a non-existing market, will dry up the orderbooks for the yards and equipment producers in several years to come (Maritimt Forum, 2021).

The domino effect of shipowners, yards and equipment producers closing down will have a catastrophic effect on the restructuring possibilities of the maritime industry. The past hundred years Norway has lived off the oceans with 70% of Norway's total export coming from the ocean industries (Norwegian Shipowners Association, 2020). To be able to keep our position as the world's foremost green maritime cluster, we have to maintain the maritime cluster complete. The technology and the competencies are essential if Norway is to restructure the maritime cluster to grasp the possibilities within renewable energy, seafood, minerals and bio marine resources.

It is within this volatile domain I teach my students.

Wobbly Sea Legs

As the maritime industry faced rough waters on March 12, 2020, I was also using the ocean to create value for me and my two sons. On that day, we were on the Sunshine Coast in Australia signing up for surfing lessons. In late 2019 I had decided to take my boys, aged 7 and 11, with me on a trip to Malaysia, Singapore, Australia and the USA to gather data for a research project that I am conducting on educational cooperation between the maritime industry and maritime universities. We were going to travel for 14 weeks from February to May of 2020. While on this trip I was going to teach and supervise my students online for the first time. I planned to hold seminars and lectures using the digital meeting platform Zoom and use the learning management system Canvas as the information sharing platform. For my students that needed supervision writing their theses, I planned on conducting face-to-face, or screen-to-screen, supervision via Zoom supplemented by the use of e-mail.

For my boys this trip was to be part of setting their sea legs as travelers and being the starting point on their journey toward becoming global citizens. We had decided to travel with few plans in place. Our only set plans were the preplanned research interviews and company visits I was doing for my project. We wanted to have few expectations and rather see where this journey would take us. This unstructuredness made it challenging to prepare as expecting something mentally prepares us for what is coming. Forming expectations makes us assume that certain sequences of actions will happen (Weick & Sutcliffe, 2007). Having travelled extensively for most of my life, I wanted this to be a journey based on my boys' premises. I did not want my expectations to guide our experience. Rather, I wanted to experience the world through my boys' eyes. For me, the control freak, this was difficult to do. I managed to meet myself halfway by booking the intercontinental flights and reserving a place to stay at our first stop in Kuala Lumpur, Malaysia.

The first challenge with no-plans travelling arose at the Oslo airport about two hours into our trip when they would not let us check in on the flight to Malaysia as we had no exit ticket from Malaysia. The next stop after Malaysia was Singapore, and since we hadn't decided which day we were to go to Singapore we hadn't gotten the bus tickets taking us across the bridge between the two countries. I could feel I was getting anxious and thinking "what on earth have I done when I haven't planned this better?" But then my seven-year-old looked at me and said, "Can't we just buy the bus tickets on your phone now?" Being used to backpack with a Lonely Planet travel guide I didn't even think about that possibility in the stressful situation of being denied check-in. But having grown up with the World in his palm, my seven-year-old solved the problem. So, while I went online to check for tickets my boys chatted with other people in the check-in line asking about their travel plans and telling them about ours. Carefree as only little boys can be. Three bus tickets ended up costing me USD two. Technology can sometimes be amazingly helpful, even if it is only a smartphone. At that moment I realized that this journey would be great. My self-efficiency was strong, and I felt comfortable with not being prepared for what was to come. We were on our way—still expecting the unexpected.

Quiet Before the Storm: Teaching While Travelling

Even if the plans for the trip in itself were close to non-existent, I did plan for the digital teaching and supervision. I had taken a course in digital pedagogy, participated in seminars on digital teaching, both online and in the classroom, and watched countless "How to …" videos of successful online teaching. I felt prepared and comfortable with using learning technology, but I had never taught online before and I was anxious to see if I could make it work well.

In my experience I love the feeling in the classroom. The classroom is my stage where I get to use language, humor, pictures, cartoons, graphs, videos and texts to teach my students about maritime management and leadership, maritime offshore technology and the bigger picture of the maritime industry. My goal is to make students fall in love with the ocean and the maritime industry the way I have. I am comfortable using technology in the classroom and had tested various digital tools such as Padlet, Mentimeter and Kahoot to make the lectures interactive when I have many students in the classroom. I also use YouTube and Spotify to utilize videos and music while teaching. I was used to utilizing these tools as a supplement to the teaching in the classroom, but I had never used them as an integrated part of online pedagogy. And I was soon to find out that teaching online was different from using digital tools in a classroom.

As in all areas of life it is not the technology in itself that matters, it is what we do with it (DeSanctis & Poole, 1994). This is especially important to keep in mind when using technology in teaching. Teaching online when I wasn't forced to, but rather something I chose myself, provided me with an opportunity to test some of the technological possibilities that I had learned about. I was using the online teaching as an experiment and I was convinced that it would be a one-time thing, so I didn't want to put more effort into it than necessary. I did spend a lot of time preparing the digital platforms but was still within my old pedagogical mindset of traditional classroom teaching. I let the technology guide the pedagogy, not the other way around.

While travelling I was the only lecturer teaching them online, the rest of their lectures, and lives for that matter, were as normal. The learning activates happened on campus with their classmates and their lectures in the classrooms. The pandemic had yet to close down the campus and the country, so I was a bit exotic—that crazy lecturer that travels with her boys while teaching from a new place each week. I started every seminar with telling them where I was, how my research was going and what we had been experiencing since the last seminar. This gave us a sense of closeness even if teaching online created a physical distance. I knew the students as I had taught them the previous year so we already had a relationship established. The teaching on Zoom went well and the students seemed to enjoy it. It was surprisingly easy to both hold presentations and to facilitate group work. Having never taught online before I did set the bar relatively low for what counted as a success, but I did feel good about myself as a digital teacher.

Returning to Safe Port

Six short weeks into my career as a cyber academic we had to return to Norway. When Norway closed down and the Norwegian government stated that they were to implement the "most invasive measures in peace time" I didn't know what to do. What was this? Were we at war? I felt like I was running right in front of a tsunami that was about to swallow us all. The information flow was overwhelming, yet the knowledge about what was happening seemed limited. Being in Australia it was the Australian news cycle that dominated, but since we were staying with a British friend, we also had the UK news updates. Neither Australia not the UK took the outbreak of the pandemic very seriously and they did predict that this would be no worse than the bird flu a few years prior. The Norwegian news cycle, on the other hand, made it sound like the world was coming to an end. I felt like I was drowning in information that pointed in all different directions and there was no clear answer on what the right thing to do was. Should I keep the travel plans "steady as she goes" or should I return to my Norwegian safe port? While trying to make sense of it all I got a message via Facebook from a friend high up in the Norwegian Ministry of Foreign Affairs. It was short and sweet: "I see you are still travelling. Looks great, but come home now! This will last a while ..." So we packed up, cancelled the surfing lessons and went home.

Returning from Australia we landed at Oslo airport which resembled a ghost town more than an international airport. Next to nobody was there. We were met by an armed military force and in a country that has unarmed police, the sight of guns was shocking. We were told to go straight into two weeks of at-home self-isolation. Returning to our house, the prospect of working from home together with two young boys I had to homeschool while being isolated from everyone else sounded like a situation that would drive me to the asylum within days. My thoughts went to Goffman's classic definition of a total institution that we so often use when describing a ship's organizational structure and culture; "A total institution may be defined as a place of residence and work where a large number of like-situated individuals cut off from the wider society for an appreciable period of time together lead an enclosed formally administered round of life" (Goffman, 1961, p. 11). Goffman's theories felt applicable because both the boys and I were required to work, learn, eat, play and sleep within the house, isolated from the rest of the world.

I worried about the boys being stuck at home without the social aspects of school and not being able to meet their friends. I worried about teaching an elementary school curriculum to my sons and about being at home 24/7. I worried about getting all my work done when daytime would be spent home schooling. I was not prepared. After a few days I felt like I was part of an experiment. I had to establish new patterns of behavior both privately and professionally, and this could not be done by comparing things to how they used to be. I was updating my ideas of the current situation, and as Weick and Sutcliffe describes it, I was "not held captive by old categories and crude renderings of the context" (2007, p. x).

When structure is missing the need for control arises. Control is a clear structure and organization of our lives; it is the power to make decisions and provide clarity. When everyone is trying to be in control, it leads to chaos because of our needs influence each other. My kids need to have a structure, my students need to have a predictable student life, and I needed control of the everyday life of me and the boys. When everyone's structure is missing, we lose control. We have to draw on our self-efficacy. People with a high degree of self-efficacy have greater ability to master new and demanding situations (Herberg et al., 2018, 2019).

What allowed me to find structure at home was, to my surprise, learning technology. Not the learning technology I used, but the boys' online classroom. The boys' school was quick to implement the use of Teams and OneNote. I had used both, but not extensively so I was of not much help. My boys had not used any form of online platform before, neither for gaming nor for school, but they embraced the use of both as if it was the most natural thing in the world. They had morning meetings with their teachers every day followed by a mix of online presentations, independent work, online lunch and chatting sessions with their friends. They even had online physical education. The structure from the elementary school forced us to establish a structure for our life in isolation.

Back at Port: Teaching from Home

Seeing how my boys embraced the digital learning technology of both Teams, OneNote and various online learning sites like Duolingo and Campus was fascinating. Since I was already teaching online during my travel, I expected minimal shift in my online classroom even if it was now taught from my home office. I was wrong. When the campus closed and all teaching went online, not just my course, something else changed. The exotic nature of having me traveling the world and in a new country every time we met online lost its novelty and I was just one among the many that taught them from my home office. I taught the same way as when I travelled, yet something changed.

Important factors to create a well-functioning learning environment, like social belonging, safety, good communication, trust and respect, are much harder to maintain when one does not meet face-to-face. My students had the opportunity to socialize with each other while the campus was open, but when all teaching became digital their forum for communication disappeared. Without the possibility of small talk the motivation to learn decreased. I too became limited because the pandemic has robbed me of my stage. We landed in a situation with black screens and monologues because no student replied to questions. For me digital education became more demanding as the black screens took away my opportunity to see if my students understood what I said or if they had lost concentration and needed a break. I was used to having all their faces to teach, the black screens made it hard to stay motivated. I typically respond to student laughter and enthusiasm (or lack thereof), and teaching to a screen with a bunch of black boxes with names on them in Zoom gave me no pleasure.

Things had to change. The online classroom was no longer my stage; it was a barrier between me and my students. How could I make the reminder of the semester, and the following semester, better? Should I continue to teach "live" online, or should I flip the classroom and prerecord the lectures?

I realized that it was more important to build the student's digital trust. Not to trust the learning management systems, nor the digital classroom as such, but to be comfortable with the digital classroom. It was their only arena for interaction with their classmates and to be able to learn trust had to be established. In the physical classroom I let the students discuss and share experiences to create interaction and unity in small groups. I made a decision to move more of the teaching into small groups using the breakout rooms in Zoom. This led to a situation where the students either logged off to not have to participate or joined in, turned the cameras back on and discussed, shared and learned. I made an active choice to make the best possible learning experience for those that took part in the online learning environment, not try to create a learning platform that was tailored to those that wanted to be offline. The students are after all adults that have chosen to go to university. It is their choice and responsibility to use the resources available to them.

Taking into consideration that the students that participated did so with varying levels of comfort, I became more conscious of the tools I used. In addition to using the breakout rooms in Zoom I started using Mentimeter, Padlet, the chat function in Zoom and live discussions in the online classroom. I decided to give the students more time than they needed to discuss the given task when I sent them into breakout rooms to provide them with a possibility to socialize as well. The idea came from the maritime industry that started having "after meeting hang outs" and "after work beer and quiz" sessions online. Slowly, but steadily, more and more students kept the cameras on when returning to the plenary sessions. The increased interaction created novel and unpredictable patterns of interaction (Tapsell & Woods, 2010, p. 542). Parallel to this I started using Mentimeter actively. This is a tool where the students can actively participate by using pools, tests and word clouds. I also increased the use of Padlet, which provides the students with the possibility to post on the same "wall." This proved to be especially useful when they worked in the breakout rooms as we could pull up all the inputs on the screen and all students had access to each other's answers. This was an excellent way of providing knowledge sharing without having to do it in a plenary session.

Reacting to the No-Structure of Korona-Life

A lot has changed due to the pandemic, and most of the news, reports and research focuses on the downsides and the negative effects. One of the upsides to the pandemic is that everyday life was turned upside down. At the time it may be stressful and overwhelming, but it also makes us more aware. Habits tend to have a dulling effect and make us do things on autopilot. The pandemic has made us more aware of what really matters. We appreciate what we took for granted yesterday and we consciously prepare for the unforeseen in the future.

Being thrown into the unknown world of digital education was obviously not unique for me. But I had to take on a new role—one that provided sensemaking for my students. I had to organize my teaching so that it provided my students with a sense of direction and helped them retain focus despite the constantly changing context (Weick, 2001, p. 91). The pandemic illustrated that we must be prepared for the unexpected. The unexpected can occur in three forms; an expected event doesn't materialize, unexpected events materialize and sometimes the unimaginable happens out of the blue (Weick & Sutcliffe, 2007, p. 24).

Normally self-organization only occur after changes in the systems (Lartey, 2020, p. 46), but my department was not prepared for this situation so there was no organized change other than that seemed to be no system anymore. We had no guidelines from the management on how to deal with our teaching. This allowed us to react to the change and generate a new structure for ourselves without having a centralized framework, and thus self-organizing (Tapsell & Woods, 2010, p. 542). Self-organization during the pandemic valued the skill of improvisation, which has traditionally not been a trait that has been seen as positive in academia, whereas preplanned and properly organized teaching is valued. Yet, improvisation creates innovation, and the pandemic gave us every opportunity to do so. Management had to trust us and support us because they had no choice. We could be creative without being vulnerable to criticism as we could blame the potential failure on the pandemic which forced us to act (too?) quickly. For me this represented the "free card." I needed to try and fail and learn to become a proper digital teacher.

Steady as She Goes?

The maritime industry is still sailing in rough waters, but they are forever optimistic and are looking for the blue horizon beyond the skies. A blue industry going green creates a lot of opportunities and challenges that will need competent employees to solve. Giving my students knowledge and skills to be part of this industry is my contribution to the development of the Norwegian maritime industry, either onboard or onshore.

Digital skills come in many forms, but the maritime industry needs them all to develop and to implement for the possibilities that lie ahead. For both the crew onboard and for land organizations, digitalization creates new tasks and new ways of interaction. By teaching online I give my students valuable digital soft skills, such as online communication, trust building, knowledge sharing on digital platforms and comfort with the use of technology—all necessary skills to work in the maritime industry when they graduate. Digital skills are needed to ensure effective operations, reduce cost, increase safety or create new services and markets (Norwegian Shipowners Association, 2021). Norway wants to be the world leader of this digital transition (Maritimt Forum, 2021), and to do so the country needs the maritime educational institutions to offer lifelong learning opportunities for the people working both onboard and onshore.

I am going to keep teaching online and trying to take progress one step further. I have started to record my lectures in short videos presenting the basics, and I am building a course focusing on problem-based learning activities, giving rich feedback, implementing both guided and independent group work, and building a trust-based learning environment. By recording the lectures, I do not replace myself, but rather the textbook. These changes will demand more from me than performing from my favorite stage, the classroom. But I believe they will create better learning activities for my students. And that is after all the most important.

We are not done with corona yet, and what happens next nobody knows. We have to be prepared for the unexpected. Through everyday life and its social activities, both we, as individuals, and the societies are wholly constructed, constituted and reproduced. Entering into the new, not yet established, everyday life opens up for reflection about what kind of working life one wants. What can I stop doing and what is it that I really want to keep doing and expanding on? Simply asking, and yet so difficult, who do I want to be? Some of this I can choose myself, some things are chosen for me. But even for the unavoidable I have to choose my response. I cannot be more prepared for the unforeseen than I am today, but I have to practice. Seek new challenges that are a bit out of the comfort zone. As we all should from time to time.

My Professional Vista

1998—Moved from Sydney, Australia, to Bodø, Norway, where I yelled at the Rector of Bodø Regional University who in return employed me to head up the newly established international office because he liked my guts.

2003—Took a year off work to do my Master of International Relations at Deakin University in Melbourne, Australia.

2007—Yelled at the Director of Competence at the Norwegian Shipowners Association (NSA) at a party in St. Petersburg, Russia, who in return headhunted me to a position as Competence Advisor at the NSA because he liked my guts and my strategic mind. I headed NSA's projects on competence, skills and recruitment for five years.

2011—Yelled at the Head of Department of Maritime Operations at Vestfold University College who headhunted me to be a project manager and lecturer at what is now the University of South-Eastern Norway.

2012—Started my higher education pedagogical journey by enrolling in courses on how to teach better at university level.

2013—Started cooperating with Liverpool John Moores University in the UK where I've been an associated part of the staff ever since.

2018—Finished my second post-graduate program, a Master of Human Resource Management which I took for two reasons; to update my knowledge about HRM and to experience being a student again to learn to be a better teacher and supervisor.

2019—Enrolled in the Professional PhD program at USN.

2022—Hopefully becoming an Associate Professor without having to yell at anyone (Fig. 6.1).

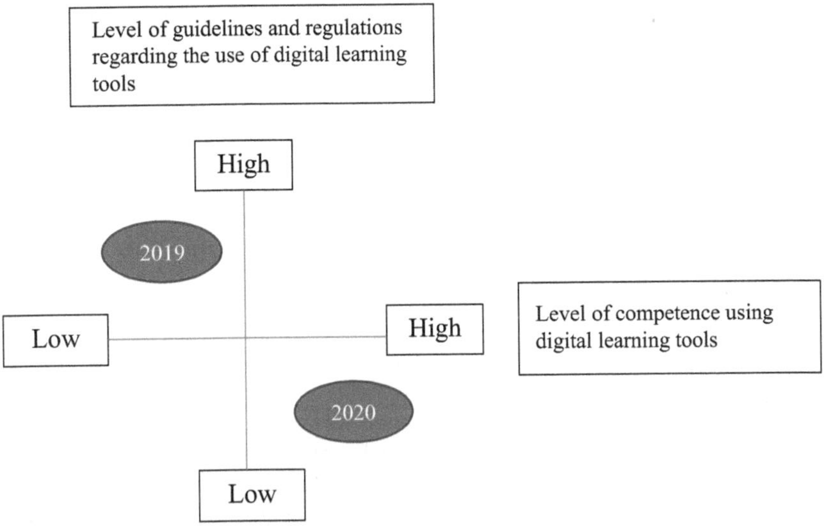

Fig. 6.1 The 2 × 2

References

DeSanctis, Geraldene, & Poole, Marshall Scott. (1994). Capturing the complexity in advanced technology use: Adaptive structuration theory. *Organization Science, 5*(2), 121–147.

DNV. (2021). Alternative Fuels Insight Platform (AFI). Found on www.dnv.com

Eksportkreditt. (2020). Newsletter on e-mail. Link to www.eksportkreditt.no

Goffman, Erving. (1961). *Asylums: Essays on the social situation of mental patients and other inmates.* Anchor Books.

Herberg, Marius, Torgersen, Glenn-Egil, & Rundmo, Torbjørn. (2018). Competence for the unforeseen: The importance of human, social and organizational factors. In Glenn-Egil Torgersen (Ed.), *Interaction: 'Samhandling' under risk. A step ahead of the unforeseen* (pp. 267–300). Cappelen Damm Akademisk.

Herberg, Marius, Torgersen, Glenn-Egil, & Rundmo, Torbjørn. (2019). Competence for the unforeseen: Social support and concurrent learning as basic components of interaction under risk. *Frontiers in Communication, 4*, 1–19.

Jacobsen, Erik W., & Espelien, Anne. (2011). *En kunnskapsbasert maritim næring.* Menon.

Lartey, Franklin M. (2020). Chaos, complexity, and contingency theories: A comparative analysis and application to the 21st century organization. *Journal of Business Administration Research, 9*(1), 44–51.

Maritimt Forum. (2020). *Maritim verdiskapningsrapport 2020.* https://www.maritimt-forum.no
Maritimt Forum. (2021). *Maritim verdiskapningsrapport 2021.* https://www.maritimt-forum.no
Norwegian Shipowners Association. (2020). *Konjunkturrapport 2020.* https://www.rederi.no
Norwegian Shipowners Association. (2021). *Konjunkturrapport* on https://www.maritimpolitikk.no
Porter, Michael E. (1998). *The competitive advantage of nations.* Free Press.
Tapsell, Paul, & Woods, Christine. (2010). Social entrepreneurship and innovation: Self-organization in an indigenous context. *Entrepreneurship & Regional Development, 22*(6), 535–556.
Torgersen, Glenn-Egil, & Sæverot, Herner. (2015). Ny pedagogikk for det uforutsettes tidsalder. In Glenn-Egil Torgersen (Ed.), *Pedagogikk for det uforutsette.* Fagbokforlaget.
Weick, Karl E. (2001). Leadership as the legitimization of doubt. In Warren Bennis, Gretchen M. Spreitzer, & Thomas G. Cummings (Eds.), *The future of leadership: Today's top leadership thinkers speak to tomorrow's leaders* (pp. 91–102). Jossey-Bass.
Weick, Karl E., & Sutcliffe, Kathleen M. (2007). *Managing the unexpected.* Wiley.

CHAPTER 7

Through the Looking Glass in a Pandemic: Inside of a Global Comms Corporation, Navigating COVID-19 on Top of Structural Change

Sarah A. Parker

This Is My Brain

I have always loved the beautiful absurdity of the Boltzmann brain argument—the idea that a brain could pop, fully formed, into existence as the universe was dying. It would hold the memories of a full human life as it once existed in said universe. It would immediately begin to decay, as all brains must when caught out in the vacuum of space.

A year of a global pandemic has brought me closer than I ever imagined I could to feeling like that fully formed brain floating out in the endless void, full of memories of things I am absolutely sure once happened. I once got in my car five days a week and sat in traffic as I commuted to my ostensibly cool tech job downtown. I had a job that I enjoyed, mostly because of the company of my coworkers. We could work from home

S. A. Parker (✉)
Austin, TX, USA

L. D. Browning et al. (eds.), *Organizational Communication and Technology in the Time of Coronavirus*,
https://doi.org/10.1007/978-3-030-94814-6_7

when we needed to and we had the necessary tools to interface with colleagues from other offices, as we were a global company.

Although we had recently been informed of an acquisition that would change company leadership (the third time in less than two years for some of us), my void brain was reasonably optimistic as it barreled unknowingly toward a life-altering pandemic in early March of 2020.

It also always misremembers "Boltzmann brain" as "Bayesian brain" which is fitting in the context of this chapter; as any self-organizing system like a brain must, it maximizes evidence of its own existence by writing about it when asked to do so.

This Is My Brain on Chaos

Similar to many of my generation, I was introduced to the idea of chaos theory watching 1993's *Jurassic Park*: Jeff Goldblum as Dr. Ian Malcolm puts water droplets on Laura Dern as Dr. Ellie Sattler's hand, asks her to predict which direction they will go, and when she can't, uses this example to illustrate that small changes in complex systems can have big, unpredictable effects. In this cinematic case, it leads to several exciting chase scenes with velociraptors and a T-Rex. In the case of this particular company's challenges during COVID-19, it certainly led to its share of chaos, but (spoiler alert!) no dinosaurs as of the time of this writing.

The key concept I wish to convey with the connection between chaos theory and this writing is this: Even in chaos there is an underlying order that can be detected. As Bütz (1997) put it in *Chaos and Complexity*,

> the phenomenon described as chaos has an underlying order and is not really chaotic at all. The behavior of what generally may be called a system, which can be anything from a chemical reaction to a business organization, may look random or chaotic, but according to this set of ideas, within that apparent randomness is order or an emerging order. The important thing to remember is that these ideas were named chaos theory because this apparently random behavior was experienced as chaos by scientists. (p. 4)

Or as experienced by employees in such a business organization that is undergoing massive change during a global pandemic. You can understand and describe a complex organization and its communication. "Chaos is seen as the unpredictable part of complexity" (Ortega & Han, 2017, p. 51), after all, but there will always be some kind of underlying order to it, even if it seems entirely random on its face.

In this case, that initial underlying order could have been reinforced as much as possible under the stress of multiple competing outside forces (leadership change, going fully remote, a pandemic, etc.) to minimize the chaos of the situation. That is not, however, what happened.

March 2020

In March of 2020 the pandemic arrived and I immediately felt lucky in one respect: I could easily work from home. The team I was on had a proven track record for putting out good work together, due in part to the strong bonds most of us formed from working together over several years and through multiple acquisitions.

Of course we all thought we'd only be working from home for a few weeks, at first. As a global company with offices in the Americas, Europe and Asia, we had tools already in place to keep everyone connected across time zones. While there wasn't an exceptionally strong remote work culture in place, it was common enough for some people to work from home frequently if they were the only person from their department in a particular office. We were therefore all familiar with the tools that would become our sole means of communication over the coming months: Zoom, Slack, the Microsoft Office Suite's various offerings. (In a previous acquisition the company I had come from grudgingly made the switch from Google Suite to Microsoft, a first sign of changing company culture from the "cool" to the "uncool with bad UX".)

Once it became clear it would be more than a few weeks of working from home, we were allowed to schedule time to come in and take what we needed from the office to be more comfortable: chairs, monitors, any personal items we left behind, rapidly expiring snacks.

We began to wonder to each other, via various messaging channels, what would happen the further we all drifted away from the various perks of our office meant to entice us to do our jobs for more hours every day: A fully stocked kitchen from which the young and ambitious could create three meals a day, the aforementioned snacks, kegs containing both beer and nitro cold brew coffee (alongside several other expensive coffee machines, some of which seemed capable of sending the user to space), catered meals, surprise treats for birthdays and holidays, regular company sponsored events and happy hours—and of course the unavoidable ping pong table found in every tech industry office. There was also the fact that we had office space downtown, close to all the places employees presumably want to be.

Those of us older than 30 wondered how our younger coworkers were going to last for more than a few weeks working from their living room floors and living off of the ramen, energy drinks, and expiring snacks they took from the office. Those with children wondered how they were going to retain their sanity. Everyone's dogs were very happy, along with a selection of cats.

As days and weeks drifted into months, we of course looked to leadership to guide us. To communicate with us. We were, after all, one of the biggest communications firms in the world! At first came the standard reassurances: We are in this together, look, this man in a position of leadership will send weekly emails meant to be relatable and endearing. Unfortunately, these often missed the mark on one or both counts; in one email he related that he hadn't learned how to properly tie his shoes until he was 40 years old. Rather than finding this anecdote funny and endearing, it raised the question to many employees reading of just how many things had been taken care of for this man throughout his whole life, so that he had only just learned how to tie his shoes? This was especially infuriating considering how much money this man made in a year compared to lower-level employees. (It was well known that the interim leadership was being extremely highly paid—my team was aware of one C-level position making $35k a month while entry-level positions on our team often weren't far above that for a year—while the company in general made the lowest market rate offers available to new hires, according to one former manager.)

This was our new senior, interim leadership; those in middle leadership positions below did the best they could to communicate with their teams and offer information—or, when not possible, informed speculation—to address issues and concerns around the business in the face of the pandemic. One such manager described it as trying to translate "the absolute silence and absurdity we were served up by the interim leaders".

Meanwhile, to find a sense of normalcy and purpose, many teams banded together to produce work at a maddening pace, perhaps in part motivated to prove that working from home did not deter us. On my team we launched, in a matter of days, a series of online events meant to help our customers talk through the communication skills that would become necessary over the coming weeks and—we all eventually realized, months—of the pandemic. These were a huge success (based on the metrics important to our team which I am being purposely vague about for anonymity's sake), highlighting everyone's need for communications guidance as well as connection around something we were all living through day-to-day.

Previously existing team leadership took the success of this project as a sign for the future of the team overall: here was proof we could accomplish anything, in any environment, given the chance.

Some of my teammates had always been workaholics and the lack of commute simply meant more time for them to work. Others just kept working because they simply didn't seem to know what to do with themselves otherwise, or had a hard time drawing boundaries between work and home life. Indeed, Pew Research reported in December of 2020 that "a third of those who are working from home all or most of the time say they are working more hours than they did before the coronavirus outbreak" (Parker et al., 2021, p. 1).

For some those extra work hours might have been an effort to prove their value as an employee, as a team player. Despite this extra effort—and the success of our initial project—the layoffs came anyway, two months into working from home, further demoralizing teams only just beginning to realize the scope of the pandemic—and the effects it would have. The communication breakdowns across the company became more apparent, as people left, were reshuffled, or laid off. Teams that had initially reached out to see how they could help one another became unresponsive or emails bounced back and that was how you found out that someone had been fired or left.

While it is obviously the model of this kind of acquisition to trim the company down and maximize its profits, some team leaders began to suspect that the interim leadership seemed to almost fear any kind of success that would make it harder for them to eliminate those teams in question. One team in particular was able to prove they had contributed over 50% of new business to the organization, a multi-million dollar business projection for the (pandemic!) year. The existing leadership of that team was labeled as redundant and eliminated in favor of a "cheaper" approach.

This approach involved hiring, among other things, a very expensive consulting firm in addition to extremely basic-level communications training and some contracted writing. All of this for a team that had already proven its value and abilities as quickly as possible in the face of uncertainty. Rather than allowing an established team to perform well on its proven terms, they chose to dismantle and demoralize it while investing significant resources in outside talent and advice. This is very arguably not a "cheaper" approach.

As for my own direct experience during this time, I was the manager of a very small team of one person other than myself and we were responsible for all of the company's content production. I tried my best to communicate everything I knew with my team, but I knew very little. I tried to help them best set themselves up for success working from home when they never had before. Fortunately, I had some experience working from home as a freelance writer early in my career so I could offer what I had learned in my own experience which was mostly what *not* to do: Work all the time, never take breaks, never go outside for walks, and only eat weird snacks over the sink instead of meals. The difficulty of the adjustment was very clear for some younger teammates because they missed the in-person connections they felt in the office and often lived alone in small spaces or with roommates who were practically strangers. People get meaning and community from the experience of doing a job with people—not having it showed just how important work life is. It is entirely possible to build this meaning and connection remotely, but that requires skill and intentional practice which wasn't being modeled or supported by the new interim leadership.

COVID-19 as an Accelerant

COVID-19 acted as an accelerant on the existing problems the company was facing; for one thing, the company was large because of many acquisitions made over many years. Some of those brands had been assimilated, but many had not, which meant there were constant conflicts with disparate company cultures, communication preferences, work styles, and more. Some continued to operate as wholly separate brands which our own customers did not even know were connected. A few seem to have been forgotten and left adrift, now just pieces of technology floating around the backend, underutilized toward that imagined final, better product.

This "culture" of fractured acquisitions created a multitude of communication problems beyond teams having different work cultures and communication preferences. People were using different tech stacks that didn't interface (Slack vs. Microsoft Teams, Zoom vs. Microsoft Teams, the ghost of G-Suite, etc.) which meant some were forced to adapt to new programs that often didn't account for their existing workflows. In some cases, these workflows were impacted enough that interim leadership postponed rollover dates to new systems so that workarounds could be established in time.

Information was siloed among various teams, sometimes on purpose because they felt it gave them some power and control in a volatile environment, and sometimes simply due to restructuring and departures along with vacated roles never getting backfilled.

Leadership was temporary and varied wildly. Tension existed between those seizing their interim leadership positions to undertake radical change within a department and those who made it clear they did not want to do anything they did not absolutely have to do while occupying their interim leadership role. Leadership styles also varied wildly, leaving teams uncertain of what to expect from different leaders they had to interact with or report to on different projects.

These interim leaders were meant to help replace themselves with "permanent" leadership, but most were barely known before everyone started working from home, which made it difficult for teams to trust they would make the best decisions in hiring new leadership. Interim leadership didn't know how these teams worked together and it was especially challenging to simultaneously learn existing dynamics and establish new ones while working remotely. Again it is entirely possible to do this and many companies who have been remote for years have put out extensive material on how to do this and do it well, but little to none of that was applied in this case whether from a perceived lack of necessity (the expectation that the pandemic was temporary) or from a perceived lack of resources to do it with (I am sure there is a consulting firm that specializes in this that could have been hired, but I do benefit from hindsight in this suggestion).

Teams were wary of any changes being made by interim leadership, knowing entire systems and modes of communication were simply likely to change *again* as the expected permanent leadership was brought in over the next weeks and months. It is the difficulty of learning and committing to something you may soon have to unlearn and to decommit.

Here is where information silos were particularly felt; leadership might make a decision to switch to a different form of messaging software based on budget without ever talking to the various teams who used it in the first place. In at least one case this led to that decision having to be rolled back repeatedly as new broken workflows emerged on a daily and sometimes hourly basis.

In one department, the interim c-suite leader made several notable firings, one long-overdue promotion and so many other questionable decisions they were ultimately let go themselves after roughly three months of chaos within that team. One of those firings was of a long-loved team leader who had been holding team morale together as best they could, scheduling regular Zoom happy hours and keeping everyone connected and motivated on projects. With that leader's exit and the increasing uncertainty around interim leadership's decision-making, most of the team began to look for jobs elsewhere. By the fall of 2020 at least ten employees had left that department for other jobs. By 2021 only two original members of that team were left, one only because their role is difficult to find in the current market.

Communication between teams was often a further challenge even when not deliberately siloed, as cultures from previous companies made through various acquisitions butted up against one another. For example, without strong leadership, our hybrid teams often failed to create new sustainable and global methods of communication, further compounded by standalone brands using different tech. The negative effect on morale, drive, and expected career progression cannot be overstated.

A coworker from another team described trying to tackle a cross-team problem this way: "Siloed information was a massive problem; you have to back channel through back channels to fix an issue. I sat through a meeting one week with lower-level managers from three different departments trying to figure out how to get a broken feature to work. Nobody from [that broken feature's team] returned emails or messages from two different messaging platforms to answer. We took an hour to figure it out, fixed the issue, then got a passive aggressive email from the [broken feature's team] 'product manager' asking to be included in these talks going forward. Because there is no ownership or accountability, it was just us being admonished for fixing an issue they refused to acknowledge." Fixes fell through the cracks. Fixers were admonished by those who created the problem. Work became less integrated, more fragmented, during Covid.

In the face of rampant uncertainty about the future across every facet of life both personal and professional, our collective morale drifted toward the bottom. The weekly emails intended to help did not help (and they became late, then less frequent). Town halls that were held in the name of transparency and communication served only to increase bitterness. Employees made three major requests that would have eased their current situations and made them feel more acknowledged and cared for by leadership:

1. A stipend for their home office set-ups (not every office was allowing employees to come in and take what they needed for a more comfortable and efficient home set-up, our office later learned).

2. For all vacation to rollover beyond the minimum standard allowed—a single week—since no one was taking any while they were at home (leadership's response to this was that we should "take time off anyway for mental health" which seemed laughable to those already juggling full-time work with full-time childcare and more).
3. Merit pay increases were suspended and employees wanted them reinstated.

All of them were denied. As a result, these announcements did not improve morale, particularly as they were not answered live during the town hall directly from leadership, but were dribbled out in a follow-up email almost certainly written by someone else and later approved. This just served to further illustrate that leadership did not care about those they were leading; they couldn't be bothered to deliver the bad news themselves, even in the form of an email.

Teams were also told that hiring was suspended, which obviously made it more difficult to backfill important roles and caused some employees to have to take on double-and-triple workloads (without increased pay). In reality, the parent equity firm was hiring new permanent leadership in a silo, *then* introducing them to existing interim leaders. This created even more confusion and further complicated communication. Reporting structures and project prioritization became increasingly unclear to individuals, further decreasing their motivation and commitment to the job.

Employees understood there would be some impact to overall company finances because of the pandemic; some customers would not be able to pay or would not be needing our various services as much as they might have before. However, the company was saving in other ways, not having to pay for stocking the kitchens, catered lunches, or events for employees. Why was *none* of this money being invested in the employees in different ways, to help them feel connected and to build trust with their new leadership while remote?

We can think about this through some example numbers. If a company was spending, let's say on average $175k a month for facilities (food, drinks, catered lunches, parking, utilities, rent, etc.) for roughly 200 employees, that would be about $2.1 million a year or $10.5k per employee. Those office perks were initially part of the attraction of the job, an expected acquisition cost. Many companies that have been operating remotely for years offer their employees a one-time home office stipend up front (anywhere from $500 to $3500 depending on if they provide hardware) plus a yearly budget for home office maintenance ($1k–$1500/year), in addition to stipends for things like employee wellness ($100/month), flexible co-working spaces (another $100/month), and perks like bi-annual meet-ups in non-pandemic times.

For a company of the same size that would mean a much lower cost-per-acquisition, less than half of the original facilities cost. If a company is making $20 million a year in ARR (annual recurring revenue), pivoting to a remote model that puts investments in employees first actually gives them more to invest in other programs since the cost-per-acquisition is so much lower. In the wake of the pandemic, many companies have realized this and are adjusting to remote or hybrid models accordingly.

This company in particular didn't seem to understand this possibility early on, even with the advantage of having much of the necessary technology in place. They still do not seem to understand it, based on the news that continues to emerge around its decisions.

What employees *did* see interim leadership investing in during the pandemic was expensive consulting firms and messaging workshops that often created frustration within teams rather than forward progress. In one example, over $1 million was allocated for a consulting firm to turn around what amounted to 1% of the business.

Again teams asked themselves, what is the point of implementing all of these new systems if they will change again—or change back—as soon as "permanent" leadership is installed? Interim leadership made no effort to talk through these concerns with teams. New permanent leadership that was installed tended to have one large team meeting, then lean on one or two people for information while never working to connect with the rest of the team, which further increased employees' feelings of isolation and being regarded as an expendable commodity. An investment could have been made in helping new permanent leadership lead remotely even if that hadn't been deemed necessary for interim leadership, but again, it was not.

There was still risk involved in looking for a new job in the middle of a pandemic, especially when employees learned that the company was suing a small startup several previous employees have gone to work for, including a request for that startup to rescind their employment offers in the middle of a pandemic. This reflected poorly from a PR perspective and so was especially confounding coming from a large global communications firm meant to specialize in such decisions.

Obviously any explicit non-competes should be communicated and enforced as expected. However, with some terminations and resignations there was no clear language around what a former employee could or could not do, particularly if they were a lower-level employee at the time of their departure.

Cease-and-desist letters were also sent to companies that had hired several former employees, citing recruitment circumstances. While this is entirely fair, overall the company should have considered the net lack of compassion they were showing—not just to former employees but to current and future prospective ones as well—to people during a pandemic, in simultaneously threatening their livelihoods and limiting their employment opportunities. This is especially stark considering their denial of employee requests for merit pay and a structure that made advancement in the current environment all but impossible.

Rumors additionally begin to circulate that the company was looking at not another acquisition, but instead a merger with their biggest competitor. Leadership refused to answer employee questions about this with anything more than obvious talking points and so employees learned about it from the press when reports emerged around possible antitrust violations.

This further decreased trust in interim leadership and in any new "permanent" leadership that had subsequently been installed.

Self-organization as It Applies to This Particular Organization

At this point it should be clear to any reader that things were chaotic within the company, compounded by the unique challenges presented by the pandemic one might have expected a large global communications firm to be better equipped to handle.

While some theories of self-organization such as complexity theory (Poutanen et al., 2016) posit that chaotic systems should be able to organize themselves from the ground up, this did not happen in these particular circumstances for several reasons suggested by this author:

1. Teams were given outside interim leadership, rather than allowing them to be led from within—on a basis of established trust—during a time of extreme stress compounded by a pandemic.
2. Interim leadership, in most cases, did not interface with existing team leadership, instead working to establish themselves and act as decision-maker with little input from the team itself (if feedback was requested it was not seen by the team as a serious request).

3. Extremely low morale brought on by all previously mentioned factors meant that teams were not motivated to do more than what they need to get through a day; fear of losing their job was counterbalanced by a lack of clear leadership or vision, complete loss of purpose and little to no connection to those making decisions.

Given the chance, employees may well have been capable of creating order from strong team bonds and their history of work. Of course, my perspective comes from a particular team in a particular office, one of many acquisitions. I do not know the full scope of the company and how many teams had strong bonds and the metrics to prove their work from the past that could be adapted in this new, more challenging environment. I do know that such a chance was never given.

My assessment reflects the idea of self-organization occurring after a change in a system (Lartey, 2020; in this case, we had multiple changes occurring at once), but all parts of the system were not allowed to react in their own ways and take on new form; outside order was incompletely applied by external forces.

At the time of this writing, the company has been back in the news several times concerning various lawsuits, the rumored merger (which did not take place after all, but was indeed a real possibility and possible antitrust violation) and now the possible sale of one of the many brands it has acquired. More members of the author's previous team have left; indeed, only a handful of those who were on the team at the start of the pandemic in March 2020 are still there, often because their roles in particular are difficult to come by in the current environment.

I myself accepted a new job in the fall of 2020.

The Author's Professional Vista

2007: Graduates from undergrad; decides to enter graduate school.

Spring 2012: Finishes graduate school with a master's degree having ridden out a recession by taking on more debt and earning no money to speak of.

Fall 2012: After several years of tumultuous underemployment undertaken while finishing said graduate degree, the author lands a "dream job": entry-level full time at a tech startup that promises it will very soon have health insurance!

2012–2018: Startup does well; author is promoted. Attends many industry events, speaks at events and guest lectures at universities.
Summer 2018: Tech startup is acquired by a larger tech startup.
Early 2019: Larger tech startup is acquired by industry behemoth.
Early 2020: Industry behemoth is acquired by a venture capital firm; author is already very tired.
March 2020: Pandemic! At the Disco.
May 2020: Layoffs affect the author's department including trusted existing leadership.
Fall 2020: Author accepts new job (Fig. 7.1).

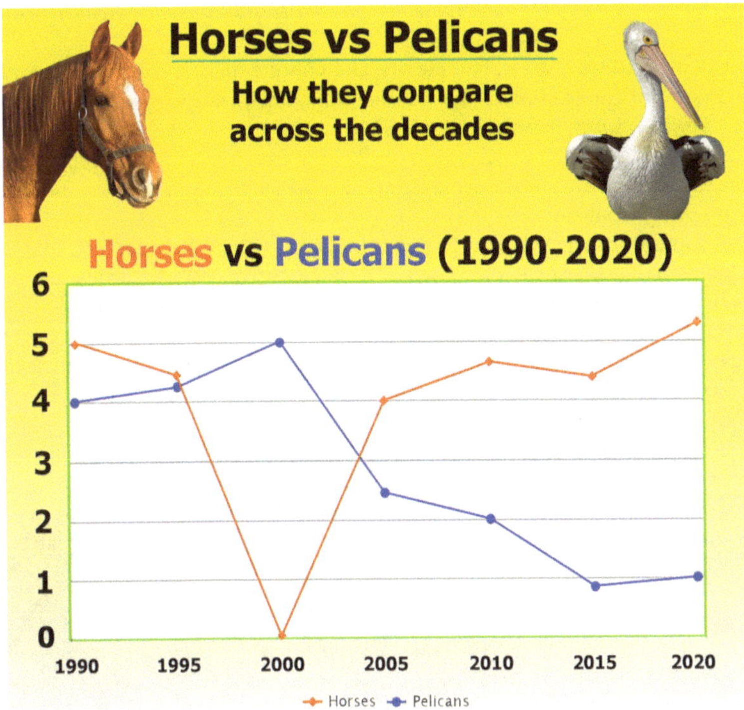

Fig. 7.1 Horses versus pelicans

Image via Sir Michael (2021) on Twitter accurately reflects for this author the sense of meaningless chaos given seemingly random order for employees of a certain large global communications firm from March 2020 through the fall of that same year.

Fittingly, Warzel (2021) recently wrote in his substack *Galaxy Brain* that Twitter from a user perspective is "mostly chaos. But Twitter is hell-bent on the notion that this chaos can be harnessed in a safe, PG-13 kind of way." That is what the approach from interim leadership felt like during this pandemic. Neither approach feels very successful to this author.

References

Bütz, Michael R. (1997). *Chaos and complexity: Implications for psychological theory and practice*. Taylor & Francis.

Lartey, F. M. (2020). Chaos, complexity, and contingency theories: A comparative analysis and application to the 21st century organization. *Journal of Business Administration Research, 9*(1), 44–51.

Ortega, Lourdes, & Han, Zhaohong. (2017). *Complexity theory and language development: In celebration of Diane Larsen-Freeman*. John Benjamins Publishing Company.

Parker, Kim, Horowitz, Juliana, & Minkin, Rachel. (2021, February 9). *How coronavirus has changed the way Americans work*. https://www.pewresearch.org/social-trends/2020/12/09/how-the-coronavirus-outbreak-has-and-hasnt-changed-the-way-americans-work/

Poutanen, Petro, Soliman, Wael, & Ståhle, Pirjo. (2016). The complexity of innovation: An assessment and review of the complexity perspective. *European Journal of Innovation Management, 19*(2), 189–213.

Sir Michael on Twitter. (2021, March 18). [Tweet]. Twitter. https://twitter.com/Michael1979/status/1372655123734929408

Warzel, C. (2021, April 13). It's not cancel culture—It's a platform failure. *Galaxy Brain*. https://warzel.substack.com/p/its-not-cancel-culture-its-a-platform

CHAPTER 8

Chaos: International Sourcing of PPE and the Covid-19 Pandemic

Frode Soelberg

The flow of commodities in the Enterprise Resource Planning system (ERP system) is linear. ERP systems integrate several business functions and track business resources (e.g., materials) and the status of business commitments (e.g., purchase orders). It is a software package that typically is based on historical data from the enterprise itself and the relevant industries involved, and it operates near real time. Thus, this system allows businesses to monitor flow, plan accordingly, and cut costs, resulting in businesses running leaner and leaner. The Enterprise Resource Planning system follows the logic of the Just-in-Time system (Sayer, 1986), in which you stock no more material than you need at hand. Predominantly, global supply chains follow the Just-in-Time logic. In effect, this reduces a business's need to stock up on materials and commodities and may, in Snowden and Boone's (2007) framework, be considered "*Best Practice*". However, learning from Gleick (1988), any linear system may reach a tipping point and cascade into chaos. Chaotic systems can, therefore, be

F. Soelberg (✉)
Business School, Nord University, Bodø, Norway
e-mail: Frode.soelberg@nord.no

L. D. Browning et al. (eds.), *Organizational Communication and Technology in the Time of Coronavirus*,
https://doi.org/10.1007/978-3-030-94814-6_8

found anywhere you care to look. A basic idea of chaos theory is that order and chaos are not always diametrically opposed, and that chaotic behavior is an intimate mix of the two (Borwein & Rose, 2012).

Resilience is a major issue in Supply Chain literature (Petitt et al., 2011). In practice, however, global supply chains are cut so lean that one tiny little hiccup may cause huge and unexpected ripple effects. On March 11, 2020, the World Health Organization (WHO) declared the Covid-19 outbreak a global pandemic, and shortly after, the well-organized, orderly and lean Personal Protective Equipment (PPE) supply chain reached a tipping point. Chaos broke loose; demand skyrocketed. The large buyers were hoarding; hospitals and health services globally were running out of face masks, gowns and protective clothing as their consumption of these commodities rose beyond imagination. Manufacturers were unable to meet this exceptional growth in demand. The terms of doing business changed: freight rates and prices soared, fake quality certificates flourished, border controls were tightened, free trade agreements were set aside, and there was intense rivalry for every container of Personal Protective Equipment commodities. Two months later (in May 2020), the turmoil was over and order had been restored. Production capacity had been ramped up, and the fear of not being able to protect health workers subsided. The flow of PPE commodities returned to normal—smooth and linear. In the following sections the chaotic months of spring 2020 are re-lived through the lens of the CEO at a small international sourcing company located in Bodø, Norway. This company stepped up as National Health Services reached out to them in a dire situation: They were running out of PPE in the midst of a global pandemic.

Flatten the Curve, Part 1

The first lockdown period, that began back in March 2020, was gradually lifted as summer approached. It appeared that the virus was less contagious during summer, when people spent a lot of their time outdoors. Looking back, the first lockdown in Norway was not that bad. The general opinion was hopeful that the virus could be contained, and the country mustered great effort to do so. Was it maybe the collectivistic ideals of Norwegian culture that helped us endure the ordeal of social lockdown? Besides, the winter of 2020 blessed the Arctic Norway with lots of snow; skiing conditions were perfect—the best in years—and I took advantage of it. March is considered part of spring elsewhere in the northern hemisphere, but in the Arctic it is very much a part of winter. Cross-country skiing is meditative and will set your head straight: Who can think about illness and disease while skiing across the snow-white rolling hills of the Bodø peninsula?

At Nord University where I work, most of my teaching chores were suspended. The semester was nearly done anyway; thus, a more student-activity-based model of teaching, which utilized mentoring rather than lecturing, was applied. It is possible to both give lectures of acceptable quality and collect data (interviews) online (using Zoom or Teams software). But I found that doing this type of work online, however meaningful, takes the fun out of it. What I really missed after a few weeks was meeting people. Later, in the early weeks of autumn, I was actually allowed to go downtown and meet with people, and it felt so energizing.

Flatten the Curve, Part 2

Today, as I'm writing up this ethnography, a second lockdown has been employed in Bodø, and I have to admit that I don't feel too happy about embarking on this second go around. It's going to be boring. On a personal level, I believe that to stay healthy in this situation, you have to focus on what's under your own control—the things you can manage and do something about; you know, family, work, healthy eating, exercising, and keeping a critical distance from social media. The experience of lockdown is nevertheless kind of lonely, and it wears your stamina down. As these thoughts run through my head, I realize that other parts of the world have been hit harder by the pandemic and that Norwegians are, in a way, seeking shelter in a privileged corner of the world. I should just shut my gob, shouldn't I?

The general public has also become more critical toward the policy of flattening the curve through social lockdown. People not only voice their distrust in the feasibility of lockdown measures; some even raise doubts concerning the rationale for containing the virus and spin their doubts into conspiracy theories. There have been a few political demonstrations, but these seem to gather support from the fringes of the political spectrum and are by no means a homogenous group of people (Skille et al., 2021). The problem is that these demonstrators create a lot of noise and draw the attention away from what's important: containing the spread of the virus while vaccination is ramping up. On top of that, the general support of anti-Corona measures has been declining as well, from a massive 93%

support in March 2020 (Klassekampen, 2020) down to 60% in January 2021 (VG, 2021a). Thus, political opinion is shifting toward more critical views, and other perspectives than just the purely medical position are gaining a foothold in the general opinion. As for me, I've decided on the more simple strategy of "sticking it out". So let's go back to September 2020 when I met with Stephen, whom I managed to interview between the two lockdowns. I'll take you there.

Stephen and I

It is a delightful 2020 Indian summer in the Arctic Norway. While lockdown has been lifted (September 2020), traffic is still very light and the city seems sleepy. The spread of the virus is not that bad this time of year. I guess people are wary and choose to work from their homes as advised, even though at the moment they are not required to do so by law. I'm actually quite anxious about having a conversation in real life with a CEO—in the flesh. He is the founder-manager of an international sourcing company with its headquarters near where I live in Bodø, Norway—70 miles north of the Arctic Circle. Parking would usually involve a bit of circling 'round the block, but not on this warm and slow September day. The sky is crystal blue, and light winds cuddle me and my few fellow pedestrians on the seafront walk that opens onto the North Atlantic Ocean and the Norwegian Sea. I'm thinking; "*If the earth was flat, I would probably see all the way to Greenland today.*" Admittedly, weird thoughts run through my head all the time. I shake it off and send a text to Stephen to let him know I'm on my way. I do hope he'll meet me at street level—I'm not too familiar with these new high-rise buildings in downtown Bodø.

The building is brand new, and Stephen's company just moved in there. He must have anticipated my confusion, and he promptly calmed me down, as he stood in the doorway holding it open with one arm and greeting me with the other. I'm still a few steps away from him, but as I'm about to greet him with a handshake, I find myself thinking: "*Is this permissible?*" I remember the all-too-familiar posters at the University: *Don't touch your face, don't shake hands, keep social distance, and use hand sanitizer*. I've known Stephen a while. A few years ago we were on the board of the local cycling club together, and we had a ball hosting the National Championship and other large cycling events. It feels strange not to shake hands. We settle for what has become the pandemic fist-bump. Social distancing doesn't feel right, not even for Norwegians.

The Sourcing Company

Having overcome this little moment of fist-bump social awkwardness, Stephen leads on toward the elevators. There are still workers inside the building, and not all the flooring has been finished at ground level. "*The process slowed down during the initial lockdown in March, and there's some finishing touches missing on these facilities,*" Stephen explains, "*but our contract at our previous location was up – we decided to move in here and just make do with the situation as it is.*" We enter the elevator that takes us to the correct floor. We talk about the general problems involved in moving into a new building, be it a professional building or a private home. There is always something big or small that has gone wrong or is not entirely finished, so you'll have to accept a period of "fixing the details". We agree on this point as the elevator *finally* manages to connect the dots and stop where we want it to. I'm thinking about translating that hilarious "voice-command-elevators-in-Scotland-joke" into a Norwegian version as Stephen gives a tour of the premises, but I resist. The company is located at one of the top floors and is a pretty big operation by Norwegian standards. I quickly estimate that there are at least ten people working there, and I know there is staff working elsewhere in Norway (Fredrikstad, South-East Norway) and abroad (China) as well. Stephen finds a conference room for the two of us, and we settle in with coffee and chocolate chip cookies. "*So, what's the story?*" I ask, hoping for a grand tour (McCracken, 1988) of what is going on.

"*We are involved in sourcing and importing goods. Preferably from China. We find producers of 'whatever' you want, perform quality control, vet exporting licenses and certificates, arrange customs clearing, transport and so on. This is not a warehouse,*" Stephen begins. He is a Norwegian of Chinese descent and speaks Cantonese. "*It doesn't help much to study at the University or to learn how to speak Mandarin or any Chinese language – well you'll survive, know how to order food and so on, but you will not cope as a manager or in negotiations with the Chinese.*" He continues: "*You wouldn't stand a chance, as you don't know their culture or understand the complexity of the language.*" He probably has an innate understanding of Chinese culture, which gives the company a competitive edge in the business of sourcing commodities in China. His family moved to Norway from

China in 1973, when Stephen was nine years old. His father was working for a major Norwegian shipping company (Wh. Wilhelmsen) at the time, and he was somewhat familiar with Norwegian culture when they moved here. Stephen carefully avoids going into detail as he lifts the veil on how it was for him growing up in Norway with Asian parents. "*I've had some problems,*" he says, and then confidently moves on. Stephen's family settled in the southern Norwegian town of Fredrikstad, and he became, to his father's dismay, a talented track and field athlete in his adolescent years. In the sprint events he was among the very elite (top ten nationwide) in his age group, but he had to give up his athletic career, as muscular problems accumulated when he was in his late teens.

The most dramatic change in Stephen's life at nine years old was leaving his Catholic boarding school in China and attending the Norwegian "*Grunnskole*" (primary education, mandatory public school). Catholic boarding school was very strict and offered little wiggle room for a child; "*but suddenly I could decide for myself what to do – it was so different and I loved it.*" He describes how, virtually from one day to the next, life changed from very restricted to very free. He has worked his way through the Norwegian education system and holds an MSc degree in Business (Nord University 1989). He has lived most of his adult life in Bodø, while making a career working for a range of companies (like Deloitte, Norges Bank/Central Bank of Norway) until founding a sourcing company in 2004 (see also Doornich, 2019). It appears this is a very successful immigrant story, though he admits to having experienced some problems.

"Everyone" knows you can get stuff cheap from China. What most people don't acknowledge is that there is an abundance of high-quality manufacturers in that country. The problem is to elicit this high-quality production every time: "*I never speak Cantonese in business meetings,*" he says with a firm look. He explains that, firstly, it would add an uncontrollable complexity to the discussion: "*Even though I make conversation – small talk – in Cantonese, I like to keep things formal and in a Western business style in meetings. When they talk among themselves, using the codes of their mother tongue, they know that I know.*" Secondly, his experience is that the quality of products is more stable when he is perceived as a foreigner; thus, he is careful not to come across as Chinese: "*I'm the only one carrying the scent of sweet cologne in business meetings,*" he laughs.

Stephen and his colleagues at the sourcing company have the knowledge, experience, network, and financial power to find, certify, and import high-quality commodities to Europe. "*We are not involved in lawn furniture – no, that's not our cup of tea.*" Stephen makes it clear that they are sourcing complex products, like boats and micro homes. He continues, "*We do things that most sourcing companies can't do.*" His sourcing company takes advantage of a highly skilled workforce, and that's the resource base that constitutes their competitive advantage. I move on to more specific questions I'd like to ask him: "*Yes, that is why it was kind of a surprise to me that you were involved in sourcing PPE to the health sector some months ago, Stephen. I read about it in the news the other day and would like to talk about that sourcing operation.*" Stephen just laughs: "*Yeah, it was a rough ride.*"

The PPE Market

Producers of PPE—clothing and equipment designed to protect the wearer from the spread of infection or injury—are predominantly located in Asia and on the Pacific rim. Key items are surgical masks, gowns, and goggles used in the health sector, and globally this market was estimated to be worth $2.5 billion in 2018 (Park et al., 2020). The production of masks is predominantly in China, whereas glove production has a more diverse distribution. In an analysis by Park and colleagues (Park et al., 2020), China appears as the world's largest exporter in commodity groups that include masks, gowns, protective suits, and goggles.

Our friend at the sourcing company continues: "*You know, we've been sourcing stuff – like boats – in China for years. And some 10 years ago we got involved in this PPE market. We had an ongoing operation until 2016, when our major customer did not find this strategically interesting anymore. We shut down and left this market – it wasn't very lucrative anyway, but we still got those relations and a history with some of the manufacturers. In China this is important.*" (Their former customer now relies heavily on Turkish manufacturers.) Stephen quickly runs through the company's history within the PPE market, and he explains that the increased focus on cutting costs has led to virtually non-existent stocks of PPE globally: "*As a rule of thumb, warehousing – you know, just putting an item on the shelf and later taking it down – would typically add 12% to total product costs.*" Like many other globally sourced items, Just-in-Time (Sayer, 1986) has become the best practice for PPE supply chains: It ensures a constant, smooth flow of commodities from producers to users, and it takes advantage of carefully planned global sourcing and manufacturing. The outcome is direct distribution, and no warehousing. The Just-in-Time supply chain aims to reduce the need for storage, which means that ideally you have no more than the material you need at hand. Just-in-Time requires a streamlined process with no excess material and minimized transactional costs. Thus, a smooth-running global supply chain may also involve free trade agreements and international product quality standards. "*But let me tell you this,*" Stephen warns. "*In the case of PPE, Just-in-Time is just talk! It doesn't work!*" The Just-in-Time system may reduce costs, but it is not designed to handle disruptions in supply or surging demand (Lagu et al., 2020) like what we saw in the PPE market in the early months (February, March, and April) of 2020. The application of best practice, however, requires a simple context (Snowden & Boone, 2007). An overlooked shift in context may, therefore, have devastating consequences for any sourcing operation.

In short, and in theory, best practice in global supply chains is employing the Enterprise Resource Planning system (ERP system). The ERP system employs both external and internal data and follows the logic of frameworks like the SOFT/SWOT analysis or PESTEL (see Grant, 2016). These are classic planning systems frameworks in the strategy literature and have for years been the hallmark of strategic analysis. Thus, in principle, an analysis of the external environment by anyone using or buying PPE commodities should make it evident that stocking up on such commodities would be a good idea as of December 2019. In practice, however, the Just-in-Time system focuses on internal efficiency and on running a lean business. Competition is usually fierce and buyers are normally inclined to choose the lowest price when acquiring standardized items (like PPE). But stocking PPE will cost money, disrupt internal efficiency, and cause diminishing profits. Therefore, the problem may be described as a matter of keeping track of the wrong issues, or failing to strike the optimal balance between internal and external efficiency, or failing to recognize the shift in context. Theory and practice are not always the same.

The Pandemic

The new Coronavirus was identified as causing what the WHO initially labeled an epidemic in December 2019 (hence, Covid-19). The WHO, monitoring the virus' spread through the early months of 2020, scaled up their warnings and declared the outbreak a global pandemic on March 11th. "*It only took one day – one day after the WHO declaration,*" Stephen erupts, "*and the head of procurement in the Norwegian Health Services* (Helse Nord) *called me, saying they'd been told that I'm pretty streetwise in*

China and asked if I could please help them with some PPE gear." He wasn't too alarmed by this call and didn't really take it too seriously: "*Maybe they're just checking what we can do,*" he says. To get a call from the Health Services in this situation may be what you expect when you run a sourcing company, but from the very top manager of procurement? Stephen would soon realize the depth of the crisis in the Norwegian PPE supply.

"*I got the call on a Friday and put together a range of relevant commodities on a website. It was business like usual. But then over the weekend, an order totaling NOK 8 million was placed by Health Service.*" That was an eyeopener, and he realized that the world today was different from yesterday. He called out at the top of his lungs in the office: "*Shit! They're not just checking out what we can do, they're running out of PPE!*" Stephen laughs out loud as he recalls the moment. He sure got his coworkers' attention on that Monday in March 2020. He had, of course, read about the outbreak in the news. His cultural knowledge of China made him worry about an increased spread of the virus in China, as travelling would become more intensified by the celebration of the traditional Chinese New Year on January 25, 2020: "*I don't think we realize (in the Western world) the impact of the Chinese celebrating New Year during the spread of the virus – I wonder if we would in fact have avoided this (the pandemic) if the initial epidemic had happened, say, in November (2019).*" The thought had crossed his mind that there might be a somewhat higher demand for PPE commodities in China, but he never imagined that the supply to the Norwegian Health Services, or to the rest of the world for that matter, would completely break down. The regular supply chain simply could not deliver. He learned in a follow-up conversation with Health Services that the Ministry of Defense was checking their emergency stockpile of PPE designed for protection in the case of chemical warfare, but this was a stockpile they'd rather not part with, and the supplies were really not ideal for surgical/health services. The supply of the desired-quality PPE was non-existent (VG, 2020a); and even worse, the problem was global (Livingston et al., 2020). These two factors—the scarcity of PPE and increasing global demand—lead (as we shall see) to a major shift in both the micro- and macro-environment; there was fierce competition over every little batch of PPE-commodity, terms of trade changed, fraud profiteering flourished, and free trade agreements were cancelled during March and April 2020.

The Chinese had been hoarding equipment since December 2019 when they knew the severity of the spread of the virus. Now the USA was hoarding—Germany, Spain, Italy, and Great Britain—everybody was hoarding face masks, gowns, goggles, and protective clothing in February 2020. Prices were soaring, as ramping up production would take two to four months, and in that period the need would only grow. "*Well, I think the problem with the Just-in-Time system is that it is still people making these decisions, and people make mistakes, mistakes that lead to us running out of PPE in March,*" Stephen explains. Retrospectively, preparations should have been made in January (2020). But they didn't do anything; either they didn't understand or they didn't realize the full potential of the outbreak. Stephen continues, "*Maybe they were too focused on the ERP-system* (Enterprise Resource Planning) *with its estimates based on the latest 10 months.*" I've got to give it to him: You can't always predict the future based on past experiences, and a key problem with best practice is the tendency to perceive complex problems as simple (Snowden & Boone, 2007). The Enterprise Resource Planning system (ERP system) is a software package that integrates several business functions and tracks business resources. The system typically employs historical data from the enterprise itself and is also linked with other partners in the value chain (see Porter, 1985). The ERP system operates at near real time and is, therefore, considered very reliable. But the smooth flow of supply and demand of PPE commodities displayed in the ERP systems did not inform decision-making in dealing with this radical shift in context: the Covid-19 pandemic.

The Sourcing Operation

In China, the sourcing company has an operation of about 20 people. They reconnected with business partners that they had been in the PPE-business with for some four years before. "*We were told there was no excess production capacity, but they made an exception as we've been doing business together before. That's China. Relations matter, and we were moved higher up on their list of prioritized customers.*" The value of the Sourcing Company's history with Chinese manufacturers became clear. Demand was way beyond production capacity, so now they had to somehow get on these manufacturers' shortlists. The previous engagement they had had, and the relations that they had been investing in, was now a valuable asset. And as Stephen points out, their history as business partners was honored by Chinese manufacturers. These relations were key to gaining a foothold on PPE manufacturers' list of prioritized customers.

Sourcing critical commodities like surgical masks requires a careful vetting process: These products must meet the desired-quality standards, and stories of faulty PPE are widespread in mass media (VG, 2020b), so they had to proceed with care. "*One of our coworkers went to visit these manufacturers. We had to see for ourselves, pick up the certificates, check them with the authorities – so we did our homework diligently – that is our competitive advantage.*" Stephen is on a roll, but I would like him to explain a bit more. "*What do you mean by homework?*" I ask. "*In China this means that you have to call the relevant authorities to have the certificate confirmed. You can't trust them at face value, and we found a lot of fake certificates,*" he replies. "*We were only interested in surgical-quality PPE, like N-95 face masks.*" Surgical quality means sterile manufacturing and packaging, plus filtering ability. There is a long list of requirements that the manufacturer must not only prove in documentation but also allow inspection of by the authorities. "*Of course, they wouldn't let us into the production facilities,*" Stephen says, "*which actually is a good sign – it's supposed to be sterile. But we proved to them that we took them seriously, and the other way around.*"

The earliest evidence of droplets as a mode of disease transmission, and the following development of personal protective equipment like face masks, dates back to 1887 (Gandhi et al., 2020). Unfortunately, masks historically carry a range of individual and culturally held beliefs, and today those beliefs are very divisive. One sphere communicates a belief in medical science, the other sphere communicates oppression, government overreach, and skepticism toward scientific principles (Ike et al., 2021). N-95 is the US standard (based on NIOSH air filtration ratings) which equals the European FFP2 and the Chinese KN95 face mask standard. These face masks have the ability to filter 95% of airborne particles. N-95 masks are manufactured using "melt blown" polymer fiber. The N-95 face mask was developed in the early 1970s and introduced by 3M in 1972. In the case of Covid-19, airborne transmission is the dominant route of spread (Zhang et al., 2020); thus, the use of face masks and social distancing are ways of avoiding transmission.

The Sourcing Company has its own engineers, and these people were responsible for controlling documentation and certificates with the Chinese authorities. I get the impression that it is normal in China that certificates must be checked, not just because of the current pandemic. But Stephen points to a new policy emerging as this sourcing operation went on. The authorities became more interested in stopping unlawful quality labeling and poor quality goods at the Chinese border (See also

Park et al., 2020). Consequently, every shipment Stephen prepared for export was held back for control of certificates and export licensing. "*But in China,*" Stephen sighs, "*these controls take time, and it's not like at home (in Norway) where you can file a complaint and someone looks into it.*" The control at the border became tighter and, in effect, every shipment was delayed—for weeks rather than days. In turn, these delays put pressure on the Sourcing Company, as it carries the liability of commodities in transit. Stephen continues: "*Now, we had done thorough preparations and all of our shipments were cleared. The risk of confiscation is, however, very real.*" Notably, confiscation would mean losing it all.

Confiscation is a financial risk. Each shipment was worth millions of NOK, and our friends in downtown Bodø were accumulating a potential for loss for every container of PPE that was stopped. The end customer usually pays on delivery, and the longer the transit takes, the higher the financial cost and risk will be. Usually, manufacturers allow some credit and these commitments are not too risky. No exceptions were made at the border, however: "*We tried to adapt by splitting shipments into smaller portions just to reduce the chance of being stopped, but no. They held back everything.*" The sourcing operation was difficult from the very start, as manufacturers did not have excess capacity, and only through long-established relations was the sourcing company able to place orders for high-quality PPE. Chinese authorities increased their inspections and the financial risk increased with the delays in delivery. Through a careful vetting process, the company avoided having any shipment confiscated at the Chinese border. However, they would soon encounter new kinds of threats and problems in their sourcing operation.

Cash on Delivery

As we've seen, the process of sourcing was difficult but fairly normal. Notably, prices had risen because of hoarding, and there was increased scrutiny at the Chinese border. This was manageable. But somewhere along the line, desperation—and maybe even a full-blown panic—started to emerge. "*We had to fight for every container of PPE,*" Stephen says. Competing supply chains started using cash to literally steal shipments of PPE at international airports: "*It turns out cash is still king in China,*" according to Stephen. When you trade in goods internationally, the normal procedure is to transfer money through the international banking system, but it takes a couple of days to complete such a transaction. "*So when* *a guy shows up in your office with $$ in hand, the choice is easy,*" he explains. "*We lost one shipment to Walmart. They seized it right under our nose, even though we had fixed everything. They just grabbed it using cash. Alright. The game had changed. We had to do the same!*" Trust had diminished, which increased the risk to a level not seen before. The terms of trade had changed to "Cash on Delivery". The traditional few days of credit that the bank transfer allowed was no longer an option, and the financial risk was further increased. An international bank transfer was considered a very safe and effective way to close any international deal. (Imagine the trouble you'd have if you could no longer pay your way with a credit card.) The banking system increased the smooth flow in supply chains by reducing transaction costs. When this was no longer accepted, it meant that the sourcing company would have to pay every shipment in cash, plus be liable for the goods in transit; "*We borrowed NOK 20 million (from a bank) because our US competitors were running around waving their cash to secure their own needs. We did that, knowing it would be the end of our sourcing company if we failed. I would not do it today, but it was too late then; we were too deeply involved.*" The sourcing company experienced path dependency in the form of lock-in (Greener, 2002) and were bound to follow through.

It dawns on me how risky this operation grew as the terms changed to "Cash on Delivery", as this increased the risk of confiscation at the border. Stephen talks about how he struggled to handle the stress: "*Sometimes I felt like I was suffering a nervous breakdown,*" he admits. Imagine yourself in his shoes, with co-workers driving to business meetings on the other side of the planet with a few million NOK-worth of cash in the boot of the car. He continues: "*I was constantly online with the guys in China, checking to see if we got the gear, if they were okay – that they've not been robbed – whether shipments came clear through customs, and so on.*" Considering the time difference between Norway and China (Bodø is UTC+1, while Beijing is UTC+8), my bet is that Stephen did not sleep much in the spring of 2020.

Free Trade and Export Restrictions

Ever since WWII, global trade has become less influenced by trade barriers, and there are both large free trade areas (like the EU) and free trade agreements (like European Economic Community [EEC], European Free Trade Area [EFTA], North American Free Trade Agreement [NAFTA]). But as the pandemic became more and more severe, export restrictions were enforced worldwide (Park et al., 2020). Both US and EU governments used emergency laws in an effort to secure their own supply of PPE. "*Our first shipment was sitting in Svinesund (the customs office at the EU-EFTA border, Sweden) for days.*" Stephen shakes his head in dismay and continues: "*Nothing ever gets stopped in Svinesund.*" The EU was confiscating everything that was in transit. Frankfurt and Leipzig are the transit hubs for global supply chains in Europe. All PPE shipments arrived there and were loaded on trucks. "*Imagine our surprise when we realized that there was no way to get the trucks through customs in Sweden. I couldn't believe it,*" he says with a laugh. The finer details of international trade politics and European relations surfaced. Norway is not a member of the EU, but she is a member of the European Free Trade Area (EFTA). The EU and the EFTA have a free trade agreement called EEC. Thus, when the European Commission adopted temporal export restrictions to stop PPE commodities in transit to all third countries (Tobler, 2020), the trucks got stuck in Sweden. I look at him, thinking, "*That was a tough one, Stephen. That's something you can't fix on your own.*" I asked him what he did next. "*Well, I contacted our local government – the mayor and her staff – and this went straight to the top. They had a meeting with the Minister of Public Health, and the Ministry took it further. There were negotiations on a governmental level between Norway, EFTA, and the EU,*" Stephen explains. "*Four days later the shipment was released.*" I'm amazed. The EU commission exempted a number of countries, among them Norway and the EFTA countries, from these export restrictions (Tobler, 2020). Stephen sure knows his way around the bureaucratic institutions, and he has the ability to take advantage of the short power distance in Norwegian culture. This is a remarkable demonstration of cultural capital (Bourdieu, 1986).

According to Park et al. (2020), more than 20 economies implemented trade restrictions and export bans during the initial phase of the pandemic, contributing to the turmoil in manufacturing and distribution of PPE. The manufacturing of PPE is distributed to a few countries, but consumption of these commodities is global. For these commodities to reach their end users, a fairly well-functioning international supply chain is a prerequisite. As seen in March through April 2020, trade barriers disrupt these supply chains. Notably, manufacturers also depend on international trade to secure raw materials. Thus, as free trade agreements were expelled, even the manufacturing capacity of PPE was affected, as the short supply of materials threatened production. After a short while of not having enough raw material, it became a struggle to keep up production, not to mention meeting the growing need of PPE in the early months of 2020. Thus, after decades of industrial adaptation to free trade agreements that allowed the comparative advantages (Ricardo, 1817) to play out, no country was able to help themselves. They all depended on international trade partners. Everybody knew this, but even those who traditionally are strong defenders of free trade—the EU and USA—resorted to protectionism, which increased the problems in PPE manufacturing and supply.

Supply and Demand

Prices were soaring during the March through April 2020 phase of the pandemic. The theoretical beauty of the supply-and-demand equation is, in reality, quite brutal. The use of PPE in hospitals took off beyond imagination, and as it became clear to the general public that the spread of the virus could be limited by wearing face masks, all kinds of businesses wanted to buy PPE. Manufacturers were running at full production capacity, and they needed a couple of months to increase production volumes. Furthermore, the supply of raw materials had similar limitations (Park et al., 2020). On top of that, protectionism only made things worse. Thus, in the short term it was not possible to increase the supply of PPE.

Scarcity drove up prices. "*Take a look at this,*" *Stephen says.* "*In 2019 one single face mask would cost about NOK 3,-. They peaked at about NOK 40,-. Prices are down to NOK 15,-, today,*" Stephen guides me through some paperwork (e-mails, invoices, etc.) from this very hectic period in his business life. He continues: "*From March through April we had to fight for every single piece of PPE, and securing one shipment of, say, goggles, felt like a victory on the battlefield. I don't think it can be described as competition.*" As buyers in the health market were in a dire situation worldwide and needed PPE immediately, all freight had to be via air. This seemingly insatiable demand for airfreight caused skyrocketing shipping rates: "*In April, one delivery to Gardermoen* (Oslo Airport) *from China would cost NOK 14 million – about seven times the normal rate.*"

The profit opportunity was something that also attracted pure profiteering. High-quality manufacturers, renowned airlines, and sourcing companies took advantage of this. Stephen's sourcing operation only involved surgical-quality PPE, but, as always, super high profits may cause some opportunism. The stories of false certificates, unlawful packaging, unlawful quality branding, and confiscation of shipments were abundant. Some of these actors are now under investigation (VG, 2020b).

Back to Normal?

Any system may cascade into chaos (Gleick, 1988). In the first days of March 2020, a call from Procurement at Norwegian Health Services made it clear to Stephen that "business as usual" was no longer an option. According to Snowden and Boone's (2007) framework, best practice was suspended by a sudden shift in context, and the Just-in-Time (Sayer, 1986) supply chain was breaking down. Stephen's decision-making was all about countering the emerging chaos and establishing some kind of order for the Sourcing Company and its sourcing operations. The Company was up against a range of hitherto unseen practices in the PPE supply chain: hoarding, non-existent supply, soaring prices and freight rates, false quality certificates, tightened border controls, expelled free trade agreements, and intense rivalry for every container of PPE commodities. An important theoretical implication is the severe limitation of the Just-in-Time logic and the lean global supply chain (see also Golan et al., 2020). The Just-in-Time supply chain is not designed to handle disruptions in supply or surging demand, as its application requires a simple context (Snowden & Boone, 2007). The experienced shift in context caused cascading failures—huge and unexpected ripple effects that eventually broke down the supply chain. It appears that PPE supply chains are optimized for efficiency, not resilience.

As of May 2020, the frenzy was over. "*The regular supply chains were catching up in May, and the market was back to normal,*" Stephen concludes. The large manufacturers had ramped up production. Chinese manufacturing output was up 10-fold, to 200 million face masks per day by April 2020. And supply chains could again deliver the needed PPE commodities to the large markets in the USA and Europe. The flow of commodities in the Enterprise Resource Planning system (ERP system) was again running smoothly. "*But we've stocked up on face masks. Come winter, and we will be at it again,*" Stephen predicts.

Today (on March 11, 2021) as I finalize this ethnography, it's exactly one year after the WHO declared the pandemic, and Stephen's prediction comes to mind. Local authorities in Bodø recommend the use of face masks by the general public, and in government buildings they are mandatory. Virus mutations are here. We're back in lockdown. The good news is that there is an abundance of PPE globally. Health services have learned a lesson about global supply chains and the Just-in-Time logic. What equals 130 years of normal consumption of PPE has been secured in additional sourcing operations (VG, 2021b). Also the vaccines are here. Still, this lockdown is going to be harder than last time. One year ago, the idea was that these extraordinary lockdown measures were going to last for only a short while; come summer, it will be over. But now it feels like we are back at Square One.

References

Borwein, Jonathan, & Rose, Michael. (2012). Explainer: What is chaos theory? *The Conversation*. https://theconversation.com/explainer-what-is-chaos-theory-10620

Bourdieu, Pierre. (1986). The forms of capital. In J. G. Richardson (Ed.), *Handbook of theory and research for the sociology of education*. Greenwood.

Doornich, June Borge. (2019). Disrupting the housing market: Simple living. In F. Soelberg, L. Browning, & J.-O. Sørnes (Eds.), *The high north in a time of transition: Gutsy narratives and wild observations*. Routledge.

Gandhi, Jignesh A., Churiwala, Jayati J., Shinde, Pravin H., & Chaudhari, Sadashivi C. (2020). Surgical masks – The Savior: From its invention to the COVID-19 era. *Indian Journal of Surgery, 82*, 278–279.

Gleick, James. (1988). *Chaos; Making a new science*. Penguin.

Golan, Maureen S., Jernegan, Laura H., & Linkov, Igor. (2020). Trends and applications of resilience analytics in supply chain modeling: Systematic literature review in the context of the COVID-19 pandemic. *Environment Systems and Decisions, 40*, 222–243.

Grant, Robert M. (2016). *Contemporary strategic analysis: Text and cases edition*. Wiley.

Greener, Ian. (2002). Theorizing path-dependency: How does history come to matter in organizations. *Management Decisions, 40*(6), 614–619.

Ike, John David, Bayerle, Henry, Logan, Robert A., & Parker, Ruth M. (2021). Face masks: Their history and the values they communicate. *Journal of Health Communication, 25*(12), 990–995.

Klassekampen. (2020, April). *Hard håndtering støttes av folket* (General support for tough measures), Klassekampen.

Lagu, Tara, Artenstein, Andrew W., & Werner, Rachel M. (2020). Fool me twice: The role for hospitals and health systems in fixing the broken PPE supply chain. *Journal of Hospital Medicine, 15*(9), 570–571.

Livingston, Edward, Desai, Angel, & Berkwits, Michael. (2020). Sourcing personal protective equipment during the Covid-19 pandemic. *JAMA, 323*(19), 1912–1914.

McCracken, Grant. (1988). *The long interview*. Sage.

Park, Cyn-Young, Kim, Kijin, Roth, Susann, Beck, Steven, Kang, Jong Woo, Tayag, Mara Claire, & Griffin, Michael. (2020). *Shortage of personal protective equipment amid COVID-19: Supply chains, bottlenecks, and policy implications.* ADB Briefs.

Petitt, Timothy J., Fiksel, Joseph, & Croxton, Keely L. (2011). Ensuring supply chain resilience: Development of a conceptual framework. *Journal of Business Logistics, 31*(1), 1–21.

Porter, Michael. (1985). *Competitive advantage.* The Free Press.

Ricardo, David. (1817). *The principles of political economy and taxation.* Dent.

Sayer, Andrew. (1986). *New developments in manufacturing: The just-in-time system.* Sage.

Skille, Øyvind Bye, Drabløs, Øystein Tronsli, & Skiphamn, Silje S. (2021, April 10). QAnon og Nazi-tilknytning på demonstrasjoner mot smitteverntiltak, (QAnon and Nazi-sympathizers against corona lockdown measures), Faktisk.no.

Snowden, David J., & Boone, Mary E. (2007). *A leaders framework for decision making.* Harvard Business Review.

Tobler, Christa. (2020). *EU corona emergency law: Restrictions on the export of protective equipment, notably from the EU into third countries like Switzerland (Regulation 2020/402). Analysis,* Efta-Studies.org.

VG. (2020a, October 12). *Kampen om Smittevernutstyret* (The Battle for PPE) Verdens Gang.

VG. (2020b, September 12). *Munnbind på grensen* (Face masks at the border – Double meaning; Poor quality face masks) Verdens Gang.

VG. (2021a, February 10). *Støtten til tiltakene har aldri vært lavere* (Support for anti-corona-measures hits an all-time low) Verdens Gang.

VG. (2021b, March 4th). *Krisekjøpte smittevernutstyr for 3,2 milliarder* (Emergency procurement of NOK 3.2 billion worth of PPE) Verdens Gang.

Zhang, Renyi, Li, Yixin, Zhang, Annie L., & Molina, Mario J. (2020). Identifying airborne transmission as the dominant route of the spread of Covid 19. *PNAS*, 14857–14863.

SECTION III

Communication Philosophy: Apprehending Opportunity in Time of Crisis

CHAPTER 9

The Fellows and a Book: Unexpected Opportunities for Practice and Theory

Jean M. Bartunek

It was the beginning of March 2020, during Boston College's spring break. I was in Finland for the week, where, with two wonderful Finnish colleagues, Ewald Kibler and Lauri Laine, I visited a Russian Orthodox monastery as part of a research project. Then, on my final full day, I gave a scholarly talk at Aalto University. It was an enjoyable and productive trip.

Except that, while I was at the University for the day, I noticed that several people were reluctant to shake hands with me. They said their reluctance was due to their fear of the spreading coronavirus, about which I had heard relatively little in the U.S. Further, the flight back to Boston, which I had expected would be quite full, as it had been when I had flown to Europe a week earlier, was almost empty.

It wasn't until I returned to Boston that I realized how serious this new coronavirus was. The universities in the Boston area were starting to send their students home from spring break for the rest of the semester. I felt

J. M. Bartunek (✉)
Department of Management and Organization, Boston College, Chestnut Hill, MA, USA
e-mail: bartunek@bc.edu

L. D. Browning et al. (eds.), *Organizational Communication and Technology in the Time of Coronavirus*,
https://doi.org/10.1007/978-3-030-94814-6_9

lucky that we at Boston College had already had our spring break and that my trip to Finland hadn't been canceled. Of course, for the rest of the semester I taught my doctoral class over Zoom rather than in person, and I continued to teach over Zoom the next school year. Such teaching required a learning curve for my students and me. (It also meant we couldn't share snacks during class breaks, which definitely took away some of the fun of being in a classroom.)

There was quite a bit I didn't realize in March of 2020. I didn't realize I would be spending virtually all of my time at home for more than a year (and counting as of this writing). I didn't realize that not one of the academic trips I had planned for the spring and summer would take place. In particular, I had been very excited about going to Vancouver in August for the Academy of Management (AOM) annual meeting. I was the outgoing Dean of the Fellows of the AOM, and I was looking forward to the last Fellows dinner I would host. I also did not realize in March 2020 that the year would give me opportunities to experience personally some of the tensions I have addressed in my scholarly work.

The Outline for This Chapter

In this chapter I will discuss how some of the tensions I have studied have played out in two major activities associated with my academic life from 2020 to 2021. One is the work I did in the summer of 2020 as Dean of the Fellows. The other is a book I began envisioning in April 2020 and then edited throughout the pandemic. The work with the AOM Fellows was completed in 2020. The book I edited was published in late 2021.

Before I discuss either, to set the stage I will describe the contextual foundation for this chapter, especially some tensions I have discussed in my scholarly work. Then I will discuss the two major activities, their underlying tensions and how I handled them.

For several decades I have conducted scholarly research addressing tensions, contradictions and paradoxes regarding organizational change and academic-practitioner relationships (e.g. Bartunek, 1984, 2006; Bartunek et al., 2000, 2021; Bartunek & Rynes, 2014). As Sara Rynes and I summarized (Bartunek & Rynes, 2014, p. 1183), "The term '*tensions*' refers to a wide variety of dichotomies, dualities, conflicts, inconsistencies, and contradictory pulls or demands experienced by those in a particular setting that … seem to require a choice of one or the other." Putnam et al. (2016, Table 1, pp. 69–72) describe contradictory pulls as "bipolar opposites that are mutually exclusive and interdependent such that the opposites define and potentially negate each other." Smith and Lewis (2011, p. 382) define *paradoxes* as "contradictory yet interrelated elements that exist simultaneously and persist over time."

Putnam et al. (2016) present three different ways people handle tensions (Table 8, pp. 125–127): *either-or*, *both-and*, and *more-than*. I have experienced each of these during the pandemic.

More specifically, Putnam et al. suggest that we may view opposites as a mutually exclusive "*either-or*" relationship in which we choose one side over the other. Or we may view them as "*both-and*" dualities that honor the interdependence of inseparable opposites, accepting both poles of tensions or contradictions, at least in part. There are several types of *both-and* approaches. *Paradoxical thinking* reflects an ability to recognize and accept the contradictory poles. *Vacillation* reflects oscillation between the contradictory poles. *Balance* involves finding equilibrium points between the contradictory poles. Finally, Putnam et al. present "*more-than*" responses that accommodate "both poles through developing a novel, creative synergy"; something new arises from and transcends the tensions.

While in my scholarly work I have addressed tensions within and between multiple types of groups, I have most often focused on several of the most frequently discussed tensions between academia and practice. In particular, Bartunek and Rynes (2014) addressed several tensions regarding the "academic-practitioner gap." These include differing *logics*, such as assumptions and frames of reference; differing *temporal dimensions*, with academics' being typically longer than practitioners'; differing *communication practices*, with academics' tending to be more abstract than practitioners'; differing *emphases* on rigor and relevance, with academics expected to emphasize rigor and practitioners to emphasize relevance; and, finally, differing *interests*. *Interests* for academics focus on scholarly contributions, while practitioners tend to focus on organization interests. These tensions are listed in Table 9.1. The activities I will discuss explicitly or implicitly reflect the tensions, and how they do so is also summarized in Table 9.1.

The Activities That Are the Focus of the Chapter

Starting in the spring of 2020, two dimensions of my work drew a great deal of my attention. One was completing my duties as Dean of the Fellows, which, thanks to COVID-19, became much more complex than

Table 9.1 Academic-practitioner tensions and their role in my activities

Tension	*My work for the AOM Fellows*	*My book editing*
Logics	Totally practitioner; get dues paid and dinner arranged	Trying to incorporate both academic and practitioner approaches
Temporal dimensions	Thinking in the immediate term	Operating out of academic temporal expectations
Communication practices	Very straightforward. "Here is how to pay your dues"	As straightforward as possible, but realizing that I speak academic language
Emphases on rigor and relevance	Banking needs to be rigorous; videos have to be done	A growing awareness that academics and consultants can both be rigorous (or not)
Interests	To keep the Fellows solvent, to provide a virtual meeting	To produce a book that is relevant and rigorous in addressing serious world issues
Either/or, both/and, more/than	Most of what I did was either/or. Donating to food banks in lieu of a dinner was more/than	A both/and impetus

in the prior two years. The other had to do with my somewhat sudden impulse to edit a book in addition to my other scholarly work.

Fellows and Fellows Dinner

The Fellows is an honorary society for a select number of AOM members, usually less than 2% of members of the AOM. As its constitution says, "The purpose of the Fellows Group shall be to recognize and honor members of the Academy of Management who have made significant contributions to the science and practice of management, and to provide opportunities for fellowship and a forum for discussion among persons so recognized and honored." I was elected a Fellow in the late 1990s. I was elected Dean of the Fellows in 2017, and my term ended at the end of August 2020.

In the early spring of 2020, I was planning for the election of a new Dean of the Fellows, an event that went smoothly under the leadership of my deputy dean, Rob Folger. I was also coordinating the election of new Fellows, following our standard processes; that election also went well.

As had been the case before, the Boston College Management and Organization department administrative assistant, Michael Smith, did most of the actual work of coordinating the online election process for new Fellows. Previously, he had been aided by undergraduate work-study students. Unfortunately, that wasn't the case in 2020 because, due to COVID-19, there were no undergraduate assistants on campus.

Dues Collection

The Fellows pay their annual dues during the summer. There are a variety of means, including web-based (PayPal and Venmo) and "real" methods (sending a check or sending cash) for doing so. The web-based methods were straightforward to use, the cash-based methods more time-consuming. Previously, I had arranged for checks or cash to be sent to my office at Boston College, and undergraduate work-study students, coordinated by Michael Smith, would do the actual work of collecting and recording all the dues collected. However, as noted just above, there were no undergraduate work-study students in the summer of 2020, and I was not going into the office; neither, for that matter, was Michael Smith. So all the checks and cash came to me at home, and I ended up depositing checks and cash in the bank on a regular basis.

Videos to Replace Fellows Dinner Presentations

The tradition has been to introduce new Fellows at the annual Fellows Dinner as well as to carry out a few other pieces of business there. The Fellow who nominated an elected new Fellow usually introduces the new Fellow to the group. I had secured a restaurant for the dinner when I had visited Vancouver in January, and I was very pleased with it as a venue.

But then in May, the AOM canceled its in-person meeting, announcing instead that the meeting would be virtual, consisting solely of online presentations. While this was not entirely a surprise, it certainly created problems for the Fellows dinner.

Because I felt it important to welcome the 11 new Fellows who had been elected rather than to put this off for a year, I decided to create some semblance of a Fellows dinner by presenting videos of every talk (including introductions of each new Fellow) that would have been given there. This included opening presentations welcoming everyone to the event, introductions of each of the new Fellows, and then a final "thank you" from me at the end. This added up to 18 videos in total, 3 of which I had

Table 9.2 Changes in my videoconferencing skills between February 2020 and August 2020

My facility with videoconferencing technologies	*February 2020*	*August 2020*
Basic use of videoconferencing technologies like Zoom, Google meet, Microsoft teams	I had some slight familiarity with Zoom; none at all with Google meeting or Microsoft teams	I was pretty good at Zoom; passable on the other platforms as long as someone else starts them. But tell me again: What is Slack?
Preparing videos for use on videoconferencing technologies	I hardly know how to record my class on Zoom. I can't imagine why I would I ever do something like this	Thank heavens for Zoom and Jel! We've made the videos! But never again

to make myself. I dyed my hair purple for the final video to signal my happiness when my work was completed.

Organizing and coordinating the videos ended up taking hours and hours of my time over the course of the summer, even though most of the individuals introducing new Fellows created their own videos and Jel Erica Hampson, whom I had hired as an assistant to the Dean of the Fellows, did the bulk of the work (sometimes with the help of her sister). For example, in some cases I had to have a Fellow giving a presentation talk to me on Zoom while we used Speaker View, and then Jel edited the video.

Table 9.2 illustrates how my facility in and attitude toward working with Zoom and similar video conferencing technologies evolved between February and August 2020. My competence (though not my desire) increased quite a bit.

The Fellows Dinner

While I was preparing the Fellows' virtual dinner, I was certainly conscious of problems with food insecurity for many in North America and elsewhere, especially during the pandemic. I was also pondering that if we were talking about a Fellows *dinner*, there should be some type of food. How could we put these two awarenesses together? At first, I thought that perhaps we could get donations from the restaurant in Vancouver at which we had reservations if the Fellows would also donate in some way, but that idea went nowhere. So did a few other ideas.

Eventually, though, I started to remember (or at least I hoped I remembered) that Dave Whetten, a Fellow now emeritus from his university, had told me several years ago that when he had retired from Brigham Young University, he had found it very helpful to talk with Rick Mowday, another Fellow who had previously retired from the University of Oregon. Rick had told him (at least I hoped he had told him) that he was enjoying doing volunteer work. I hoped that the volunteering had something to do with a food bank.

I contacted Rick to see if some food distribution center that I hoped he was connected with would make some contribution that the Fellows could match. Rick and his wife, Mary, had a better idea: The two of them would match contributions to their food bank up to $1000 of Fellows' donations to any food banks or equivalent services. That ended up working extremely well. The Fellows, under Rick's guidance, raised more than $10,000 in food donations, with Food for Lane County, in Eugene, Oregon, quite properly being the biggest beneficiary.

The Tensions Associated with Collecting Dues and Preparing the Videos

As noted above, the Fellows are very successful scholars, definitely on the "academic" side of the academic-practitioner divide. So I guess it is a wonderful irony that in order to collect dues and to have a Fellows dinner of sorts, I had to become almost entirely a practitioner. My approach was definitely *either/or*. As the tensions in Table 9.1 suggest, I was operating almost exclusively out of a practitioner frame-of-reference. I was focused on how to collect dues and prepare videos on time, sometimes communicating bluntly. ("This is a reminder that you haven't paid your dues yet," or "You haven't made your video yet; I need it by Friday.") I was rigorous about dues (just as banks are rigorous about money), but recognizing the impossibility of perfection, I was just trying to get the videos made in a passable form for presentation at the dinner. (Fortunately, Jel made the videos look much better than many deserved.) My aims were that the Fellows would remain solvent, the new Fellows would feel welcomed, there would be some semblance of the meeting part of the Fellows dinner, and that all of this would be available online by the time of the virtual AOM meeting. We accomplished these.

I don't know of any management or organizational theory that could have helped me (though I'm sure academics can tell me there are some).

In fact, I found it hard to do academic work while I was focusing on collecting dues and making videos about people being celebrated for their scholarly achievements. The purely academic side of me would never have had purple hair at a Fellows dinner.

The Tensions Connected with the Fellows Dinner

Inviting the Fellows to contribute to food banks and equivalent charities did involve a complex holding of a tension, although the tension was not of the academic/practitioner variety. The original question was: How can we have the Fellows dinner be about food even when it's not possible to eat (together)? Figuring out how to handle such a contradiction, and to link it with food insecurity, required reflexivity, a term that Macintosh et al. (2017, p. 7) describe as "critically engaging with self-knowledge to recognize boundaries and limitations and move beyond them." I reflected on this issue through several drafts of ideas. These eventually led to the possibility of action—contributing to food banks—that transcended our usual way of thinking about the "dinner" part of the Fellows dinner. It also included bringing back "from retirement" someone who could lead our efforts. In this way, it illustrated a *more/than* approach.

Editing a Book

Events of April 2020. In early April 2020, some of my friends and colleagues were taking initiatives to respond to the coronavirus, now also being referred to as COVID-19. It was also around this time that I reread Albert Camus' (1947/1948) book *The Plague*, which has been particularly meaningful to me ever since I read it in a moral philosophy course in college. (I still have a copy from my college days, given to me as a gift from a college roommate.) The book describes a plague that suddenly hits a town in Algeria called Oran. After devastating the town and killing many of the townspeople, almost of its own accord, the plague faded away. The narrator in the book is Dr. Bernard Rieux, a physician who had cared for plague-stricken victims in Oran. A few sentences on the last page have spoken to me all my adult life:

> [Dr. Rieux] knew that the tale he had to tell [about the plague and its ending] could not be one of a final victory. It could be only the record of what had had to be done, and what assuredly would have to be done again in the

> never-ending fight against terror and its relentless onslaughts, despite their personal afflictions, by all who, while unable to be saints but refusing to bow down to pestilences, strive their utmost to be healers.

As I reread the book in 2020, I was also inspired by another paragraph on the last page:

> Yes, the old fellow had been right; [after the plague the citizens of Oran] were "just the same as ever." But this was at once their strength and their innocence, and it was on this level, beyond all grief, that Rieux could feel himself at one with them. And it was in the midst of shouts rolling against the terrace wall in massive waves that waxed in volume and duration, while cataracts of colored fire fell thicker through the darkness, that Dr. Rieux resolved to compile a chronicle, so that he should not be one of those who hold their peace but should bear witness in favor of those plague-stricken people; so that some memorial of the injustice and outrage done them might endure; and to state quite simply what we learn in a time of pestilence: that there are more things to admire in men than to despise.

This paragraph gripped me. The doctor wanted to write about the plague to honor those who had suffered, and so there should be a memorial of their suffering.

Also in April 2020, Ed Schein, who had been a distinguished professor at MIT for several decades and now, in his early 90s, was living in a retirement home in Palo Alto, California, sent me an email saying, "Hi Jean—Would you take a look at this rant and tell me whether it makes any sense and whether something like this needs to be distributed to some of (the AOM) divisions or even more broadly." Ed's "rant" was a call to action for social scientists. It included statements like this:

> As Social Scientists we need to speak up:
>
> The next pandemic will be global warming and the collapse of pieces of the global environment. We already see early symptoms with the heat waves, the floods, the uncontrollable wildfires, hurricanes and other weather changes.
>
> The current virus pandemic will force some shift from rampant competition among countries, states, hospital units, and systems based on economic well-being rather than global health, to inventing processes of collaboration that protect the common resources pertaining to health.
>
> Will we recognize that we need to use or invent methods of collaboration on a global level to deal with the global environment as a finite resource that

> we are currently depleting by encouraging or at least sanctioning competition among countries, industries, and political parties?

I was grateful that Ed had written to me and excited that he was arguing that we, as social scientists, have something important to say about issues like the pandemic or other global crises; it's not just the natural scientists who can contribute.

My immediate response was to set up an email group discussion that included both academics and consultants, and many lively exchanges occurred over the course of a couple weeks. I didn't contribute much myself beyond organizing the exchange, but I found the conversations energizing. It reminded me that I had originally gone into social and organizational psychology because I had been a recipient of some awful organization development consulting when I had been a high school teacher, and I thought that such consulting could be done better (Bartunek, 2006). Over time, as an academic, I'd become much more interested in studying organizational change than practicing it. Fortunately, a few years ago, Bob Marshak had gotten me involved in a conference organized by some OD practitioners, and I'd had a chance to meet up again with some consultants I knew and admired. So I was more sensitive to concerns of practice than I had been.

Shortly after I had received Ed's call for action, I was spending some quiet time pondering all that was going on. As I was doing this, four pieces of information came into focus. One was Ed's rant/call to action. A second was that I wanted to do something on my own initiative to respond to COVID-19, even if I had no idea what it would be. A third was the line(s) from *The Plague* about the importance of compiling a chronicle, "*so that he should not be one of those who hold their peace but should bear witness in favor of those plague-stricken people*". A fourth was remembering that I am one of the editors of a "short form" series on scholarly impact on practice, being published by Routledge, https://www.routledge.com/Management-Impact/book-series/IMPACTM.

The Resulting Initiative

Slowly, just being present to all of these ideas and hovering over the different pieces, it occurred to me that maybe I could edit a book for the Routledge series in which I could invite both respected academics with interest in practice and respected consultants with interest in academia, to write their own chapters regarding the importance of social science having an impact on the handling of global issues and crises. The book would have to be accessible to both academics and change agents. Each chapter would have to include some theorizing and some direct implications for practice. This would be different from the usual approach of the series, which so far had included work by academics themselves. But it sure could (I hoped—and still hope as of this writing) be impactful.

I let this play around in my head for a little while, talked it over with Ed Schein, who was very excited about the prospect, and contacted the other editors of the Routledge Impact series (Cary Cooper and Nic Beech) as well as Terry Clague, a senior publisher at Routledge who is in charge of the series. I thought of several possible people who might write chapters, and I submitted a proposal for the book, first informally and then formally, where it was accepted. (It helped that, in addition to being one of the editors for the series, I had recently edited a book for Routledge with Jane McKenzie [2018] and still remembered what to do.)

Then I had to start writing to possible authors, asking them to submit chapters, which was quite anxiety-producing. In fact, I wrote in my notes on May 4:

> WHY did I decide to edit a book? I must be nuts. But then I talked with Ed, and he was very enthusiastic about the book. That gave me a ton of energy, and by yesterday afternoon I had invited everyone. Having the invitation out has been particularly positive. Now I hope that people will respond.

I am very lucky that almost all of those I invited said yes.

Though the book was inspired by the pandemic, other issues emerged over the summer of 2020 and into 2021 that confirmed its potential importance. There have been any number of serious events that have happened since last April concerning climate change, Black Lives Matter and other forms of racism, election fairness in the U.S., insurrections in multiple countries, and other issues that reinforce what I hope will be the value of the book.

I am completing this chapter shortly before publication of the book, titled *Social Scientists Confronting Global Crises* (Bartunek, 2022). I'm also realizing more and more that I'm not sure that I personally have anything original to say on the main topics the book chapters address other than creating ways that academics and consultants can contribute together to addressing global concerns. But at least I have gathered both sets of voices together in ways that enable each to say what matters to them. Maybe that is my contribution.

Working on this book has been rewarding; however, it has been in addition to my other full-time workload, and my life became very busy. I made several notes to myself while the book was in progress during the past several months, commenting: "Feeling overwhelmed with work stuff"; "I'm aware of how overcommitted I am"; "I have a ton more work to do."

Tensions Associated with the Book

The way I have approached the tensions in editing this book is summarized in Table 9.1. I am trying to appreciate both academic and consultant logics. This requires varying versions of theory and practice in each chapter. My temporal dimensions somewhat meld academic time and practitioner time, in that the book will have been published within 19 months after the original invitations went out. (I have learned that academics are no worse than consultants at getting drafts of chapters in by my deadlines.) My communication with the authors is as straightforward as it can be within the parameters I have set for the chapters. However, I have realized that the decades I have spent reviewing for academic journals has meant that my comments to authors are probably much more detailed and picky than some authors, who are not academics, are used to.

The book has made me aware that academics and consultants both can be rigorous in their work and that there is a rigor appropriate to successful consulting that academics may not recognize. Thus, my hope is that this book truly is both rigorous and relevant to our times, one that asserts and stimulates important contributions from social scientists on dealing with global concerns.

Editing the book resulted from "hovering" over several different elements—including a desire to respond to the coronavirus in some unspecified way, rereading a book by Camus, Ed Schein's rant, and my co-editorship of a book series—in a way that led to joining academic and consultant voices on, essentially, the same side of a tension, while leaving each free to contribute their own insights. Thus, the resulting book reflects a *both/and* approach to academic and practitioner contributions and collaboration.

Some Final Reflections

In reflecting on these experiences my guess is that I've been viewed by others I've been involved with as quite competent in organizing—in collecting dues, in putting together a virtual Fellows dinner, in setting up a discussion of Ed Schein's rant, and in editing a book. Some of those at a distance probably also are under the illusion that I've stayed calm. This is largely because I've made public only the outcomes of what I've been doing. I doubt that any of the Fellows had any idea how much work I put into collecting dues or my angst about making the videos for the Fellows dinner. I doubt that those contributing to the book have been fully aware of my anxieties about it or how overwhelmed or worried I have sometimes felt about it.

Putnam et al. (2016) state clearly that tensions are not just abstract differences; they necessarily involve stress, anxiety and discomfort on the part of those experiencing them. This is something I (and many people who write about contradictions and paradoxes) do not discuss very much. However, I have often experienced stress, anxiety and discomfort while dealing with the tensions associated with the Fellows work and the book I am editing, sometimes simply from the amount of extra work they entail. Fortunately, sometimes there have also been moments of excitement and elation: hovering over possibilities of responses to COVID-19; Rick Mowday's leadership and Ed Schein's encouragement; and in reading some excellent book chapters that I'm excited about making public.

In reflecting on these experiences, I've also had a chance to think again about the tensions Sara Rynes and I discussed in 2014. In doing so, I've come to realize that the academic-practitioner tension that is most frequently discussed—that practitioners don't care about rigor—is a ludicrous stereotype. Some academics care less about rigor than others, and some practitioners care more about rigor than others. The consultants who have written for the book I edited have very rigorous standards and are upset by consultants who do not have such standards.

A few years ago, Lily Crosina and I (2017) had written about the fact that academics and practitioners who engage in reflective practice (Macintosh et al., 2017; Schön, 1983) were actually more similar to each other than scholars and practitioners who did not engage in such practice. Editing the book during the pandemic has taught me that academics and practitioners who are rigorous in their work are also very similar to each other in ways that have not adequately been appreciated.

Fortunately, the time period of the pandemic has not entirely been driven by tensions. There have been positive and replenishing events as well. I will end with one very prosaic positive event that had nothing to do with my work.

I grew up in a suburb of Cleveland, Ohio, and still identify with the city in many ways. Professional sports teams from Cleveland have almost always been unsuccessful in recent decades. But we experienced a minor victory in January 2021: Cleveland's (American style) football team, the Cleveland Browns, actually won one playoff game, something that hasn't happened in forever. My brothers Bob and Tom and I were texting each other from our homes throughout the game while watching it individually on our devices. We started with the assumption that Cleveland would probably lose, leading to texts like "Is there any realistic reason to keep watching this game?" when the other team scored first, and "Someone has to play some defense." But eventually the texts turned to "For the first time tonight I feel a little confidence," to "That might do it," to ultimate victory. Smiling, however briefly, and for whatever reason, is a fine way to end this chapter.

References

Bartunek, Jean M. (1984). Changing interpretive schemes and organizational restructuring: The example of a religious order. *Administrative Science Quarterly, 29*(3), 355–372.

Bartunek, Jean M. (2006). The Christmas gift: A story of dialectics. *Organization Studies, 27*(12), 1875–1894.

Bartunek, Jean M. (2022). *Social scientists confronting global crises.* Routledge.

Bartunek, Jean M., & McKenzie, Jane (Eds.). (2018). *Academic-practitioner relationships: Developments, complexities and opportunities.* Routledge.

Bartunek, Jean M., Putnam, Linda L., & Seo, Myeong-Gu. (2021). Dualisms and dualities in the ongoing development of organization development. In M. S. Poole & A. H. Van de Ven (Eds.), *The Oxford handbook of organizational change and innovation* (2nd ed., pp. 50–76). Oxford University Press.

Bartunek, Jean M., & Rynes, Sara L. (2014). Academics and practitioners are alike and unlike: The paradoxes of academic–practitioner relationships. *Journal of Management, 40*(5), 1181–1201.

Bartunek, Jean M., Walsh, Kate, & Lacey, Catherine A. (2000). Dynamics and dilemmas of women leading women. *Organization Science, 11*(6), 589–610.

Camus, Albert. (1947/1948). *The Plague* (Stuart Gilbert, Trans.). Vintage.

Crosina, Eliana, & Bartunek, Jean M. (2017). The paradoxical mystery of the missing differences between academics and practitioners. In *The Oxford handbook of organizational paradox* (pp. 472–489). Oxford University Press.

MacIntosh, Robert, Beech, Nic, Bartunek, Jean M., Mason, Katy, Cooke, Bill, & Denyer, David. (2017). Impact and management research: Exploring relationships between temporality, dialogue, reflexivity and praxis. *British Journal of Management, 28*(1), 3–13.

Putnam, Linda L., Fairhurst, Gail T., & Banghart, Scott. (2016). Contradictions, dialectics, and paradoxes in organizations: A constitutive approach. *The Academy of Management Annals, 10*(1), 65–171.

Schön, Donald A. (1983). *The reflective practitioner: How professionals think in action*. Basic Books.

Smith, Wendy K., & Lewis, Marianne W. (2011). Toward a theory of paradox: A dynamic equilibrium model of organizing. *Academy of Management Review, 36*(2), 381–403.

CHAPTER 10

Mindful Management of the (Un)expected

June Borge Doornich

Crisis Management of a Faculty Through a Pandemic

I am the Vice Dean of Education at the Business School at Nord University in Bodø, a compact coastal city of roughly 52,000 souls located on the Norwegian Sea just north of the Arctic Circle, at latitude 67°. Here we learn to endure long, dark winter months, yet the breathtaking scenery compensates us, bringing us beautiful polar nights with endless variations of playful polar light. This light offers us glimpses of the sun on the dark sky and spreads colorful shadings from deep green and blue to glowing yellows and reds. The city is therefore familiarly known as Bodø by Light, where the long summer months of total brightness set off the azure sky and ocean and the green majestic mountains, all of which bring out the sporting nature of our people well into the evening hours. Our city is therefore also known as Bodø by Night. And whether by light or by night, it always stands bordered by the Gulf Stream, so the sea is never frozen and thus spared the need of an ice cutter.

J. B. Doornich (✉)
Business School, Nord University, Bodø, Norway
e-mail: June.b.doornich@nord.no

L. D. Browning et al. (eds.), *Organizational Communication and Technology in the Time of Coronavirus*,
https://doi.org/10.1007/978-3-030-94814-6_10

But today, an emotional darkness blankets the city. Although the sun has started to rise again to light up Bodø and its people, the darkness of the pandemic inevitably penetrates the body and the soul.

One year ago, I had stepped into the role of crisis manager for the Business School faculty at Nord University. It was a natural role for me as I had already overseen the faculty's education activities and thus had an overview of all the activities related to teaching and exams. Thus, theoretically, I could rearrange activities quickly to ensure that all eventualities and their consequences could be met before they became unmanageable. I was to be the normalizer; as near as possible, we would maintain business as usual, even during a pandemic.

But managing a crisis primarily via communication technology did not come easy for me. When management and my life suddenly unfolded in the digital space, I needed sensemaking in order to navigate this unfamiliar space, not just adequately but properly.

Managing the (Un)expected

My pandemic wakeup literally occurred in the hallway outside my office. I had just concluded a meeting with a colleague about our research paper, but before facing my computer with new editing ideas, I decided I needed a quick hit from the office coffee machine, so off I went. And now, with my fresh warm coffee mug in hand, I walked back down the corridor, and as I passed by colleagues' offices, I detected a pronounced tonal change in their conversations. Their normal cheerfulness had morphed into a worried and insecure mood, their voices so muted that I could decipher just fractions of their conversations—references to things like "food stocking," "fuel tanking," "face masks," and "home offices." Whoa! We were clearly now in a different world.

A colleague, noticing me, glanced at me and warned in a low voice, "It's now happening!" My nervous system reacted with immediate resignation, and my body slumped. Instantly I knew I faced managing an immense crisis looming over the upcoming days. Sure enough, as if on cue, on the morning of the 12th of March 2020, the Norwegian government implemented a national lockdown in order to stem the pandemic. All white-collar workers were forced to leave their offices and continue their work at home. Little did we suspect that such full-bore crisis protocols would last not just for weeks but for months.

For all of us, unexpected events, seemingly out of the blue, appear regularly (Weick & Sutcliffe, 2007). Yet managing them requires a prepared response. To reduce the surprise of the unexpected, we need to constantly notice the unfolding events in our organizational life and surroundings. By bracketing observations, information, and experiences, we provide an unconscious proactive readiness to respond to events that have not yet happened.

One such event had occurred on a Monday morning in mid-January, two months before the Norwegian government imposed its lockdown. I had stepped outside of a meeting room at the Business School only to notice that a group of students from China had entered our main hallway and were on their way to their first lecture. They had arrived in Norway just two days prior, and I was startled, for they had just come from the very country where the virus was born and which it now ravaged. I thought we had decided that these students were to stay in voluntary quarantine at their dormitory for a week.

At that time, the virus had not yet been detected in Europe. That didn't occur until late January, in Italy, when an Italian brought the virus back home with him after visiting China. The virus wasn't discovered in Norway until late February, while the greater outbreak occurred early in March, after several people had spent their winter holidays in Italy.

But now, in mid-January, while the virus had not yet turned up in Europe, I was immediate concerned about the possibility of my being the first leader having to announce the virus's arrival on Norwegian soil. Not only could it potentially infect our students and employees, it could also critically damage our organizations' reputation. My concerns were hardly lessened by the sight of all these Chinese students wearing surgical masks. From several travels to China, I knew that mask-wearing is normal there, thanks to the heavy pollution from industry emissions and carbon-heavy coal heating. The Chinese rely on masks to filter the air and also to stop airborne germs. So face masks have for years become a part of their culture—certainly long before COVID-19 appeared there. But here in Norway, with its pure air and very scattered population, masks have been a rarity except in some industrial contexts. I knew that most of our native Norwegian students and employees at the Business School were unaccustomed to observing people using masks and were unaware of their frequent use in China.

I was unsure of how to respond. Before the Chinese students' arrival, we had already discussed a voluntary quarantine for them. Their contact person at their home university had emailed my colleagues at the Business School who oversaw the student exchange, recommending that the students remain in their dormitories for voluntary quarantine throughout their first week here. And we had agreed. So I was startled to see them here, right on campus, that Monday morning. Being responsible for all our students, I thought that these Chinese visitors should politely be stopped before they had strolled around the whole campus, encountering who knows how many people and rooms.

For advice on the matter, I immediately contacted our university's Chief Security Officer, as he was experienced in dealing with crises and also had the authority to act. This was a situation that, I later acknowledged, I had created—as there is no crisis before someone brings it into existence and pushes actions in motion. The Security Officer responded by establishing a crisis meeting that also included, among other people, the university's Chief Risk Officer. I had yet to be introduced to the Risk Officer and I had seen the RO role to be quite anonymous at the university—a person who is only visible when a crisis or emergency occurs, but otherwise has a low profile that is limited to those involved in the situation. The crisis meeting covered whether and how the situation should be approached. From the outset I felt alone with the opinion that the students should be asked to return to their dormitories.

We discussed several actions, such as whether to send a text message to all our students, plus issue a press announcement to reduce public speculation. We conferred with the local health authorities, who viewed the situation as low risk and thus requiring no action. Determining the wisest response was difficult at this juncture, as we had first-year students just arriving in an unfamiliar country, plus a budding university, just four years old, with few established relations on which to depend. Meanwhile, during all our initial discussions, the Chinese students had already started moving across campus and enjoying their lunch in the canteen together with Norwegian students. Those at the crisis meeting concluded that we should not react to the situation. The students already had moved across campus, and there seemed a low risk that the students brought with them the virus to Bodø.

I was an outlier on this decision. I personally believed that we should ask the Chinese students to return to their dormitories. But after the decision was made to not act on the situation, I ran into a part-time professor at the Business School who was scheduled to give the first lecture in the Chinese students' study program. This professor has extensive experience working abroad in the high-risk petroleum business and on foreign policy at the Norwegian Ministry of Foreign Affairs. He is highly respected for his experience and wisdom in dealing with demanding situations in foreign countries. I knew he had the experience to give me wise advice on how to act on the situation, and I was still doubting myself about the proper response when I ran into him. After hearing me out, he asked me reflectively, Would you be comfortable if there was one chance of a 100 likelihood that one of these students is infected with COVID-19? That hypothetical convinced me that the students should return for voluntary quarantine, as even the small likelihood of infection could bring huge consequences for the entire country. Feeling reaffirmed, I promptly contacted the Security Officer again, hoping to convince him that we should act on the situation. But his response was curt: "We can't stop every person travelling from China into Norway."

This initial experience with the Chinese students' arrival in my home city taught me that sensemaking, especially in the face of vague questions with muddled answers, is made yet more uncertain with peoples' varied interpretations about unexpected events and the appropriate response. Does it call for laissez-faire or command and control?

In retrospect, the mid-January of 2020 decision to not act on the situation was most likely the right one. Although we did have knowledge about the virus's spread in China, it had not yet arrived in Europe and our attention to it was therefore very low. But the situation gave me an early experience with COVID-19 and left me with lots to reflect on. It also gave me a foretaste of what was to come.

Making Sense of Unfolding Events Over Time

Given humans' escalated travel habits, plus our destruction of nature, diseases from animals will continue to transfer into our habitat, perhaps with even stronger virus outbreaks in the years ahead. In the case of COVID-19, though governments across the world imposed restrictions on peoples' mobility and interaction in the society due to the pandemic to come, the virus had already found its way in and established its power over our human habitat. Extraordinarily adaptive, it learned quickly how to effectively spread from one human to another, and from one country to another. The virus forced everybody into crisis management—governments, organizational leaders, and individuals. Everybody was engaged in sensemaking in order to anticipate how the virus might affect their own life.

When the outbreak occurred in Norway in March of 2020, I was forced into crisis management of the Business School. With its 2700 students and 170 teachers spread out over four cities, and with Bodø being both its main campus and my home turf, I felt a great responsibility to ensure continued good teaching for the students and good facilitation for the teachers to continue their teaching and holding their exams during the outbreak. Crisis management was particularly intense for the first three weeks of the national lockdown due to the novelty and complexity of the situation. Nobody really grasped the scattering behavior of the virus, nor its strength to influence humans' respiratory functioning, nor how long we might need to shut down the country to win this war.

During these first weeks, it was necessary to engage in rapid communication and make important decisions on how to handle the situation, including how to adjust our teaching and examination activities. The university formed several forums where approaches were discussed to ensure a common, aligned management of the crisis. My calendar was quickly filled with formal meetings of the university management team, plus meetings of the university's five faculties and several departments. Meetings were also frequently held with the management team at the Business School, plus the faculties' fifteen line managers who are responsible for our various study programs. They report to me, as I have overall responsibility for all our programs and students.

Invitations for meetings would often appear in my Outlook email only an hour before they were to start. This reflected our many uncertainties with COVID, plus the sudden changes in regulations, from both the national and local governments, that needed to be discussed so that we might anticipate necessary changes in our teaching activities. Decisions on how to approach the crisis seemed invariably fraught, all of them with potentially great consequences for both our students and teachers. Meetings on weekday evenings and even Sunday morning were necessary to keep up with our ever-changing environment. Staff meetings were required to update teachers and administrative personnel on important decisions. Pre-pandemic, staff meetings had been a rather rare phenomenon, but now, active attendance and support from the employees were essential to ensure a smooth implementation of decisions.

In between the meetings, I needed to update myself on the virus's behavior and regulations that affected our activities at the university. I would search national and international news media and journals to gain a greater understanding of the virus—how it spreads and how to fight it. I watched every press conference from the national and local government with deep concentration and concern for how my organization was affected and what we needed to act upon. The crisis demanded frequent and fast analysis of potential scenarios and consequences for our activities, which required both a deep and broad understanding to learn appropriate decisions.

In the fourth week of the government's national lockdown, we entered a week of Easter holidays. With no leisure time during those first weeks, I could finally take a break from crisis management and snooze in the mornings, take longer hikes in our beautiful mountains, and enjoy the company of my closest friends. But the Norwegian government required that we limit our in-person gatherings to just two persons. As I live alone in a two-room apartment, social distancing became my new norm with little interaction even with friends living close by. And I still needed to monitor the activity of the virus both nationally and internationally.

Sensemaking is my conceptual guide. For me as for others, it is activated when we "notice, perceive, and act" on certain discrepant cues in the present moment that interrupt stability and trigger a need for making sense of what is going on. Sensemaking begins when we notice and bracket information as we "chop moments out of the continuous flows [of events] and extract cues from those moments" (Weick, 1995, p. 43). These cues are "seeds from which people develop a larger sense of what may be occurring" (Weick, 1995, p. 50). My early experience with the students arriving from China in mid-January was the first cue I noticed and acted on; it raised my awareness of the immediacy of the virus and increased my effort in noticing and interpreting the flow of information and events for months thereafter. This experience made me realize how quickly the virus could travel and that we probably should expect a major spike in Norway. It certainly made me better mentally prepared when we experienced the outbreak in Norway and when I was forced into crisis management.

When the summer of 2020 arrived, the virus required less crisis management effort. The international society had learned more about COVID-19's behavior—how it spread and how it affected humans. Still, everybody knew that crisis management would remain a part of our working lives for months to come. With an understanding that the virus would continue to spread for the foreseeable future, and with our expectation of a new spike during the summer holidays, the university needed to somehow plan for predictability for the upcoming autumn semester in an unpredictable environment. We needed for both teachers and students to have more stability in the uncertainty of the now defined pandemic.

Managing Change and Stability

Uncertainty about the mercurial behavior of the virus forced leaders to constantly readjust their response to the unfolding events. Crisis managers like me had to remain vigilant and defensive. The uncertainty challenged us to balance our response over time to ensure at least minimal stability and a response. Like funambulism—the art of walking a tightrope—we attempted to achieve a delicate balance between stability and change. While it is true that "the acrobat maintains her balance," it is no less true that "the acrobat constantly adjusts her posture" (Tsoukas & Chia, 2002).

Looking ahead to the autumn semester in 2020, leaders at the university sought to achieve a balance between stability and change, with the main goal being that students should have in-person teaching activities as long as circumstances allowed. Our experience during the spring semester, when we offered only online instruction, taught us that the students felt alone, and several student groups saw an increase in mental-health issues. The pandemic had challenged their mental well-being, so we needed to bring them back on campus within national and local restrictions and for as long as the virus did not spread in the four cities where we had activities. Restricted to using just 30% of our auditoriums' capacity, and required to keep 1.5 meters distance between people, we planned for physical teaching for several students groups. But we needed to make a comprehensive plan for what types of student groups we wanted to be granted physical teaching.

Our larger classes got divided into two groups, one of which got physical and the other group digital. Each student group got two classes they could attend physically; their other two classes they could follow digitally. Students in their first semester at the university, either bachelor or master students, were given priority for physical teaching to ensure that they could network and establish close friends from the outset of their studies. Students on executive education—the more senior students with full-time jobs alongside their studies—had to make do with online classes. For those students attending us from other cities in Norway, we wanted to reduce their commuting hassles by providing them only online classes. Our comprehensive planning for physical teaching gave us some stability in the crisis for the upcoming semester and let us reserve greater in-person teaching for the most fragile student groups.

In my ten years at the university, I have learned that stability is the norm and change is the pain. There seems a silent resistance to change and a comfort with the known. As Orlikowski (1996) says, "for decades, questions of transformation remained largely backstage as organizational thinking and practice engaged in a discourse dominated by questions of stability" (p. 63). Our approach to teaching has been based on a settled agreement about the physical classroom: offering person-to-person contact, it is the main arena where the teacher conveys their knowledge to students. Pre-pandemic, discussions about full online study programs found little teacher support. Only a few of our faculty were already fully online with their teaching. But that simply reflected their private preference for meeting students digitally. The majority of our teachers feared that without face-to-face interaction, students' learning would suffer, their grades would drop, and their capacity to use their knowledge and competence when entering the business world would decrease.

Because of our faculty's minimal experience with online teaching, we also had minimal know-how with respect to using the needed technology just when the virus forced us to teach with it. I was surprised, then, to see how willing most of our teachers were to adapt and also to learn from each other. They seemed to enjoy sharing their expertise. I suspect that their commitment to the students was the driving force behind their embracing the new technology. Were it not for the virus suddenly governing our approach to teaching, it would have taken most of us years, if ever, to adopt the wholesale use of technology in teaching.

Proactive Technology Enactment

When we were forced onto digital platforms, my use of technology escalated quickly and my life suddenly unfolded itself in the digital space. All the small varieties of impressions that we get when moving freely in the physical space were gone. Gone, too, were the small exchanges of conversations and smiles to people passing by in our hallways and cafeteria. These quotidian interactions that daily confirmed our membership in a larger human habitat were not there anymore.

My technological life had been limited to my office computer, with my Outlook email and phone being my main tools for communicating and interacting with colleagues. I had few apps on my private phone, as apps and the regular ping of notifications stress me. At home, my use of the internet and TV was also rather low as I preferred quiet downtime from my office computer.

But now, I needed to act on the crisis through technology.

From mid-March till the beginning of August, every employee at the university was forced to work from home. So for nearly half a year you'd find my computer, keyboard, and headphones adorning the dining table in my living room, a full half of my two-room apartment. The fall semester of 2020 saw us all finally allowed to return to campus. But that proved a brief reprieve, for the entire spring semester of 2021 saw us exiled to our homes once again.

Given these turnabouts, and given our forced reliance on technology, now we needed to really upgrade our use of it. Our calendars now were filled with Teams invitations, and new Teams groups were established as a communication platform for the faculty. The broad forum for communicating with managers at the university was dialog on Teams. Teams brought together a big group of managers who previously had rarely common dialogues and meetings. We could now enjoy direct contact with decision-makers at the top management group at the university, which meant that we were plugged into the departmental decision-making about how to plan for and arrange exams. We could plan for departmental help with student mobility, thanks to assistance from the IT department, whose members understand all such arcana.

The forum promoted fruitful dialogues between many people unused to venturing beyond their own area of responsibility and expertise. This interaction created a rich understanding of the appropriate response to the virus and to the government's effect on our activities.

Thanks to the continuity afforded by the forum's many meetings, the relationships between the leaders of the faculties and departments at the university were significantly strengthened. When participating at the Teams meetings with the cameras on, it soon felt as though we were meeting in person. Leaders whom I had never met, or seldom met, were suddenly seen rather frequently. Technology, far from distancing us from each other, ironically had the opposite effect. It created an extensive collaborative network within our organization that reduced the previous silos that had existed before the crisis—silos that often had promoted misunderstandings of each other's challenges with little generosity. We got to know each other's managerial principles and concerns, and that created a bond for common ambitions during the pandemic.

Communication through technology also increased with my own faculty. Email became my primary means of communicating with our teachers and administrative staff. I also held staff meetings on Teams and used Teams group for communication and interaction, but email remained my bread and butter. I preferred it because it encouraged me to reach out to all employees and also left less room for misinterpretation about what I wanted conveyed.

But there was a downside to this: It was commonly understood that any emails sent from the management team or from the general email account at the Business School were seldom read by our employees, who dismissed them as either spam or not their business. The administration and I often experienced this. We'd have teachers approach us with concerns about issues that we had already provided detailed information about, precisely to head off any misinterpretation. Such emails might have explained important deadlines, like registering one's curriculum, or dates for teaching and exams, or changes in regulations and governing documents that each teacher needed to conform to.

With around 200 very busy employees on our faculty, I knew that these emails needed to be crafted smartly to catch their attention and to limit misunderstandings. Which meant I needed to compose my thoughts extra thoughtfully before any email was sent out. And I came to rely heavily on graphics. For example, I'd highlight dates and deadlines to ensure that decisions were followed and quickly implemented. I'd write certain words in FULL CAPS, or in bold red, or in highlighter yellow—anything to arrest the eye. I also sought help from a good colleague to preview my emails and advise me on whether my message was unmistakable. Fortunately, our teachers' attention improved, as did my memo-writing, and there were fewer misunderstandings.

My proactive enactment of technology during the crisis changed the technology from being a support function to playing a central part in how we communicated and interacted. As a result, technology has become a part of our work processes, not only in regard to teaching but in the dialogue between our employees and the faculty. We have also integrated technology into a way of working and cooperating. We make technology a part of our daily working life in a much more positive way than we did before the pandemic. We now take advantage of all that the technology has to offer in renewing, simplifying, and improving our processes.

Mindful Management

The pandemic imposed great psychological stress on us as individuals, and it also challenged the mental health of our whole society. Social restrictions and limited interactions left many of us depressed and anxious and feeling cut off. Realizing the toll COVID was taking, we put the concept of mindfulness on our agenda to help minimize such negative feelings.

Mindfulness is "an awareness that emerges through paying attention on purpose to the present moment and non-judgmentally to the unfolding of experience moment by moment" (Kabat-Zinn, 2003, p. 145). It is a mental state characterized by nonjudgmental awareness of our present-moment experiences, while also encouraging openness, curiosity, and acceptance in ourself and others (Stedham & Skaar, 2019). Mindfulness enhances our capacity of attention and awareness to unexpected events and builds a capability to respond appropriately (Weick & Sutcliffe, 2011).

My approach to crisis management during the pandemic has been influenced by my private practice of mindfulness. In the summer of 2018, I attended a yoga retreat in Spain. For one week I practiced MediYoga, which promotes awareness to the present moment and to the self, and builds mental strength. Before this, I had been practicing and teaching Iyengar Yoga to build physical strength. Because of my deep experience with MediYoga, I conducted a teacher-training course in Denmark to get certified as a teacher. I started to run courses and practiced MediYoga on a regular basis with its slow meditative movements and active meditation.

MediYoga became a crucible to the way I practice management. "Crucibles" can be regarded as critical experiences, like tragedy, trauma, or blessings, that are catalysts for major breakthroughs (George & Gergen, 2015). They are events that are central to one's life story—anchoring events for a reference point for change. MediYoga become important for me, as I got in contact with my inner peace. It lowered my restlessness and my need to always be on the move toward something. It taught me to be present in the moment, and more deeply connected with both myself and others. MediYoga became a blessed crucible and made me a better manager by enhancing my capacity to remain mindful even in the midst of a storm.

In the summer of 2019, I experienced a traumatic crucible that changed my way of living. I experienced the sudden loss of a close friend. Over the last ten years we had been soulmates able to feel the joy and pain of each other's experience, even when not close in distance. We supported each other, even in times of struggle. No one else knew the depth of my soul, only him. The shock and the grief of my loss were painful in the extreme. After weeks of suffering, I needed to get back to my office as I could no longer stretch my vacation. I needed self-healing quickly. I turned to MediYoga and started to practice meditative movements and meditations every morning for thirty minutes—waking up at 6:30 and performing the same set of yoga each day, to heal my broken heart. MediYoga became my daily practice, and my mental health became stronger than ever. It was a silent improvement of my own mental well-being that healed the trauma and previous life struggles. I became calm and safe in my own presence. It was a traumatic crucible that taught me how to handle setbacks in life and to manage with a more mindful approach.

When my panicky colleague warned me with "It's now happening!" I was not only prepared because of my experience in January of 2020 with the students arriving from China. I was also mentally strong, calm, and resilient—qualities forged from my blessed meeting with MediYoga and the traumatic loss of my soulmate. I was ready to confront and manage a new crisis—one that for me was actually much smaller in scale than the loss of my soulmate.

I believe my mental state of mindfulness made me better at managing the pandemic. I was able to maintain a sustained focus over time, with a rich overview of all eventualities and their consequences for our education activities. My awareness of the unfolding events from moment to moment improved my focused attention with sustained commitment to the problem of interest. The management guru Karl Weick stresses that good management of the unexpected is mindful management. My approach to crisis management can be summarized by a quote from Weick and Sutcliffe on management qualities from mindful sensemaking during unfolding crises:

> It involves the combination of ongoing scrutiny of existing expectations, continuous refinement and differentiation of expectations based on newer experiences, willingness and capability to invent new expectations that make sense of unprecedented events, a more nuanced appreciation of context and ways to deal with it, and identification of new dimensions of context that improve foresight and current functioning. (Weick & Sutcliffe, 2006, p. 516)

During the pandemic, mindfulness raised my responsiveness to the ongoing national and international events and to information about the virus. It created a willingness to interpret and make sense of the unknown in the blast of a chaos, with few rushed decisions that were not based on conscious analysis of the situations. I questioned the unknown and sought to view the flow of events and information from various angles, aiming to get a richer and nuanced understanding about the crisis to improve decisions and lessen the potential bad consequences. Mindful management during the crisis made me better at making analyses and decisions to ensure that we could maintain "business as some sort of usual" during the pandemic.

Resilience

Mindfulness creates resilience in times of crisis. Resilience denotes our ability to maintain business as usual by stretching without breaking, by maintaining and preserving functioning despite adversity. Also to recover quickly, by bouncing back rather than collapsing in the aftermath of a crisis. Resilient managers are actively seeking to expand their knowledge about a given situation in order to reduce the surprise and to dampen oscillations over time. Resilience builds the capacity to "maintain its function and structure in the face of internal and external changes and to degrade gracefully when it must" (Weick & Sutcliffe, 2007, p. 95).

For the first month of the intense crisis management I established a new routine to ensure a sharp and sustained attention with endurance. I woke up at 6:30 a.m. as usual. But now I began my morning with a walk down to the harbor in the city center. I stepped outside to get some beautiful daylight and to clear my head before the new dawn. After my office hour, I again stepped outside for a longer walk to clear my head again and to savor the cold winter weather. A new evening session was then performed in front of the computer, before I took a night walk to calm down once again and to prepare for a good night's sleep.

This structured routine made me take pauses during the long working day—pauses that made me better able to observe my own state of mind. It made me step out of the crisis management, leaving me only witnessing what was occurring within myself in the interaction with my chaotic surroundings. That connection with my inner self ensured that my body gave me subtle signals for when I needed to rest, to get some fresh air, and when I needed to step out of crisis management for a while.

Even though the pandemic changed my everyday life and took up most of my time during its outset, my resilience kept me going and sustained my attention and awareness on crisis management. That resilience increased my ability to notice cues and to adapt to the unfolding events. I have always had the capacity for high resilience during pressure, to stay calm and focused, when others panic and lose control or perspective. But I have also always known when to push the pause button and to recognize when resilience is lost.

Because of the many hours of work and scant social networking during the first months of the pandemic, I knew I had to find a new hobby to get my mind focused on something new. I also knew it had to be an outdoor activity, to get me once again connected better with nature. So I started playing golf. Golf had gotten great attention in Norway in 2019 and 2020 because of national representatives in the higher international league. During the first weeks of May I participated in a course to take the green card, that allows you to play on the green grass. The first day of the course, a light snowfall was drifting horizontally due to strong winds. But the enjoyment was big, and I quickly got hooked. During the summer and autumn, I played up to three times a week. It became a new blessed crucible, a drift from reality, away from my role as a crisis manager, a place where I could calm my head and socialize with new people unassociated with my work. This new hobby helped strengthen my resilience without breaking as I got a pause in the natural world with my mind drifting away from crisis management.

Resignation

Near the end of 2020, people began looking forward to a new year with hopes of a fresh start and an end to the virus. It had spread minimally in Norway in December and Bodø had experienced no large outbreaks of it, so, like many others, I was hoping that the new year really would prove a new year—returning us to a normal society requiring little crisis management. I was also planning to resume a research project that had been put on hold for all of 2020 due to little access to informants and the amount of energy already required of me for crisis management.

But at 4:30 a.m. on a Saturday night, two days before our first week of work in January of 2021, I was caught off guard. I had had some friends over for a late wine night. In the morning I randomly checked the national news media on my phone. To my surprise there had been an announcement from the government earlier that evening: they would hold a new press conference on Sunday morning announcing new measures because of an uptick in the virus. For me, it occurred out of the blue. With all the increased mobility during the Christmas season, I should of course have expected a new outbreak, but my resilience had gotten worn down.

On that Sunday morning, the government once again enforced new restrictions on universities. There would be no in-person teaching for the first two weeks of January. After that, only those students who needed to be in an actual classroom setting to gain their learning outcome could be invited back to their classrooms—but with the further restriction that there could be only twenty students in each room. Once again, my calendar was filled up with Teams meetings, the first occurring that very Sunday evening. I was back into intense crisis management.

In retrospect, I acknowledge entering the new year with high hopes that it would bring normal days with minimal crisis management. But my fantasy was just that. With dreams of normal days, I had stopped looking for, and noticing, cues about how the pandemic unfolded and how it could affect our organization, which caused me to overlook significant information and signals about a new outbreak during the Christmas holidays. During Christmas and the first days of the new year, I had mentally resigned from my responsibility and my role as a crisis manager of the faculty during the pandemic. My focused attention with conscious awareness to the pandemic was simply not as intense as it had been the year before. I had not only taken a Christmas vacation, I had taken a vacation from updating myself on the pandemic.

Fast forward six weeks to the middle of February—the national and local government had just made several changes to how we could perform our teaching activities. With less resilience to crisis management, it started to be difficult to follow all the frequent changes and detailed regulations they implemented. I was less engaged in seeking information about the virus, which lowered my overall picture of the crisis I was to manage. I communicated only the most important information so that the faculty could operate within the regulatory framework and to ensure that both teachers and students remained updated. I started to rely more on the decisions made by the university management team, which reduced my critical thinking and questioning. In the new year, I was less engaged with crisis management, although it remained a big part of my everyday working life.

In a meeting with the line managers of the faculty's study program, I became annoyed upon learning that the participants were not updated on the regulations even though they had been informed through emails. I was also frustrated that the line managers did not stretch as far as we'd wished to engage with the students even though we were once again forced to teach online. I was in no mood to hide the irritation in my voice, and after the meeting, I phoned one of the attendees to confirm that, yes, my irritation was noticeable.

Some days later, after reflecting further on how the meeting had unfolded, I realized that I had lapsed from my mindful approach to crisis management. My resignation continued to grow through mid-February. I was not on top of my responsibility and role, but now at least I was conscious of it and looking for ways to manage my slippage.

Mindlessness Management

Mindlessness is a mental state that offers "limited information processing, rigid categorical thinking, single perspectives, and failure to recognize context" (Burgoon & Langer, 1996, p. 107). It is characterized by perspectives and interpretations that rely on automaticity and reactivity toward what occurs in the moment. My management of the crisis had become mindless when we entered 2021.

For weeks I had failed to note my resignation to my role responsibilities for the pandemic. I was in a mindless mental state. I operated with less attention and awareness toward the crisis and my own management of it. I did not pay attention to the unfolding events and information about the spread of the virus and the ever-changing regulations by our national and local governments. The available cues about the virus were ignored as I stopped attending to the events and information available. Rather, I managed the crisis based on my experiences from the year before—managing with little consciousness to myself and the environment. I did not question or critically assess the situation or my own management of it, behaving more in an automatic fashion. My decisions relied on familiar decisions made in the previous years. Thus, I lost the opportunity to reassess decisions made in the previous year and to make better ones when we again experienced an outbreak.

In meetings with the broader forum at the university, I kept a more silent role compared to the year before. I did not question assessments or decisions in the same manner. I raised my voice only when I felt it was absolutely necessary. I did not contribute with analysis of potential scenarios and consequences, as I did not have a tight grip on the virus and the government and local regulations. When a decision was made, above me, I simply affirmed the decision and immediately implemented it without registering my own opinion about the decision. I only questioned decisions when they were unclear and could be interpreted in several ways.

My communication with teachers and administrative personnel at the faculty was reduced—mostly due to an expectation of my own manager to reduce the amount of emails sent to employees at the faculty. The restriction placed on me made me less proactive since my assessment of the overall picture was no longer required. I was not invited to update the employees at faculty meeting, thus I no longer needed to have a constant update on the pandemic. These restrictions made me take a step back from my proactive crisis management and influenced my mindless management of the pandemic.

I believe my mindlessness state also gradually appeared as I had neglected to look after my own mental health the last few months. I scrapped my morning routine of waking up at 6:30 each morning to do yoga or walk down to the harbor. Because of the long winter months in the High North, I no longer played golf in the beautiful scenery that nature had gifted us since late autumn. Meanwhile, my social activity remained limited due to national regulations. Although I became aware of my own resignation and mindless state, it took a month before I was back in a mindful mental state—just before the outbreak in Bodø in March, a year after the pandemic triggered a national lockdown the year before.

Management and the State of Mind During Crisis

Mindfulness prepares managers for unexpected events and increases their readiness to respond proactively. Mindful management practices promote an enhanced capacity for noticing and bracketing information and events that require a trigger for sensemaking and responsiveness. Crisis management based on mindfulness ensures openness, curiosity, and acceptance of what is occurring, thereby increasing one's capability to respond to the crisis. But when management of a crisis is based on mindlessness, responses to the crisis are based on previous similar experiences and beliefs about what is appropriate management.

A manager's state of mind influences their ability to perform effective crisis management. Resilient managers ensure that their organizations stretch without breaking during a crisis and maintain functioning despite adversity. Resilience also ensures that the organization bounce back after a crisis rather than collapsing. During a crisis this capacity is necessary both to ensure that the organization experiences business as usual and to direct the organization forward past the crisis (Fig. 10.1).

Fig. 10.1 State of mind

References

Burgoon, J. K., & Langer, E. J. (1996). Language, fallacies, and mindlessness-mindfulness in social interaction. *Communication Yearbook, 18*, 105–132.

Fountain, Jane E. (2001). *Building the virtual state: Information technology and institutional change*. Brookings Institution.

George, B., & Gergen, David. (2015). *Discover your true north*. New York: John Wiley & Sons.

Kabat-Zinn, Jon. (2003). Mindfulness-based interventions in context: Past, present, and future. *Clinical Psychology: Science and Practice, 10*(2), 144–156.

Orlikowski, Wanda J. (1996). Improvising organizational transformation over time: A situated change perspective. *Information Systems Research, 7*(1), 63–92.

Stedham, Yvonne, & Skaar, Theresa B. (2019). Mindfulness, trust, and leader effectiveness: A conceptual framework. *Frontiers in Psychology, 10*, 1588.

Tsoukas, Haridimos, & Chia, Robert. (2002). On organizational becoming: Rethinking organizational change. *Organization Science, 13*(5), 567–582.

Weick, Karl E. (1995). *Sensemaking in organizations*. SAGE.

Weick, Karl E., & Sutcliffe, Kathleen M. (2006). Mindfulness and the quality of organizational attention. *Organizational Science, 17*(4), 514–524.

Weick, Karl E., & Sutcliffe, Kathleen M. (2007). *Managing the unexpected. Resilient performance in an age of uncertainty* (2nd ed.). Wiley.

Weick, Karl E., & Sutcliffe, Kathleen M. (2011). *Managing the unexpected: Resilient performance in an age of uncertainty* (3rd ed.). Jossey-Bass.

CHAPTER 11

Compassion, Burnout, and Self-care During COVID-19: On the Collective Impact of Self-soothing Super Highways

Sarah J. Tracy, Brianna L. Avalos, Laura Martinez, B. Liahnna Stanley, Sophia Town, and Alaina C. Zanin

What fires together, wires together. The habits we practice over a lifetime become a superhighway in our brain. No bumps. No pot-holes. Smooth sailing. Unless we activate energy to forge alternate routes, that well-traveled highway is where our mapping software guides us every time. And it's the auto-pilot route we use when times get tough, uncertain, and chaotic.

* * *

S. J. Tracy (✉) • B. L. Avalos • L. Martinez • B. L. Stanley • A. C. Zanin
Arizona State University, Tempe, AZ, USA
e-mail: sarah.tracy@asu.edu; blavalos@asu.edu; lauramartinez@asu.edu; blstanl1@asu.edu; azanin1@asu.edu

S. Town
Fordham University, Bronx, NY, USA
e-mail: stown@fordham.edu

L. D. Browning et al. (eds.), *Organizational Communication and Technology in the Time of Coronavirus*,
https://doi.org/10.1007/978-3-030-94814-6_11

I'm not nostalgic. I'm not a keeper. Yet, I still have my baby blanket. It's tucked safely into a 20-gallon plastic tub, squeezed between my sixth-grade sticker collection and worn 1980s penny loafers. The blanket is a soft yellow waffle knit, edged with a 1970s polyester satin trim. One of the four satin corners is a silky ripped-up mess. Every night, after my mom turned out the light and left me alone in my frigid cavernous Wisconsin bedroom, I clutched and rhythmically rubbed one satin corner. Night by night, I caressed that silky trim between pudgy fingers into a damaged wreck. My tiny toddler voice couldn't form the word "silky" (ˈsilkē), so instead, I begged Mommy to find "kee kee" corner. Kee kee corner became my beloved and reliable friend. My own untidy melody. It helped me traverse the uncertainty of the night and arrive safely into the soft yellow morning sunshine.

Today, professional productivity is my (Sarah Tracy's) adult version of kee kee corner. It's also my superhighway. Sure, some days I activate the energy needed to travel a side-road and trudge into uncharted waters. On those occasions, I may hike a local trail rather than tune into my virtual fitness class. Or maybe I'll tinker on the piano or sing along to an 80s playlist, rather than return another email. But, if I'm in doubt, I'll work harder. Not sure what to do today? I head to the computer. Under threat? I eat an ugly frog and immediately feel in control again.

Indeed, even as a 51-year-old, much of my self-value is wrapped in the cloth of achievement, planning, and hard work. I maintain an hour-by-hour calendar, annually revise my academic vision, and can tell you six months out whether I'm available to meet. I juggle multiple deadlines, rotate five different office desk configurations to ward off carpal tunnel syndrome, and dutifully update my 73-page academic vita every couple of months. These workaholic activities galvanize neither pride nor embarrassment. One thing middle age grants is telling the truth to myself.

The notion that productivity equates with self-worth is its own story—one that was triggered in my childhood and cultivated over years of young adulthood in which I strove to prove myself as worthy and lovable (Tracy, 2016). Here, I want to tell another story: how someone with such an identity coped in the time of complete chaos and uncertainty that comprised the first few months of the 2020 COVID-19 pandemic in 2020—and how these habits of work and productivity resulted in a range of effects, including self-soothing, compassion for others, and the reification of structures of burnout and ideological productivity norms.

This is not just my story, but also a larger story of how to be humane—to ourselves and others—in the face of uncertainty and upset. And how such efforts, despite innocuous intentions, can result in problematic consequences. It's a story of how we piece together remnants of familiarity and habit to protect us from the storms in life. And how our self-soothing habits can provide comfortable warmth for ourselves and others—while also occasionally exacerbating cold realities that sediment chaos and pain.

My working habits during Spring 2020 took on the contours of a collaborative research project called "COVID Stories and Sensemaking" or "S&S" for short. This story would not be possible without the contributions of my collaborators, all of whom are listed as coauthors in this chapter. They have been instrumental in this tale through their ways of being, their thought leadership, and their vulnerable sharing about how I showed up in the process of our work together. Although the story is told from my (Sarah Tracy's) point of view, they contributed feedback, commentary, and visualizations of their own self-soothing superhighways.

This chapter opens by sharing a timeline and academic narrative vista that chronicles crucial turning points that lead to this particular narrative (Franzosi, 1998). The heart of this chapter describes how the S&S research project unfolded—and how our team purposefully foregrounded emotion within ourselves, each other, and our participants. Along the way, I share how aspects of the story intersect with the organizational communication research associated with compassion (Miller, 2007; Way & Tracy, 2012) and burnout (Maslach et al., 2001; Tracy, 2017). Furthermore, I include some lessons regarding how the situation problematizes assumptions about what typifies "good" research and the complexity of judging and choosing appropriate, ethical, and kind actions during a time of uncertainty.

This chapter closes with a scatterplot that pictures the relationship between habitual ways of caring for ourselves and how this might affect the structural care for others (Sarikaya & Gleicher, 2017). This scatterplot graphically illustrates how different "go-to" self-care strategies, especially when brought to the extreme, have diminishing returns and can result in harmful repercussions for ourselves and others. Finally, this chapter returns to my narrative vista, reimagining a future timeline that opens up alternate possibilities. The existence of well-traveled highways suggests likely future routes. But, even the almost inevitable future can never obliterate the alternate and yet unforged path. Becoming aware of well-grooved patterns (and thanking them for their service) is a first step in having a choice. And then, if desired, the opportunity for choosing otherwise.

A Narrative Vista of Overwork

Some aspects of an individual's past are merely interesting catalyzing fodder, while others serve a cardinal and crucial function (Franzosi, 1998), serving as hinge events that are risk-laden and likely to significant impact one's identity and path (Barthes & Duisit, 1975). The following cardinal events in my journey of productivity situate the current story.

1993—I take my first "real job" at a public relations firm in Los Angeles, regularly working 60 hours a week for a $21,500 salary (Tracy & Redden, 2019). Six months in, I call to my favorite undergraduate professor at University of Southern California, Dr. Eric Eisenberg. I want to be a Dean. He says there are a few steps. I apply to graduate school.

2000—I graduate with a Ph.D. in organizational communication from University of Colorado-Boulder. My research focuses on stress, burnout, and emotional labor. I'm hired along with a cohort of seven other assistant professors into a tenure track communication position at Arizona State University, Tempe. At 29 years old, I shine green and get right to work.

2002—I teach qualitative research methods for the first time at the doctoral level. Midway through the semester, multiple students express disdain at the time commitment required by course assignments. They are overwhelmed. I stand firm. One student breaks down in tears and tells me how she would like to be a professor one day but just can't keep up. I smile and spew hope, but doubt colors my soul. She drops out of the program a couple years later.

2006—The Arizona State University (ASU) president names me as one of six "exemplars" across the university. I'm a "rising star" in organizational communication, with a research focus on workplace problems such as burnout and workplace bullying. In addition to being awarded tenure, I am featured in ASU news stories, on the provost website, and awarded a substantial extra raise.

2008—I train for and compete in a full IronMan triathlon. My 20+ training hours a week mean that I miss out on several work commitments. I worry whether I'm doing enough at work and double down. I tell people that my tiny diamond IM pendant stands for "IronMind."

2009—An advisee is managing the exhaustion of her dissertation, single-mother parenting, and a recent miscarriage. During a mentoring session, she begins to weep, then stops herself saying, "I'm sorry. I know crying makes you uncomfortable." I protest. But it's true. I want her to stop crying. Several months later, another student drops me as advisor. She says it's because my expectations are a mismatch for her goals. I'm heartbroken.

2011—I take a personal self-development course. For the first time I consider how childhood decisions I made—equating achievement with lovability—are those I have uncritically dragged through life. I share my vulnerabilities with several close friends. One tells me, "Sarah, people like you not *because* of your achievements. People like you *despite* your achievements." Another says, "You don't realize how intimidating you can be." Scales and tears fall from my eyes. In the Wittgenstein (1980) way, I am STRUCK. Through a series of these "aha" moments, I am moved to critically unsettle my guiding life frameworks.

2012—Spurred by a student's doctoral dissertation in the context of hospice, and my attendance at an ASU guest lecture by pioneering positive organizational scholar Dr. Jane Dutton, my scholarship moves toward positive and flourishing aspects of emotional communication, like compassion at work.

2019—On the recommendation of a professional coach, I opt-out of Google Scholar citation emails and other such things that I label "academic achievement ego anchors." I begin paying closer attention to the suffering of others and how I (through my practice and scholarship) might create more compassion and connection. I realize that without being compassionate with myself, it's going to be difficult to be compassionate to others.

2020—I am named a National Communication Association Distinguished Scholar, an award for excellent career achievement. I'm stunned, as they've never before awarded it to someone so young. Furthermore, I'm conflicted, due to me perpetuating the history of whiteness of the award. I tell myself, "It is what it is. Just take it. You can rest now." But I'm not sure if I believe all that.

The preceding ten events serve as a narrative timeline of how I arrived to the place where I am today, and the current story of overwork, the COVID S&S research study, and how self-care, compassion, and burnout interrelates.

Self-care, Compassion, and Burnout in a COVID Research Team

When the pandemic hit the United States, I was in the midst of teaching (for the12th? time) the ASU advanced doctoral course on qualitative research methods. All of us suddenly had to transition our courses online. Due to the social distancing orders, many of my ten students' projects were immediately disrupted. They were in shock, angry, and already overwhelmed with the course. I learned later that some viewed their coursework as an escape. But at the time, it was clear that many needed an escape from the coursework.

So, I went to work fixing. Too overwhelmed? O.k., me too, let's cancel the midterm. Worried about your semester project? Totally fine for you to skip the fieldwork and make it an interview-only project via Zoom.

But wait, I took it another step by kick-starting an interview project and institutional review board (IRB) protocol precisely about COVID. If the students' regular semester projects were ruined, no problem. They could join me in this other project. I was going to make this disruption productive. One week after the course transition, I was ready to submit the IRB application and asked if anyone in the class wanted to be part of it. Two of them said yes, but kept their semester class projects intact. Three other colleagues joined as well.

Meanwhile, on Academic Twitter, I saw tweets like, "I can't work right now" and "Everyone who is going on with life and work as normal right now should just stop it. Like really, STOP IT."

I carried on. I skimmed material about the stages of grief (Kübler-Ross & Kessler, 2005), which is a process that includes denial, anger, bargaining, depression, and acceptance. It seemed I had skipped a couple of steps. Sure, I had been in denial, anger, and bargaining for several days (when I couldn't bear to cancel a trip to Australia and kept thinking, "if only ..."), but I was immune to the depression. It felt like I was already in "acceptance." Business as usual. The protestants I went to church with as a Wisconsin youngster would have been proud of my stiff upper lip.

But as days turned into weeks into months, I began to wonder whether what I thought was acceptance was just a protracted denial. It wasn't that I was resilient and "bouncing back" (Buzzanell, 2010). No, I was seeking comfort in the superhighway of what made me feel agentic and in control: Work. In a sea of questions (e.g., should I wipe down my groceries, visit my mom across town, or reroute my plane ticket *again*?) seeing something like an accepted IRB protocol felt familiar, good, moral and right.

But, of course, that was because work was my "kee kee corner." There was nothing inherently good about it. But it soothed me. It helped me deal with the uncertainty. It's what I knew, my good old faithful.

Indeed, as I began to closely observe those around me, it seemed clear that in the path of the pandemic, people were becoming *more* rather than *less* like their typical selves. Colleagues who were characteristically contrarian spouted devil's advocate conspiracy theories and doubled down on questioning popular opinions. Fitness buddies posted enthusiastic, "you can do it" home fitness videos. Weekend chefs outdid one another as they posted photos of beautifully scored sourdough bread boules and air-fried popcorn shrimp.

And, indeed, working harder and better was just part of me becoming more like myself—finding a place of agency and control in a sea of chaos. I was definitely in the grief stage of "denial" rather than "acceptance."

Regardless, along the way of creating this work, one thing was different than my typical way of being: as leader of the COVID S&S project, we purposefully centered emotion and feeling with one another and with our participants. Whether consciously or not, we applied aspects from two key areas from my familiar organizational communication research: burnout and compassion. Burnout is characterized by emotional exhaustion, depersonalization, and decreased efficacy (also known as a diminished sense of personal accomplishment) (Tracy, 2017). Compassion is characterized by *recognizing* others' suffering through presence and listening, *relating* empathically through vulnerable disclosure and reframing, and *(re)acting* in ways that addressed or even ameliorated the suffering (Way & Tracy, 2012). (Re)acting can come in the form of communicatively constructing hope (Tracy & Huffman, 2017), providing instrumental and informational support (House, 1981), as well as through nonverbal presence, immediacy, and acts of service (Huffman, 2017). Application of these two research streams emerged both in our research project meetings and in how we chose to sample and interacted with participants.

In every research meeting, we checked in with one another and honestly shared how we were coping with the pandemic and social distancing. During these discussions, we disclosed the sicknesses in our families, our difficulties in keeping up with work and school, and the upset in having to cancel plans or do without. We laughed. We cried. We talked over each other and didn't mute ourselves. We were authentically curious about each other's everyday lives. Many of these meetings took place in May 2020—after the academic semester was complete and during a period when many of us were facing an expanse of unscheduled time due to canceled summer plans. As such, some of us enjoyed a strange "snow-day" like luxury. When we eventually talked specifically about the research project, we agreed that the *process* of the research project needed to be as meaningful as the outcome. And, at this time, the end goal was amorphous. Mostly, we thought, "let's talk to people about COVID and see what happens" and "let's keep checking in with one another."

Second, we made the conscious choice to forego a strict "sampling plan" for the study and instead forged ahead with this question in mind: "Who do we personally want to speak with about their sensemaking and coping strategies?" This sampling choice was foundational for two reasons. First, it actually allowed us to move forward with the study in our time of great upset and sidestep aspects of burnout. This right-sizing of expectations helped us avoid emotional exhaustion or the feeling that we were not accomplishing enough (Ray & Miller, 1991). The precious little emotional energy of the team was expended toward our own individual sensemaking and coping while still carrying on with the project.

Additionally, this more easy-going interview approach allowed us to engage authentically and compassionately with our interviewees at a deeper level. We chose to interview our friends, family members, and colleagues. Although team members shared a similar interview guide, we gave each other permission to deviate and focus in on the questions that seemed most meaningful to ourselves and our participants. Interviewees opened up about their own struggles and coping techniques. And we shared our own. This helped us recognize and be with others' suffering, compassionately relate, act and react through presence, reframing, and hope-building, and contributed to our own sensemaking frameworks. As time went on, the energy generated in our collective conversations allowed us to have the will to expand and diversify the interview pool.

Indeed, an important lesson in this story is reconsidering what equates with rigorous research. The project emphasized the notion that there is no one ideal sampling plan or interview stance that equates with high-quality qualitative research (Tracy, 2010). Although some might decry the "convenience" sampling method, our plan was also the most ethical and, arguably, because of the depth and authenticity of our interviews, ended up creating the context that resulted in the study's rich dialogue and reflection. As such, the disruption caused by COVID served as an opportunity for us as scholars to pause and question typical protocols of quality research and imagine a range of priorities. What would it look like if we defined research quality by considering the ways the research process served to create flourishing and care among participants and researchers? What if we decried scholarship that left the researchers burned out and bereft? What if we cared as much for the ways that research might positively impact and transform the researcher as much or more as we cared about its impact and transformation on others (Lopez & Tracy, 2020).

A related lesson learned from this process is the sheer joy of scholarly activity when it's unattached to preconceived outcomes. In so much research, we are focused on the end prize—the semester paper, the conference presentation, or academic gold, the peer reviewed journal article. In such a framework, the hours, weeks, and months of the research process is relegated to an endured purgatory punctuated by the nagging worry of whether we'll actually reach that prize. In our collective process with this project, in contrast, I did not feel that attachment. This might be a luxury of my age and full professor tenure, granted. But it is a lesson learned, and one that I'm taking with me into the future. And, I think most of us would make wiser choices if we viewed the process as important and life-giving as the outcome. Indeed, as they say, today is the first day of the rest of your life.

Despite our early lack of attachment to the specific results, we as a team did create outcomes that we feel good about. Over the course of a couple months, we engaged in almost 30 hours of conversations with 44 people. As a team we transcribed and engaged in early analysis and then found a small grant to fund two team members as they transcribed the rest. As I left for sabbatical Fall 2020, the other team members acted compassionately toward me by taking the lead on analysis and writing. That break of several months from regular scholarly expectations was filled with long walks on the beach and afternoon naps—allowing me to avoid what likely would have become a full-blown case of personal burnout. What's more, my absence probably did them (and all my other colleagues) good. As of Fall of 2021, we developed two conference papers based on the project which then led to two publication submissions (Stanley et al., 2021; Zanin et al., 2021).

Let me say more about the biggest lesson I feel I've learned from this process. As indicated by the opening vignettes, my immediate rush toward familiar work productivity served as my own personal coping and denial device. In a time filled with overflowing uncertainties (Should I buy more toilet paper? When will the price of masks go down? How the hell do I share my Zoom screen? What will happen if I cancel this trip?), working was my self-soothing "kee kee corner," buoying me in stormy uncharted waters. What's more, I believe the compassionate process of our study served as a steady space of sensemaking for my collaborators and the research participants.

That said, even though the microcosm of our team thoughtfully engaged and applied concepts from the field of burnout and compassion, developing this chapter triggered me to critically self-reflect upon how kick-starting a research project and overdriving my work ethic during a historic time of upset and stress likely had more complex effect at the structural level. Said more simply, I'm beginning to consider how my workaholism contributes to burnout at a structural level.

Certainly, my actions in May 2020 as a full professor and informal school leader sedimented the idea that it was possible and proper to carry on with research and academic productivity even as the world tumbled around us. My activities suggested that one could (should?) simply power through. And, although I sat "with" the pain of my close colleagues (at least for the first portion of research meetings and classes), I was also task oriented—focused on productivity when instead I could have purposefully dialed back. Although some research suggests that organizational leaders can be "happy workaholics" themselves but still encourage flexible work-life balance for others (Friedman & Lobel, 2000), followers second guess themselves when their behavior doesn't match that of their mentors.

Indeed, if a person desires to effectively be with and relate others who are in pain, then a key ingredient for doing so is vulnerability (Brown, 2015). My difficulty in experiencing my own upset and disappointment—in this instance and others throughout my life—suggests that I have it all together, and that, ostensibly, others should as well.

Indeed, in preparation for this chapter, I asked the COVID team members, "What did you learn about your collaborators on this project?" Liahhna said,

> The folks on this team are, or appeared to be, fairly skilled in bracketing (and when they weren't, they were honest about it). I am not, and I forgive myself for the days that I kept trying. We—ourselves, each other, and the lands that shape us—are interdependent and integrated wholes. The pain of the suffering before us, the suffering in which we are complicit, is not "out there" or "over there," it is right here. I learned I am not very good at compartmentalizing.

Apparently, I am a compartmentalization expert. Early in my career students told me that they felt an expectation to act extraordinarily professional, organized, and content when they were around me. Over the last ten years, this has softened and, at this point, I get more comments such to the effect that people *were* intimidated to talk to me—but only at first, and that as they got to know me, they realized they could open up. Regardless, what I'm seeing is how this "intimidating / having it all together" first impression stunts the chances that others will share their suffering with me. This, in turn, compromises one's ability to relate empathically and react effectively (Tietsort, 2021).

Case in point, in one particular late April 2020 class, as COVID became a reality, I faced a litany of questions and misgivings from my doctoral students about their semester project. I reserved extra time for discussion in class, softened deadlines, and created more detailed explanations of assignments and multi-page rubrics. I tried to show them that I heard their pain, and endeavored to show that I would fix it. But, soon after class I realized how, in many ways, I essentially met their searing upset through a sandpaper salve of little boxes, directions, and checkmarks. That night after class, I sat with the muck of this "remedy." I thought about how I had buried myself in work as a way to deny the complete and utter ontological unmooring of the pandemic. My superhighway, my "kee kee corner," my golden hammer of working harder proved to have diminishing returns. I finally sent this email (edited slightly for length and clarity):

April 27, 2020

Greetings students:

I sit here, again, alone on a Monday morning. This week for some reason feels tougher than the rest. I'm feeling sorry for myself, unmotivated, and irritated that the world doesn't seem like it's going to heal itself anytime soon. I feel like I've disappointed myself and others.

And, it's clear, that if I'm feeling that way—as a tenured professor with a steady paycheck and no huge expectations in the next few weeks—then graduate students are feeling this and MORE in terms of overwhelm and stress.

To reiterate, all the expectations on final papers and presentations are relaxed. I created the very detailed paper tips sheet and rubric with the idea that doing so would be helpful. I'm now having second guesses of whether that is actually the case or whether it just serves as more of a constraint, a jungle gym of "have tos."

So, just do the work that feels inspiring to you. If the paper structure feels useful, lean on it. If it doesn't, please put it aside, tear it into tiny pieces, use it as a dart-board—and then do what feels right.

The last two weeks of the semester, with looming papers, deadlines, teaching, are among the toughest for grad students during ANY year. Right

> now, when you are separated from so many of your typical outlets for venting and social support, and uncertain of what the future holds, completing PhD level academic work may feel next to impossible.
>
> So, do what you can do. And, know that YOU are amazing people outside of any work done or not done. Anyway, my apologies if this message seems non-academic. And, perhaps it hits you as completely off base, and you're o.k. And, maybe I needed to send it more for myself than for you. So, for that, I thank you for reading.
>
> I'm here if you want to, together, co-complain, or talk, or tell stupid jokes, or talk through anything related to COM 609, grad school, etc.
>
> SJT

In response to this message, I received a couple emails of thanks and relief. But also, miraculously, I also received something I did not know I needed: words of comfort ... for ME. One kind soul simply said, "Dr. Tracy, know that we all see and honor your struggle, too."

I reread the words. Again and again. And, I wept.

I was struggling. And it was o.k. to feel it. And it was also o.k. to show it.

Having it all together and doubling down on work was not the solution here. What I had turned to as a silky "kee kee corner" had become a sandpaper salve.

A Story of Unintended Consequences of Self-care

So, what is this a story of? It's a story of how our self-soothing "kee kee corners" and superhighways increase as uncertainty and upset increases. In my case, when things get uncertain, I double down on work. That's what feels moral and right and familiar and good. More importantly, it's a story about how our self-soothing superhighway behavior not only affects ourselves, but can impact the larger collective. And that some of these behaviors, no matter how helpful to the individual, may have unintended and problematic consequences on the collective.

So, let's try to visualize the relationship between environmental uncertainty and self-soothing behavior, and then take it one step further in charting the relationship between self-soothing behavior and consequences on the collective. A scatterplot design can serve as a "sandbox" for visualizing an argument (Sarikaya & Gleicher, 2017, p. 2). Visually speaking, on a scatterplot, the relationship seems linear. The more the environmental uncertainty and upset, the more of the self-soothing and superhighway mindless behavior. See Fig. 11.1.

Fig. 11.1 Scatterplot

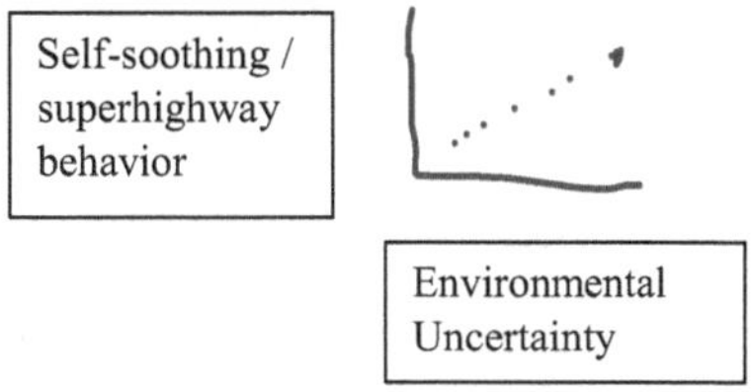

Fig. 11.2 Scatterplot

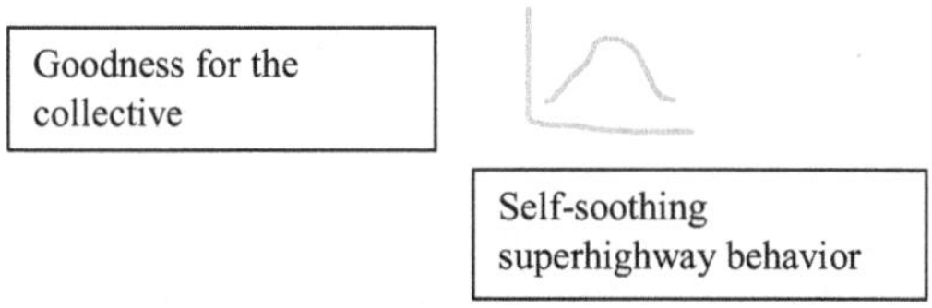

But what about the relationship of the behavior and the goodness of the collective? So what we see here is a bell curve. Just shutting down without doing any work likely would have caused harm to the collective. However, more work (even though that's where uncertainty pushes me) has diminishing returns. See Fig. 11.2.

If I want to be responsible to the collective, I've got to have some restraint when it comes to my own self-soothing habits of overwork. Further, I can mindfully develop some side-roads of new self-soothing habits that would not have the same type of harmful effect on others even when I must flex them for my own personal wellbeing.

As the great statistician and data visualization expert John W. Tukey famously said, "The greatest value of a picture is when it forces us to notice what we never expected to see" (Wainer & Lysen, 2009, p. 272). In the case of the second scatterplot, "what we never wanted to see" is how our own self-soothing devices, how silky and wonderful they may feel to ourselves, can be sandpapery and problematic for others when practiced to the extreme.

Indeed, input from my coauthors about their own "kee kee corners" and superhighways illustrate the range of ways self-coping devices may impact the collective.

Alaina's kee kee corner is planning and scheduling. When COVID hit, in addition to the typical stressors, she also faced losing two grandparents, negotiated fertility concerns, and—in the wake of Jacob Blake's shooting—watched historical buildings burn and Black Lives Matter protestors murdered in her Wisconsin hometown. She avoided the grief of these losses by planning her calendar down to the last second. Whether it was training for a virtual half-marathon or collaborating on 11 different research projects, her sticky notes, calendar, and white board reminded her that she was in control. Such planning allowed Alaina and those around her to dream together and accomplish goals. However, her planning also created arbitrary rules and timelines for what constituted success.

Likewise, Sophia turned to overwork and pleasing others. In the wake of COVID, she accepted almost every request and invitation. In doing so, maintained the notion for herself and others that she was tough, capable, and in control—something that was top of mind in a new job as a tenure track professor. While saying yes to many long-term projects, she also turned to teaching activities and virtual workshops as short-term projects with near instant gratification. Along the way, she found comfort in aesthetics, making sure she looked her best as she edited video lectures, posted affiliated photos on social media, and overall presented a competent and put together person. These activities—similar to those by myself and Alaina—served to help her feel in control, liked, and respected. However, at the structural level, these actions contribute to the expectation that more work is the most moral, ethical, and praiseworthy prize.

Brianna soothes herself by focusing on others' needs. She was able to turn her attention toward others (like her parents) as well as with research collaborators. From this, she can deny the problems in her own environment. So, her self-soothing strategy seems to have a positive correlational effect in terms of positive impact on those around her—at least for the short term. However, caring for others often means neglecting the nurturing of one's own self (a member of the collective). What's more, there is a fine line between comforting and controlling. Brianna admitted that some of her help toward her parents could also be overly controlling.

Finally, Liahnna admitted that as someone with chronic depression and anxiety, that in times of deep upset like COVID, it's a lot easier for her to dig herself deeper into holes than climb out. The malaise of Spring and Summer 2020 for Liahnna was intricately intertwined with the ongoing racial, colonial, and carceral violence at the intersections of difference. However, Liahnna turned to an activity where joy has always persisted, and that is community work. Liahnna became buried in antiracist committees, graduate student taskforces, and with Indigenous communities—consumed by imagining possibilities so that lives could be more livable. This collaboration with like-minded folks facilitated survival especially during a time of Liahnna's critical reflection on the limits of what can be accomplished in academia, another organ of a neoliberal repressive state. The laughing, dreaming, crying, and sitting in silence with others was simultaneously healing and also a place of grief, loss, and suffering. In reflection, although this activity is definitely a contribution to a collective, Liahnna is less sure of whether these activities served as "self-soothing kee kee corners"—or even whether they would choose this particular framing of self-care.

Liahnna's reflection on this topic recalls Audre Lorde's (1988) quote: "Caring for myself is not self-indulgence, it is self-preservation, and that is an act of political warfare" (p. 130). Indeed, if we are not caring for themselves, nor looking after our own spirits, it seems unlikely that we are able to energize meaningful care and change for the collective.

Future Narrative Vista

Now that we have considered multiple effects of self-soothing tactics on the larger collective, let us double back to the value of writing personal narratives like this one. Certainly, one aspect of sociological introspection (Ellis, 1991) is critically reflecting on the unintended consequences and impact of certain self-coping mechanisms on the larger collective. What's more, research shows that deep reflection into the past—including the timeline of key turning points and consideration of key guiding habits and values—leads to a temporary elongation of future time horizons. Coined by Professor Omar El Sawy as the "Janus Precedence Effect," leaders who first reflect on the past are better able to learn from mistakes, consider key milestones, and then look further into the future (Kouzes & Posner, 2012).

So, perhaps in writing this tale, I'm able to better reflect on my own narrative vista as it arcs to the future. As I thought about the future, I realized how much I am going to need to resist typical habits and ego anchors in order for it to come to fruition. Here's a thoughtful guess of what the future may hold for Sarah J. Tracy.

2021–2022—I decline to apply for editing one of our discipline's most prestigious journal. I reacquaint myself with childhood practices that my body associates with joy, flourishing, and whimsy—such as singing, dancing, and playing.

2023–2024—I create an "academic adjacent" consulting business focused on individual and organizational flourishing. It brings joy and enough extra income to regularly spend every summer in a house by the beach. I visit the ocean at least three times a week, where I viscerally feel the vastness of the world and the smallness of my own concerns.

2025–2040—A coauthor joins me in writing the third edition of my book "Qualitative Research Methods" and over the next several editions and 15 years, transitions to being first author.

2026–2029—I write regularly on compassion, productivity, and the cult of achievement, cultivating a blog, podcast, and culminating in a popular book that helps others create practical wisdom and value in their own lives and organizations.

2030—My passions turn toward serving others as a primary activity. I become director of a related program or center, putting all my work related to organizational flourishing, leadership, and phronesis into practice.

2035—I return to tenure track full professor full time.

2040—I retire at age 70, move to live full time at the beach, and visit the ocean every day.

Conclusion

In late May 2020, a colleague and informal mentor, Art Bochner, brought to my attention an Atlantic Monthly essay that poignantly captured what many of us felt but could not yet articulate about the effects of the pandemic:

> A pandemic, if you are fortunate enough not to be hospitalized or killed by it, wears you down by other, more subtle measures. It administers, by a thousand cuts, a kind of spiritual and psychological incapacitation. It sends you away on a malevolent holiday, open-ended, enough to make you crave the rhythms and ardors of labor. By stripping you of the most basic knowledge that the world will remain predictable, stable in the morning, it makes you all too aware of just how good you once had it—and that no such assurance was ever promised to you in the first place. // It is our great strength as well as our terrible weakness to live most fully in the past and in the future. But pestilences rob us of the sanctuary of both of these states, forcing us into the totalizing uncertainty and silence of the present. A pandemic, then, is an opportunity, at last, to see ourselves and our condition more clearly. If there is one, this is the virus's silver lining. (Chatterton Williams, 2020, n.p.)

One of the important truths that Williams reveals in this passage is how much most of us live in the past and future, rather than the present. And how being thrust into the present is such an uncomfortable place. We must grieve all the things that we accomplished in the past that were going to set us up for a present that never came to fruition. And we must be with ourselves exactly as we *are* and exactly as we are *not* right now. But, as Art posted on Facebook when reflecting on this article:

> The upside of this pandemic is the chance it provides to see ourselves, our condition, and the people, ideas, and things we love, more clearly. If this is, indeed, "the silver lining of coronavirus," we must seize the opportunity. Don't you think? Instead of imagining what you will do as soon as Covid-19 is gone—perhaps magical thinking—can you allow yourself to settle in and consider living "with" Covid-19 now and forever. Imagine you were born into a world of Covid-19 and couldn't imagine living in any other world. What then?

So, in the light of reflecting on these two passages this story ends. It ends with someone discovering how upset leads us to our superhighway "kee kee corners." And how our self-soothing devices create a range of both intended and unintended effects on ourselves and others I find that awareness offers looseness and choice.

> Rather than my working gripping me, I can have more say over and with work.
> And choose play. And whimsy. And flourishing.
> And forge a new path.
> And thank the potholes and bumps along the way.
> After all, there's an ocean by my side.

References

Barthes, Roland, & Duisit, Lionel. (1975). An introduction to the structural analysis of narrative. *New Literary History, 6*(2), 237–272. https://doi.org/10.2307/468419

Brown, Brené. (2015). *Daring greatly: How the courage to be vulnerable transforms the way we live, love, parent, and lead*. Penguin.

Buzzanell, Patrice M. (2010). Resilience: Talking, resisting, and imagining new normalcies into being. *Journal of Communication, 60*(1), 1–14. https://doi.org/10.1111/j.1460-2466.2009.01469.x

Chatterton Williams, Thomas. (2020, May 31). A malevolent holiday. *Harper's Magazine*. Retrieved at https://harpers.org/archive/2020/06/a-malevolent-holiday/ 6-2-2020.

Ellis, Carolyn. (1991). Sociological introspection and emotional experience. *Symbolic Interaction, 14*(1), 23–50. https://doi.org/10.1525/si.1991.14.1.23

Franzosi, Roberto. (1998). Narrative analysis—Or why (and how) sociologists should be interested in narrative. *Annual Review of Sociology, 24*(1), 517–554. https://doi.org/10.1146/annurev.soc.24.1.517

Friedman, Stewart D., & Lobel, Sharon. (2000). The happy workaholic: A role model for employees. *Academy of Management Executive, 17*, 87–98. https://doi.org/10.5465/ame.2003.10954764

House, James S. (1981). *Work stress and social support*. Addison-Wesley.

Huffman, Timothy P. (2017). Compassionate communication, embodied aboutness, and homeless young adults. *Western Journal of Communication, 81*(2), 149–167. https://doi.org/10.1080/10570314.2016.1239272

Kouzes, James, & Posner, Barry. (2012). *The leadership challenge: How to make extraordinary things happen in organizations* (5th ed.). Jossey-Bass.

Kübler-Ross, E., & Kessler, D. (2005). *On grief and grieving: Finding the meaning of grief through the five stages of loss*. Simon and Schuster.

Lopez, Cary, & Tracy, Sarah J. (2020). Anchoring the big tent: How organizational autoethnography exemplifies and stretches notions of qualitative quality. In A. F. Herrmann (Ed.), *The Routledge international handbook of organizational autoethnography* (pp. 383–398). Routledge.

Lorde, Audre. (1988). *A burst of light*. Ixia Press.

Maslach, Christina, Schaufeli, Wilmar B., & Leiter, Michael P. (2001). Job Burnout. *Annual Review of Psychology, 52*, 397–422. https://doi.org/10.1146/annurev.psych.52.1.397

Miller, Katherine I. (2007). Compassionate communication in the workplace: Exploring processes of noticing, connecting, and responding. *Journal of Applied Communication Research, 35*(3), 223–245. https://doi.org/10.1080/00909880701434208

Ray, Eileen B., & Miller, Katherine I. (1991). The influence of communication structure and social support on job stress and burnout. *Management Communication Quarterly, 4*(4), 506–527. https://doi.org/10.1177/0893318991004004005

Sarikaya, Alper, & Gleicher, Michael. (2017). Scatterplots: Tasks, data, and designs. *IEEE Transactions on Visualization and Computer Graphics, 24*(1), 402–412. https://doi.org/10.1109/TVCG.2017.2744184

Stanley, B. Liahnna, Zanin, Alaina, Avalos, Brianna L., Tracy, Sarah J., & Town, Sophia. (2021). Collective emotion during collective trauma: A metaphor analysis of the COVID-19 global pandemic. *Qualitative Health Research, 31*, 1890–1903. https://doi.org/10.1177/10497323211011589

Tietsort, Cristopher J. (2021). *Uncertainty, expressed suffering, and cultivating compassion at work: An exploration of employee's experiences of workplace compassion and compassionate leadership* [Unpublished doctoral dissertation]. Arizona State University.

Tracy, Sarah J. (2010). Qualitative quality: Eight "big-tent" criteria for excellent qualitative research. *Qualitative Inquiry, 16*, 837–851. https://doi.org/10.1177/1077800410383121

Tracy, Sarah J. (2016). Buds bloom in a second spring: Storying the male voices project. *Qualitative Inquiry, 22*, 17–24. https://doi.org/10.1177/1077800415603397

Tracy, Sarah J. (2017). Burnout in organizational communication. In C. Scott & L. Lewis (Eds.), *The international encyclopedia of organizational communication* (pp. 166–174). Wiley-Blackwell.

Tracy, Sarah J., & Huffman, Timothy P. (2017). Compassion in the face of terror: A case study of recognizing suffering, co-creating hope, and developing trust in a would-be school shooting. *Communication Monographs, 84*, 30–53. https://doi.org/10.1080/03637751.2016.1218642

Tracy, Sarah J., & Redden, Shawna M. (2019). Emotion and relationships in the workplace. In *Movements in organizational communication research* (pp. 155–174). Routledge.

Wainer, Howard, & Lysen, Shaun. (2009). That's funny… A window on data can be a window on discovery. *American Scientist, 97*(4), 272–276.

Way, Deborah, & Tracy, Sarah J. (2012). Conceptualizing compassion as recognizing, relating and (re) acting: A qualitative study of compassionate communication at hospice. *Communication Monographs, 79*(3), 292–315. https://doi.org/10.1080/03637751.2012.697630

Wittgenstein, Ludwig. (1980). *Remarks on the philosophy of psychology*, Vols. 1 and 2. Blackwell.

Zanin, Alaina C., Avalos, Brianna L., Town, Sophia, Tracy, Sarah J., & Stanley, B. Liahnna. (Online First, 2021). Discursive, communal, and individual coping strategies: How US adults co-constructed coping during preliminary COVID-19 stressors. *Health Communication*. https://doi.org/10.1080/10410236.2021.2010347

CHAPTER 12

Improvisation in Public Diplomacy During the COVID-19 Pandemic

Susan Szmania

Thursday, March 12, 2020, marked the end of my week at the Public Affairs office in the U.S. Embassy in Jordan. To set the scene, it had been a busy time for me, and I was looking forward to a long-planned celebratory retirement luncheon for a Jordanian colleague. She had been a trusted partner since I arrived in Jordan in the summer 2018 for a four-year tour of duty as a Public Diplomacy Officer, and she helped me get acquainted with Jordanian culture and meet professional contacts. The previous week, we concluded a two-day conference for three hundred government, military and civil society contacts. The event represented months of work, setting up speakers, finalizing topics and making logistical preparations. Although one American speaker canceled his travel to Amman due to COVID-19 travel

Disclaimer: The views and opinions expressed in this chapter are those of the author and do not necessarily reflect the official policy or position of any agency of the U.S. government.

S. Szmania (✉)
Independent Scholar, Dulles, VA, USA

L. D. Browning et al. (eds.), *Organizational Communication and Technology in the Time of Coronavirus*,
https://doi.org/10.1007/978-3-030-94814-6_12

warnings, the conference ran as planned for the majority of Jordanian audience that attended.

Back in the office after the conference, I spent the early part of the week typing up an official report about the event. I drafted the performance evaluation for my retiring colleague, and I sorted through other issues that had piled up while my attention was focused on the conference. An American colleague forwarded Ramadan menus from a local hotel for April celebrations, when the Embassy traditionally hosted parties for Jordanian contacts. We promised to review options later in the week, planning ahead for what is normally a busy social season in the Muslim world. I offered feedback on the written testimony of our American Ambassador-designate, awaiting U.S. Senate confirmation. I made a request for an official car to take me to Irbid, a city in northern Jordan, to visit a grant recipient conducting a women's violence prevention training program. I scheduled a meeting with a university researcher to discuss concerns about another funded project's progress. I emailed a contact about a youth activity facing some challenges, and I received two new grant proposals, which I would need to review and make a recommendation on funding.

Apart from these more routine aspects of my job, there were small indications of impending disruptions caused by the COVID-19 cases. On March 10, I sent a message to a government contractor in Boston who was planning to come to Jordan. I forwarded official Embassy guidance explaining that only essential travel would be permitted in Jordan due to COVID and suggested that he plan his trip later. Another American researcher, traveling to Jordan to conduct a research project on refugees, cancelled her trip because of new international travel warnings in the United States. On March 11, I exchanged emails with a State Department colleague proposing that a mid-April technical visit be rescheduled in June when I expected "things were more certain." That same morning, I received notification about an afternoon virtual Town Hall for Embassy employees to provide updates on COVID-19 along with the unusual instructions that the event, according to the email invitation, would "only be streamed via a website, and not a physical meeting." Usually, employee Town Hall meetings at the Embassy took place in the newly remodeled cafeteria with folding chairs arranged to accommodate at least one hundred employees. This was perhaps the first sign the "business-as-usual" attitude at the Embassy was changing.

On the morning of March 12, I heard rumors from various WhatsApp groups, the preferred means of informal communication in Jordan, that the government would make an official country-wide lockdown announcement to slow the spread of COVID-19. When I arrived at work, the first emails I received came from my boss, instructing Public Affairs staff to take online training to become "telework eligible." My job, up until that point, had been specifically designated as "not eligible for telework" by the U.S. Department of State. My boss followed up with instructions to print out email contacts in hard copy in case we could not access them from our computers at home. She then requested that staff send her official "telework training certification" and provided guidance for how we could log on to our government network from our home computers. She also sent a form to fill out entitled, "Safety Checklist for Teleworkers" with helpful recommendations such as ensuring a home workstation is set up with an adjustable chair, preferably with wheels and sturdy legs, or that a "multi-use" fire extinguisher is readily available. Additional guidance from the Embassy came in the early afternoon with instructions on how to manage potential symptoms from COVID-19 as well as guidance on how to check out an official government laptop to work from home.

Amid the flurry of information that day, our office of about thirty people collectively decided to postpone the retirement party for our colleague. Faced with a mountain of technical requirements to complete, we scrambled to take the required online trainings, fill out paperwork and determine what other needs we might have for working from our houses. If that was not enough, the weather worsened. I recall looking out my bullet-proof office window from inside the Embassy as a dust storm swept through the streets, bending the palm trees and blurring visibility. Looking around the open-concept office where we all furiously worked, I sensed a new urgency to finish up work and go home. Before I left work that day, more cancellation email messages followed: the university meeting with researchers, the discussion on the youth program and the trip to the city of Irbid, about two hours north of Amman. As my husband and I walked home from work that night, the dust storm had passed, and it was dark. We stopped at an Indian restaurant nearby the Embassy, our last dinner inside a restaurant until summer. We did not wear face masks or worry about the other tables of diners around us. We talked about a few days or maybe weeks of disruption. At the time, Jordan had not reported any COVID-19 cases. We had no idea how much life would change in the coming days and weeks.

Learning to Communicate as a Diplomat

When I completed my doctoral dissertation in Communication Studies in 2004, I did not envision that my career would be in government. After graduation, I accepted a tenure track position in a Communication Department in a large state university. As an assistant professor, I taught courses in peace studies, conflict communication and discourse analysis. I continued my doctoral research on mediation in the prison system, and I participated in the usual junior faculty member departmental service requirements. I published a few academic articles, carefully keeping track of journal rankings to fulfill tenure, but I never considered transitioning in what has become known as an "alternative academic career" track (Nowviskie, 2010, para 1). Instead, my shift to government work occurred because of life circumstances: marriage to a diplomat meant I needed move overseas.

To become an American Foreign Service Officer who serves as a diplomat overseas, prospective diplomats normally take a written test and submit a writing sample. Successful applicants take an oral assessment, followed by a battery of medical and security clearances. Finally, the new diplomat travels to Washington, D.C. for several weeks of training and then receives their first assignment, eventually moving abroad. My husband completed this process while I continued to teach and conduct research in the university. I traveled occasionally to visit him in Mexico, where he was posted for his first assignment, and he would come to visit me. The arrangement worked well until he received a job in Sweden as his second assignment.

With this news, I realized that commuting between the United States and Sweden would not be as easy as commuting to Mexico. I remember discussing whether I could continue to teach online at my university while living in Sweden. I researched the cost of traveling back and forth to America a few times a year. I worked on a pitch to the faculty to consider the arrangement; however, they ultimately turned down my request, citing the need for assistant professors to be physically present on campus in order to fulfill their expected duties. It became clear that I would need to eventually quit my tenure track position and plan for a permanent relocation. To ease the transition, I negotiated a year of teaching online as an adjunct and also applied for a small research grant to work on a research project with refugees. Once I arrived in Sweden, I immersed myself in the new project and online teaching, but a few months later, a non-career job opened up at the U.S. Embassy in Stockholm. After much consideration, I accepted the offer to become a political analyst in the government and quit my teaching position at the university.

The U.S. Department of State is a particularly hierarchical organization, where positions are based on rank, experience and connections. Inside the organizational culture, embassies function like satellite offices to a central headquarter location, and each one has its own unique organizational culture based on organizational expectations as well as host-country norms. Navigating these dynamics is challenging under normal circumstances. In many ways, my academic communication training in conversational analysis and theories of interpersonal communication prepared me to manage the change from an intellectual standpoint. Professionally, I had worked my way up into a faculty position in academia. At the Embassy in Stockholm, I fell to the bottom of the hierarchy and started over. On practical level, I faced an entirely foreign work environment that required wholesale changes in how I acted.

From the first day on the job, my academic title was dropped. No one asked about my personal research interests or what papers I was working on, a question I had been accustomed to answering as an assistant professor. My first task in the Embassy was to edit a daily news summary translated from Swedish into English. I corrected the document for grammar and clarity, ensuring that the report highlighted key information in bold face type or underlined essential issues that might be consequential for foreign policy decisions. My new boss, the Political Counselor, explained that "busy Washington readers" did not have time to sift through deep analysis or discussion. They only wanted to see the "bottom line up front," a refrain that government workers use to ensure the most important information is made clear at the beginning of a paper, not at the end.

I learned the expected style guide for government writing, not from an academic manual with written rules and style conventions, but by sitting side-by-side my boss as he edited my writing using a pencil. I became accustomed to the expectations of "getting clearance" on written documents, requiring a supervisor's review of written materials as well as approval signatures from other units across the Embassy with a stake in the issue. At meetings, I sat on the "back bench," which meant situating myself on the periphery of a room and not at the main conference table. I learned to provide quick briefings for the Ambassador, succinctly answering questions about an event or planned activity often while driving in an armored vehicle. I attended official meetings, taking official notes while my boss conducted business. I also honed the art of "backchanneling" information, sharing preliminary but potentially contentious information with colleagues over the phone or in preparatory meetings, so that a final decision could be made more quickly in a formal meeting.

Through these communicative practices, junior diplomats learn State Department communication expectations and establish what is known as their "corridor reputation," or an individual's assessment "based on the views of peers and Bureau's leadership" (United States Senate Committee on Foreign Relations, 2020, 45). While this assessment includes a consideration of technical skill, it is also an evaluation of how State Department employees navigate their interpersonal relationships inside and outside the organization. The phrase itself is derived from the physical architecture of the headquarters—the corridor refers to the long and complex maze of hallways that snake through the State Department's Washington, D.C. office building. Establishing one's "corridor reputation" is the foundation for career advancement within the State Department.

Improvisation in the Workspace

While there are clear checklists for career diplomats to manage their own professional advancement and build their "corridor reputation," my role as a non-career professional came with no guidebook. Coming from the academic field where I had been so focused on advancement toward tenure, it was jarring to find myself at a loss for making sense of the organizational routines I confronted. Like a well-trained academic, I recall logging into the State Department's online library to look up articles about diplomacy and the work for diplomats. I also returned to some of the readings that had most impacted me during my graduate studies. Above all, Bateson's (1993) essay, "Joint performance across cultures: Improvisation in a Persian garden," made a deep impression on me when I read it for the first time in a graduate seminar on interaction analysis. In the essay, the author, an American anthropologist, describes her experience of attending a religious ceremony involving the sacrifice of a sheep in Tehran, Iran. In this new and unfamiliar situation, Bateson discusses how she tries to explain the events to her young daughter, taking on the roles of "a learner, as an observer, [and] as an outsider" (p. 115). I re-read this article during the early days of my own professional transition into a federal bureaucracy and applied the model as I made sense of my place in the new organization. As a learner and communication scholar, I took on tasks of a typical junior diplomat: writing daily reports, drafting official speeches, and preparing an Ambassador's briefing book. As an observer and ethnographer, I came to enjoy frequent assignments as a notetaker during official meetings. Recognizing my role as an outsider also brought much-needed perspective, giving me freedom to put distance between and expected organizational demands. Now, after more than a decade of work at the State Department, I still view myself as an outsider and non-career professional.

Overtime, Bateson's (1993) essay has allowed me to continuously examine my non-traditional career and allowed me "turn" my story "at different angles" to make sense of the seemingly disparate work (p. 113). A key element of the Bateson essay centers on the metaphor of improvisation as a way of "combining skills that are not given in existing models" to make sense of her experience in the Persian garden and other aspects of her personal and professional life (Bateson, 1993, p. 120). While I am certain that Bateson did not think to extend her ideas to my own situation—an academic turned non-career diplomat—I have found that her reflection on improvisation stretches and adapts to my own personal experiences, "putting together different elements, [and] dealing with the unknown in a way which sustains performance and connects it with other systems of meaning" (Bateson, 1993, p. 120). This metaphor has helped me navigate a career trajectory that has taken unexpected turns while, at the same time, grounding and unifying this work in my training as a communication scholar.

Public Diplomacy Through Cultural Diplomacy

My job at the U.S. Embassy is a Public Diplomacy Officer. There is a lot to be said about what public diplomacy is, the unique history of public diplomacy in foreign policy, and more specifically, American public diplomacy. Not surprisingly, much of that discussion deals with the official, state-level engagements between high-ranking government officials and the ways that public diplomacy has been used to achieve foreign policy goals. While this history and analysis is informative for students of international affairs and an area where Communication Studies scholars have made important theoretical contributions (e.g., Belanger & Szmania, 2018), my focus for this chapter will be on the working-level actions that Public Diplomacy Officers do in their daily activities, usually behind the scenes from official representation. By focusing on these everyday actions, which are rarely documented, I describe how improvisation altered the organizational norms in fundamental ways.

To situate my work, it is important to start with the structure of a typical American Embassy abroad. Large or small, American Embassies are staffed by an Ambassador who oversees a range of diplomatic activities in a foreign country. Foreign Service Officers, assigned to an Embassy or Consulate for a few years, rotate while local workers typically stay at Embassies in their jobs for many years. The work at an Embassy ranges from technical jobs, like adjudicating visas for travelers or managing housing for diplomats in the local country, to the more analytical jobs of political or economic officers who report on the political and economic climate of the country. Additionally, Public Diplomacy Officers administer media engagement and cultural affairs programming, which can range from hosting visiting performers and artists to sharing American culture with foreign audiences or through support for teaching English programs. In this regard, cultural diplomacy is described by Joseph Nye as "soft power" or the ability "to build partnerships, advance agendas, and work in the international space" (Cull, 2019, p. 16). Cultural diplomacy activities may also involve capacity building and dialogue training, which is the kind of work I do in Jordan.

I am a Community Engagement Officer, a constructed title for my non-career position which normally involves arranging face-to-face meetings with officials, leaders and young activists to learn about community issues and concerns to better understand local context and issues. I visit local organizations, attend official gatherings at government agencies and occasionally participate in conferences. In some cases, these engagements lead to projects and activities administered through government-sponsored grant or exchange programs to advance policy goals such as boosting economic opportunity or supporting civil society development. Strikingly, most of this work relies on in-person engagement. After all, the very reason that diplomats are stationed abroad is to engage in these direct encounters. Public diplomacy is by its very nature a "communication-centric" practice (Wang, 2020). Yet, almost overnight, the pandemic threw these fundamental features of cultural diplomacy practice into disarray.

Cultural Diplomacy During Lockdown

On March 19, the Jordanian government imposed a state of emergency in the Kingdom due to the COVID-19 pandemic (Mimoune, 2020). All international borders closed, workplaces shut down, group gatherings of more than ten were limited, and citizens could not leave their homes (Human Rights Watch, 2020). On March 21, the Jordanian military imposed a nationwide curfew (Gavlak, 2020). Though the strict do-not-leave-home orders lasted only a few days, the government extended a nationwide curfew, allowing movement only between the hours of 10 am and 6 pm, a defense order which lasted for over a month.

During these first few weeks of lockdown, my Embassy work ground to a halt, and my focus turned inwards to the immediate needs of my own family. My husband and I followed local news announcements and government directives so that we could know when stores would be open to buy food. We helped our daughter with online first grade and tried to keep our energetic toddler occupied in the house. We were fortunate to be able to stock our pantry with non-perishable milk, pasta and beans even though it took several days to order. In spite of these restrictions, we tried to make a routine for our daughters. I posted activity lists on the kitchen door during lockdown days to break up the monotony of being cooped inside, hoping to hide the fact that we would not be going outside to the park or piano lessons. Like Bateson (1993) in the Persian garden, I found myself trying to objectively explain to my daughters why air raid sirens blared each night and why they needed to be inside the apartment immediately after they heard the alarm. I tried to reassure them about safety when they saw armed police on the sidewalk outside our apartment building. "They are here to make sure we follow the rules," I told them, omitting the fact that we could be fined or jailed for not adhering to the lockdown measures. Our world narrowed to the confines of our apartment, which thankfully provided us safety unlike so many others who were less fortunate during the outbreak of the pandemic.

Locked inside, I logged on to my government work account from my personal computer, something I had never done before. As an academic, I always found it challenging to set boundaries between work and home life. In my first job at a university, I had a home office where I graded papers or worked on my writing late into the night. As a junior tenure track faculty member, I recall feeling a sense that I always needed to work, keeping research materials in my bedroom to review or stacking books around the house to stay current with the new research in my field. In government, I did not have home computer. For security reasons, I rarely brought home work to do at night. Aside from occasionally checking my email from my work phone, I did not have a designated office space or papers at home, and my bosses had no expectation that I would have the ability to log in and do government work from my house. Yet, in mid-March 2020 these long-held institutional expectations changed.

My immediate professional task focused on trying to figure out how the civil society groups I worked with would be impacted by the government lockdown. Their work, funded through U.S. government grants, depended on in-person engagement, whether it involved meetings, trainings, events or activities. Although it took a few days to get a better sense of the lockdown parameters and its impact on work in Jordan, headquarters colleagues sent general guidance to Embassies to gather information about how our government-sponsored programs were impacted by the severe restrictions and government directive. The first emails I sent after logging into my office account from my home computer were to local program partners. I inquired if previously planned travel might be affected, what events had to be cancelled and what effects these cancellations might have. Headquarters also asked us to gauge the financial impact of these measures on the programs' intended goals and objectives. As I compiled a list of the responses to send back, I remember thinking about how much remained unknown and uncertain. How long did we expect the delay to last? Would in-person meetings be able to take place in a few weeks or a few months? Should large meetings be cancelled or postponed? Could money be spent on masks, gloves and thermometers? Was travel permitted?

Looking back over March and April 2020, my work calendar chronicles few activities. Whereas in previous months I scheduled nearly forty meetings with contacts all over Jordan, these early pandemic calendar entries are noticeably brief, only listing a name and a cell phone number to call. I usually made the phone calls while sitting in my living room, looking out at our apartment's walled garden, a typical Middle Eastern garden with cypress, cedar and palm trees, but shielded from the "not so hospitable" world around (Bateson, 1993, p. 114).

Improvised Public Diplomacy Practices

Of these new routines developed by diplomats around the world, foreign policy scholar Pierre Vimont (2020) observes,

> Mostly confined at home, without the technical support of security networks for confidential conversations, diplomats had their workspace limited to virtual conferences and webinars. They had to adapt and learn to live within the constraints of this new reality. (The improvised diplomatic practices in days of lockdown, para 1)

Without a doubt, the State Department's transition from a formal brick-and-mortar office culture to a work-from-home environment represents a massive shift in the way American diplomats posted abroad conduct business. Before the pandemic, very few meetings occurred online, directly reflecting the value that diplomats place on the security of face-to-face meetings. As the impact of the pandemic caused international shut-downs and prevented in-person meetings, diplomats adjusted but also underwent a transformation in the practice of their profession, both internally and externally.

Like all other organizations faced with the problem, the State Department worked quickly to adopt new technology to support remote working. Part of this evolution involved making available tools that diplomats had not been approved prior to the pandemic. In addition to the enormous task of identifying these new technologies and securing them for official-use, the organization also underwent a massive shift in the expectations of daily operations. In the pre-COVID context, diplomats placed great importance on planning and preparing the physical set-up of meetings. They carefully devised seating arrangements to dictate speaking roles for senior officials while more junior members of the team sat on the sidelines. In a virtual setting, these visual cues disappeared and new issues arose. For example, physical meetings rooms often have limited space for attendees. Virtual meetings offer potentially limitless space for participants, including those who are not co-located in the same Embassy. This new ability to bring together employees from around the world created a new opportunity for information sharing.

For the most part, the pandemic's impact on the use of technology in diplomacy has ushered in new openness and inclusiveness to the profession. This is not just seen in internal staff interactions but also through official external engagement with host-country partners. Long before the pandemic, public diplomacy officers had already begun to experiment with the "digitalization of diplomacy" (Manor, 2017, p. 4). This typically occurred through one-off events or webinars. However, the COVID-19 pandemic hastened the acceptance of using technology not just to support routine institutional communication but also to engage directly with foreign audiences. In my own public-facing work with civil society organizations, some of this work came naturally. One grant implementer quickly adopted an online learning platform to deliver a community training on media literacy. Originally the project involved several weeks of in-person training for over two hundred participants with requisite conference rentals, transportation for participants, overnight costs for their travel, and budget lines dedicated to food and hospitality. With large meetings prohibited, many of these costs were reallocated to covering the internet costs of participants' online participation from their homes. For projects that involve knowledge transfer and the potential to reach larger audiences in remote geographic area, this online adaptation proved successful.

Conversely, a more challenging online adaptation has been how to organize a project's official closing ceremony. Typically, high-level leaders like a government minister or an ambassador speak to a seated audience to congratulate participants on their achievements. Press may attend formal ceremonies in which participants receive official certificates. Now, in lieu of bringing several hundred people together in a room, these events turn into a virtual "talking heads" platform and much of the individual recognition of achievement is lost. Certainly, there are options for designing virtual events that allow for participant recognition, but at the moment, meaningful models for these celebratory virtual events are yet to be designe.

In managing issues like event planning or meeting, I have learned to consider the balance of how to organize in new ways, relying on improvisation to guide my decision making. While virtual meetings make sense for introductions or knowledge acquisition, face-to-face meetings are better suited for finalizing plans or discussing more sensitive matters. Recently, I met with a contact for coffee at an outdoor café. In this setting, we could discuss a few issues that related to political dynamics while at the same conduct business in a mostly private environment. These kinds of decisions about how, when and where to host meetings are part of the normal diplomatic work that even the most junior officers learn to manage. Taking COVID-safety measures into account adds another layer to the preparation work before arranging meetings and other activities. By drawing on familiar routines but adding in some extra considerations, diplomatic practice expands to address the current pandemic conditions.

Wang (2020) recognizes that there is a good deal of diplomatic re-skilling that must done to meet this new reality. While improvisational practices have been helpful as the COVID-19 crisis has unfolded, diplomats need to expand their professional communication skills to manage the multidimensional diplomatic environment of the future. Public diplomacy will no longer consist of a single physical event—an art show or musical event—with some traditional or social media coverage to highlight the cultural significance. Instead, events will routinely have both digital and physical components that can be recycled on different platforms and in different formats over the course of days or months. Official meetings may be held online, which requires virtual leadership skills to design agendas, arrange speaking turns and share notes efficiently. Public diplomacy officers will also need to apply more sophisticated evaluation tools to assess the impact of these activities. It is no longer sufficient to simply count the number of attendees who came to an activity or administer pre- and post-test assessments to determine learning after an in-person training.

There will also need to be a reimagining of public diplomacy audiences beyond geographic borders. At most U.S. Embassies, public diplomacy work typically engages citizens living in one country. With the digitization of public diplomacy, this geographic boundary is greatly expanded. There is no doubt that diplomats will continue to focus on content that primarily is targeting a specific audience, but there are new opportunities for targeting secondary and tertiary digital audiences like diaspora communities, regional audiences that may share the same language and possibly even individuals interested in the topic of a specific program. Expanding the potential universe of how public diplomacy officers engage with global audiences offers exciting new opportunities for cultural exchange and understanding at a much greater scale than before the pandemic.

Despite these opportunities, there are important limitations that remain, chiefly regarding security. In diplomacy, particularly for high-level engagement, some conversations require security and confidentiality. In these cases, hosting meetings in open-air cafes or on unsecured virtual platforms is not permitted. More security and discretion is needed. While the pandemic has given diplomats more flexibility to work from non-secure locations, there remains a need for better options to engage with foreign counterparts and other colleagues through secure communication channels that are easily accessible outside of the Embassy compound. When these systems are developed, it will be important to review the physical architecture of Embassies, which function as the centerpiece of most diplomatic missions abroad. These structures are notorious for being highly secure buildings designed to be protected from outside attacks

(Adams, 2020). As the pandemic has forced many employees to work from home, these buildings stood nearly empty on the inside, working with limited or rotating staff. In newer buildings, such as the U.S. Embassy in Amman, the open-office floor plans, large cafeterias and bullet-proof windows pose significant challenges for maintaining health and safety protocols. When pandemic health concerns subside, this space might be repurposed in new ways or to meet the expectations of a changed work environment.

Improvisation and Resilience in Uncertainty

The pandemic has upended many assumptions about the fundamental practices of public diplomacy. Yet, as I have described in this chapter, much of this outward-facing work has continued through creative approaches. Looking forward, I hope that the U.S. State Department will institutionalize the improvisational learning that has occurred since early 2020. This might be done by sharing good practices internally, rewarding innovative digital programming efforts and ensuring that diplomatic training includes hands-on technological skill-building opportunities. When health and safety conditions permit, it is likely that some traditional diplomatic rituals will return; there are simply no substitutes for official State dinners, international exchanges or cultural engagement events like art exhibits or concerts. These soft-power tools are essential to American diplomacy. However, as I have shared here, the improvised digital diplomatic practices that have emerged during the pandemic deserve attention

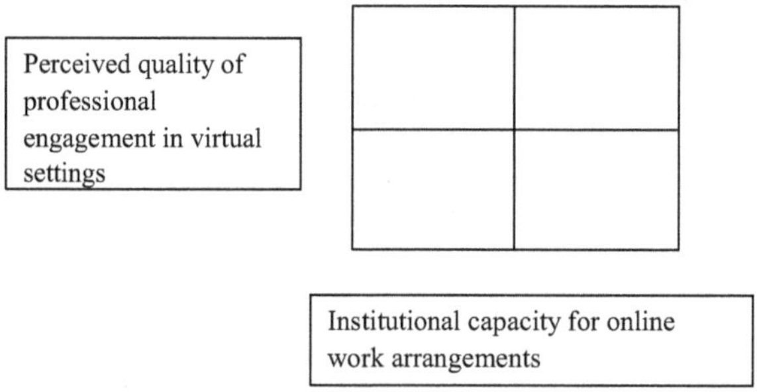

Fig. 12.1 Acceptance of telework

and review. Telling these stories will advance the theory and practice of diplomacy to meet the world of the future.

More profoundly, the institutions where I have worked have undergone a dramatic shift in their acceptance of telework (Fig. 12.1). Early in my career, even when there was growing use and acceptance of online teaching in academia, I could not continue to work remotely as a full-time tenure track faculty member. This reality meant that I forged another career path, albeit in an organization that required work to be done in-person at Embassies abroad. Both institutions placed a high value in direct face-to-face engagement, in part because of the sense of security that physical settings provide and the belief that virtual engagement would somehow degrade the quality of the work provided. The pandemic has shown that an institution's ability to allow some work online—both internally and externally—provides employees with new tools to experiment and improvise with new approaches and organizational patterns to complete work requirements. In a time of crisis, this flexibility has brought expanded opportunity and has not negatively impacted work relationships in most cases. While it will be nice to return to the office when conditions permit, I assume that many jobs at the Embassy and in other professions that have resisted the shift to virtual work will remain at least partially "telework eligible" in recognition of this fact.

Lately, I have been reflecting on how Bateson's (1993) description of improvisation seems somewhat incomplete in the prolonged crisis we face. Before proposing improvisation as a way of pulling together different roles in her life and learning to adapt to unfamiliar settings, Bateson considers another common metaphor of juggling the different roles we play in life, an act which she views as anxiety-producing. In the months since the pandemic started, I have found that the constant and continual need for improvisation feels tiring. There are seemingly endless issues that need to be addressed, from managing personal family life and work obligations, often at home. The need to improvise is never-ending. An alternative that has come to mind is resilience, which certainly is an over-used concept in academic literature, but it offers a lens for deeper scholarly investigation of good practices for integrating personal and professional skills to manage emergencies like the COVID-19 global pandemic.

In the coming year, my family and I will reach the end of our four-year assignment in Jordan. We will need to make myriad decisions about jobs, housing and family life. There is a good deal of uncertainty and insecurity ahead. If nothing else, the pandemic has made clear that there is an impermanence to all the routines and rituals of our daily lives. As we wait, I continue to turn and re-examine the improvisational lessons I discovered in the Persian garden: learning, observing and reflecting.

Professional Vista

May 2004	Graduate with Ph.D. in Communication Studies from the University of Texas at Austin
August 2004	Start tenure track assistant professor position at the University of Wisconsin, Milwaukee
May 2008	Quit tenure track position, move to Sweden, conduct research about refugees seeking asylum and teach online adjunct courses
June 2009	Take U.S. State Department job in Sweden as a political analyst and develop programs to counter violent extremism among diaspora groups
November 2011	Take U.S. State Department job in Spain as a political analyst and serve as the staff aide to the U.S. Ambassador to Spain and Andorra
February 2015	Take a research position at the University of Maryland's National Consortium for the Study of Terrorism and Responses to Terrorism to create terrorism prevention training for law enforcement
September 2015	Take an academic detail position with U.S. Department of Homeland Security
April 2016	Appointed to the interagency Task Force for Countering Violent Extremism to draft policy and oversee federal programs
September 2018	Take U.S. State Department job in Jordan as a Community Engagement Officer
June 2022	Depart Jordan. Plans to be determined.

References

Adams, Eric. (2020, January 3). How the US prepares its embassies for potential attacks. *Wired*. https://www.wired.com/story/how-us-prepares-embassies-potential-attacks/

Bateson, Mary Catherine. (1993). Joint performance across cultures: Improvisation in a Persian garden. *Text and Performance Quarterly, 13*(2), 113–121. https://doi.org/10.1080/10462939309366037

Belanger, Patrick, & Szmania, Susan. (2018). The paradox of source credibility in Canadian and U.S. domestic counterterrorism communications. *International Journal of Communication, 12*, 1459–1480. http://ijoc.org/index.php/ijoc/article/view/5638

Cull, Nicholas J. (2019). *Public diplomacy: Foundations for global engagement in the digital age*. Polity.

Gavlak, Dale. (2020, April 7). Covid-19 diaries: Strict curfew in Jordan holding down infections. *Voice of America News*. https://www.voanews.com/science-health/coronavirus-outbreak/covid-19-diaries-strict-curfew-jordan-holding-down-infections

Human Rights Watch. (2020, October 28). Jordan: State of emergency declared. *Human Rights Watch*. https://www.hrw.org/news/2020/03/20/jordan-state-emergency-declared

Manor, Ilan. (2017, August). *The digitalization of diplomacy: Toward clarification of a fractured terminology*. https://digdipblog.files.wordpress.com/2017/08/the-digitalization-of-diplomacy-working-paper-number-1.pdf

Mimoune, Nejla Ben. (2020, December 16). Policy and institutional responses to COVID-19 in the Middle East and North Africa: Jordan. *Brookings*. https://www.brookings.edu/research/policy-and-institutional-responses-to-covid-19-in-the-middle-east-and-north-africa-jordan/

Nowviskie, Bethany. (2010, January 10). #Alt-Ac: Alternate academic careers for humanities scholars. *Bethany Nowviskie*. http://nowviskie.org/2010/alt-ac/

United States Senate, Committee on Foreign Relations. (2020, July). *Diplomacy in crisis: The Trump administration's decimation of the State Department*. https://www.foreign.senate.gov/imo/media/doc/Diplomacy%20in%20Crisis%20%2D%2D%20SFRC%20Democratic%20Staff%20R

Vimont, Pierre. (2020, September 2). Diplomacy during the quarantine: An opportunity for more agile craftsmanship. *Carnegie Europe*. https://carnegieeurope.eu/2020/09/02/diplomacy-during-quarantine-opportunity-for-more-agile-craftsmanship-pub-82559

Wang, Jian. (2020, July). Rethinking public diplomacy for a post-pandemic world. *The Foreign Service Journal*. https://www.afsa.org/rethinking-public-diplomacy-post-pandemic-world

SECTION IV

Techno-Ethnography: Using Social Science Methods to Study the Virus

CHAPTER 13

Internal Communications During the Pandemic: Challenges and Implications

Martin N. Ndlela and Jens Petter Madsbu

On March 12, 2020, the Norwegian government announced a sweeping national lockdown, described by the prime minister as the "strongest and most intrusive measures" Norway has ever seen in peacetime.[1] As she further warned, the new measures would have huge consequences on personal freedoms, everyday life, and on how society functions. The measures would have major consequences across all facets of Norwegian society, including the higher-education sector. In one stroke, the country was placed on lockdown, with various forms of preventive measures and requirements put in place to restrict the movement of people during this public health emergency. The overarching goal of these measures was to control and slow down the rate of person-to-person infections through

M. N. Ndlela (✉)
Inland School of Business and Social Sciences, Inland Norway University of Applied Sciences, Elverum, Norway
e-mail: martin.ndlela@inn.no

J. P. Madsbu
Inland Norway University of Applied Sciences, Elverum, Norway
e-mail: jens.madsbu@inn.no

L. D. Browning et al. (eds.), *Organizational Communication and Technology in the Time of Coronavirus*,
https://doi.org/10.1007/978-3-030-94814-6_13

isolation, quarantine, and social distancing. The immediate implication of the lockdown measures was that, with the exception of specified essential services, non-essential organizations had to shut down their premises or reduce the number of employees in their premises. For the higher-education sector, this meant closure of campuses, the end of in-person teaching, dispersion of students, and the use of home offices for the staff and faculty. Some of these groups were not dimensioned or even minimally prepared to work from dispersed spaces such as home offices. An important question within the higher-education sector was what to communicate and how to communicate it to each diverse stakeholder—staff, students, faculty, and other service providers. Another question was how to maintain continuity in providing essential services given the limitations on physical interactions.

The lockdown brought physical disruption to the organizational system as a whole, and even upset its existential core. Organizations were suddenly, almost without warning, thrust into a complex environment. Even though the virus had been detected in Wuhan Province in China in December 2019, the lockdown announcement brought the elements of suddenness, surprise, uncertainty, and time compression to organizations (Hermann, 1963; Lerbinger, 1997). The pandemic brought sudden ruptures to the organizations' internal and external environments, thereby generating a wave of uncertainties and/or unknowns. Managers and employees alike got little or no time to integrate the complexities of the new unstable environment.

The crisis created an unprecedented demand for organizations to make decisions (faster than normal) in very uncertain conditions. As Sanders et al. (2020) note, organizations and employees have been forced to transform their operational routines virtually overnight. This rapid transformation of routines required a full redeployment of organizational communication: firstly, to facilitate crisis communication messages from national, regional, or local authorities and what those meant to the sector; and secondly, to facilitate communication from principals, deans, and/or heads of department to the lower levels of the organization and from the lower levels to the upper levels. A considerable amount of communication from the different levels of university management focused on compliance to national guidelines, with measures concerning access to university buildings, hygiene rules, and the need to rapidly shift to online teaching, given that the regulations barred face-to-face teaching. The upward-bound communications focused on individual concerns, including concerns about performing duties in a changed environment. The communications not only focused on how the crisis communication messages from leaders were formulated and received, but also included work-related messages.

The pandemic generated an unprecedented need for information and communication across all strata of the organization, thus emphasizing the importance of internal communications. The importance of communication is captured in Goldhaber's (1993, p. 5) metaphorical descriptions of organizational communication as: "the life blood of the organization," "the glue that binds the organization," "the oil that smooths the organization's functions," and "the thread that ties the system together." Communication is central to organizations which, by nature, operate in unstable environments where they must constantly evaluate how they interact and communicate with their stakeholders, be it internal stakeholders (i.e. employees and management) or external stakeholders (i.e. customers, local communities, media, and other interested parties) (Coombs, 2019; Ndlela, 2019; Stephens et al., 2005). Crises often generate a huge demand for information by the organization's stakeholders, hence heightening the demands for effective communication of critical decisions (van der Meer et al., 2017).

During any crisis, organizational communication is put under stress. The recent pandemic challenged various aspects of organizing work, including organizational communication. This chapter examines the internal communication challenges experienced by universities during the pandemic, as well as how institutions responded to these disruptions and the new dispersed communication environment. What digital transformations did universities make on internal communications, and what are the implications for the future of the workplace.

Digital Transformation

Digital transformation has been shaping organization communication with increasing intensity in the past decade, especially with the growing importance of social media communications. Social media has been a major component of a shifting communications landscape since the mid-1990s and has lately become "ingrained in our culture and in the ways that people look to communicate with the organizations that matter to them in their lives" (Doorley & Garcia, 2010, p. 115). Social media started as an online platform for social networking, content creation, and microblogging. In its earliest stages, it did not attract the attention of corporate users, as it was perceived as just a social networking platform for use by individuals in their private capacities. But as technology evolved, so did the functions and purposes of social media. While the medium retains the social media name, the concept has evolved to encompass many other functions that are not social. In addition to the social networking aspects, we can talk of a multitude of other functions engrained in social media: content creation and distribution, messaging, and digital marketing tools. It later became evident that corporations could not afford to ignore social media, as all their stakeholders were already there. Organizations reluctantly started adopting social media platforms, mainly for marketing and sales purposes. The higher-education environment has experienced great changes and, as Bolat and O'Sullivan (2017) note higher-education institutions need to be managed more and more as corporate brands. This involves an elaborate leverage of social media and other digital communications in an environment that is increasingly digital.

Of late, social media is emerging as an important arena for organizational communication, with companies now using it for overall communication with the external environment. This includes communication with all stakeholder groups, strategic communication management, branding, image building, relationship building, corporate promotion, market news, customer services, financial reporting, and integrated marketing communication. The higher-education environment has experienced a high increase in the deployment of integrated marketing communications activities seeking to leverage the opportunities in digital communication and social media. Some organizations have also experimented with the use of social media for internal communications. In a way, social media and other forms of digital communication are changing the way organizations communicate and interact with their stakeholders, be they employees, advocates, partners, suppliers, the media or the public, and vice versa. However, as Doorley and Garcia (2010) note: "Social media does not replace most other forms of communication; it complements, expands and enriches organizational communication" (p. 115). Social media can thus be considered a hybrid component of the corporate communications mix, characterized by a fragmented media landscape.

Digital Organizational Communication

Digital organizational communication is about delivering communication content to constituent stakeholders, both internal and external, through digital communication platforms. It encompasses "a mode of communication where the information or the thought is encoded digitally as discrete signals and electrically transferred to the recipients." Information flows in digital form to the recipients (pc, mobile, and tablet) within a fraction of a second. The concept "digital communication" is often used to cover a broad area of communications, mostly the technical aspects of digital transmission. Developments in digital communication have revolutionized the way companies communicate and interact with their publics. It is changing the interfaces between organizations, society, and stakeholders. It is an incontrovertible fact that we are now in the midst of revolutionary changes in the sphere of digital communication, characterized by extensive connections via mobile devices. Social media has evolved, since its inception, into a complex and potent force for digital organizational communication. Digitalization opens up a plethora of communication channels between the organization and its stakeholders. It incorporates real-time communication capabilities such as voice, video, and messaging into their interactions with their stakeholders. Channel digitalization has expanded the number of communication channels available for corporate communications.

Digital communication is one of the most commonly used modes of organizational communication. For many organizations, the challenge has been how to integrate the wide variety of technologies (social media, applications, etc.) into their channel portfolio, not just to improve external communications, but also to enhance employee-to-employee communications. Digital communication is changing the dynamics of "organizational communication," defined as: a set of activities involved in managing and orchestrating all internal and external communications aimed at creating favorable point of view among stakeholders on which the company depends (Van Riel & Fombrun, 2007). Organizational communication entails a set of communication activities, such as public relations, marketing, advertising, investor relations, and employee communications. It focuses on the organization as a whole and the important task of how an organization is presented to all its key stakeholders, both internal and external (Cornelissen, 2004). Digital organization's communications stand today in contrast to the traditional communications paradigm in terms of communication flow, control of the message, as well as the sender-receiver relationship. Tools and strategies for corporate communication have changed tremendously since the emergence of social media.

Methodological Considerations

The design for this study falls under ethnographic studies. We wanted to find meaning in the events being studied by describing the events in detail, uncovering patterns, and then interpreting them (Wolcott, 1994). Our empirical field is the university we work in, and our empirical material is email exchanges between the faculty's central management, middle managers, and employees. The emails analyzed in this study were exchanged between March 2020 and March 2021. There were 39 emails from the faculty management to the employees (approx. 47 A4 pages of text). There were approximately 35 emails between the Head of Department (HOD) and the employees at the department (included in the analysis). In addition, information from the central administration level is included in the interpretations, but not systematically in the same way as the emails. Here, the University College's web pages on Covid-19 information have been used.

Ethnographic studies open up the possibility of going into the depths of a phenomenon, and in that way describe changes in relationships and roles for the actors involved. Thick descriptions are possible (Geertz, 1973). Ethnographic methods are typically used where one wants comprehensive phenomena descriptions, preferably about conditions that have either not been studied in detail before, and/or where changes have taken place that may have had a major impact on the context in which the actors live. The pandemic year is a very good example of such an expected changed context, where an ethnographic approach is relevant and appropriate.

The emails, as empirical material, form the basis for text analysis; therefore, the analytical principles we use in interpreting the empirical material are that there are texts. When we, as researchers, are to understand how actors within this study justify and understand the different consequences of Covid-19, for example, reduction of uncertainty in the organization, this is about us interpreting the actors' own interpretations. Interpreting an already-interpreted reality is described by Anthony Giddens as double-hermeneutics (Giddens, 1984). For us as social scientists, our task is to interpret interpretations, which entails requirements for both the systematics of the empirical material and for various principles used in analysis of meaning content.

Inspired by Wolcott (1994), we have therefore divided the analysis process into three phases, which so far overlap, but which, purely analytically, have different purposes. The goal of the first phase is systematization of the various aspects of the phenomenon descriptions, primarily by structuring the emails, and the simple and obvious systematization principle is chronology. In this way, the course of events follows the order in which it happened. Ethnographic studies are also well suited when critical events are in focus, such as Covid-19. The actors involved will almost automatically justify their choices and positions when the events are unusual or critical. This provides a relevant vehicle to understand the internal form of communication in the organization, precisely by focusing on what was communicated and how it was communicated.

The goal of the second phase is to try to grasp the content elements of the interpretations and understandings of the Covid-19 pandemic that the emails represent. This is achieved by transforming the content of the emails into narratives or stories, while the goal of the third phase is to synthesize the actual content of these stories in the light of relevant theoretical perspectives so that new general and theoretical knowledge can be established. A relevant analysis of meaning content requires relevant theoretical standpoints. As long as we set our empirical findings against theoretical considerations, and the analysis has followed recognized principles for systematization and interpretation, and that the research process itself is accounted for, it is common to claim that the findings have a conceptual generalizability (Tjora, 2018). The purpose of ethnographic research is often to develop insight into selected phenomena and then to link this understanding of phenomena to theoretical concepts that can help us explain and interpret social patterns and relationships. And it is when we connect our empirical findings (phenomenon descriptions) with theoretical concepts (general concepts) to a logical and valid interpretation (phenomenon understanding) that we can claim we generalize our findings; we elevate the findings from descriptions of individual events to theoretically interpreted phenomena.

The Lockdown: Continuity and Disruption

The lockdown generated one of the most difficult conundrums for internal communications. The following account captures the experiences of a Head of Department in a medium-sized university college. In order to preserve anonymity, the name of the informant has been changed. In the following account, "John" details accounts of his experiences in the aftermath of the lockdown.

John is a Head of Department (HOD) of a newly established department, and he oversees a staff complement of approximately 40 full-time faculty and administrative support. The staff is spread between two campuses, separated by a two-hour car or train journey. The organizational structure of the department is a complex hybrid system, with elements of function-based and matrix organizations. The department is highly decentralized. It necessarily contains the characteristics of distance management with aspects of employees at a distance, where the staff is separated geographically. Lack of face-to-face communication is often cited as one of the frustrations of distance work. Due to its structure, the department depends on a robust system for internal communication with campuses linked through video-conferencing facilities. In each of the respective campuses, meeting rooms are fully equipped with a video-conferencing system, and the meeting rooms are linked together. The HOD, hence, conducted his hybrid meetings across the campuses, with people in two separate rooms and virtual links for those employees working from home or other places. Besides video-conferencing facilities, the HOD uses other communication forms, such as Skype For Business, telephone calls, and email communications. Therefore, internal communications, coordination of work, and decision-making were partially technologically driven even before the pandemic.

The pandemic brought several disruptions to these internal communication structures and cultures. The vast majority of employees were only familiar with Skype For Business as a digital tool for communication, and this solution was first used in one-to-one communication, with and without a camera. In the immediate aftermath of the lockdown, Skype For Business was used for management meetings. However, it was then not technically geared for complicated departmental and/or management meetings. Management and department meetings were shifted to a relatively new digital platform: Zoom. The platform was new to everyone in the department, and expectedly the institute experienced somewhat of a chaotic start. In the first few meetings, much of the initial meeting time was used to explain what John referred to as "digital discipline." The first versions of Zoom did not have the ability to "mute" the other meeting participants, so they had to be asked to turn off their own microphones. As the leader of the meetings, John always started with such rules of conduct for digital-meeting behavior. (It was always the same people who forgot to turn off their own microphone.) In addition, he had to introduce rules for "raising your hand" to be recognized. Zoom was early on equipped with a "raise hand" function when someone wanted to speak, but this function was, for some reason, little used. Instead, the chat function was used, where the employees who wanted to speak put a star in the chat box or wrote in their name. It was challenging to both lead meetings and, at the same time, take care of the chat function, but still this became a practice that established itself.

The structure of the meeting was fundamentally affected. The meetings became very much one-way in format, and "very effective"; effective because their duration was significantly shortened. "We halved the time we spent at the meetings, there were few discussions, mostly because the employees were unfamiliar with the digital medium, and the meetings were largely characterized by one-way communication." Paradoxically, even though John was frustrated by the lack of dialogue during the departmental meetings, the vast majority of employees appreciated that the meetings were short.

In addition to departmental meetings, which were held every four weeks, John established a more informal digital "breakfast coffee" hour every week. These informal, hour-long chats were held in the beginning of the pandemic. However, because of the number of employees in the department, the group became too large to allow any kind of small talk between different groups. They could have tried to divide into smaller groups in so-called break-out rooms, but this was not done. They still held several such informal meetings the first time, and the initiative was appreciated, even though the format worked relatively poorly. The same people talked every time and, therefore, a few were influencing these informal meetings a lot.

Instead, John gradually conducted a combination of short, information-oriented departmental meetings where he oriented the staff; followed by a small discussion; and then he held longer, more seminar-oriented digital gatherings that lasted over half a day. Here, he used the options in Zoom for group discussions and presentations in plenary. The feedback he received was that this combination worked well.

Frequent and Uncertain Communication

As John describes the aftermath of the lockdown, there was a sudden surge of demands for information, and frequent and uncertain communications. At the same time, the communication channels were not equipped to handle extraordinary and multifaceted communications. The first challenging issue was understanding the communication channels available to communicate with the different target groups. The emergency management team needed to find a way to communicate with all the employees. The most important communication medium for finding out information about the consequences of the closure was through the University College's email systems. Immediately after the national shutdown on March 12, 2020, communication with the faculty and department went through the existing email protocol Listserv. Relatively quickly, on the same day as the closure on March 12, another email Listserv was established principally for communications related to the crisis. The main reason for separating the Listserv was to streamline all emergency-related communication into one channel; hence, leaving the other email channels free for everyday uses. The emergency email address was to be used by employees at the facility. At the separate faculty level, another email Listserv was created to handle communications related to the business school, where employees would receive information that specifically concerned their faculty. It is also this address that was to be used to ask questions which could not be answered by the immediate manager. At the same time, the University College strengthened the use of its intranet.

The second challenge pertained to the implications of lockdown restrictions. Information provided at the beginning of the pandemic was not about infection control but about practical organization of the work, closure of premises, and restricted physical access to the University College's premises, including its own offices and workplaces. In addition, an attempt was made to control communication between management and the employees by using the above-mentioned common address.

On the same day that the campus closed, a new email was sent to employees at the facility stating that employees and students "are asked to take relevant items needed to work and study at home" (Email 2 from the emergency management, 12.3.20). In addition, they were informed that a way would be provided for employees to access their workplaces so that they could obtain the necessary equipment to be able to continue their work. All campuses were now completely closed until March 26, 2020.

A third email was sent the day of the shutdown on March 12. Here, it was expressed that the management was impressed with the way employees had handled the unexpected situation. At the same time, they were informed that a schedule would be prepared to collect items and necessary equipment from the campus. In addition, they were informed that the spring exams would be converted to digital home exams and that solutions for digital teaching were being worked on. This was also the first email with a link and reference to the National Infection Control Councils, and an invitation to the employees to follow them.

"We Can Manage This"

On March 13, a relatively comprehensive email was sent from Emergency Management at the facility. It emphasized that everyone was to work from home. Permission to gather necessary equipment from campus offices was granted on March 13, but it was emphasized that employees had to stay in the workplace for as short a time as possible. Students were encouraged to travel back to their homes or stay in their own dormitory or apartment. Both students and staff abroad were contacted with the stated wish that they should interrupt their studies and get home to Norway as soon as possible. Emergency Management acknowledged that working from home would disrupt existing communication lines and even make communication more complicated.

Different Concerns

John describes how overwhelmed he was. With 35–40 employees under his control, enquiries were certainly expected. One major concern pertained to requests for dispensation to use the work offices. Access to one's own workplace was, first of all, as John experienced it, about access to the workplace itself, with access to the tools and resources required to carry out the job on a purely practical basis. In addition, and just as much, this closure represented a significant intervention in the employees' autonomy and self-determination. The workplace is of great importance to employees, not the least of which is in terms of professional identity and belonging. The transition to a home office was also about different issues for different groups of employees; for example, parents of young children experienced different problems than the older workers.

As John recollects, at the same time as the University College closed down, practically all other workplaces, schools, and kindergartens were also closed down. As a leader, he received many inquiries from this group of employees (parents of young children), where they expressed concern about how they would be able to complete their own work tasks and, at the same time, give their children the help they needed to complete a digital school day on Teams. In addition to that, they shared cramped spaces with other family members and had restricted access to workplaces where they could work in peace. It was also difficult to have meetings or teach because there were often several people present in the same room, who each had their own work tasks to take care of, and who had to participate in their own meetings. An average Norwegian home is not equipped with work facilities capable of covering all the family's needs at the same time. For many, internet bandwidth was also a challenge when everyone, both children and parents, was dependent on using the Internet at the same time.

Therefore, John received many inquiries from parents of young children in the first period after the closure, with questions about whether they could gain access to the workplace. The answer was easy to give: it was "no." The central guidelines provided very few exemptions:

The starting point is that all campuses are still closed until 13 April. We therefore ask that everyone do their utmost to find other solutions, before they possibly apply for a dispensation! If you still find that you have to apply, the application must be sent by email … (email from Emergency Management 20.3.20).

Concerns of the older employees were slightly different. Most of the employees at the department John leads are between 50 and 60 years old. This group of people are used to a large degree of autonomy; at the same time, they seem to have a strong identity associated with the workplace itself. This group raised issues related to infection control. Their argument was, as they had little or no social interaction during the shutdown period, that they should therefore be able to go to work and sit in their one-room offices, and that they, in very little degree, would contribute to the spread of infection. These arguments also made little progress. It was pointed out that infection control considerations placed great demands on the cleaning and disinfection of common areas, and that this would be very resource-intensive if many people were physically present at work, and that it could potentially expose cleaning personnel to an unnecessarily high risk of infection.

Nevertheless, there were some differences when it came to inquiries from the various study places. At one of the campuses, most employees live relatively close to the workplace, while at the other campus, they commute. There were far more, and more frequent, requests for access to the campus where employees lived close by, while there were relatively few from the other campus to which most commuted. This is hardly surprising, and it seems quite obvious that those who live in relatively close proximity to the workplace have in every way a closer connection to that workplace, while those who are used to commuting have probably already established some form of home office for themselves.

Digital Teaching: Unprepared Faculty

For the vast majority of lecturers, teaching digitally was a completely new and unknown experience. Therefore, as the immediate manager, John received a number of inquiries regarding the basics. Most inquiries concerned practical information about how the connections should be made, how the tools and applications for digital teaching worked, and how teaching itself should be carried out with, for example, PowerPoint presentations. Other inquiries concerned whether employees could be required to carry out digital training, about who was responsible for relevant training, as well as questions concerning technological matters such as bandwidth and necessary equipment, for example, camera and headset. How can I teach when I do not have the equipment to implement digital solutions? Even though the faculty allowed employees to take equipment home, some could not do so for various reasons. Some employees were also reimbursed for the additional costs of upgrading bandwidth at home.

There were employees who expressed great frustration over the situation that had arisen and who thought they could not be compelled to do online teaching. However, this resistance met strong opposition from other colleagues, who regarded such demands as being counterproductive and failing to take into consideration students' needs and demands for continued instruction. John described how he handled this difficult situation: Firstly, by showing an understanding that this was a demanding and difficult situation, but also emphasizing that the students' right to receive instruction took precedence over any rights of the employees; and secondly, by giving them "an offer that they could get personal guidance from me as a leader, since I had already familiarized myself with how such teaching worked, and that I also possess relatively good digital competence." This strategy was successful, as evidenced by the number of people who sought and received help from John. One-on-one, step-by-step tutoring was well received, and the principle that students' right to education takes precedence over any employee's right to not have to teach digitally was accepted. John personally supervised between five and ten employees online. For him, this was a manageable number that was not too resource-intensive to mentor personally. They were all employees who could be called older workers (well over 50), and they weren't considered to have great digital skills. Nevertheless, they acquired the necessary skills relatively quickly and were able to carry out digital teaching on their own. And, of course, strong opposition to digital teaching ceased relatively quickly. True, some of the employees clearly stated that physical education surpassed digital education in quality, but they still completed the digital education as planned, and as assumed.

Changes in Administrative Routines and Processes

The closure of the workplace naturally led to changes in administrative routines as well. For John, as a middle manager with economic responsibilities, this meant that changes had to be made in certifying bills for payment. University College introduced electronic solutions for certifying electronic invoices, but not for physical vouchers, which largely consisted of salary forms for part-time teachers, external examiners, and guest lecturers. These pay forms are filled in manually by the hourly paid employees themselves before they are printed out and physically signed by the manager. Fully digital routines for these administrative conditions had not been established, and the argument was that such forms required a physical signature of the manager who held financial authority. Here, a very simple digital solution was established relatively quickly: Instead of a signature, it was now acceptable for the administration to scan the pay slips and send them electronically to the managers, via email, for reading and forwarding for payment by email.

A Typical Workday

A typical day for John, as Head of Department, is largely about sitting in Zoom digital meetings. Many of these meetings—about half during the day—are one-on-one meetings with management, colleagues, or other employees. The meetings are organized and convened by sending a Zoom link via email. Zoom is integrated with our email system and Outlook, and the times for the meetings are either agreed upon by using the calendar function in Outlook, or via email exchange, or by phone call.

The pandemic situation has led to an increased use of the electronic calendar function in Outlook. Employees can see a full overview of John's calendar, when he has free time or is busy. This is an obvious advantage for those who want to arrange meetings with him, but it means that John leaves the management of his time to others.

Discussion and Analysis

John's narrative provides a good background for analyzing the implications of the pandemic on internal organizational communication. The crisis exerted enormous stress on organizations across the world, setting dampers on business operations, effectiveness, and viability. The pandemic led to a "massive, unexpected, and sudden disruption to billions of employees around the world" (Sanders et al., 2020, p. 289). Lockdown compelled employees and their managers to abruptly leave their office spaces and to work from their homes, some of whom had never worked from home before. Changes in the way the workplace functioned during the pandemic put internal communication practices into the fore, showing how intertwined work, organizations, and digital technologies are. Employee communication is considered the lifeblood of any organization, and digital technology is the glue that binds everything together. In general, this pandemic context created new communication challenges and required new digital innovations in order to adapt to the changed context. Some of these challenges are imminent, from our narrative account.

Disruption of Communication Structures and Cultures

Just like any crisis, the pandemic and its associated lockdown measures created an insurmountable need to convey a huge amount of information across organizational levels. The pandemic disrupted fundamental organizational communication structures and culture. Organizations are often characterized by formal communication structures and channels of communication, be it vertical or horizontal communications. The communication flows are often structured along designated lines such as email listserv and intranets. The pandemic truncated these existing communication channels. Traditional internal communication channels, such as face-to-face conversations, physical notice boards, or printed newsletters, were no longer feasible. This necessitated the need to adopt digital communication platforms. Hence, organizations have adopted digital communication solutions, where managers communicate information and any other messages via multiple channels including, but not limited to, email, intranet, video conferencing, and other tools. The reduction or elimination of all possible means of physical contact compelled organizations to opt for digital communication solutions. Digitalization became compulsory by default as all other possible means were eliminated.

Enforced Digital Transformation

Digital transformation has, for some time, been on the agenda for many organizations in Norway as a direct response to the government's digitization process. However, the pace of digital transformation has been slow in the university sector. For example, while digital solutions for remote teaching had improved considerably, its adoption for teaching purposes had been very slow. The pandemic dramatically changed the situation, as both the students and lecturers were compelled to conduct their activities in digitally enabled environments, in particular, in new video-conferencing platforms like Zoom and Microsoft Teams. The previous administrative practice of sending documents—for example, letters, bills, and invoices—by ordinary mail was no longer a viable option. As noted in our narrative, John's department completely digitalized their practice and routines in certifying these kinds of documents. Since the whole organization had to interact digitally, every employee had to be part of the bandwagon.

Domestication: Negotiation and Appropriation

The adage "technology changes society and society changes technology" captures the intersection between organizations, technology, and work. A full year of lockdown restrictions has allowed for speedy adoption, adaptation, and experimentation with new digital platforms. Organizations have experimented with different communication and work platforms on a huge scale and with great tempo as they scrambled for solutions to the multifaceted challenges ignited by the pandemic. In the above narrative, we witnessed how John's department harnessed new communication and collaborative work platforms. To explain John's experience, we can use the domestication theory paradigm as a theoretical framework. We use this theory to explain how technology has adapted to everyday work life and how it has contributed to changes in working life. The paradigm explains how new technologies are adopted, and also discarded, when new options become available. In John's account, we see an attempt by a middle manager to run a department via digital management platforms. We notice the partial shift from Skype For Business to Zoom, as well as attempts to domesticate the new tool to serve both the organizational management processes (e.g. meetings, teaching) and all the socio-cultural processes (e.g. social meetings). Workplaces have a social dimension that is created and nurtured through physical spaces. In the absence of these physical spaces, the virtual spaces become an option. A coffee-hour social meeting on Zoom is one such initiative aimed at replicating physical spaces. The limited success of this initiative shows the limitations of technology platforms. They are not geared to allow for multi-conversations, as is normal in everyday life. Too many people using the digital space at the same time without controlled mute/unmute functions leads to chaotic outcomes. Digital spaces cannot sustain or mirror everyday life conversation, especially when many people are involved in the conversation. Nevertheless, we note a full integration of new technologies and an introduction of new digital cultures. Zoom, Teams, and other communication tools now constitute a vital aspect of working life. The tools now constituted a vital part of the organization's communication ecology.

Uncertain Futures in Digitally Saturated Environments

The coronavirus pandemic crisis subjected society and organizations to unchartered territories. The pandemic accelerated the degree of digitization of internal organizational communication. Organizations, including the educational sector, have developed a new normal for working and, in our case, for communication. Today's workplace is changed or is changing; so too are the dynamics of internal communication. The pandemic changed the way organizations communicate, what they communicate, how often they communicate, and what channels they use to communicate through. When the pandemic is over, organizations will have to deal with a new set of internal communication challenges arising from the profound structural and technological changes that they are now working under.

These challenges have short-, medium-, and long-term implications for internal communications. Organizations have invested huge resources in a number of new communication platforms, and their employees have become competent in their utilization. New communication cultures, processes, and styles have emerged as employees have become digital natives in these new technological contexts. For example, now that employees are digital natives in digital platforms like Zoom, Teams, or Skype, would they revert back to the old system? What foreseeable changes are likely to remain after the pandemic? Which traditional internal communication channels are likely to come back when normality returns? Some pundits would argue that past communication behaviors might become redundant. What compelling reasons will organizations have to revert to old systems when digital systems work equally well? For internal communication, the question now is how to cope with the sheer number of digital communication media that have emerged.

Note

1. Government Press release 12.03.2020 https://www.regjeringen.no/no/aktuelt/nye-tiltak/id2693327/ (Accessed 24.03.2021).

References

Bolat, Elvira, & O'Sullivan, Helen. (2017). Radicalising the marketing of higher education: Learning from student-generated social media data. *Journal of Marketing Management, 33*(9–10), 742–763. https://doi.org/10.1080/0267257X.2017.1328458

Coombs, Timothy W. (2019). *Ongoing crisis communication: Planning, managing, and responding.* Sage.

Cornelissen, Joep. (2004). *Corporate communications: Theory and practice.* Sage.

Doorley, John, & Garcia, Helio F. (2010). *Reputation management: The key to successful public relations and corporate communication.* Taylor & Francis.

Geertz, Clifford. (1973). *The interpretation of cultures: Selected essays.* Basic Books.

Giddens, Anthony. (1984). *The constitution of society: Outline of a theory of structuration.* Polity Press.

Goldhaber, Gerald M. (1993). *Organizational communication.* McGraw-Hill.

Hermann, Charles F. (1963). Some consequences of crisis which limit the viability of organizations. *Administrative Science Quarterly, 8*, 61–82.

Lerbinger, Otto. (1997). *The crisis manager. Facing risk and responsibility.* Lawrence Erlbaum.

Ndlela, Martin N. (2019). *Crisis communication. A stakeholder perspective.* Palgrave Macmillan.

Sanders, Karin, Nguyen, Phong T., Bouckenooghe, Dave, Rafferty, Alannah, & Schwarz, Gavin. (2020). Unraveling the what and how of organizational communication to employees during COVID-19 pandemic: Adopting an attributional lens. *Journal of Applied Behavioral Science, 56*(3), 289–293. https://doi.org/10.1177/0021886320937026

Stephens, Keri K., Malone, Patty C., & Bailey, Christine M. (2005). Communicating with stakeholders during a crisis: Evaluating message strategies. *Journal of Business Communication, 42*(4), 390–419. https://doi.org/10.1177/0021943605279057

Tjora, Aksel H. (2018). *Viten skapt: kvalitativ analyse og teoriutvikling.* Cappelen Damm akademisk.

van der Meer, Toni G. L. A., Verhoeven, Piet, W.J. Beentjes, Hans, & Vliegenthart, Rens. (2017). Communication in times of crisis: The stakeholder relationship under pressure. *Public Relations Review, 43*(2), 426–440. https://doi.org/10.1016/j.pubrev.2017.02.005

Van Riel, Cees B. M., & Fombrun, Charles. (2007). *Essentials for corporate communication. Implementing practices for effective reputation management.* Routledge.

Wolcott, Harry F. (1994). *Transforming qualitative data: Description, analysis and interpretation.* Sage.

CHAPTER 14

The Impact of Trust in Time of Covid-19: Trust in Crisis Management and Crisis Communication in Inland Norway University of Applied Sciences

Åse Storhaug Hole and Bjørn Tallak Bakken

Introduction

Inland Norway University of Applied Sciences (INN University) suddenly locked down on March 12, 2020. The Norwegian government had just announced a national lock-down, with large consequences for working life and everyday life. Our students and employees got little preparation time and we were ordered to leave campus and our offices at 1800 on that day, and to take our computers, headsets, devices, and books with us. Within days, most of the teachers had changed their teaching methods, from

Å. S. Hole (✉) • B. T. Bakken
Department of Organization, Leadership and Management, Inland Norway Business School, Inland Norway University of Applied Sciences, Elverum, Norway
e-mail: ase.storhaug@inn.no; bjorn.bakken@inn.no

L. D. Browning et al. (eds.), *Organizational Communication and Technology in the Time of Coronavirus*,
https://doi.org/10.1007/978-3-030-94814-6_14

classroom meetings to communicating and teaching digitally. The seven campuses in our institution are geographically spread over large distances, and our six faculties offer very different study programs: business administration, health care, teacher education, ecological and agricultural education, to mention some. Academics accustomed to autonomy were arranged into a situation where a central emergency management group directed everybody. In an instant, our working lives were changed from autonomous employees to loyal order-followers. Few said anything or protested, at least not loudly. Why did this "transformation" go so smoothly, at least under the first phase of lock-down? Most of us worked many extra hours weekly to cope with all the changes. Yet, complaints were rare. How did we manage to adapt so quickly to the huge changes forced upon us?

This chapter reflects upon organizational trust and loyalty in management in time of crisis. We will explore both formal and informal organizational contracts between management and employees. We propose that high trust based on relational factors between management and employees was a prerequisite for this disruptive change to take place so smoothly as a contractual agreement. Since contracts can be both formal and informal, we ask: What kind of formal contracts and informal psychological contracts existed between management and employees, and how did formal and informal contracts and trust change over time through the different phases of the pandemic? In answering this question, we will also reflect upon how this crisis might influence organizational trust and loyalty in the future. The corona crisis represented a disruptive change to how we live, communicate, experience, and learn in a quite new setting. Perhaps our experiences from the pandemic can help us to respond more effectively to challenges in an unpredictable future.

We begin with a brief description of the Norwegian context and governance in higher education, where we focus on the traditionally high trust in government and the legitimacy of state. Further, we argue that there has traditionally been high trust between employer and employees in the Norwegian working life, built on the Nordic model of cooperation. Then we turn to a brief description of the national authorities' strategic crisis communication and how our institution responded to restrictions and meaning-making efforts from national authorities. We focus on both formal and informal organizational structures and mechanisms which have an impact on trust-building in time of crisis, as a starting point of our analyses and discussion of trust in crisis management and communication in INN University. Quantitative and qualitative data collected in the spring and autumn of 2020 are our empirical materials. Last, we share our reflections and lessons learned from the pandemic crisis, "the new normal" for our institution.

Theoretical Backdrop

Trust in crisis management depends on many factors, especially type of crisis, type of organization, the actors involved, and the organizational context. The covid-19 crisis proved to have similarities as well as differences between countries. For a better understanding of trust in management and how the crisis unfolded in our institution, we start out with a brief backdrop explaining the Norwegian context, where trust in government is traditionally high.

The Norwegian Context: Trust in Government and Legitimacy of State

Citizens of Norway have overall high trust in government (Christensen & Lægreid, 2020). The Nordic countries have the highest levels of generalized trust and social capital in the Western World under normal circumstances, and these high levels have been stable for decades (Rothstein & Stolle, 2003; Svendsen & Svendsen, 2015). Social capital, as explained by Coleman (1988, p. 119), consists of three main forms: trustworthiness concerning obligations and expectations, information-flow capability of the social structure, and norms accompanied by sanctions. Social capital can lead to a society's ability to cooperate without written rules and extensive contracts and may therefore be linked to a population's trust and commitment to follow guidance from the authorities. Norway is a high trust country, has a well-developed welfare state, and has an open and transparent government. Citizens' trust in government is high, and mutual trust relations between government authorities are higher than in many other countries (OECD, 2017). The stock of social trust is an important reason for the successful Norwegian welfare state.

Christensen and Lægreid (2020) have analyzed the arguments presented by central and local government leaders in Norway in the spring of 2020 to justify the measures introduced to restrict contact between citizens, and to seal Norway off from the rest of the world. This radical decision involved closing businesses and public institutions, such as schools and universities, and it prevented movement of people within and across regions. The effectiveness of the government in controlling the pandemic was due to the suppression strategy, a collaborative decision-making style, successful meaning-making in the communication with the public, and the high level of citizens' trust in government (Christensen & Lægreid, 2020). Crisis management in our institution followed the recommendations from the national authorities, as did the other universities and university colleges in our country during lock-down.

Higher Education Governance in Norway

Traditionally, there is low power distance between leaders and employees in Norway, and horizontal relations between colleagues and management is especially common in academic institutions. This "collegial management style" of distributed leadership has been customary in the Norwegian school-system (Brundrett, 1998; Harris, 2010; Møller & Ottesen, 2011), as well as in higher education. Over the last years, however, more formal control systems have been applied (Ferlie et al., 2008), but the informal systems based on mutual trust are still dominant. At least we like to think so. Researchers have found that an important prerequisite for trust between management and employees in the Nordic countries is "the Nordic model" of cooperation in working life (Hvid & Falkum, 2018).

The Nordic Model of Cooperation in Working Life: The Role of Union Representatives and Safety Representatives

Local cooperation between partners is a basic element in the Nordic working-life model. The representative participation of the unions and the participation through safety representatives, together with the individual participation, form this system of collaboration. A prerequisite for the Norwegian or the Nordic model for working-life cooperation is nationwide collective agreements stated in the Working Environment Act (2005). Institutional arrangements are both a legal supplement and a prerequisite for inter- and intra-organizational trust (Trygstad & Andersen, 2021). In our institution, union representatives take an active part in management and they were also central actors in crisis management during covid-19.

Prior to discussing aspects of the concept of trust, we present a brief overview of crisis management and the impact of trust in crisis management.

Crisis Management and Crisis Communication

Boin et al. (2005) explain that crisis is the result of multiple causes, which interact over time to produce a threat with devastating potential due to unintended consequences of increased complexity caused by the inability of a social system to deal with the disturbance (Boin et al., 2005, p. 5). Crises are events that have escalated to the extent that they become a surprise to the organization—which means there are no available plans that have been properly rehearsed and exercised for managing the crisis. Hannah et al. (2009) distinguish leadership in extreme contexts from other crises and contexts. What type of crisis is a pandemic?

Health authorities worldwide are not unfamiliar with influenza outbreaks that could lead to epidemics and even pandemics. Pandemic as a high-risk event has occupied the top-right corner of the Norwegian matrix of "societal risks" for more than ten years, unsurpassed by every conceivable natural disaster and industrial accident. For example, in Norway, a pandemic is regarded much more likely than an earthquake in a city, and with more severe consequences than large floods and forest fires (Norwegian Directorate for Civil Protection, 2019). The reason pandemics are located at the very top of the risk matrix is due to the way risk in crises is defined and measured. What makes a pandemic an extraordinary, high-risk situation is that an infected person might show no symptoms for a longer period (the incubation time), and accordingly it is harder to prevent spreading of the virus. Combined with the biological reproduction mechanisms of the virus, the virus will spread and grow exponentially. A pandemic tends to spread in waves or cycles. In a complex and enduring crisis such as the Covid-19 pandemic, governmental authorities will continuously have to balance trust with control, in order to gain a perceived risk level that ensures compliance from the population. If there is too much reliance on trust, the situation can veer out of control when people no longer see the point in following strict regulations, either because the measures taken are not working as expected or because the spreading of the disease appears to be lowering from natural causes. Conversely, having too much control can undermine the positive effects of trust, leading to public disobedience, uproar, and riot.

The greater responsibility for the crisis external actors attribute to the management, the more responsive managers should be in crisis communication to minimize reputation loss and strengthen legitimacy (Coombs, 2011). Communication strategies are categorized depending on where they are placed on the continuum between defensive and responsive strategies. A distinction is made between denial strategies (denying the crisis vs. dealing with the incident), reduction strategies (reducing the perception that there is a crisis or a reprehensible condition), and reconstructive strategies (acknowledging the crisis and apologizing). While nobody is responsible for causing the pandemic outbreak (although that is debated), the ability or lack of ability to take appropriate measures may be criticized and scrutinized by the public, thus paving the way for denial, reduction, or reconstructive strategies. Thus, trust is an important asset in crisis management.

Trust

In the following section we outline the importance of trust in interpersonal and inter-organizational relationship in general, and more specifically, the importance of trust in crisis management.

Trust enables cooperative behavior; it promotes networks, reduces conflicts, and promotes effective responses to crises (Meyerson et al., 1996; Miles & Snow, 1992). The different aspects of trust can include different levels: individual, group, firm, and institutional levels. Trust can be within and between organizations; trust can be a cause, an outcome, and a moderator (Dirks & Ferrin, 2001, 2002; Rousseau et al., 1998). There are different ways to conceptualize trust, but there are some common interpretations and explanations: willingness to be vulnerable, willingness to rely on another, confident, positive expectations, a positive attitude toward others, preconscious expectations (Mayer et al., 1995; Rousseau et al., 1998). Summing up different views from scholars, Rousseau et al. agreed on the following definition of trust: "Trust is a psychological state comprising the intention to accept vulnerability based upon positive expectations of the intentions of another" (Rousseau et al., 1998, p. 395). Two central conditions for trust to arise are risk and interdependence. Uncertainty about whether the other party intends to, and will react properly, is a source of risk. Interdependence means that the interest of one party cannot be achieved without reliance upon another. As interdependence increases, risk and trust change. In other words, the context of the relationship matters. The more we depend on another, the higher risk we take when trusting one another.

Trust changes over time; it develops, builds, and declines due to different circumstances (Rousseau et al., 1998). It is not a question of either trust or distrust, but rather a dynamic and changing phenomenon. According to Rousseau et al. (1998) understanding the following phases of trust can help our understanding of trust: Building trust in the first phase means that trust is formed or reformed, stability in the second phase means that trust already exists, and dissolution in the third phase means that trust is declining. Trust can be violated in many ways, and trust can be repaired (Kim et al., 2009). Violation of psychological contracts (psychological contract breaches) is also violation of trust (Morrison & Robinson, 1997; Robinson & Rousseau, 1994). In a long-lasting pandemic, we suppose that trust in crisis management can be built, and trust can decline. As the different phases of the crisis unfold, uncertainty can spread among employees and in the public. Maintaining trust in crisis management and crisis communication is being put to the test. In the aftermath, when the crisis management measures prove to be successful, people might question the strictness of the rules and regulations: "We didn't need them, the rules were too strict."

Another aspect of trust is that trust can arise from different motivations. Different forms of trust are deterrence-based trust, calculus-based trust, and relational trust. Deterrence-based trust refers to low trust, nearly distrust, emphasizing the costly sanctions in place for breach of trust. Sitkin and Roth (1993) have raised the question of whether deterrence-based trust is trust at all. Beliefs in absence of negative intentions are not the same as positive expectations of good intention, which is a prerequisite for trust. Calculus-based trust is based on rational choice, characteristic for interactions based upon economic exchange. Trust emerges when the trustor perceives that the trustee intends to perform according to what is viewed as beneficial, such as receiving credible information about the intentions or the competences of another party (Barber, 1983). Relational trust is based on reliability and dependability of previous interactions between the parties, and it derives from repeated longer-term interactions over time. This kind of trust is also referred to as "affective trust" (McAllister, 1995) and "identity-based trust" (Coleman, 1988). Identity-based trust is relational trust at its broadest. Relational trust entails not only the beliefs in the positive intentions of another party but also in the absence of negative intentions. Some scholars have used the term fragile trust and resilient trust, pointing at resilient trust as parallel to relational trust (Nilsson & Mattes, 2015). Institution-based trust can be viewed as both control and trust. Institutional control mechanisms as laws and sanctions can serve as a springboard for the creation of trust, and societal controls can function both as a means of controlling behavior and as a basis for supporting the development of control. Relational and resilient trust is important when it comes to crisis management. However, in crisis management you also need institutional control systems to secure that safety measures function. Schoorman et al. (2007) warn against pairing trust with too much control, which we may see as the double-edged sword of using a control system versus relying on trust in an organization:

> when the risk in a situation is greater than the trust and the willingness to take risk and rely on another party declines, a control system can bridge the difference by lowering the perceived risk to a level that can be managed by trust. If there is a very strong system of control in an organization, it will inhibit the development of trust. Not only will there be few situations where there is any remaining perceived risk, but trustworthy actions will be attributed to the existence of the control system rather than to the trustee (Schoorman et al., 2007, p. 346).

Mayer et al. (1995) identified three factors of trustworthiness: competence (ability), integrity, and benevolence. Ability refers to competencies and skills of the trustee. Benevolence refers to the extent the trustor believes the trustee has a positive orientation toward the trustor beyond an egoistic profit motive. Integrity implies that the trustee acts in accordance with values and principles the trustor finds acceptable. How does trust develop between actors in a virtual setting and in virtual teams? Concerning trust in virtual settings, Breuer et al. (2020) found five main categories of perceived trustworthiness (ability, benevolence, predictability, integrity, and transparency) and three main categories of risk-taking behavior (disclosure, reliance, and contact-seeking). The categories were identified both in face-to-face and in virtual team situations. The need for understanding the influence of spatiality for trust-building has become more important under the pandemic, when we communicate digitally on distance.

Woolthuis et al. (2005) explored the relation between trust and control in inter-organizational relations, and they found that trust is a precondition and a prerequisite for successful contracts. Trust and contracts can be both substitutes and complements, and trust can successfully substitute contracts. Sitkin and George (2005) discuss the concepts legalistic trust-building and relational trust-building. Legalistic trust-building could include environments where individuals are linked with transactional contracts (Rousseau, 1995), or by highly legalistic and formal relations. Relational trust-building, which can lead to resilient trust, is possible in environments where individuals are linked with relational psychological contracts and they will seek to gain and maintain relational trust. In the following section we will turn to discuss how trust relates to the informal and unwritten psychological contracts.

Psychological Contracts

A psychological contract contains the individual's perceptions about the reciprocal relationship with their employer (Rousseau & Tijoriwala, 1998). In a psychological contract, the employer and employee are engaged in a contractual relationship in which both parties feel they owe each other something. This "something" can refer to training, promotion, recognition, trust, fair pay, and a good working environment. An important part of the contract is that in exchange for good work, the employee will expect something in return, such as further training or a promotion. Thus, a psychological contract implies that there is a reciprocal relationship between the parties. The premise is that without the promise of a future exchange, neither party has incentives to contribute much of anything to the other, which may result in a strain or termination of the relationship (Robinson & Rousseau, 1994).

Most research on psychological contracts has focused on the consequences of contract breaches and has found connections to many work-related outcomes, such as job satisfaction, organizational commitment, turnover intention, in-role performance, and organizational citizenship behavior (Zhao et al., 2007). The consequences of breaching a psychological contract are substantial, meaning that handling breaches and knowing the content of the psychological contract (what exactly was breached) are important to prevent these negative consequences (Restubog et al., 2007).

Research on the substance of the psychological contracts shows that there is an important distinction in the literature between transactional and relational contracts (Rousseau, 1990). A transactional contract is composed of specific, short-term obligations entailing limited involvement of the parties, as for a seasoned worker, who exchanges money for work. Employees' motivation for working extra hours during the covid-19 crisis depends on their awareness of the transactional psychological contracts. Employees will gradually begin to expect rewards and pay-back for their efforts. A relational contract entails broad, open-ended, long-term obligations, and is based on mutual trust and loyalty (Morrison & Robinson, 1997, p. 229), for example, the permanent worker who exchanges lifetime work for loyalty to the company. According to Rousseau (2004), employees with a relational contract tend to put more effort into their job, help colleagues, and support changes in the organization. This is important factors in time of crisis, especially when authorities use the slogan "we will work together."

A third type of psychological contract is called a value-based or ideological contract. It involves working for a higher cause or ideology, fulfilling expectations toward an overarching goal of the organization (Thompson & Bunderson, 2003). Employees with such a contract have been shown to exert more extra-role behavior (Vantilborgh et al., 2014). In an academic institution, we expect that ideological contracts can exist among academic staff and students, in disciplines involving health care, pedagogy, sustainability, ecology, to mention some that are ideologically based. Employees with ideological contracts will perhaps also show more pro-social behavior in crisis (Grant, 2008), because of their loyalty toward their organization.

Much of the literature on psychological contracts has focused on the individual perceptions about the terms of the exchange relationships. However, employees may collectively agree on terms, and these contracts are called normative contracts. When co-workers agree among themselves on the terms of their individual psychological contract with the employer, the agreement becomes a normative contract. Normative contracts are products of social integration, discussion, and interpretation, creating similarity in the way people see their organization and their relationship to it (Rousseau, 1995). Normative contracts are relevant related to the common beliefs among employees concerning their trust in colleagues and trust in their employer. Employees can agree among themselves about the trustworthiness of their management, both top-management, and their nearest department leader. We assume that transactional, relational, ideological, and normative psychological contracts are relevant when analyzing the impact of trust in crisis management.

Through our literature review we have intended to shed light on the various interpretations of the concept of trust, and we define trust as the intention to accept vulnerability based upon positive expectations of the intentions of another party. Further, we have explained how trust is built and how trust is sustained, how trust can decline and be violated, and how trust can be rebuilt. We have discussed the importance of both trust and control in crisis management, and especially the importance of balancing trust and control. Building on the theory outlined in the previous sections, we will now take a closer look at how trust has an impact on crisis management, in general, and on the corona pandemic, in particular. On this background, we have formulated the following research questions:

What is the impact of trust on managing a profound and prolonged societal crisis such as the corona pandemic?
How is trust built and maintained before and during a crisis?
What is the impact of informal psychological contracts and formal contracts on the decision-making processes?
How can our experiences from the crisis influence organizational trust and loyalty in the future?

To answer our research questions, we analyze qualitative data collected in the spring and autumn of 2020. In the next section we discuss our methodological approach.

Methodological Approach

Our empirical base for analyzing crisis management and communication during the corona crisis is mainly qualitative data collected during the lock-down in the spring semester 2020 and the beginning of the autumn semester 2020 (Bakken et al., 2020). The aim of our study was to evaluate the crisis management and crisis communication in INN University during lock-down in the spring of 2020. We combined qualitative and quantitative research methods. Eight semi-structured group interviews with key-informants were carried through in June 2020. We include three of these group interviews in our analysis including technical/administrative staff, academic staff, and Union representatives. All interviews were transcribed before the coding and analyzing process started. Open categories were included in a questionnaire designed to explore the respondent's experiences in more detail. About 437 employees answered the questionnaire, and the response rate was 43%. And 626 free text answers from academic staff and administrative and technical staff are included in our analysis. The data collection steps were as follows:

- Group interviews were carried out in May–June 2020.
- Data from eight group interviews were transcribed and analyzed in May–June 2020. The purpose was the following:

1. A starting point for the design of our questionnaire
2. Collecting in-depth qualitative data as supplement to the questionnaire.

- The interview guides were based on the six dimensions outlined below (page 11). Qualitative analyses of three group interviews is included in this article (interviews with Union representatives, administrative/technical staff, and academic staff)
- Questionnaire data collected in September–October 2020.
- Quantitative analyses combined with qualitative analyses. Qualitative data collected from free texts is included in this article.

The following dimensions of crisis management were central guidelines when designing our interview guide and questionnaire. Situational awareness (SA) and common mental models are about having an overview of the situation—how it has arisen, how it develops, and what are possible and probable future events (Bakken, 2020). Management and organization include the four principles of crisis management: Responsibility, meaning that the organization which is responsible for a subject area in a normal situation, is also responsible for necessary emergency preparedness and for handling extraordinary incidents in the area. Equality, meaning that the organization you operate with during crisis should in principle be as similar as possible to the organization you have in ordinary administration of the organization. Proximity, meaning that crises must be handled organizationally at the lowest possible level. Cooperation, meaning that authorities, companies, and agencies have an independent responsibility to ensure the best possible collaboration with relevant actors. Decision-making during crises must often be made under high time pressure, great degree of uncertainty, and lack of relevant and accurate information. The effectiveness of the decision-making process depends on the decision-makers' competence and preferences and the complexity of the situation (Bakken & Hærem, 2020). Cooperation and team-processes are important in crisis management, and effective emergency teams consist of team-members who know each other well and trust each other. Internal and external communication are central processes in crisis management.

Demanding factors are connected to choosing of communication channels, and making decisions about what, how, and when to inform (Ndlela, 2019).

Qualitative Research Method and Text Analyses

To analyze reactions and comments means to interpret the participants' own interpretations. Interpreting an already interpreted reality is described by Anthony Giddens as double-hermeneutics (Giddens, 1984). As methodological approach for analyzing the texts, we use thematic analysis, as described by Braun and Clarke (2006).

Our analysis started by identifying the central themes in our material describing trust in crisis management and trust in crisis communication at all levels. The quality of our analysis depends on our ability to capture the most important themes in our material, both concerning prevalence, meaning and relevance for understanding trust in crisis management and communication. The reflections and answers from employees were sorted into the following themes:

Trust and crisis communication and information
Trust and management and organization
Trust and digital teaching and digital transformation
Trust and control
Credibility and reliability

Credibility of the data refers to the accuracy of understanding, interpretation, and representation of research results (Lincoln & Guba, 1985; Ritchie et al., 2013). The use of triangulation in methods secures multiple sources of data, which gives a better accuracy of understanding when collecting data. The Credibility of interpretation is satisfactory as we looked at the empirical data from different theoretical perspectives (Ritchie et al., 2013). We have formulated our analytic categories based on what characterizes organizational trust and trust in crisis management. In our theory section we outline these theoretical aspects. By using quotations from the free text answers, we aim to strengthen the credibility of representation. In addition, we have the quantitative data from the questionnaires as background check and validation.

Analysis

In the following sections we will reflect upon some of the challenges and experiences our institution has faced through the last year. We have analyzed three group interviews and 626 free texts written by employees in a large survey carried out in the spring and autumn of 2020. We explore the experiences of employees during three phases of the pandemic, spring, summer, and autumn 2020, with focus on the impact of trust in management and authorities in time of crisis. In the theory section, we discussed the importance of different dimensions of trust (Rousseau et al., 1998; Sitkin & Roth, 1993; Mayer et al., 1995), and how relational trust is a prerequisite for maintaining relational psychological contracts (Rousseau, 1995). Psychological contract breaches may affect a person's motivation and commitment and affect work performance in a negative way (Robinson & Rousseau, 1994). Formal and informal control systems can support the building of both inter-organizational trust and intra-organizational trust in time of crisis (Woolthuis et al., 2005; Sitkin & George, 2005).

Results from the quantitative study evaluating crisis management and communication showed a generally high degree of satisfaction with crisis management from the institution. Crisis management and crisis communication from the institution have been characterized by clarity, trust, and security (Bakken et al., 2020). The transition to digital teaching methods has worked out satisfactory. Younger employees are most satisfied with management under the lock-down. With regard to different job categories, administrative and technical staff are more satisfied than academic staff with leadership and crisis management. PhD students were critical of how crisis management was carried out at all levels.

As explained in our method section, we emphasize the qualitative data in this chapter, because we want to go behind the survey numbers, seeking for explanations and reasons in more detail than our quantitative data can explain (Blaikie & Priest, 2019). In our thematic analysis of the impact of trust in crisis management, we identified the following central themes connected to the impact of trust in crisis management: Information and communication, management and organization, transition to digital teaching, and workload.

Trust in crisis management seems to be strong when (1) expectations of being taken care of are met, (2) information comes on time and is precise, (3) self-managed work during the crisis is appreciated by colleagues and management. Trust declines when expectations are violated, consciously or unconsciously. We explain more in depth in the following sections why these themes are central for understanding how trust can be built and how trust can decline. Examples from the interviews and the free texts are used as documentations and illustrations.

Information and Communication

When it comes to crisis management and communication, there were both positive and critical comments in the interviews and the free texts. On the positive side, employees expressed satisfaction with crisis management on the institutional level. On the department level, however, there were many critical comments concerning the timing of the information, the content of the information, the different channels of information, and difficulties with the interpretation of the information. (1) Multiple channels = ambiguity and different interpretations. Examples: "Written information on the intranet could have been structured in a better way." "Too much information on various websites and emails. We were expected to log into the intranet several times a day." (2) Information overload, and too much was left to our own interpretation. Examples: "I would have preferred more precise information. Tell me what to do, please!" "Messages arrived too late in the start of the pandemic." (3) Different interpretations of common information at the nearest management level. Example: "Redundant information in the webinars, one-way communication, there were no dialog or involvement." "Inconsistent correspondence between institutional level and faculty level."

Management and Organization

The four principles of crisis management and organization (organization, proximity, equality, and cooperation) are important to address, but perhaps difficult to carry through in an enduring pandemic. We observed that the principle of proximity (handling of the crisis at the lowest possible level) has been demanding for many of the frontline leaders. It seems that leaders were not aware of the unwritten expectations from their employees, how they missed personal contact with their colleagues and nearest leader. The levels in the ordinary organization did not work as usual during the crisis. Our respondents experienced differences between institutional intentions and how it was interpreted and carried through operationally. They ask for more involvement from leaders at the lowest levels: faculties and departments. As some of their examples express, "We were told to find all the information on the Intranet, but I would prefer more information from my department boss." "Huge distance from the operational level and up to the institutional level."

However, some were very satisfied with crisis management, and they hope the changes we have been through will help us cope better in the future: "Positive mobilization! Take good care of this momentum!" "I am left with an experience of being taken care of." "The crisis management at INN University has been exemplary!"

The union representatives were satisfied with the way they had been involved at the institution level, and they mention that an important reason for that was initial trust between the parties. They had already experienced a positive and constructive cooperation. However, one of them called for a more proactive strategy for including the safety representatives, and others mentioned that the organization had been unprepared for the crisis. "The management have listened to us, and they have been very responsive. We know each other well from years with cooperation." "Trust and loyalty are already established." "We must focus on competence in the future so we can be better prepared. When crisis strikes, it's too late."

Administrative staff was more satisfied with crisis management and the consequences of the crisis than the academic staff: "Cooperation between campuses and faculties have been better than before, now we meet on zoom on a more regular basis."

Transition to Digital Teaching and Workload

Adapting to changes is normally demanding, and in higher education the academic staff are not the earliest adapters. The disruptive change to digital teaching appeared to be quite a shock for many people. However, the transition to digital teaching seems to have gone well. Employees express satisfaction with the technological support and online learning through webinars. However, as the crisis went on, impatience seems to grow. Some examples of this were: "An extremely demanding situation. All the extra work was not paid for." "The 'dugnad' lasted for too long." "Too much responsibility for difficult issues left to the individual." "Why didn't anybody ask us about our research and development work? Their only focus was on teaching!"

There were many comments on the lack of support from nearest leader, many people had felt left alone in a demanding situation. They were not prepared for making decisions on their own concerning digital teaching methods, care for students' well-being and students' motivation. Many experienced the situation as unpredictable and uncertain. It seems that especially between semesters and in matters concerning exams, critics were many. The different experiences are due to individual differences in personality, competence, and motivation. There are differences in a normal situation, and perhaps in crisis extra attention must be payed to the individuals, as one person wrote: "I wish somebody had called to see how I was doing. It was difficult to ask for help."

Differences between campuses and between departments appeared in our qualitative analyses. Study programs in health care and teaching are normally organized with close contacts between teachers and students, due to practice and training periods. Programs in agriculture and ecology are also examples of programs which need practice and fieldwork. Examples of statements from teachers were: "Lack of precise information." "Important decisions concerning practice periods and registration of students' absence came far too late." "Delegation of decisions from top management to front line teachers made differences between study programs, which was frustrating." These statements differ from business studies which normally has larger groups of students, with less contact between teachers and students, and teaches in business administration seem to have had a less demanding situation concerning these issues. However, our impression is that most of the academic staff independent of faculties and campuses experienced significant increase in workload. They were also less satisfied than the administrative and technical staff with crisis management and communication at all levels.

Discussion

Trust in crisis management on the Institutional level and the department level: The quantitative and qualitative data show high degree of trust in crisis management and crisis communication on the institutional level. Employees responded to the regulations and restrictions with loyalty, and protests were rare, at least the first weeks. However, trust is not a static phenomenon (Kim et al., 2009; Rousseau et al., 1998). Trust is built and trust is violated. The characteristics of a pandemic make it difficult to measure results especially that are long-lasting. Trust in crisis management can decline in different phases of the pandemic. Under lock-down we find that trust is high, and very few doubted central authorities' competence, benevolence, and integrity (Mayer et al., 1995). However, comments are more critical during transitions between phases, for example, between semesters. Both academic staff and administrative staff express frustration about ambiguous information and conflicting information in different channels in transition periods between semesters. We interpret that their need for predictability was not met (Breuer et al., 2020). To keep people well informed in transition periods is a potential for improvement for both central and local crisis management. Trust declines when the parties are not aware of the importance of maintaining trust through dialog and cooperation (Chen et al., 2014).

On the department level, we find more critical comments, both concerning lack of information (competence in communication strategies), attention and care from nearest leader (benevolence), and consistent and predictable leadership (integrity) (Mayer et al., 1995). One reason for that might be that the communication was exclusively digital. The maintenance of trust in virtual settings is demanding because of several reasons. Two important factors are the need for transparency and predictability (Breuer et al., 2020).

Leaders on the lowest levels who relied upon their employees found the information from the institutional level to be good enough (Fernandez & Shaw, 2020). According to the principles of proximity and equality, crisis management should be handled at the lowest possible level (Bakken & Hærem, 2020). In a large and hierarchic organization, the distance from the top level to the frontline is vast.

Most digital meetings on Zoom, Teams, and other digital platforms have been asynchronous, and dialogues have been rare. Dialogue and involvement are important to secure common interpretations and to clarify expectations toward one another (Robinson & Rousseau, 1994). In addition, care for employees' well-being is an important task for a department leader, especially in time of crisis. Individuals respond differently, and in crisis these differences might become more evident (Betsch et al., 2020). The outcomes of a pandemic crisis depend on the appropriate behavior of each individual as well as on collective behavior. To manage the crisis effectively, management must rely on individual behavioral responses. Accordingly, mutual trust on the individual level is an important asset in crises.

Information strategies are crucial to build and maintain trust in crisis management (Ndlela, 2019). We have underlined the importance of dialog and involvement. However, the formal information systems prove to be as important as the informal. Some of our informants experienced ambiguous, conflicting, and unclear information in different channels, especially in transition periods between semesters.

The Influence of Psychological Contracts

In the beginning of lock-down, academic and administrative staff acted properly and responded with loyalty to the strict regulations and extra work forced upon them by the covid-19 crisis. We interpret that this trust and loyalty in management is due to the relations and normative contracts established at the workplace (Rousseau, 1995). In addition, the strong tradition in Norway with participation of union representatives in the management group seems to have built trust. People trusted each other before the pandemic (Hvid & Falkum, 2018). Differences in behavior can be explained by normative contracts as well. Reasons for suspiciousness and skepticism to crisis management might arise among employees through normative psychological contracts in working environments where trust between management and employees are low. Some of the reactions to strain and workload during lock-down were employee's demand for compensation for extra working-hours and extra time spent on on-line attending digital teaching courses. The lack of pay-back for the "voluntary" extra work during lock-down could be interpreted as a breach of a transactional contract (Rousseau, 1995; Robinson & Rousseau, 1994). In Norwegian we use the word "dugnad," meaning voluntary working together without getting payed. This was a slogan used by the Norwegian government during lock-down, and Christensen and Lægreid (2020) explain this as one of the successful efforts of meaning-making during the pandemic. However, when a "dugnad" becomes the normal, people react with frustration and disappointment. A voluntary work without being payed is typically for a short time. We interpret this to be a breach of both relational and transactional contracts between employers and management (Restubog et al., 2007; Robinson & Rousseau, 1994).

Further, many employees had expected more direct support from their nearest leader, as well as from colleagues. The feeling of being left alone with the responsibility and extra working-hours informing students, teaching online, making new exams fit for exams from home, and so on, are other examples of relational psychological contract breaches (Morrison & Robinson, 1997). The lack of support from nearest leader and lack of contact with colleagues was not what people had expected. In reality "the working together"-slogan meant "working alone without extra support and payment" for many employees. However, protests were rare, but our results show that people reacted differently.

Colleagues can share the same normative psychological contract at the workplace (Rousseau, 1995). Among our colleagues we interpret there are such unwritten contracts. We have the same expectations concerning what is appreciated concerning work performance. For example, among academic staff there is a dilemma concerning the time you are willing to spend on teaching and the time you are willing and motivated to spend on research activities. There are also common expectations between academic staff that academics work autonomously; we are not used to being told how to do things. At least we expect to be involved in decisions (Ferlie et al., 2008). In times of crisis it is important to help colleagues to manage at the same time as you try to cope with changes yourself. When working from home, colleagues may feel isolated and left alone, and you will perhaps wait for others to take initiatives concerning cooperation and support. In this situation a breach of a normative contract can occur; many employees experienced that their nearest boss and their colleagues did not contact them (Rousseau, 1995). This can also be interpreted as a breach of a horizontal psychological contract between colleagues and vertical contracts between employees and employers (Sverdrup, 2012; Hole & Sverdrup, 2020).

Ideological psychological contracts involve working for a higher cause and fulfilling expectations of an overarching goal of the organization (Thompson & Bunderson, 2003). Employees with this kind of contract tend to show more extra-role behavior, intrinsic, and pro-social behavior (Vantilborgh et al., 2014; Grant, 2008). In an extraordinary situation like a pandemic, the organization needs people who are willing to "walk an extra mile." It is therefore of great importance to maintain this kind of intrinsic motivation and engagement among employees, by strengthening the contracts, rather than weakening them.

Trust and Control

Resilient trust is important in crisis management (Nilsson & Mattes, 2015). Resilient trust is built and sustained through relationships. During the corona crisis personal contact between leaders and employees and between colleagues has been reduced. This might lead to a decline in trust. Many employees interpreted crisis management as top-down, with large distance between organizational levels. Regulations and restrictions in crisis are necessary, but formal control systems must be supplemented by trust (Schoorman et al., 2007; Woolthuis et al., 2005; Rousseau et al., 1998; Sitkin & Roth, 1993). Lack of relational trust, also referred to as affective or identity-based trust (McAllister, 1995; Coleman, 1988), opens for more use of managerial control. If there is a very strong system of control in an organization, it will inhibit the development of trust (Schoorman et al., 2007). Our analyses show that this was the case at times in our institution. At the same time, frustration may occur during crisis if too many decisions are delegated to the frontline. Accordingly, crisis management needs to balance between trust and control.

Concluding Remarks

It is too early to sum up the worldwide consequences of the Covid-19 pandemic. It appears that the Norwegian authorities have chosen appropriate strategies to deal with the pandemic. Norway has kept critical societal functions operational—such as health services, pharmacies, and even grocery stores—and the government has provided financial compensation to companies that were struggling. In the future, it will be debated whether the correct measures were applied—in the right amount, time, and place. Did the authorities rely too much on public trust, or should one rather have exerted more control? In a complex and enduring crisis such as the Covid-19 pandemic, the governmental authorities will continuously have to balance trust with control, in order to gain a perceived risk level that ensures compliance from the population (Betsch et al., 2020; Schoorman et al., 2007; Sitkin & George, 2005). If there is too much reliance of trust, the situation can come out of control when people no longer see the point in following strict regulations, either because the measures taken are not working as expected or because the spreading of the disease appears to be lowering from natural causes. Conversely, having too much control can undermine the positive effects of trust, leading to public disobedience, uproar, and riot.

Experiences and Lessons Learned

First, our experiences with managing the corona crisis have widened our knowledge and skills about crisis management and communication. Trust in crisis management and communication has been resilient in our institution during covid-19 crisis, due to the high trust in government in our society and our traditions in Norwegian working life with cooperation and involvement in decision-making processes. However, trust is fragile when expectations of predictability and care for people's well-being are not met. Second, we have learned much about the strength lying in building strong relationships with colleagues. Development and maintenance of psychological contracts between colleagues and between leaders and employees are important, especially during crisis. Third, the way we use digital communication and digital teaching methods today has been a disruptive innovation in our institution. Digitalization has opened borders between campuses and faculties and made our communication more effective. Digital teaching methods have made teaching more flexible and we are now able to include more student groups when teaching on digital platforms. Last, we have learned lessons about the impact of both organizational trust and individual trust in time of crisis. Our teaching methods and ways to communicate have been changed forever, and we have learned a lot about how to adapt to sudden changes and how to respond to crises. What we have experienced will contribute to a more resilient organizing, better inter- and intra-communication strategies, better student welfare strategies, better teaching methods, and better internal and external collaboration. We will not "go back to normal." Some of the ways we are working together today will be the "the new normal."

From a stable situation for our department and our institution, to an unstable situation, and from there moving to a new equilibrium, not like the situation we left and not yet stable—we do not know what comes next, but we are sure we will not go back to things like they were before March 12, 2020. Czarniawska (2000) sites Todorov (1977, p. 111): "An 'ideal' narrative begins with a stable situation, which is disturbed by some power or force. There results a state of disequilibrium; by the action of a force directed in the opposite direction, the equilibrium is re-established; the second equilibrium is similar to the first, but the two are never identical ..."

References

Bakken, Bjørn Tallak. (2020). Between chaos and control: The practical relevance of military strategy in fighting and recovering from a pandemic outbreak. In Samir Rawat, Ole Boe, & Andrzej Piotrowski (Eds.), *Military psychology response to post pandemic reconstruction* (pp. 585–599). Rawat Publications.

Bakken, Bjørn Tallak, & Hærem, Thorvald. (2020). Adaptive decision making in crisis management. In Marta Sinclair (Ed.), *Handbook of intuition research as practice* (pp. 14–26). Edward Elgar.

Bakken, Bjørn Tallak, Hole, Åse Storhaug, Malasevska, Iveta, Kårstein, Asbjørn, & Lund, Per Olav. (2020). Evaluation of crisis management and communication in Inland Norway University of Applied Sciences during the covid-19 crisis. Inland Norway University of Applied Sciences.

Barber, Bernard. (1983). *The logic and limits of trust*. Rutgers University Press.

Betsch, Cornelia, Wieler, Lothar H., & Habersaat, Katrine. (2020). Monitoring behavioural insights related to COVID-19. *The Lancet, 395*(10232), 1255–1256.

Blaikie, Norman, & Priest, Jan. (2019). *Designing social research: The logic of anticipation*. Wiley.

Boin, Arjen, t Hart, Paul, Stern, Eric, & Sundelius, Bengt. (2005). *The politics of crisis management: Understanding public leadership when it matters most*. Cambridge University Press.

Braun, Virginia, & Clarke, Victoria. (2006). Using thematic analysis in psychology. *Qualitative Research in Psychology, 3*(2), 77–101.

Breuer, Christina, Hüffmeier, Joachim, Hibben, Frederike, & Hertel, Guido. (2020). Trust in teams: A taxonomy of perceived trustworthiness factors and risk-taking behaviors in face-to-face and virtual teams. *Human Relations, 73*(1), 3–34.

Brundrett, Mark. (1998). What lies behind collegiality, legitimation or control? An analysis of the purported benefits of collegial management in education. *Educational Management & Administration, 26*(3), 305–316.

Chen, Ying-Hueih, Lin, Tzu-Pei, & Yen, David C. (2014). How to facilitate inter-organizational knowledge sharing: The impact of trust. *Information & Management, 51*(5), 568–578.

Christensen, Tom, & Lægreid, Per. (2020). The coronavirus crisis—Crisis communication, meaning-making, and reputation management. *International Public Management Journal, 23*(5), 713–729.

Coleman, James S. (1988). Social capital in the creation of human capital. *American Journal of Sociology, 94*, 95–120.

Coombs, W. Timothy. (2011). *Ongoing crisis communication. Planning, managing and responding*. Sage.

Czarniawska, Barbara. (2000). The uses of narrative in organization research. *GRI reports*.

Dirks, Kurt T., & Ferrin, Donald L. (2001). The role of trust in organizational settings. *Organization Science, 12*(4), 450–467.

Dirks, Kurt T., & Ferrin, Donald L. (2002). Trust in leadership: Meta-analytic findings and implications for research and practice. *Journal of Applied Psychology, 87*(4), 611.

Ferlie, Ewan, Musselin, Christine, & Andresani, Gianluca. (2008). The steering of higher education systems: A public management perspective. *Higher Education, 56*(3), 325.

Fernandez, Antonio Arturo, & Shaw, Graham Paul. (2020). Academic leadership in a time of crisis: The coronavirus and COVID-19. *Journal of Leadership Studies, 14*(1), 39–45.

Giddens, Anthony. (1984). *The constitution of society: Outline of the theory of structuration*. University of California Press.

Grant, Adam M. (2008). Does intrinsic motivation fuel the prosocial fire? Motivational synergy in predicting persistence, performance, and productivity. *Journal of Applied Psychology, 93*(1), 48.

Hannah, Sean T., Uhl-Bien, Mary, Avolio, Bruce J., & Cavarretta, Fabrice L. (2009). A framework for examining leadership in extreme contexts. *The Leadership Quarterly, 20*(6), 897–919.

Harris, Alma. (2010). Distributed leadership: Evidence and implications. In T. Bush, L. Bell, & D. Middlewood (Eds.), *The principles of educational leadership and management* (pp. 55–60). Sage.

Hole, Åse Storhaug, & Sverdrup, Therese E. (2020). The influence of psychological contracts on decision-making in whistleblowing processes. In P. J. Svenkerud, J. O. Sørnes, & L. Browning (Eds.), *Whistleblowing, communication and consequences: Lessons from the Norwegian National Lottery* (pp. 185–200). Routledge.

Hvid, Helge, & Falkum, Eivind. (2018). *Work and wellbeing in the Nordic Countries: Critical perspectives on the world's best working lives*. Routledge.

Kim, Peter H., Dirks, Kurt T., & Cooper, Cecily D. (2009). The repair of trust: A dynamic bilateral perspective and multilevel conceptualization. *Academy of Management Review, 34*(3), 401–422.

Lincoln, Yvonna S., & Guba, Egon G. (1985). *Naturalistic inquiry*. Sage.

Mayer, Roger C., Davis, James H., & Schoorman, F. David. (1995). An integrative model of organizational trust. *Academy of Management Review, 20*(3), 709–734.

McAllister, Daniel J. (1995). Affect-and cognition-based trust as foundations for interpersonal cooperation in organizations. *Academy of Management Journal, 38*(1), 24–59.

Meyerson, Debra, Weick, Karl E., & Kramer, Roderick M. (1996). Swift trust and temporary groups. In R. M. Kramer & T. R. Tyler (Eds.), *Trust in organizations: Frontiers of theory and research* (pp. 166–196). Sage.

Miles, Raymond E., & Snow, Charles C. (1992). Causes of failure in network organizations. *California Management Review, 34*(4), 53–72.

Møller, Jorunn, & Ottesen, Eli. (2011). *Rektor som leder og sjef: om styring, ledelse og kunnskapsutvikling i skolen*. Universitetsforlaget.

Morrison, Elisabeth W., & Robinson, Sandra L. (1997). When employees feel betrayed: A model of how psychological contract violation develops. *Academy of Management Review, 22*(1), 226–256.

Ndlela, Martin. (2019). *Crisis communication. A stakeholder approach.* Palgrave Macmillan.

Nilsson, Magnus, & Mattes, Jannika. (2015). The spatiality of trust: Factors influencing the creation of trust and the role of face-to-face contacts. *European Management Journal, 33*(4), 230–244.

Norwegian Directorate for Civil Protection. (2019). *Analysis of crisis scenarios* (pp. 68–71). https://www.dsb.no/globalassets/dokumenter/rapporter/p2001636_aks_2019_eng.pdf

OECD. (2017). *Government at a glance: Trust in government.* https://www.oecd-ilibrary.org/sites/gov_glance-2017-76-en/index.html?itemId=/content/component/gov_glance-2017-76-en

Restubog, Simon Lloyd D., Bordia, Prashant, & Tang, Robert L. (2007). Behavioural outcomes of psychological contract breach in a non-western culture: The moderating role of equity sensitivity. *British Journal of Management, 18*(4), 376–386.

Ritchie, Jane, Lewis, Jane, Nicholls, C. M., & Ormston, R. (2013). *Qualitative research practice: A guide for social science students and researchers.* Sage.

Robinson, Sandra L., & Rousseau, Denise M. (1994). Violating the psychological contract: Not the exception but the norm. *Journal of Organizational Behavior, 15*(3), 245–259.

Rothstein, Bo, & Stolle, Dietlind. (2003). Introduction: Social capital in Scandinavia. *Scandinavian Political Studies, 26*(1), 1–26.

Rousseau, Denise M. (1990). New hire perceptions of their own and their employer's obligations: A study of psychological contracts. *Journal of Organizational Behavior, 11*(5), 389–400.

Rousseau, Denise. (1995). *Psychological contracts in organizations: Understanding written and unwritten agreements.* Sage.

Rousseau, Denise M. (2004). Psychological contracts in the workplace. Understanding the ties that motivate. *Academy of Management Executive, 18*(1), 120–127.

Rousseau, Denise M., & Tijoriwala, Snehal A. (1998). Assessing psychological contracts: Issues, alternatives and measures. *Journal of Organizational Behavior, 19*, 679–695.

Rousseau, Denise M., Sitkin, Sim B., Burt, Ronald S., & Camerer, Colin. (1998). Not so different after all: A cross-discipline view of trust. *Academy of Management Review, 23*(3), 393–404.

Schoorman, F. David, Mayer, Roger C., & Davis, James H. (2007). An integrative model of organizational trust: Past, present, and future. *Academy of Management Review, 20*(3), 709–734.

Sitkin, S. B., & George, Elisabeth. (2005). Managerial trust-building through the use of legitimating formal and informal control mechanisms. *International Sociology, 20*(3), 307–338.

Sitkin, Sim B., & Roth, Nancy L. (1993). Explaining the limited effectiveness of legalistic "remedies" for trust/distrust. *Organization Science, 4*(3), 367–392.

Svendsen, Gunnar L. H., & Svendsen, Gert T. (2015). The puzzle of the Scandinavian welfare state and social trust. *Issues in Social Science, 3*(2), 90–99.

Sverdrup, Therese E. (2012). *The strength of reciprocity: Exploring horizontal psychological contracts in work groups.* Unpublished doctoral dissertation, NHH Norwegian School of Economics, Bergen.

Thompson, Jeffery A., & Bunderson, J. Stuart. (2003). Violations of principle: Ideological currency in the psychological contract. *Academy of Management Review, 28*(4), 571–586.

Todorov, T. (1977). *The Poetics of Prose*. Blackwell.

Trygstad, Sissel C., & Andersen, Rolf K. (2021). Medbestemmelse og medvirkning i krisetider. (Participation and involvement in decision-making during crises). Fafo-Report, 2021.

Vantilborgh, Tim, Bidee, Jemima, Pepermans, Roland, Willems, Jurgen, Huybrechts, Guy, & Jegers, Marc. (2014). Effects of ideological and relational psychological contract breach and fulfilment on volunteers' work effort. *European Journal of Work & Organizational Psychology, 23*(2), 217–230.

Woolthuis, Rosalinde K., Hillebrand, Bas, & Nooteboom, Bart. (2005). Trust, contract and relationship development. *Organization Studies, 26*(6), 813–840.

Working Environment Act. (2005). *Act relating to working environment, working hours and employment protection, etc* (LOV-2005-06-17-62). Lovdata. https://lovdata.no/dokument/NL/lov/2005-06-17-62

Zhao, Hao, Wayne, Sandy J., Glibkowski, Brian C., & Bravo, Jesus. (2007). The impact of psychological contract breach on work-related outcomes: A meta-analysis. *Personnel Psychology, 60*(3), 647–680.

CHAPTER 15

The Role of Communication, Institutional Trust and Reputation to Health Advice Adherence: Lessons from a Case Study of the Norwegian Institute of Public Health During the COVID-19 Pandemic

Prosper Ameh Kwei-Narh and Leif Rydstedt

As the psychosocial and economic consequences of the COVID-19 pandemic accumulate (Xiong et al., 2020), and a section of the public wavers in its adherence to the COVID-19 health guidance, one wonders how much worse it can get before it gets better. This global crisis is putting societal endurance and government crisis management to the test. The

We thank Mr. Jan Behrens at Ipsos for arranging access to their dataset. We also thank Dr. Kirsti Jylha for initial discussions and ideas.

P. A. Kwei-Narh (✉) • L. Rydstedt
Faculty of Business & Social Sciences, Inland Norway University of Applied Sciences, Elverum, Norway
e-mail: prosper.kwei-narh@inn.no; Leif.Rydstedt@inn.no

L. D. Browning et al. (eds.), *Organizational Communication and Technology in the Time of Coronavirus*,
https://doi.org/10.1007/978-3-030-94814-6_15

COVID-19 pandemic and its management, as a crisis, call into question institutional trust, institutional reputation, public adherence to health guidelines and adherence to subsequent directives from these institutions. For starters, institutional trust—the positive expectation that an institution will do what is right for its stakeholders—is jeopardized if the general public does not perceive the government and state institutions to be doing what is required to deal with the crisis or acting in the public's best interest (Meredith et al., 2007). Institutional trust reflects stakeholders' confident beliefs in an institution's ability to deal with a crisis (Cerna, 2014; Gilson, 2006). The track record of trustworthy actions also contributes to institutional trust. According to Cerna (2014), reputation is related to trust because it involves direct experience with the institution. Finally, managing the COVID-19 crisis so far involves individuals adhering to regulations communicated with the aim of protecting the public from the risks of the COVID-19 pandemic. Most of these regulations, such as social distancing, regularly washing hands and using "uncomfortable" face masks, are very stringent and unprecedented restrictions. Nonetheless, the continued qualified success in managing the COVID-19 pandemic in certain parts of the world suggests that the various stakeholders—governments, institutions and the public—have collaborated very well.

Contextualizing the full COVID-19 crisis management story involves accounting for the nature of institutional trust, reputation and adherence behaviors among these stakeholders. We aim to complete this accounting by examining theoretical aspects of crisis management, communication and public perceptions in examining the work of a critical stakeholder, the Norwegian Institute of Public Health (NIPH), during this crisis. As we will show, existing crisis communication models will be reintegrated to develop a coherent narrative. The COVID-19 pandemic is a specific type of crisis, a "creeping crisis" (Boin et al., 2020); nevertheless, it has triggered context-specific crisis intervention needs and activated varying risks to institutions and the public. As a result, we combine this evolving theory of creeping crisis (Boin et al., 2020) with existing situational crisis communication theory (SCCT; Coombs, 2006; Coombs & Holladay, 2002) to investigate how institutional trustworthiness and reputation influence adherence to health advice in a case study of the NIPH.

There is no doubt at this point that this COVID-19 pandemic is a crisis—a situation that can cause unexpected harms to various stakeholders and values (Coombs, 2010; Lyon & Cameron, 2004). Within any crisis is the attribution of responsibility for the crisis (Coombs, 2006), and based on this attribution, the organization develops a crisis management strategy. Existing crisis communication theories, however, must be re-evaluated when applied to the COVID-19 pandemic because this crisis does not fall neatly within the core frames of most crises; that is, to identify who is responsible for the crisis and whose reputation is most at risk. In adopting Coombs' situational crisis communication theory (SCCT), the COVID-19 pandemic falls under the victim cluster. Within the victim cluster, neither the government/institution nor its stakeholders are to blame for the crisis, but some stakeholders face reputational harm regardless of culpability (Coombs, 2010). For example, the government and health institutions must meet significant public expectations (Finset et al., 2020). Governments are expected to be proactive, open and caring (Finset et al., 2020; Moss & Sandbakken, 2021). Health institutions must be seen as sharing relevant information in a timely manner, demonstrating care and consistency in behavior. Health experts have a special responsibility to provide accurate information and to implement measures that safeguard the public (Finset et al., 2020; White et al., 2021). The implicit assumption within SCCT is that crises can be clearly defined by a starting and ending period. The COVID-19 pandemic may have a definite start date, but it appears to be a creeping crisis—a slowly evolving crisis with precursor events and varying degrees of success at managing the crisis (Boin et al., 2020). Managing this crisis involves responsible stakeholders establishing public confidence through health communication that builds trust (Palenchar & Heath, 2002; Seeger et al., 1998).

Persuasive health communication is predicated on trust, particularly institutional trust (Devine et al., 2020; Peters et al., 1997). Institutional trust reflects confidence that an institution is meeting expectations. According to Shockley-Zalabak and colleagues, the drivers of trust include competence, openness and honesty, concern for employees and stakeholders, reliability, and identification (Shockley-Zalabak & Ellis, 2006; Shockley-Zalabak & Morreale, 2011). The specifics of these drivers of trust are as follows: The *competence* dimension reflects how effectively the organization handles the crisis and survives after the crisis. Because this crisis is ongoing, competence is an evaluation of the effectiveness of plans and advice. *Openness and honesty* reflect the sincerity, quantity, sufficiency and appropriateness of the information during the crisis. The information must be evolving and relevant for particular moments in the public space, such as holidays and cultural events. When there is a forthcoming holiday, information pertaining to social distancing or travel will be a useful indicator of openness and honesty. *Concern* reflects the sincerity of the institution's effort in attempting to understand stakeholders' feelings during a crisis. The institution must be seen to be *reliable*, as demonstrated by the consistency and dependability of their actions. Finally, *identification* reflects signals that tie in with the common goals, norms, values and beliefs associated with the organization (in this case the society). When combined, these factors point to how institutions are perceived as trustworthy during the crisis.

In Norway, various agencies work in collaboration with the government in managing the COVID-19 pandemic. The NIPH oversees the gathering and dissemination of epidemiological information regarding COVID-19 to the public, as well as advising the Norwegian government on policy. This organization is an important node in understanding COVID-19 management because they have the technical competence and state mandate to make recommendations to the public and to the government. The NIPH does its work through connecting with laboratories and through a networked system of alerts and reports both nationally and internationally. How this institution has acted in the past, the effectiveness of its crisis communication in evoking trust and its public reputation all have an impact on public adherence to health guidelines (Meredith et al., 2007). Lapses in these factors could have an impact on adherence to health advice (Siegrist & Zingg, 2014).

In general, institutional trust is both distinct from, yet based on, general societal trust, and Norwegian society normally scores very high on measures of social and institutional trust (Oksanen et al., 2020). All the same, even within the same society, different institutions can have different degrees of public trust (Ward, 2017). Furthermore, the NIPH has always scored high on measures of trust. However, trust can easily be lost when the issue is important for stakeholders (Devine et al., 2020). For example, trust could be lost in this COVID-19 pandemic if relevant institutional communication and behavior did not demonstrate competence, openness, care and concern. The very nature of this pandemic poses a challenge to trustworthiness. The lack of knowledge at the beginning of the pandemic limited the ability to demonstrate competence (Devine et al., 2020). Even though virus infection specialists had some knowledge about the COVID-19 virus, much was unknown during the early phase of the virus (NIPH, 2020), and thus, the public perception of institutional competence was perilous. When an institution is faced with uncertainty, they may be cautious in releasing information and thus risk being perceived as nontransparent. Any indication of a lack of transparency or concern for the public would have undermined institutional trust. As the COVID-19 virus prevails in society and information from other sources becomes available, the NIPH has to continually show through their communication that they can revise their earlier conclusions and limit their guidelines to the emerging facts in order to maintain trust (Smith, 2017). The public will have the general expectation that they are not being unnecessarily placed under strict demands out of fear, but through a genuine evaluation of the evidence and the risks confronting society. Indeed, the public will expect that decisions are made for their interests in order to maintain institutional trust. It also seems that trust is enhanced when there is more information rather than less information, because crisis creates a strong need for information in order to reduce uncertainty.

When the public distrusts institutions, they are less likely to adhere to the health regulations and advice that will be given by these institutions (Devine et al., 2020). For instance, low institutional trust has been linked to higher mortality during this COVID-19 pandemic (Oksanen et al., 2020). Eventual plans to enhance vaccine uptake also depend on the level of trust in the health institutions (Carlsen et al., 2020; Vinck et al., 2019). Organizational reputation also plays a key role as members of the public revise their beliefs and expectations of the Institute as a result of their exposure to NIPH in the media. The NIPH has to be seen as modelling the right expectations in order to convince stakeholders of the genuineness of their advice. To be clear, we do not claim that the NIPH is the only/most important actor for the adherence to COVID-19 guidelines, but we chose to analyze this institution because in comparison with the government, it is perceived as being more neutral and as having the technical competence to inform the public on the right strategies.

Based on the foregoing, we aimed to build a holistic, theoretically informed account of crisis communication and its association with adherence to COVID-19 health guidelines. We relied on multiple theoretical positions and triangulated data sources to create a rich account of a key stakeholder in the crisis management of COVID-19. Our theoretical contribution will be to integrate situational crisis communication theory (SCCT) with the creeping crises framework to understand a creeping crisis that includes issues of reputation, trust and public adherence to health advice. Our practical contribution is to the agencies that manage various slow-paced crises. To these agencies, understanding the dominant element of trust in their communication will be key (White et al., 2021). Although an organization may not be responsible for a crisis, their reputation plays an important role, and they need to gather information from multiple sources to leverage effective communication targeted at public compliance (Holmes et al., 2009).

Theory

The Challenges of Fitting the COVID-19 Pandemic into a Coherent Crisis Communication Theory and Proposing an Integrated Perspective

There is no question that the practice of crisis management relies on communication and trust, but a lot of the studies undertaken on the topic are primarily atheoretical. Many crisis communication theories exist (Siegrist & Zingg, 2014), but we consider the COVID-19 pandemic to evoke issues of responsibility and reputation/trust. Responsibility in this case is not about who caused the problem, but who can enable stakeholders to make meaning within the crisis. We therefore adopt situational crisis communication theory for our purposes. Situational crisis communication theory—SCCT—(Coombs, 2006, 2010; Coombs & Holladay, 2002) articulates that within any crisis are two core issues: responsibility and risks to reputation. Developed from attribution theory, SCCT seeks to prescribe ways in which an organization can match their crisis response to the attribution of responsibility. SCCT constructed a typology of crisis responsibility and associated prescriptive strategies. To begin, once the public has been informed about how to handle the crisis, the organization must seek a communication strategy that manages its reputation based on public perception of crisis responsibility. The SCCT categorizes a crisis into three core stages: pre-crisis (plans and preparations in place before the actual crisis); crisis (i.e., the event whose onset destabilizes the organization); and post-crisis (Coombs, 2006). We will, in this chapter, focus only on the pre-crisis and actual crisis stages.

As the public witnesses a crisis, they evaluate who is responsible for the crisis and how the responsible organization is treating crisis victims. SCCT therefore suggests that the organization must adopt a strategy that demonstrates that it cares for the victims of the crisis and knows the acceptable way to behave, thereby meeting public expectations. The theory details how the severity of a crisis and institutional performance history all contribute to the attribution of responsibility for the crisis. If a crisis is severe and an institution has a poor performance history in the area in which the crisis is concerned, stakeholders will regard the institution as responsible. Coombs and Holladay (2002) classified the range of crises, from natural disasters to sabotage, into three clusters: victim, accidental and preventable. We find that crises such as natural disasters are in the victim cluster, where both the organization and its stakeholders are victims. Accidental crises are defined as unintentional actions by the organization, such as technical breakdowns, for which the organization bears a moderate degree of crisis responsibility. The third cluster, preventable crises, includes, for example, organizational misdeeds or human communication breakdowns, where the crisis is caused by an organization's intentional actions that put stakeholders at risk.

Surprisingly, an organization's reputation can suffer whether or not the crisis is the result of its actions. The SCCT model is very useful in explaining fast crises ('t Hart & Boin, 2001), which are crises with a definite onset and resolution. When the crisis slowly escalates, it may not evoke the same response from organizations, but it may cause reputational damage all the same.

Creeping Crisis

Boin et al. (2020) catalogued a number of crises that started slowly and thus escaped public attention until they reached raging proportions (Boin et al., 2020). These creeping crises are exemplified by pandemics like HIV/AIDS, the European migration crisis and the COVID-19 pandemic. According to Boin and colleagues (2020, p. 122), a "creeping crisis is a threat to widely shared societal values that evolves over time and space, is foreshadowed by precursor events, subject to varying degrees of political and/or societal attention, and impartially or insufficiently addressed by authorities." These creeping crises may emerge in one location and spread to several locations, although the public and policymakers may not notice it as a crisis. Nonetheless, one can trace the root causes and the process by which a creeping crisis is activated into becoming a full-fledged crisis. Indeed, this framework is a useful lens for relating the nature of the victim cluster (in SCCT) to reputational threat according to SCCT theory.

The creeping crisis framework (Boin et al., 2020) can be used to explain why, as suggested by SCCT theory, organizations can become victims in times of crisis. Here, the organization is a victim because it is not directly responsible for the outbreak of the crisis. The unanticipated crisis may begin in a different location and thus escape the attention of the organization until it is too late. When the organization finally recognizes the crisis, the initial crisis management strategies may be insufficient and thus put the organization at risk of reputational damage. The organization, through its actions, can communicate intentions and behaviors which may help maintain their reputation and increase institutional trust in the organization. In this case, trust and reputation are dependent not only on the history of trust of the organization but on the sincerity and transparency of the organization's conduct during a crisis.

Trust Building Communication, Institutional Confidence and Institutional Reputation in Crisis Management

According to Shockley-Zalabak and Ellis (2006, p. 49), "trust is communication based. It influences and is the outcome of communication behaviours such as providing accurate information, giving explanations for decisions, and demonstrating sincere and appropriate openness." While trust is relational, institutional trust is demonstrated by public confidence in an institution's ability to manage an issue such that the public's expectations are met (Tonkiss, 2009). When people are being asked to make sacrifices, as they are in this COVID-19 pandemic, then trust is even more important (Hetherington, 2005). For example, trust has been associated with compliance to health advice during the Ebola outbreak in West Africa in 2014–2016 (Blair et al., 2017), and likewise during an H1N1 flu outbreak in Italy (Siegrist & Zingg, 2014).

As the NIPH institution engages in disseminating information and providing advice about the COVID-19 virus/pandemic, we can see that their work will be given attention and thus is important to the public. According to Hetherington and Husser (2012), trust is driven by policy saliency. If, over the course of the pandemic, the decisions made and the actions taken (even in the moments of uncertainty) are proven justifiable, public expectations will be met and indicated by higher institutional trust and reputation. Trust in this sense is not static, but rather dynamic—easily lost when the public expectations are not met, but also easily increased when the expectations are met. Crises create desire among stakeholders for information necessary to tackle the crises. Thus, stakeholders who are gatekeepers for this information have a high responsibility to meet. Honesty and consistency of information are central drivers in increasing trust in public health services during emergencies (Meredith et al., 2007). The public, as stakeholders, will need adequate information from the institution, who themselves are handicapped by uncertainty regarding the COVID-19 pandemic. The public is not relying on the NIPH exclusively for information during this COVID-19 pandemic but on other sources both national and international (Naeem & Bhatti, 2020). However, timeliness of communication and continued access to information play important roles. NIPH must be perceived as providing timely information and making fact-based decisions, which in turn further enhances institutional trust. The stakeholders have information asymmetry, and in this case the experts do not have all the information needed. In communicating this information, the themes of honesty and transparency come to the fore. Honesty during a crisis involves full transparency regarding all the known and unknown issues within the COVID-19 pandemic and consistency regarding the nature and framing of reports. Furthermore, institutional trust is also about the extent to which stakeholders feel their interests are represented, and this predicts their adherence to health information about avoidance behaviors to avoid virus outbreaks (Vinck et al., 2019).

Adherence to COVID-19 Containment Measures

In treating the pandemic, measures such as self-isolation, regular handwashing and using face masks are key impositions placed on the public aimed at minimizing the spread of the virus. However, these adherence interventions are not automatically accepted by the public; rather, the public considers multiple factors, such as institutional and political trust. For example, in Denmark, willingness to socially distance is related to political trust which also predicts compliance to health advice (Olsen & Hjorth, 2020, May 4). Likewise, Prati et al.'s (2011) telephone survey in Italy after the H1N1 virus in 2009 examined risk perception, trust and compliance with health recommendations during the pandemic. Their results showed that respondents who adopted recommendations were those who trusted the health authorities. In the current instance, a NIPH-led survey examined adherence to getting tested for COVID-19 when respondents manifested symptoms of the COVID-19 disease. Less than 50 percent of respondents voluntarily tested for COVID-19 when they had symptoms of the disease. Yet, when these same respondents with COVID-19 disease symptoms were tested, 65–72 percent were later quarantined.

Context of the Study

The NIPH is a government agency that reports directly to the Ministry of Health and Care Services. The NIPH has expertise in a wide range of health topics and provides technical advice to the government, the health service, the judiciary, the media and the public. It is primarily responsible for disease diagnosis and prevention, and in relation to COVID-19, it oversees monitoring and communicating about the pandemic to the government and the general public (NIPH, 2020). The NIPH also conducts research in order to disseminate information to the public. It has traditionally been at the forefront of national interventions in dealing with various national health issues such as the seasonal flu and provides advice on international health issues that may affect Norway. During the ongoing COVID-19 pandemic, it performs this function by issuing weekly risk assessment reports. This COVID-19 risk assessment report summarizes evolving knowledge on the pandemic, with a focus on data from accredited medical laboratories in Norway and the most recent research from the rest of the world. The NIPH monitors the epidemiological situation in Norway by using a number of messaging systems, alerts and laboratory input, and integrates these inputs into a centralized system, MSIS (Meldingssytemet for smittsomme sykdommer). They also rely on hospitalization records in assessing the COVID-19 infection rates. NIPH frequently concludes the report by offering advice based on accumulated knowledge. For the purposes of this chapter, we used communication issued through the NIPH website as crisis communication information. We also report our own survey of a convenient sample of informants on their trust in NIPH, and we reanalyzed relevant aspects of the Ipsos reputation survey (IPSOS, 2020).

The COVID-19 Pandemic in Norway and NIPH Communication About the Pandemic as Sourced from Their Website

When news broke out regarding the outbreak of the COVID-19 pandemic, the government assured citizens that Norway was prepared to handle the pandemic (22.01.2020, via vg nett-). The NIPH was quick to issue a 13-page risk evaluation report on 28.01.2020 about the COVID-19 epidemic (NIPH, 2020) with special attention to the areas of uncertainty about COVID-19 (NIPH, 2020, p. 4). Thereafter, the NIPH issued a weekly COVID-19 risk report which can be accessed on their website (http://www.fhi.no). We relied on reports between January 2020 through November 2020 which overlaps with our primary survey and the Ipsos reputation report.

The Evolving Nature of NIPH Communication

Part of NIPH duties is to gather and disseminate epidemiological data and advice to the government and to the public. We do not have unbridled access to all internal communication and discussions regarding this coronavirus, but their public communication gives a reliable indication of their guiding policies (Allen & Caillouet, 1994) and strategies to the government and the media. A more detailed report on the internal and external aspects of NIPH's role during this COVID-19 pandemic is found in the Koronakommisjon-report (Helsedirektoratet, 2021). For our purposes, we conducted a content analysis (Holladay, 2009) of NIPH weekly reports, which they began issuing to the public in order to generate a comprehensive understanding of communication that evokes trust. We limited ourselves to weekly epidemiological reports available between 21.03.2020 and 15.11.2020, which overlaps with our quantitative data collection. We conducted a real-time analysis of the communication environment to determine what was being communicated to the public (Savoia et al., 2013), thus guiding the public trust in and high reputation of the institution.

During the content analyses, we segmented four key moments in the pattern of communication. These moments in a progressive series are (i) an early phase characterized by preparatory strategies and establishment of systems; (ii) an emergent phase, where uncertainty still prevailed but was marked by NIPH issuing advice in their summaries; (iii) a growing phase of convergence in understanding the nature of COVID-19; and (iv) further convergence in understanding and a re-interpretation of the data in addition to definite conclusions. These moments are further elaborated below because of their relevance to trust-based communication. The first report was issued on 18.03.2021, containing information and data that was gained from laboratories and health institutions. The core aspects of the epidemiological information they reported on will not be included here due to space limitation and to minimize the scope of the discussion.

An Uncertain Early Phase (Weeks 12–18)

The uncertain phase was marked by preparation for handling the crisis, an oscillation in the testing criteria, the establishment of centralized systems, and attempts at managing expectation and stating areas of uncertainty. *Preparation* involved establishing roles and internal meetings held within the NIPH. Lab data was also used to check the strains of the virus: s- for original and L- for the mutated strains. NIPH used this method to identify clusters of infections at various stages (e.g., one cluster of infection was localized to Oslo University Hospital). The report also discussed strategies of improving the quality and quantity of epidemiological reports from the laboratories and health institutions and the establishment of MSIS. They also created a system where the public could report suspected symptoms of the disease. The *oscillation* in the testing criteria was characterized by excluding patients with some symptoms from mandatory requirements to test and later including those patients with symptoms within mandatory requirements to test. For instance, people with mild symptoms returning home after foreign travels were no longer required to be tested. They also described that testing for SARS-CoV-2 started on 23 January 2020, with the first reported case on 26 February 2020. In addition to primary data sourced from the laboratory and health systems, they established mathematical models to estimate potential rates of infection and incidence of COVID-19 cases. The areas of *uncertainty* identified in their reports concern how the prevailing testing criteria may influence weekly infection rates from the laboratory data and a lack of an accurate total number of infected cases. While the true extent of the penetration of the disease was unknown, NIPH opined that a more stable picture of infections are from hospital records, which often have a time lag of two weeks before being updated in the centralized system. A marked quality here is that the NIPH did not make any comments beyond the analyses of the core elements of the reports: infection rates, biographical information on those testing positive, those in intensive care units and total fatalities.

An Emergent Phase (Weeks 19–22)

We call this next phase "emergent" in that while there remains uncertainty, the NIPH began to issue tentative public advice. This week was also leading to the most important day in the Norwegian calendar, the yearly National Day celebrations on 17 May. While the epidemiological information was presented, the NIPH report anticipated that there could be more infections due to the gradual reopening of society. Indeed, infection rates were not dramatically changed in the subsequent weeks, but the NIPH was definite that the infection case counts would likely change as more tests were conducted.

A Growing Phase of Convergence on What the COVID-19 Entails (Weeks 23–39)

This phase reflects the areas of clarity and understanding in how the COVID-19 infection occurs and good practices for the local communities to adopt to control the pandemic. Over time, the NIPH weekly reports included all the relevant epidemiological details. They added that there was a need for tighter regulation within local communities involving contact tracing, isolation of the sick, increased testing capacity and rolling out of quarantine strategies within prevailing boundaries. They also gave attention to summer travels, which increase the risk of imported cases. Indeed, this period witnessed lower infection cases nationally. Through their analyses, NIPH was able to identify that most infections were spread through close contacts, travels and local outbreaks in clusters. They recommended tighter contact tracing within the local communities where infections were identified, and interventions focused within these communities. Indeed, this strategy was helpful in zoning cases of local outbreaks in three Norwegian cities (Bergen, Sarpsborg, and Oslo) and later infections carried by travelers originating from other countries.

A Bigger Picture Emerging, Characterized by More Detailed Analysis and Prognoses Beyond the Data (from Week 40)

We consider this stage the big-picture stage because it is noticeable that the NIPH had developed more robust mathematical models to estimate the rates of infection. We also noticed the reports contained more details and health advice. The report, though, contained some changes in the weekly infection numbers which were not explained; this was probably due to lagged data trickling in on a weekly basis. For instance, in the main Week 41 report, 1044 new cases were reported; but in Week 42, the infection figure for Week 41 was reported as 1058. (This seemed to be the case in several subsequent weeks.) This varying figure could be due to the weekly report being issued on Wednesdays, but it could also be due to some data being reported later into the MSIS (recall, there is a lag of about two to three weeks). NIPH's mathematical models indicated that throughout the pandemic until that date, the case diagnoses were as little as 1:5 or 1:7 as reported into the MSIS system. At the later phase, the cases identified shot up to 1:2 or 1:3. Their later analysis involved more confident conclusions on earlier data dating back to the beginning phase of the pandemic.

Reputation

The Ipsos organization conducts a yearly appraisal of institutional reputations (IPSOS, 2020), and the NIPH was one of the highest-scoring public institutions in the 2020 assessment (IPSOS, 2020). The reputation scores are computed on perceptions of the institution's social responsibility, financial effectiveness, openness and access to information, and competence. Social responsibility perception details the institute's ability and willingness to act responsibly toward the general public and to keep public confidence. Financial effectiveness reflects the perception that the institution performs its activities within budgets. Openness and access to information is the perception of ease in accessing the institution's work and how well the institution communicates about itself to the public. Lastly, competence reflects the perception of the institution's expertise within their domain.

We focused on reputational scores from 2017 to 2020, thus telling a more nuanced story. We noticed that the scores between 2017 and 2019 are similar; however, there was a dramatic increase in NIPH's reputation measured in 2020. As a basis for comparison, 1034 respondents were surveyed in 2019; 62 percent had a "very good" or "somewhat good" impression of NIPH. In 2020, of the 1019 people polled, 82 percent reported having a "very good" or "somewhat good" impression of NIPH. Below, we reproduce NIPH scores averaged over the years according to respondents' perception of the NIPH. These perceptions are due to NIPH's presence in the media and the central role they have been playing in managing the COVID-19 pandemic. Figure 15.1 highlights the dramatic changes and positive reputation that the NIPH attained during its role in the COVID-19 pandemic. The average of those with "very good" or "somewhat good" impressions of the NIPH was very high, and the number of respondents with no knowledge of the NIPH reduced in 2020. In explaining these figures, Ipsos remarked that apart from the perception

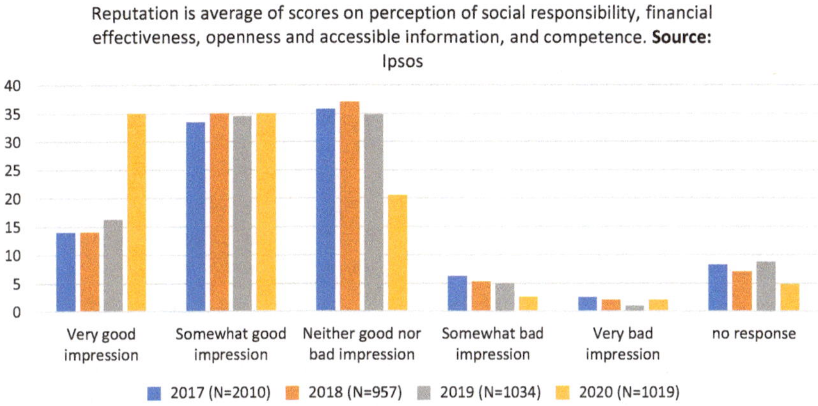

Fig. 15.1 Reputation of NIPH 2017–2020 in percentages on a 6-point Likert scale

that the agency is doing its work, NIPH's leaders have remained relatively free of scandals. All these contribute to the positive reputation the NIPH enjoys.

Quantitative Survey

Sample and Procedure

A convenient sample of respondents were sourced using a mixture of the snowballing technique and respondents from the first author's social network on Facebook, LinkedIN and telephone contacts via SMS. Individuals were invited to participate in a web-survey examining how COVID-19 has affected attitudes toward social institutions. The questionnaire was created in *nettskjema*, and participants were assured anonymity. Data were collected at two time points: March–May 2020 and September–November 2020, to ensure capturing trajectories of changes in variables of interest. We attempted to ensure that an equal number of respondents were sourced for each sample (March–May data, $N = 146$; September–November data, $N = 141$), making a total sample size of 287 (70 percent female). The age distributions within the sample were: 18–25 (37 percent), 26–40 (40 percent), 41–60 (18 percent) and 5 percent over the age of 60. In terms of the highest level of education, 23 percent reported having completed compulsory education, high school or other types of non-academic studies, while 77 percent reported some form of advanced academic education.

Trust in NIPH

Different stakeholders and institutions responsible for managing the COVID-19 virus were presented to the respondents, who then responded to a single item—measure of trust—on a 5-point Likert scale; that is, "*What trust do you have in these institutions and authorities when it comes to handling the coronavirus (COVID-19) in Norway?*" Here, since measurement took place after the first months of the pandemic, "trust" refers to the institution having met expectations. Responses ranged from 1 = very low to 5 = very high. In the entire sample, 10 percent of the participants reported *very low*, *low*, or *neither low nor high* trust in the NIPH, while 68 percent reported *rather high* and 22 percent *very high* trust in NIPH ($M = 4.09$; $SD = .46$; $\alpha = 0.70$). The trust in NIPH increased considerably between the two data collection points (from $M = 3.85$ and $SD = .48$ in Sample 1, to $M = 4.35$ and $SD = .71$ in Sample 2). This difference is significant with higher mean scores on the second data point as compared to the first data collection ($t = -5.35$; $df = 2.79$; $p < .001$).

Adherence to Health Advice

The Norwegian government, in consonance with other nations, issued several health guidelines intended to protect public health. In Norway, some of these included social distancing, regularly washing hands, using face masks, reduced use of public transport and staying home when sick. Participants were asked to rate how they adhered to these health guidelines on a 5-point scale (ranging from 1 = *I do not adhere at all* to 5 = *I totally adhere*). These items have acceptable internal consistency and are therefore grouped together to create the adherence scale ($M = 3.82$, $SD = .89$, Cronbach $\alpha = .70$).

What Is the Relationship Between Trust in NIPH and Adherence to Health Advice?

A one-way analysis of variance (ANOVA) showed that the measure of confidence in NIPH related significantly to adherence behaviors ($F_{4/282} = 2.63$;

$p < .05$). Thus, the stronger their confidence in NIPH the participants reported, the more they tended to follow the recommended measures.

What Is the Nature of Institutional Trust and Adherence Behaviors from Early Phase of the Pandemic to Later Phase?

As our analyses below show (Table 15.1), the patterns of adherence were inconsistent. While the reported institutional trust in NIPH was already fairly high at the first time point (April–May 2020), it increased considerably at the second time point (September–early November 2020). Furthermore, there was a significantly positive relationship between the reported confidence in NIPH and participants' COVID-19 knowledge (*Spearman rho* = 0.134, $p < .05$). When we examined all 12 recommendations, we noticed that adherence to the recommendations was not

Table 15.1 Adherence to recommendations at early phase (March–June 2020) and later phase (September–November 2020) of the COVID-19 pandemic

	March–May Sample (1)		*September–November Sample (2)*		*Mean difference*
Recommendations	*Mean*	*Std.D*	*Mean*	*Std.D*	$t_{1,2}$
Keep at least 1 meter distance	4.32	0.57	4.06	0.92	2.86**
(Will) stay at home when feeling ill	4.67	0.55	4.57	0.68	1.37
Often wash my hands with soap and warm water	4.71	0.53	4.51	0.71	2.13*
Often use disinfectants to keep my hands clean	*4.10*	*0.95*	*4.55*	*0.74*	*−4.39***
Coughs and sneezes in the elbow or in a paper tissue	4.54	0.54	4.54	0.57	0.11
Avoid touching my eyes, nose or mouth	3.18	0.98	3.23	0.95	-0.37
Use mouth-bind when I am out	*1.04*	*0.23*	*2.22*	*1.25*	*−11.1***
Avoid crowds	3.95	0.93	3.71	1.00	2.13*
Avoid social gatherings (e.g., parties)	4.35	0.96	3.68	1.12	5.47**
Avoid public transport	4.23	1.16	3.35	1.47	5.64**
Inform others about how to avoid spreading of COVID-19	2.89	1.09	2.77	1.03	0.99
Reduced my social contacts	4.34	0.87	3.64	1.09	5.99**

N = 287, 5-point Likert scale (1 = "not true at all" to 5 = "perfectly true"), * p<0.05, ** p<0.01

uniform. Adherence behaviors were significantly higher in the early phase than the September–November phase on the following behaviors: keeping at least one-meter distance, handwashing, avoiding crowds, avoiding social gatherings, avoiding public transport and reducing social contacts. On the other hand, there were significant increases in two behaviors during September–November when compared to March–May: respondents used more disinfectants to keep their hands clean and reported an increased use of face masks. Indeed, as at the time when the data was collected, the use of face masks in Norway was not a mandatory policy. There were three behaviors where we did not see any significant changes between the first data and the second data: staying at home when sick, coughing and sneezing into elbows, and informing others about how to avoid the spread of COVID-19.

One can only speculate about the causes for these somewhat contradictory findings. During the summer and early autumn 2020, the number of new cases dropped markedly compared to the initial first wave and were still relatively low compared to the second wave (FHI.no). Furthermore, the spread of the virus in Norway was relatively limited compared to most other European countries. Taken together, the way that the NIPH had managed to handle the pandemic up to that time seems to have strengthened public trust and confidence in the competence of NIPH. But since the pandemic had already been ongoing for quite a long period when the second questionnaire was distributed, it can be assumed that many people were fed up with the often intrusive restrictions and advice, such as keeping physical distance or avoiding all sorts of social contacts, which were the recommended behaviors that dropped the most between the two time points. On the other hand, use of face masks and disinfectants were possibly seen as less restrictive behaviors. As of the time of this data collection, the use of face masks was not mandatory government policy, so the personal choice to wear a mask is highly commendable. The use of disinfectants understandably increased, because they were made available at all public spaces.

Discussion

The purpose of this chapter was to examine the role of the NIPH in managing the COVID-19 crisis in Norway. We argued that as a central actor in managing the COVID-19 pandemic, NIPH's ability to influence the public to adhere to health measures hinges on communication that both inspires trust and maintains the good reputation that it enjoys. Pursuant to this objective, we triangulated data from three sources: NIPH's own communication, accessible on their website; our primary survey of a convenient sample and the Ipsos reputation survey. We contextualized our discussion by integrating situational crisis communication theory with the creeping crisis concept as the theoretical frame for our discussion. We highlight that theoretically, a crisis where all stakeholders are victims still carries a reputational cost. Nonetheless, institutional actions considered by the public as open, competent and caring altogether enable trust and development of reputation. The COVID-19 pandemic falls within the victim cluster crisis (in situational crisis communication theory), yet when an institution has no direct responsibility in a crisis, its reputation may suffer because responsibility is not just due to the initiation of a crisis but also the management of a crisis. In situations where there are clear mandates involved, stakeholders' actions enable crisis management through timely and adequate communication. Our data triangulation study of the NIPH during the (ongoing) COVID-19 pandemic revealed interesting insights that have both theoretical and practical implications. Below, we note some observations before highlighting the theoretical and practical implications.

What Is the Nature of Trust and Adherence Behaviors?

When crises occur, stakeholders are not only interested in who created the crisis but also who can manage the crisis (Christensen & Lægreid, 2020). When institutions are mandated to manage planned and unplanned crises, shirking this crisis management responsibility is not an option. How an institution manages the dual issues of stakeholders' perception of an institution (reputation) and how the institution is performing its role and meeting stakeholder's expectations (institutional trust) is fundamental to ensuring that stakeholders obey crisis management guidelines. Under the COVID-19 pandemic, institutional trust (Shockley-Zalabak & Ellis, 2006) and reputation are seen as game-changers in ensuring the public adheres to the challenging guidelines issued (Devine et al., 2020). In Norway, institutional trust is historically high, and the NIPH has traditionally scored high on trust and reputation (IPSOS, 2020). Intriguingly, high trust and reputation were further accentuated during the COVID-19 pandemic. When we examined how institutional trust in the NIPH and its reputation affect adherence behaviors, our data showed that institutional trust increased from its existing high levels. Interestingly, this accompanying increment in high trust was not accompanied by a corresponding increase in adherence to all the restrictions, apart from the use of face masks and sanitizers. The use of face masks was at the time not mandatory, so respondents' desire to use them may reflect a conscious decision around convenience and accessibility.

Face masks can be conveniently carried in pockets and handbags and used when coming in contact with others. At shopping malls and in public places, these face masks are worn and then discarded later. Although face masks were originally costly, they became cheaper over time. Related to convenience, disinfectants were available in small bottles which could be transported around. In addition, supermarkets and all public places installed antibacterial dispensers which enabled easy use of these sanitizers. We think the combined factors of accessibility and convenience explain the increase in adherence to these prevention regulations.

As the later cases of sporadic COVID-19 outbreaks at the national level will indicate, not all the regulations were adhered to, and this is mirrored in our findings. We see that there were significant differences in adherence to the guidelines from April–May 2020 to September–November 2020 (NIPH, 2020). Indeed, respondents in the second sample reported lower adherence to social distancing behaviors, handwashing, avoiding crowds, avoiding social gatherings, avoiding public transport and reducing social contacts. We propose that these adherence behaviors belong to two distinct clusters: a personal hygiene cluster (e.g., handwashing) and a social connection cluster (e.g., reducing social contacts). Personal hygiene guidelines, such as regular handwashing, are not as intrusive as minimizing social connections, which are very intrusive. For some respondents, handwashing may have seemed to mimic the benefits of applying antibacterial sanitizers and this may explain why respondents increased their use of hand sanitizers but reduced their reported handwashing. In addition, handwashing is associated with dryer skin, and some respondents may just prefer to use hand sanitizers.

The other cluster of adherence behaviors—the social connection cluster—is the behaviors that demand reducing social contacts through avoiding public transport and public gatherings. It was especially challenging for respondents to reduce their social contact or to avoid public transport. Understandably, a large percentage of our respondents were young and lived in cosmopolitan areas. This combination may be associated with lower access to private cars, and thus the use of public transport would be unavoidable. There seem to be other considerations involved; for instance, the NIPH conclusively reported that clusters of infection were mostly occurring among individuals with shared networks. The fact that our second sample reported lower adherence to social contact speaks to this observation. Indeed, there were several infractions of the adherence guidelines, as reported in the media. While the public often disavows non-adherence behaviors, it seems that instead of convening in large gatherings, some people found ingenious ways of maintaining contacts with their close networks, which speaks to the centrality of social contacts to both our need to make sense of our crises and to get support during these crises (Siegrist & Zingg, 2014). Social connections are fundamental to social wellness, and while there are significant consequences to breaking the social distance regulation (about 20,000 NOK), yet people nonetheless took risks.

Continuing this intriguing theme on adherence behaviors, we see that there were some behaviors which witnessed no significant change when comparing our first and second samples. Specifically, we identified three adherence behaviors which witnessed no significant changes: staying home when sick, coughing into the elbow and informing others about COVID-19. We can speculate that good healthcare, coupled with strong worker unions in Norwegian society, means being absent from work when sick is usual. In addition, personal hygiene and civility values, meaning coughing directly into one's elbow, is not fundamentally restrictive. We noticed that our respondents generally refrained from telling others about the COVID-19. This is a good practice because it reduces the diffusion of false beliefs about the COVID-19 and enables experts to do their work. Our overall conclusion when we examined the second data is that the pandemic had already been going on for quite a period when the second questionnaire was distributed. Probably many people felt fed-up with the intrusive restrictions and advice—such as keeping physical distance or avoiding social contacts; however, respondents adhered to the less restrictive and personal hygiene recommendations. This seems to suggest that respondents made choices based on convenience of guidelines and access to resources such as face masks and hand sanitizer.

SCCT Integrated with Creeping Crisis: Victim Cluster Crisis Is Also Reputational Crisis

When Coombs and colleagues (2006) formulated their SCCT and proposed strategies for managing the different clusters of crises, there was no specific proposal for dealing with the victim crises cluster. The ideas contained in the creeping crises framework are central for understanding the victim clusters. Central to both SCCT and creeping crisis is the issue of attention, which is the point at which an organization realizes the extent of a crisis and begins to plan for it. As we uncovered in our analyses, the NIPH and Norwegian media first reported the COVID-19 global infections in January 2020, but it was in late February 2020 before serious attention was given to the infections. During the planning stage, there were uncertainties regarding what criteria to use and whether or not individuals from hotspots but who were asymptomatic should be tested. The NIPH nonetheless demonstrated proactivity in creating systems where individuals could privately report symptoms of the disease. As will be seen later, these were all missed opportunities to identify points of contact and ensure local contact tracing. When the NIPH overcame their initial uncertainties and swung into full action, some of their effective tactics were to identify, test and engage in contact tracing in local communities. As Boin et al. (2020) pointed out, this revising and reviewing of initial assumptions highlights the central characteristics of creeping crises.

Despite the challenges to attention and planning during the COVID-19 pandemic, we also know that the NIPH is solely mandated to monitor epidemiological developments within and outside Norway. It is assigned the central role in acquiring information and making recommendations to the government. There was marked increase in its reputation, as indicated by the IPSOS survey and our own data which showed that respondents considered the NIPH to be meeting their expectations. Considering this data was gathered concurrent to the COVID-19 pandemic, there exists no external attribution for this sudden increase in reputation and trust beyond the public's perception of the extent of NIPH's management of the COVID-19 pandemic. Indeed, the core aspects of access to information, competence and social responsibility were scored very high in the responses we collected and also reported by Ipsos. Our analyses of NIPH public communication indicated frequent communication with the public and regular media engagement every week. In addition, the government included the NIPH in all critical public updates, thus highlighting public engagement.

Our analyses of the NIPH communicative activities talk about not only the frequency and salience of their activities, but a communication that is regularly in sync with and matches public expectations (Holmes et al., 2009). Of central importance was how NIPH adapted their messages to reflect the public's need for information around the periods leading to the National Day celebrations (May 17) and the summer holidays. The leadership of NIPH modelled the central aspects of their message in that, in examining the materials available to us, there were no top leaders from NIPH caught infringing on the health regulations, unlike other institutional leaders, such as the politicians. This degree of modelling is a relevant aspect of the trust process, further enhancing NIPH's reputation.

Limitations of the Study

Our study used a convenient sample of respondents recruited from social networks. It is likely some respondents participated in both data collection activities. With the intention to ensure participant anonymity, there was no way to link individual responses together to examine individual effects in the variables of interest. Our analyses also did not check for clustering of shared variance. Furthermore, since the study was designed as a panel study, including different participants at two points in time, the between-subjects analyses had less statistical power than the within-subjects design would have given. Nevertheless, the significant increase in confidence in the NIPH between the two time frames used in this study was in line with the findings in IPSOS' larger and more representative opinion polls. Additionally, our claims regarding adherence behaviors may not be generalizable. However, NIPH's own data confirm our results of an increase in selective adherence to the health guidelines, as captured in the second sample.

Conclusion

The foregoing discussion has detailed the benefits of institutional reputation and trust on adherence behaviors. Our data suggests that these are very useful and important considerations to make in future health interventions.

References

Allen, Myria W., & Caillouet, Rachel H. (1994). Legitimation endeavors: Impression management strategies used by an organization in crisis. *Communications Monographs, 61*(1), 44–62.

Blair, Robert A., Morse, Benjamin S., & Tsai, Lily L. (2017). Public health and public trust: Survey evidence from the Ebola Virus Disease epidemic in Liberia. *Social Science & Medicine, 172*, 89–97. https://doi.org/10.1016/j.socscimed.2016.11.016

Boin, Arjen, Ekengren, Magnus, & Rhinard, Mark. (2020). Hiding in plain sight: Conceptualizing the creeping crisis. *Risk, Hazards & Crisis in Public Policy, 11*(2), 116–138. https://doi.org/10.1002/rhc3.12193

Carlsen, Ellen Ø., Caspersen, Ida H., Trogstad, Lill, Gjessing, Håkon K., & Magnus, Per. (2020). Public adherence to governmental recommendations regarding quarantine and testing for COVID-19 in two Norwegian cohorts. *medRxiv*, 2020.2012.2018.20248405. https://doi.org/10.1101/2020.12.18.20248405

Cerna, Lucie. (2014). *Trust: What it is and Why it Matters for Governance and Education.* (EDU/WKP(2014)7). OECD Publishing. Retrieved from https://www.oecd-ilibrary.org/content/paper/5jxswcg0t6wl-en

Christensen, Tom, & Lægreid, Per. (2020). The coronavirus crisis—Crisis communication, meaning-making, and reputation management. *International Public Management Journal, 23*(5), 713–729. https://doi.org/10.1080/10967494.2020.1812455

Coombs, Timothy W. (2006). A theoretical frame for post-crisis communication: Situational crisis communication theory. In M. J. Martinko (Ed.), *Attribution theory in the organizational sciences: Theoretical and empirical contributions* (pp. 275–297). Information Age Publishing.

Coombs, Timothy W. (2010). Parameters for crisis communication. In W. T. Coombs & S. J. Holladay (Eds.), *The handbook of crisis communication* (pp. 17–53). Blackwell Publishing Ltd.

Coombs, Timothy W., & Holladay, Sherry J. (2002). Helping crisis managers protect reputational assets: Initial tests of the situational crisis communication theory. *Management Communication Quarterly, 16*(2), 165–186. https://doi.org/10.1177/089331802237233

Devine, Daniel, Gaskell, Jennifer, Jennings, Will, & Stoker, Gerry. (2020). Trust and the coronavirus pandemic: What are the consequences of and for trust? An early review of the literature. *Political Studies Review, 1*(12), 1–12. https://doi.org/10.1177/1478929920948684

Finset, Arnstein, Bosworth, Hayden, Butow, Phyllis, Gulbrandsen, Pål, Hulsman, Robert L., Pieterse, Arwen H., Street, Richard, Tschoetschel, Robin, & van Weert, Julia. (2020). Effective health communication – A key factor in fighting the COVID-19 pandemic. *Patient Education and Counseling, 103*(5), 873–876. https://doi.org/10.1016/j.pec.2020.03.027

Gilson, Lucy. (2006). Trust in health care: Theoretical perspectives and research needs. *Journal of Health Organization and Management, 20*(5), 359–375. https://doi.org/10.1108/14777260610701768

Helsedirektoratet. (2021). *Koronakommisjonens rapport om myndighetenes håndtering av koronapandemien*. Helsedirektoratet Retrieved from https://www.helsedirektoratet.no/nyheter/koronakommisjonens-rapport-om-myndighetenes-handtering-av-koronapandemien

Hetherington, Marc J. (2005). *Why trust matters: Declining political trust and the demise of American liberalism*. Princeton University Press.

Hetherington, Marc J., & Husser, J. A. (2012). How trust matters: The changing political relevance of political trust. *American Journal of Political Science, 56*(2), 312–325. https://doi.org/10.1111/j.1540-5907.2011.00548.x

Holladay, Sherry J. (2009). Crisis communication strategies in the media coverage of chemical accidents. *Journal of Public Relations Research, 21*(2), 208–217. https://doi.org/10.1080/10627260802557548

Holmes, Bev J., Henrich, Natalie, Hancock, Sara, & Lestou, Valia. (2009). Communicating with the public during health crises: experts' experiences and opinions. *Journal of Risk Research, 12*(6), 793–807. https://doi.org/10.1080/13669870802648486

IPSOS. (2020). Profilundersøkelse av norske etater 2020, 17. gjennomføring-Folkehelseinstituttet. Retrieved from https://www.ipsos.com/nb-no/knowledge/overview

Lyon, Lisa, & Cameron, Glen T. (2004). A relational approach examining the interplay of prior reputation and immediate response to a crisis. *Journal of Public Relations Research, 16*(3), 213–241. https://doi.org/10.1080/1532-754X.2004.11925128

Meredith, Lisa S., Eisenman, David P., Rhodes, Hillary, Ryan, Gery, & Long, Anna. (2007). Trust influences response to public health messages during a bioterrorist event. *Journal of Health Communication, 12*(3), 217–232. https://doi.org/10.1080/10810730701265978

Moss, Sigrun M., & Sandbakken, Ella M. (2021). "Everybody needs to do their part, so we can get this under control." reactions to the Norwegian government meta-narratives on COVID-19 measures. *Political Psychology, 42*(5). https://doi.org/10.1111/pops.12727

Naeem, Salman B., & Bhatti, Rubina. (2020). The Covid-19 'infodemic': A new front for information professionals. *Health Information & Libraries Journal, 37*(3), 233–239. https://doi.org/10.1111/hir.12311

NIPH. (2020). *Risikovurdering av og respons på 2019- nCoV-infeksjon i Norge*. Retrieved from Oslo: https://www.fhi.no/contentassets/c9e459cd7c-c24991810a0d28d7803bd0/vedlegg/risikovurdering-av-og-respons-pa-2019-ncov-infeksjon-i-norge-28.01.2020.pdf

Oksanen, Atte, Kaakinen, Markus, Latikka, Rita, Savolainen, Iina, Savela, Nina, & Koivula, Aki. (2020). *Regulation and trust: A social science perspective on COVID-19 mortality*. Available at SSRN 3569845.

Olsen, Asmus, & Hjorth, Frederik. (2020, May 4). *Public opinion and social distancing in the COVID-19 pandemic*. Retrieved from osf.io/uanhg

Palenchar, Michael J., & Heath, Robert L. (2002). Another part of the risk communication model: Analysis of communication processes and message content. *Journal of Public Relations Research, 14*(2), 127–158. https://doi.org/10.1207/S1532754XJPRR1402_3

Peters, Richard G., Covello, Vincent T., & McCallum, David B. (1997). The determinants of trust and credibility in environmental risk communication: An empirical study. *Risk Analysis, 17*(1), 43–54. https://doi.org/10.1111/j.1539-6924.1997.tb00842.x

Prati, Gabrielle, Pietrantoni, Luca, & Zani, Bruna. (2011). Compliance with recommendations for pandemic influenza H1N1 2009: The role of trust and personal beliefs. *Health Education Research, 26*(5), 761–769. https://doi.org/10.1093/her/cyr035

Savoia, Elena, Lin, Leesa, & Viswanath, Kasisomajula. (2013). Communications in public health emergency preparedness: A systematic review of the literature. *Biosecurity and Bioterrorism: Biodefense Strategy, Practice, and Science, 11*(3), 170–184. https://doi.org/10.1089/bsp.2013.0038

Seeger, Mathew W., Sellnow, Timothy L., & Ulmer, Robert R. (1998). Communication, organization, and crisis. *Annals of the International Communication Association, 21*(1), 231–276. https://doi.org/10.1080/23808985.1998.11678952

Shockley-Zalabak, Pamela S., & Ellis, Kathleen. (2006). The communication of trust. In *The IABC Handbook of organizational communication: A guide to internal communication, public relations, marketing and leadership* (pp. 44–55). San Francisco, CA: Jossey-Bass, ISBN 0-7879-8080-3.

Shockley-Zalabak, Pamela S., & Morreale, Sherwyn P. (2011). Building high-trust organizations. *Leader to Leader, 2011*(60), 39–45.

Siegrist, Michael, & Zingg, Alexandra. (2014). The role of public trust during pandemics: Implications for crisis communication. *European Psychologist, 19*(1), 23–32. https://doi.org/10.1027/1016-9040/a000169

Smith, Carly P. (2017). First, do no harm: Institutional betrayal and trust in health care organizations. *Journal of Multidisciplinary Healthcare, 10*, 133–144. https://doi.org/10.2147/JMDH.S125885

't Hart, Paul, & Boin, Arjen. (2001). Between crisis and normalcy: The long shadow of post-crisis politics. In Uriel Rosenthal, A. Boin, & L. K. Comfort (Eds.), *Managing crises: Threats, dilemmas, opportunities* (pp. 28–45). Charles C. Thomas.

Tonkiss, Fran. (2009). Trust, confidence and economic crisis. *Intereconomics, 44*(4), 196–202. https://doi.org/10.1007/s10272-009-0295-x

Vinck, Patrick, Pham, Phuong N., Bindu, Kenedy K., Bedford, Juliet, & Nilles, Eric J. (2019). Institutional trust and misinformation in the response to the

2018–19 Ebola outbreak in North Kivu, DR Congo: A population-based survey. *The Lancet Infectious Diseases, 19*(5), 529–536. https://doi.org/10.1016/S1473-3099(19)30063-5

Ward, Paul R. (2017). Improving access to, use of, and outcomes from public health programs: The importance of building and maintaining trust with patients/clients. *Frontiers in Public Health, 5*(22). https://doi.org/10.3389/fpubh.2017.00022

White, Sarah J., Barello, Serena, Cao di San Marco, Eugenia, Colombo, Cinzia, Eeckman, Edgard, Gilligan, Conor, et al. (2021). Critical observations on and suggested ways forward for healthcare communication during COVID-19: pEACH position paper. *Patient Education and Counseling, 104*(2), 217–222. https://doi.org/10.1016/j.pec.2020.12.025

Xiong, Jiaqi, Lipsitz, Orly, Nasri, Flora, Lui, Leanna M. W., Gill, Hartej, Phan, Lee, et al. (2020). Impact of COVID-19 pandemic on mental health in the general population: A systematic review. *Journal of Affective Disorders, 277*, 55–64. https://doi.org/10.1016/j.jad.2020.08.001

SECTION V

Understanding the People at Risk

CHAPTER 16

A Mosaic of Researcher "Back-Stories" and Oral History "Front-Stories": COVID-19 and Metro Detroit BIPOC Entrepreneurs' Resilience

Rahul Mitra, Allison Lucas, Sheryl Johnson-Fambro, Claire Van Raaphorst, and Shelby Lasky

During the Fall 2020 semester, a graduate class at Wayne State University's Department of Communication decided to gather oral histories from Black, Indigenous, and other People of Color (BIPOC) entrepreneurs in the Detroit region on their experiences navigating the COVID-19 pandemic. The class was COM 6250 Organizational Communication: Rahul was the course instructor, and Allie, Sheryl, Claire, and Shelby were students in the class (along with five others). Our focus was on the problems faced by local BIPOC entrepreneurs during the first months of the pandemic and the ensuing quarantine.

R. Mitra (✉) • A. Lucas • S. Johnson-Fambro • C. Van Raaphorst • S. Lasky
Wayne State University, Detroit, MI, USA
e-mail: rahul.mitra@wayne.edu; hc9621@wayne.edu; shelbylasky@wayne.edu

L. D. Browning et al. (eds.), *Organizational Communication and Technology in the Time of Coronavirus*,
https://doi.org/10.1007/978-3-030-94814-6_16

Detroit (and SE Michigan more broadly) had emerged as an early hotspot of the novel coronavirus in the U.S. that summer, and Black and Brown communities were especially hard-hit—and continue to be so, as per the numbers on the spread of infection, hospitalization, and deaths (Centers for Disease Control and Prevention, 2020). Michigan's governor, Gretchen Whitmer, had moved relatively early to shut down schools, businesses, and public gatherings in an effort to slow the spread of the virus, as our hospitals and clinics were overwhelmed and people were dying. But this shutdown came at a cost. Protests against the quarantine orders and economic shutdown grew, and the governor's orders were criticized for being an overreach of executive authority. People were afraid. Stores, startups, and small businesses floundered, and several of these shut down, especially those in the service industries that rely on face-to-face interaction (Farrell et al., 2020; Kuckertz et al., 2020). Small businesses owned by Black and Brown entrepreneurs, which were already at a severe disadvantage in securing capital and in participating in crucial informational and social networks in the entrepreneurial ecosystem, and other factors, were suffering the most (Beer, 2020).

So our COM 6250 class decided to take on a collaborative project that would highlight the stories of resilience among BIPOC small business owners and entrepreneurs in our metropolitan region. All the students—composed of seven MA and two Ph.D. students drawn primarily from the southeast Michigan area—completed mandatory human-subjects behavioral research training from the university's Institutional Review Board (IRB). Peppered through our reading list for the semester were scholarly articles by organizational communication researchers on entrepreneurial identity, career trajectories, and other challenges especially pertaining to Black and Brown individuals. We discussed how societal discourses of entrepreneurship were raced, gendered, and classed in ways that reflected privileged white male, hi-tech subjectivities, and dominated by geographical hubs on the east and west coasts of the U.S. (e.g., Allen, 2011; Gill, 2014; Gill & Larson, 2014; Haseki et al., 2020; Jones, 2017; Shumate et al., 2014).

Rahul reached out among his contacts from a prior, unpublished research project to set up a panel session for the class. It consisted of three local entrepreneurs (two of whom were BIPOC), all deeply rooted in the Detroit entrepreneurial ecosystem, who were committed to helping other small businesses with minority owners launch and succeed in their ventures. The panel discussion in the course enabled the COM 6250 students (and Rahul) to engage in frank conversations, to situate their scholarly learning in the "real world," and to reexamine their (our) own biases and locations of privilege before we reached out to interview participants for the project.

In the end, we opted to engage not in an IRB-approved social science study, using qualitative interviews with research participants, but instead to participate in a public humanities project (Brooks, 2014) that centered on oral histories with community narrators. Chief among the reasons for our shift, despite our IRB training and completion of a protocol ready for submission, was our recognition of the historical nature of the crisis that had impacted—and was continuing to impact—our community and these Black and Brown small business owners whose stories we wanted to highlight. In our preparatory conversations with entrepreneurial support organizations and the entrepreneurs themselves, we were constantly asked what we were going to do with these stories and how we would ensure that these stories would remain "alive" in the public's and policymakers' consciousness. Individuals wanted to share their stories of despair, heartache, anxiety, precariousness, and resilience with us, but they were less eager to do so if these stories were destined to be hidden away under the cloak of IRB anonymity, and the lived experiences and emotions at their core were not saved for students, both present and future, to know these histories. COVID-19 had impacted BIPOC communities and entrepreneurs in an unprecedented way, and the onus was on us, as researchers, to respect these narrators by recognizing the historical importance of their experiences and adopting historical methods of conducting oral interviews: archiving them, making them freely accessible to the public, and analyzing them as vital social artifacts (Ritchie, 2015). Methodologically, this meant bypassing epistemic debates of transferability versus generalizability of social science research (Tracy, 2020), and delving deep into the specific social, locational, and temporal contexts of the histories that we were recording with our narrators.

Thus, we do not claim that these stories and experiences are transferable to other contexts or groups of people; rather, these are the historical accounts, orally narrated, by nine specific minority small business owners in Metro Detroit. Their stories tell how they first encountered the COVID-19 pandemic during its "first wave" in Michigan, between the months of March and May of 2020, and how it impacted their health, wellness, families, communities, and businesses. Our first oral history interview was conducted on November 3, 2020, with Ashley Mattison, who co-owns a cheer- and dance-coaching business and is also a flight attendant. We completed eight additional interviews in November and December of 2020 since then. These narrators are Thea and Mark Parker, (November 10) who run a gym; Jade Miller, (November 10) who owns a hair beauty business; Tyrik Davis, (November 16) who owns a clothing and lifestyle brand; Pamela Hilliard-Owens, (November 19) who owned a copywriting consulting business during the summer of 2020; Toney Hughes, Sr., (December 5) the long-time owner of an antiques and art framing shop; Robin Kinnie, (December 7) who owns a recording studio and podcasting business; Kwaku Osei-Bonsu and Lloyd Talley, (December 14) who started a restaurant during the pandemic; and finally, Reva Germain, (December 14) a fitness instructor and gym owner. Each of these interviews was conducted on Zoom, and the conversations included the narrator, Rahul, and one of the COM 6250 students.

We had not planned to write a collaborative essay on our own emotions and experiences during these oral history interviews, but when we received the invitation from the editors of this collection to contribute a chapter on how the discipline and practice of organizational communication was being shaped in the era of the COVID-19 pandemic, it seemed like an ideal vehicle to explore our own subjectivities in relation to our narrators. Some might consider this collection itself an oral history project, preserving, as it does, stories and impressions from scholars and students in the field of organizational communication who have experienced the pandemic from multiple perspectives, temporalities, and locations. This helps us better understand the nuanced and intersecting impacts that define us even as we seek to define *them* through our words, images, graphs, and vistas. Accordingly, our chapter explores mutual dialectics of narrative constitution—between researchers and oral history narrators, and between the field of organizational communication and its practitioners—through reflections that seek to better understand these interconnecting strands. We grappled with the following guiding questions as we re-read the oral history transcripts and penned our personal narratives: *(1) How did you find and why did you select the person for an interview? How do/did you relate to this person? What is the nature of your ties to him/her/them? (2) What stood out most for you during the interview? (3) Can you recall what was going through your mind as the participant was speaking? How did you feel after the interview was concluded? (4) How have you been impacted by the pandemic in your personal and professional life? What has helped you navigate the past few months?* With the aid of these questions, as we began engaging with the narrators' oral histories, we gradually came to see how our own lives intersected with theirs in multiple ways. Some of us are BIPOC entrepreneurs or their long-term customers or are married/related to small business owners; while others have tested positive for the coronavirus or know friends/family who have fallen sick or died from COVID-19; while yet others are completely new to the Detroit region and thus must traverse a difficult space as "outsiders" peering in. By connecting the "back-stories" of our multiracial class and research team with the "front-stories" of the entrepreneurs, this chapter thus demonstrates the mosaic of resilience and storytelling that characterizes organizational communication research amid this pandemic.

We use "mosaic" in another sense while writing this chapter, namely, to give form to the "back stories" that form the remainder of this chapter. Our fragmented mode of storytelling draws from "new" or postmodern (auto)ethnographic writing (Cushman, 2002; Goodall, 2000) to highlight the varied modes of sense-making social phenomena and to juxtapose these narratives of moving from the "back" to the "front" of the oral history interview experience. These fragments have not been randomly arranged, however; they have been positioned to tell a story—multiple stories, really, depending on how you read them—of resilience, adaptation, care, concern, and vulnerability. Temporally, they tell an alternative story of our project—from conception through execution and back to more planning—in what might seem to be an ongoing spiral echoing the flux of the pandemic itself.

Rahul's Story: "Swinging into Action"

The pandemic hit home for me in more ways than one. I first started realizing how big and devastating it could be while on a layover in Hong Kong on my way back from India, where I'd gone to visit my ailing grandmother and my father, who'd just had a pacemaker installed in his heart in late February 2020. Because of delayed flights in Asia, I missed my connecting flight to the U.S. and was put up in the airport hotel for a night. But this was a far cry from the bustling city of Hong Kong I remembered from previous trips. The airport was practically deserted, and the local people wore face masks. In the newspaper, I read about how schools had been cancelled and teachers were teaching students remotely: a harbinger of things to come a few weeks later here in Michigan. Thinking back to the eerie sensations I felt—the strange feeling in the pit of my stomach, because I knew things were horribly wrong and that they would get worse but couldn't predict how, exactly—I realize that that was why I deeply wanted to know how my oral history narrators first experienced the gravity of the COVID-19 pandemic. "Tell me when the pandemic—all of this—first seemed real to you; like that moment in time when you knew that this would be a big deal for your business, your family, and your life. When was that moment? What was that like?" I asked during our interviews.

My sabbatical leave occurred between January and May 2020, so I didn't have to make the pivot to remote teaching right away, at least not until the Fall 2020 semester. Between March and September, as I watched the pandemic sweep through Detroit, Michigan, and the rest of the U.S., I threw myself into my research, advocacy, and family life. My ex-husband is an interior designer and owns a small boutique company in a Detroit suburb, and when Governor Whitmer decided to shut down nonessential businesses, we worried about how the pandemic might affect his company and our livelihood. I realized how lucky and privileged I was to still be able to retain my job and not be furloughed or laid off. Detroit was severely impacted by the novel coronavirus in those early days of what we now call the "first wave" of the pandemic, and Black and Brown communities, low-income and fixed-income folks, seniors, and healthcare workers were falling sick in droves and dying. A cousin of a colleague passed away. He had been a healthy, young Black man in his early 40s with no previous health complications. Then, a friend of a friend. And then, a friend. And another. I was deeply inspired by collaborators and friends, with whom I had served in our Detroit Water Stories oral history and advocacy project, rallying to deliver water, food, and hygiene supplies to people who were suddenly cut off from the world—in some cases, without access to running water due to unpaid bills. I wrote op-ed pieces urging the governor to ban water shutoffs, I helped write grants for student organizations which allowed them to donate supplies to those in need, and I wrote statements in support of environmental justice and Black Lives Matter (BLM) when protests erupted following the murders of Breonna Taylor and George Floyd.

Even as all this was unfolding, I kept track of the rollout of unemployment benefits and the Paycheck Protection Program (PPP) to aid laid-off workers and shuttered small businesses, along with noting the many problems in this rollout of support. My ex-husband needed to apply for a PPP loan, and so I followed the news media coverage long before the program went live, keeping him informed about the controversies arising.

Columnists bemoaned how the PPP terms misunderstood the fundamental situation for most small business owners—and especially BIPOC owners—who could not afford to hire staff on payroll, but predominantly used contract workers (Reese & Kerrigan, 2021). A report from the Brookings Institution noted that Black and Brown small business owners were also not as well-connected to banks and other financial institutions that served as the main vehicles of the PPP rollout—which resulted in several BIPOC entrepreneurs missing out or not even being notified about how to apply for these funds (Liu & Parilla, 2020). My ex-husband received a small PPP loan—he is white and we live in Royal Oak, a fairly diverse suburb just north of Detroit—but I knew from friends and the news coverage that BIPOC entrepreneurs were suffering, and I wanted to use my expertise to do something to help.

Sometime during the summer—perhaps May or early June—even as I'd decided I was going to deactivate my Facebook account for good in a month or two—I messaged friends both at Wayne State University and within the community with a tentative message: If I designed a project or led a team to examine the impact of COVID-19 on BIPOC entrepreneurs, starting in the Fall semester, would they be interested in collaborating? I received a strong affirmative within minutes from Ned Staebler, CEO of TechTown Detroit, the city's largest entrepreneurial support organization and incubator, who also informed me they were designing a fund to help Metro Detroit small business owners. I had worked with TechTown since 2016 on various teaching and research collaborations, and I was exhilarated at the thought of working with them again to help address this problem. I also heard back from entrepreneurs I'd been in touch with, who pledged to connect me with participants for the project, as well as collaborators in other disciplines at Wayne State. Slowly, a motley crew coalesced that started giving shape to a collective vision and we migrated our conversation from Facebook to Microsoft Teams (Fig. 16.1). (I deactivated Facebook in mid-July 2020, arguably my best pandemic decision.)

On Teams, we brainstormed over what our underlying goals and research questions would be, as well as a potential timeline and funding opportunities. We realized that most extramural, and even internal, funding windows would be in early- to mid-2021. We decided to take a two-pronged approach: The team would continue refining the details of a study that would collect both quantitative and qualitative data for a

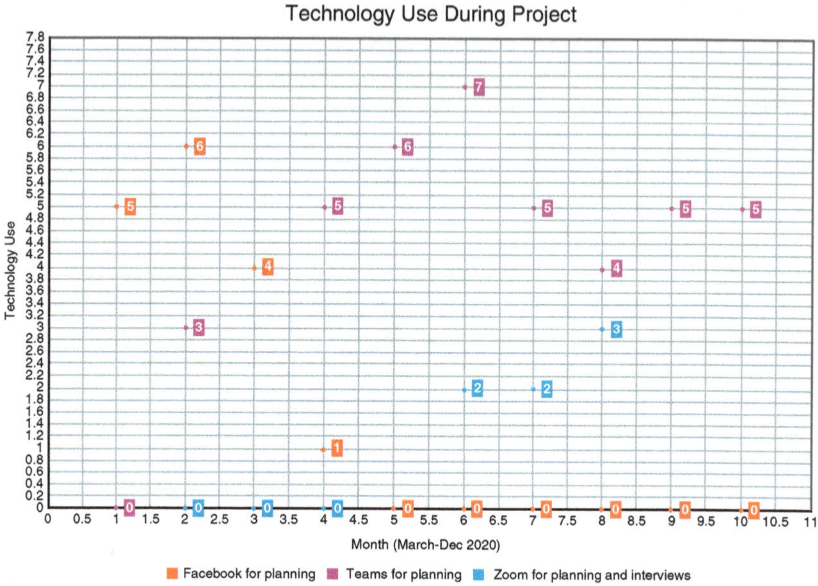

Fig. 16.1 Use of Facebook, Microsoft Teams, and Zoom during March–December 2020 for the project

regional or even national study, while my colleague Marijo Upshaw and I would design a protocol for qualitative interviews that we would kick into gear that Fall with my COM 6250 graduate seminar. I had blended teaching and research before, with my Detroit Water Stories project (see http://www.detroitwaterstories.com), and it would be quite similar this time: Marijo and I would work with my students to recruit and interview BIPOC entrepreneurs in Metro Detroit. When Marijo's teaching load increased during the Fall 2020 semester, however, and then she contracted COVID from her husband who was a doctor, she stepped back from the interview project. Nevertheless, the COM 6250 students remained committed and were raring to go. It was almost cathartic for both them and me: our first semester together, our first semester learning/teaching online, and our first semester during a pandemic. We desperately needed to make a difference.

Claire's Story: "Coming Face-to-Face with Privilege"

When first asked to find a BIPOC entrepreneur to interview, I have to admit, I was a little stumped. I'm from a northern suburb (exurb, really) of Detroit with very little diversity, and I had only recently moved close to Detroit where there was more of a chance to possibly know someone who might be a BIPOC entrepreneur. I felt a little embarrassed to not be able to think of anyone at first; it felt like my lack of experience with diversity was showing through, even though no one could actually see. But I had an epiphany, and I thought of someone. Just prior to the COVID-19 pandemic, I had been chatting randomly with some women I met at a brewery, and they suggested a local gym run by Mark and Thea Parker. But then, of course, the world shut down for months while we grappled with what to do in this situation. By early June, I was itching to get back into a gym, as mine was closed. At the same time, the deaths of George Floyd and Breonna Taylor ignited my interest and enthusiasm to support the Black community and Black business owners. I saw that Mark, who is Black, was running outdoor fitness classes and it seemed like a perfect fit. Slowly, I got to know both him and his wife, Thea, who helped run the gym. I am so grateful to them for agreeing to an interview with me for COM 6250.

What stood out to me the most from our interview with Mark and Thea was just how precarious their situation was—and is. They had opened their gym a few years prior and were just really starting to hit their stride a few months before the pandemic hit. To be honest, it made me feel uncomfortable and sad to hear him describe their situation. My father is also a small business owner, albeit as a dentist. When his practice was shut down for many months, it was kind of a "vacation" for him. There was no question that my parents could survive without his salary for a few months. It was difficult for my dad to navigate various rules and legislation that impacted his business, like the PPP system, and to locate personal protective equipment, like masks and gloves, but he had an office manager to deal with all of that. Hearing about Mark and Thea supporting their children and grappling with some of the same barriers, but having a *much* more difficult and stressful time overcoming them, made me truly feel and grapple with my own family's privilege.

I was in awe at their faith in themselves and in their partnership to make it through.

Shelby's Story: "Helping Hands"

COVID-19 changed our world in ways I had never dreamed possible. Like most Americans, social distancing was totally foreign to me, and I had never worn a face mask until I became extremely sick at the end of February 2020 and was given one at the doctor's office. Although I was not tested for COVID, the panic I felt realizing I may have contracted the novel coronavirus was indescribable. The fear and panic have never really gone away, and I remain deeply worried about my friends and family getting sick.

I applied to Wayne State for my MA in Communication while in quarantine, and my first semester taking classes was Fall 2020. I come from the central part of Michigan, so I am new to the Detroit area and did not know any local small business owners—BIPOC or otherwise—to approach for this project. I ended up helping Rahul interview Pamela Hilliard-Owens for the project, though, and something that immediately struck me as she talked was her experience of losing so many friends and acquaintances to the pandemic. Although no one in her immediate family had gotten sick, "Facebook turned into an obituary page," she said. Several of my own family members and friends had tested positive, but luckily, everyone made a quick recovery. Perhaps that is why hearing about our interviewee Pamela's losses was difficult: Her experience with seemingly endless announcements of positive tests, hospitalizations, and deaths on social media served as a harsh reminder of the toll this pandemic has taken and of the social inequities that have disproportionately impacted Black and Brown communities.

Pamela's story is so incredible. She was able to not only adapt her business approaches but also to recognize changes in the field or in the needs of her clients and offer unique solutions to them. This skill has helped her continue to offer assistance during the pandemic. For example, she was able to help several clients with their messaging on newly installed COVID-19 policies. Even just asking customers to wear a mask while in a store can be controversial; creating store signage informing customers of COVID-19-related policies is tricky for store owners who want to keep their employees safe while also keeping their customers' likes and dislikes in mind. Knowing that she had an unusual comfort with filling out government forms and documents, Pamela offered her help to clients who were having difficulty applying for small business loans such as the PPP during the pandemic. For her, this was intensely personal, and not just providing a service to paying clients. Acknowledging how lucky she was that her business was not negatively impacted by COVID-19, she felt it was her due to support other Black-owned businesses by purchasing a birthday cake for her husband from a local bakery, for example, or buying clothes and jewelry from a neighborhood boutique, or continuing automatic payments to her yoga studio although it was closed due to the shutdown. Her willingness to support others in the community who were struggling was an important reminder of how we are all connected and the little ways we can all chip in. During the pandemic, it can be hard not to feel helpless, but recognizing the small things we all can do to support our local business owners can make all the difference, especially for a family-owned enterprise.

Pamela's story offers just a glimpse into the incredible community that is Detroit. On the surface, it can feel like we are completely powerless against this virus, but her story foregrounds the willingness of ordinary people to reach out and support one another. Whether that is through virtual lunches with coworkers, helping clients navigate the many unique challenges they faced during this time, or spending some extra money (if we are fortunate enough to not be financially affected) supporting a small business, these small acts are proof that we can all get through this together.

Allie's Story: "Dare to Be"

I knew Tyrik Davis through previous work connections and had been following his story since he first launched his company, DARE to be/ Yer'self/. During our oral history interview, I enjoyed getting to know more about the origins of his brand and what goes on "behind the scenes." As he recounted his story of being a new entrepreneur, just finding his footing when the pandemic took hold, I gained an appreciation for his ability to maintain optimism and hope, and to continue to express gratitude despite compounding challenges.

On social media and through our previous work-based interactions, his public persona generally comes across as optimistic, gracious, and uplifting. As we talked about his life and work in our interview, I came to understand that this was a more strategic and calculated front, however, which required a concerted effort to sustain as an intrinsic part of his character.

He was motivated to maintain positivity and assume a sunny disposition because he was a new entrepreneur working diligently to grow his business—and this was, perhaps, intensified because of the particular challenges he faces as a Black gay man.

As I watched him speak, I realized how his identity had played an integral role in his entrepreneurial venture, both inspiring him to create the business in the first place and subsequently guiding its mission. As he put it, "'DARE to be/Yer'self/,' the message doesn't only speak to me, right? being a black gay man? 'Dare to be yourself' speaks to anyone." This courage of conviction was invaluable in helping him pivot and create new products during the pandemic's early days, such as his "Dare to Frontline" clothing line, which celebrated the millions of essential and frontline workers who put their (predominantly Black and Brown) bodies on the line for the U.S. economy to remain partially open. Nevertheless, when Black Lives Matter protests flooded the country during the summer of 2020, following the deaths of George Floyd and Breonna Taylor at the hands of the police, and Ty sought to use his brand to stand up to white supremacy, he came up against stiff institutional resistance. It became painfully clear that a lucrative corporate collaboration fell through because of his support for BLM—a cause that was integral to his very being. "A lot of companies don't want to take a stance for Black Lives Matter, and that's what the collaboration was about," he sighed. With the election of President Joe Biden and Vice President Kamala Harris, the first Black woman ever to earn that title, Ty experienced additional tensions—intense joy and pride, mixed with concerns that disclosing his political beliefs or positions on social justice issues would cause further harm to his fledgling company—at a time when he could least afford it. "To know that we have people in there who support Black Lives Matter and who support equality, that is what matters to me, right? And I would never say that publicly."

These instances emphasized a truly precarious position: to be empowered and inspired, but to have an acute awareness of how expressing those emotions, even via personal channels, can have lasting effects and tangible costs. The irony of this suppression in the context of a brand based on the idea that everyone should feel empowered to live authentically is particularly tragic—but perhaps not uncommon for BIPOC entrepreneurs and workers (Allen, 2011; Grimes, 2002; McDonald & Kuhn, 2016).

Sheryl's Story: "Changing in Place"

This project provided me with an opportunity to feature the neighborhood of my youth through the voice of Toney Hughes. The Sherwood Forest Art Gallery, which he owns, is nestled in the northwest corner of Detroit on the Avenue of Fashion, a six-block stretch of Livernois just south of Eight Mile Road. Detroit was in the waning days of white flight during my school years of the 1960s, and I have a vivid recollection of white school administrators openly bemoaning the fact that our schools were becoming "inner-city" schools. (No, it wasn't really much of a code back then, either.) As times changed and auto factories closed, eliminating shifts and, thereby, the middle-class opportunities that went with it for those holding only a high school diploma, many of the stores I grew up visiting were also impacted. Neighborhoods on both sides of Livernois changed. The upper middle-class areas on the east side became less Jewish, and the lower middle-class neighborhoods on the west side fell slowly into poverty.

During our interview with Toney, I was stunned to hear that our paths most certainly had crossed long before I ever became a customer at his art gallery and framing store. He described a thirty-plus-years career as a Detroit firefighter—leading me to wonder whether he'd been at the frontline during the 1967 rebellion—while managing supplemental business(es) on the side. I learned that he was a hustler like my dad, who also held a full-time job while selling cars over the phone, running a small cosmetics company, and, at one point, operating three fully staffed barber and beauty shops. Men like my dad and Toney were driven to take charge of their own lives to make ends meet for their families.

Toney spoke of how his business evolved through the ups and downs, and unexpected crises like the COVID-19 pandemic. As his earlier embroidery business declined, he decided to open a printshop with his son, which is their art gallery today. Converting their store to a gallery enabled father and son to keep the building they owned viable as a business, and they subsequently expanded to purchase an adjoining building. Considering the era that Toney first purchased property on the previously exclusive Avenue of Fashion during the 1990s, he probably obtained it at auction or for taxes, just as Dad did when he purchased his commercial building.

Proudly, Toney noted that his son was "the brains of the operation," a boast any business-owner dad would like to attribute to his son. Both of them have taught each other, as they relied on each other to build the space and their brand—and increasingly embrace the Internet, online orders, and out-of-state shipping to adapt to the changing conditions of the pandemic. Diversifying their core business, from antiques to selling and framing art, and expanding their clientele beyond the City of Detroit helped them weather the unstable winds of the virus. Sherwood Gallery also functions as a "B2B," or in a business-to-business capacity, with other galleries in the city, wholesaling artwork and performing other services on their behalf, which provided new streams of revenue.

The success of Toney's cozy, family-owned cultural center reflects the resilience of this city and neighborhood. That is not to imply similar stories are not happening throughout Detroit's 200-plus neighborhoods during this pandemic. My city—and Toney's business—will both change through (and along with) changes shaped by demographics and economics, but as long as they are nurtured from the deep wells of struggle and opportunity, they will thrive.

Our Story: "A Sort of Epilogue"

Our collective epilogue here has two main goals.

In the spirit of organizing disorder, or its inverse—finding chaos in organization—we note that the "back stories" we arranged in this chapter represent the process of resilience, as it were, that was mirrored in the narratives from our oral historians. Resilience is a slippery concept that has been addressed in different disciplines. While definitions of resilience vary, it broadly addresses positive adaptation in the face of adversity, and early scholarship focused on personality traits that emphasize "in-spite-of" responses to difficult situations (Bachay & Cingel, 1999). This predilection toward personality traits eroded over time toward a process-based approach, so that Luthar et al. (2000) defined it as "a dynamic process encompassing positive adaptation within the context of significant adversity" (p. 543), while Richardson (2002) saw resilience as "the process of reintegrating from disruptions in life" (p. 309). Scholars have increasingly adopted grief and trauma-informed perspectives that see resiliency as a pattern of positive adaptations to adversity, shaped by familial, communal, and social interactions of a person in their environment (Hernandez et al., 2007). At the same time, we must be careful to guard against the "medicalization" of trauma in affected populations, so that a sole focus on deficits and problems can obscure the strengths and resiliencies that trauma survivors can individually and collectively display and, in doing so, inadvertently pathologize actors (Rothenberg, 2012). Madsen and Abell (2010) thus focus on protective measures to enact resilience, which are defined as "positive qualities within the cognitive, emotional, environmental, social and spiritual experience of a person, which are associated with and cumulatively facilitate resilience" (p. 224).

In line with this perspective, Communication scholars concentrate on the communicative practices that constitute resilience in relational contexts. Lucas and Buzzanell (2012) defined resilience as "meaning-making through everyday messages and stories that enable reintegration from life's disruptions" (p. 190). And the Communication Theory of Resilience (CTR; Buzzanell, 2010, 2018; Buzzanell et al., 2009) adopts an explicitly social and relational stance on the possibilities of recovery from disruption, compared to the traditional coping literature that focuses on individual-centered stress management (e.g., Lazarus & Folkman, 1984). CTR specifies five interrelated communicative processes by which people enact resilience: crafting normalcy (e.g., maintaining and/or creating new routines), affirming identity anchors, maintaining and using communication networks, constructing alternative logics (e.g., reframing and using humor), and foregrounding productive action while backgrounding negative emotions. Importantly, these processes are not straightforward and do not pan out exactly the same way for everybody, or even in the same sequence, but are often manifested as push-and-pull dialectics (Wieland, 2020). They are tensions to be navigated amidst enormous stresses of everyday life and trauma, and they cumulatively build up adaptation and hope, even through moments when hope seems, quite frankly, absent (Buzzanell et al., 2009).

Although we have not yet undertaken a systematic qualitative analysis of the narratives from our oral historians, this adaptive tensional picture is what emerged through our discussions and conversations within our little group and with our everyday historians; and this is the mosaic that we have sought to put together, imperfectly but painstakingly, in this short chapter. Our intersecting stories of resilience show us thus "swinging into action" (Rahul's story), but then stopping short, realizing the almost bottomless depth of fear, hesitation, anger, emotion, and privilege that we needed to navigate, and wondering if we were equal to this task. "Coming face-to-face" (Claire's story) seemed almost like a cruel joke in this age of Zoom, Facebook, Teams, and other remote conferencing technology. We desperately wanted to visit places and people, to bear witness in person, yet we were held back because we were scared for everyone involved. We floundered; we reached out for understanding; we sought to read, feel, talk, and share; we lashed out in desperation and in empathy, and there were many failed "restart" attempts. But somehow, we realized there were "helping hands" (Shelby's story), people who wanted to and could offer help, and we gratefully reached out to accept that help and, in turn, to help out when we could. Our oral historians stunned us with their courage and bravado, even as they negotiated their own dark spaces of fear and anger. Quite simply, they had little option but to regroup and to recharge, as their stories of "daring to be" who they were (Allie's story) inspired them to push these boundaries, even as they sought to protect themselves with what rhetorical cover they could afford. Their resilience is quiet, calm, and silent; not the charging of the Light Brigade or an emphatic sounding of trumpets, but the behind-the-scenes pivot and "changing-in-place" (Sheryl's story) that enabled them to shift, evolve, and hustle along with their changing neighborhood, city, and clientele.

Our mosaic-based storytelling approach in this chapter highlights the tensional push-and-pull processes underlying resilience for BIPOC entrepreneurs, who must deal with not only the personal and professional traumas of COVID-19 but also with the structural inequities of race, gender, class, and geography that permeate American life. We use storytelling about the stories BIPOC entrepreneurs recount to steel themselves amidst such adversity. This "meta" approach to resilience storytelling encourages one to put yourself in the Other's place and can potentially provoke empathy—a deeply affective and emotive response, in line with the goals of "new" ethnography (Cushman, 2002; Goodall, 2000). At the same time, we must be careful that in our goal to complement the voice of the Other, we do not end up supplanting her.

Our collective epilogue points to the ongoing march of time for both the oral historians and for those of us who gathered these stories (Table 16.1). At the time of writing this chapter, the entrepreneurs whose oral histories we gathered are hard at work, already ensconced in the next crisis their livelihood is facing. They are seeking to redefine their business and make it "stand out" for potential customers, as the U.S. economy rebounds slowly, more and more people are vaccinated, and a sort of "post-COVID" picture emerges on the horizon (as fuzzy and muddled as it may be, especially given the hardships faced by BIPOC entrepreneurs even pre-COVID). They have received a white paper, produced by a group of undergraduate students in Rahul's Winter 2021 senior capstone course, outlining the main responses and lessons gleaned from their stories. These

Table 16.1 Professional vista—Rahul Mitra

Event	*Significance*
2005–2007	Started switching jobs from business news media to public relations and investor relations, in Mumbai (India), realizing that I was unhappy and looking for a change in vocation and career; began considering applying for a MA in organizational communication and public relations to a U.S. university, with little understanding about what that meant. Did not want to be an academic, but thought about working in Corporate Communications with the MA degree
Aug 2007	Started MA program at Bowling Green State University, OH (U.S.); was much more comfortable with the idea of being an academic, but still not sure about what that meant. Focused on organizational communication more clearly, and attracted by research with an applied bent that is focused on helping communities and organizations directly
Aug 2009	Started PhD program at Purdue University, IN (U.S.); decided to focus on environmental sustainability, corporate social responsibility, and leadership
June–Aug 2013	Graduated from Purdue with PhD and joined Wayne State University in Detroit MI as a tenure-track assistant professor, with a research agenda focused on environmental organizing and sustainability
2015–2016	Started collaborating with TechTown Detroit and other entrepreneurial support organizations in Metro Detroit; my initial focus was on the broader implications of the emerging entrepreneurial ecosystem for including diverse small business owners, and especially Black and Brown folks, for long-term and sustainable community development
Sep 2019	Received promotion and tenure at Wayne State University
Mar–Jun 2020	COVID-19 hit; started planning and designing the BIPOC Entrepreneurs Resilience in COVID public humanities project
Summer 2021	Published White Paper based on initial nine interviews collected during the Fall 2020 semester with COM 6250 students; obtained grant funding for collecting additional oral histories and larger public humanities project using Digital Diaries
Fall 2021	Worked with collaborators to design digital diary platform for data collection
Jan–Dec 2022	Finish analyzing oral histories and submit manuscript to interdisciplinary journal; launch digital diary data collection and set up public archive of oral histories from Metro Detroit collected during 2020–2021 with the Reuther Library at WSU
Mar 2023	Conclude data collection from larger funded project with collaborators; start creating informational material with community partners to be distributed among participants, policymakers, and other stakeholders
2023–2024	Work on manuscripts based on larger project to be submitted to scholarly journals and create multimedia monograph

stories have also been shared with policymakers and entrepreneurial support organizations in the hope that they can learn and prepare better for the next crisis to affect BIPOC entrepreneurs in our city. In 2022, we launched a website (see www.https://wsuresilientproject.wordpress.com) embracing the public humanities component of this project, as we strive to reach the broader public with our scholarship (Brooks, 2014).

Meanwhile, the student authors of this piece have pushed themselves into another semester of coursework, new readings, and writing final papers. They have taken the time to reflect on their experiences of gathering the oral histories and have penned a few paragraphs of this chapter, but most of them/us will probably detach themselves from this project over the next few weeks once the submission is complete. A couple of the student authors continue to work with Rahul on grant submissions expanding on this oral history project and on negotiations with Wayne State University's Reuther Library (famous for its archives on labor records), to convert these oral histories into a special archive that will ensure that these stories remain accessible to the public. We continue to gather new oral histories with more BIPOC entrepreneurs and small business owners in Metro Detroit, learning from their wealth of experiences and recording these for posterity. In 2022, we will undertake a systematic analysis of these histories and submit a manuscript to an interdisciplinary scholarly journal. Some of our newer collaborators have broached the idea of a monograph—perhaps in electronic format to allow for greater dispersal and reach—in our efforts to ensure that these stories of resilience are not lost and so that they can serve as a learning tool for future crises.

Collectively, we look to the motto of the city of Detroit, emblazoned on its seal—penned by a French Roman Catholic priest in 1805 after the city endured a devastating fire that burned much of it to the ground:

> *Speramus Meliora… Resurget Cineribus*
> We hope for better things…. It will rise from the ashes.

References

Allen, Brenda J. (2011). *Difference matters: Communicating social identity.* Waveland Press.

Bachay, Judith B., & Cingel, Pamela A. (1999). Restructuring resilience: Emerging voices. *Affilia, 14*(2), 162–175.

Beer, Tommy. (2020, May 18). Minority owned small businesses struggle to gain equal access to PPP loan money. *Forbes*. Retrieved from https://www.forbes.com/sites/tommybeer/2020/05/18/minority-owned-small-businessesstruggle-to-gain-equal-access-to-ppp-loan-money/#41df154f5de3
Brooks, Peter. (2014). *The humanities and public life*. Fordham University Press.
Buzzanell, Patrice M. (2010). Resilience: Talking, resisting, and imagining new normalcies into being. *Journal of Communication, 60*, 1–14.
Buzzanell, Patrice M. (2018). Organizing resilience as adaptive-transformational tensions. *Journal of Applied Communication Research, 46*, 14–18.
Buzzanell, Patrice M., Shenoy, Suchitra, Remke, Robyn, & Lucas, Kristen. (2009). Intersubjectivity creating resilience to foster human dignity and hope. In Pamela Lutgen-Sandvik & Beverly D. Sypher (Eds.), *Destructive organizational communication: Processes, consequences, & constructive ways of organizing* (pp. 530–576). Routledge.
Centers for Disease Control and Prevention. (2020, June 25). *COVID-19 in racial and ethnic minorities*. Retrieved from https://www.cdc.gov/coronavirus/2019-ncov/need-extraprecautions/racial-ethnic-minorities.html
Cushman, Ellen. (2002). Postmodern ethnographies. *Journal of Advanced Composition, 22*, 925–934.
Farrell, Diana, Wheat, Chris, & Mac, Chi. (2020, June). Small business financial outcome during the onset of Covid-19. *JP Morgan Chase & Co. Institute*. Retrieved from https://www.jpmorganchase.com/institute/research/small-business/small-business-financial-outcomes-during-the-onset-of-covid-19
Gill, Rebecca. (2014). "If you're struggling to survive day-to-day": Class optimism and contradiction in entrepreneurial discourse. *Organization, 21*, 50–67.
Gill, Rebecca, & Larson, Gregory S. (2014). Making the ideal (local) entrepreneur: Place and the regional development of high-tech entrepreneurial identity. *Human Relations, 67*, 519–542.
Goodall Jr., Harold L. (2000). *Writing the new ethnography*. Altamira Press.
Grimes, Denise S. (2002). Challenging the status quo? Whiteness in the diversity management literature. *Management Communication Quarterly, 15*, 381–409.
Haseki, Müge, Scott, Craig R., & Gailliard, Bernadette M. (2020). Communicatively managing multiple, intersecting identities among immigrant women entrepreneurs. *International Journal of Business Communication, 58*, 282–303.
Hernandez, Pilar, Gangsei, David, & Engstrom, David. (2007). Vicarious resilience: A new concept in work with those who survive trauma. *Family Process, 46*(2), 229–241.
Jones, Natasha N. (2017). Rhetorical narratives of Black entrepreneurs: The business of race, agency, and cultural empowerment. *Journal of Business and Technical Communication, 31*(3), 319–349.
Kuckertz, Andreas, Brändle, Leif, Gaudig, Anja, Hinderer, Sebastian, Reyes, Carlos A. M., Prochotta, Alicia, Steinbrink, Kathrin M., & Berger, Elisabeth

S. C. (2020). Startups in times of crisis—A rapid response to the COVID-19 pandemic. *Journal of Business Venturing Insights, 13*. https://doi.org/10.1016/j.jbvi.2020.e00169

Lazarus, Richard S., & Folkman, Susan. (1984). *Stress, appraisal, and coping*. Springer.

Liu, Sifan, & Parilla, Joseph. (2020, September 17). New data shows small businesses in communities of color had unequal access to federal COVID-19 relief. *Brookings*. Retrieved from: https://www.brookings.edu/research/new-data-shows-small-businesses-in-communities-of-color-had-unequal-access-to-federal-covid-19-relief/

Lucas, Kristen, & Buzzanell, Patrice M. (2012). Memorable messages of hard times: Constructing short and long-term resiliencies through family communication. *Journal of Family Communication, 12*, 189–208.

Luthar, Suniya, Cicchetti, Dante, & Becker, Bronwyn. (2000). The construct of resilience: A critical evaluation and guidelines for future work. *Child Development, 71*, 543–562.

Madsen, Machelle D., & Abell, Neil. (2010). Trauma resilience scale: Validation of protective factors associated with adaptation following violence. *Research on Social Work Practice, 20*(2), 223–233.

McDonald, Jamie, & Kuhn, Timothy R. (2016). Occupational branding for diversity: Managing discursive contradictions. *Journal of Applied Communication Research, 44*, 101–117.

Reese, Lexi, & Kerrigan, Karen. (2021). Why aren't struggling small businesses taking more PPP? *Entrepreneur*. Retrieved from: https://www.entrepreneur.com/article/366797

Richardson, Glenn E. (2002). The metatheory of resilience and resiliency. *Journal of Clinical Psychology, 58*, 307–321.

Ritchie, Donald A. (2015). *Doing oral history* (3rd ed.). Oxford University Press.

Rothenberg, Nancy J. (2012). Surviving violence and trauma: Resilience in action at the micro level. In Roberta R. Greene (Ed.), *Resiliency: An integrated approach to practice, policy, and research* (2nd ed.). NASW.

Shumate, Michelle S., Atouba, Yannick, Cooper, Katherine R., & Pilny, Andrew. (2014). Two paths diverged: Examining the antecedents to social entrepreneurship. *Management Communication Quarterly, 28*(3), 404–421.

Tracy, Sarah J. (2020). *Qualitative research methods: Collecting evidence, crafting analysis, communicating impact* (2nd ed.). Wiley.

Wieland, Stacey M. B. (2020). Constituting resilience at work: Maintaining dialectics and cultivating dignity throughout a worksite closure. *Management Communication Quarterly*. https://doi.org/10.1177/0893318920949314

CHAPTER 17

Even Heroes Need Help: The Impact of COVID-19 on Physicians Already at Risk for Burnout

Ana M. Aquilar and Dawna I. Ballard

A hero is an ordinary individual who finds the strength to persevere and endure in spite of overwhelming obstacles.
—Christopher Reeve

Growing up in a rural area in California, the child of immigrant Spanish-speaking parents, navigating healthcare was often challenging for the lead author on this chapter. In our various discussions about how to write this chapter in a way that offers context to the hero metaphor we heard so much in the early days of the COVID-19 pandemic, she felt a personal tie to the story. Below, we begin with her story to frame the chapter.

A. M. Aquilar (✉) • D. I. Ballard
Department of Communication Studies, The University of Texas at Austin, Austin, TX, USA
e-mail: ana.m.aguilar@utexas.edu; diballard@utexas.edu

L. D. Browning et al. (eds.), *Organizational Communication and Technology in the Time of Coronavirus*,
https://doi.org/10.1007/978-3-030-94814-6_17

> My family was relatively low income, their wages below the federal poverty level and my dad's job offered no benefits, which meant we relied on federally qualified health centers (FQHC). Stemming from a family with low health literacy in addition to language barriers, which meant that I acted as a translator at a very young age, I thought physicians were extraordinary. My mom would defer to the doctor's knowledge and would completely rely on the physician's decision making in treatment plans. At medical appointments, the physician was the authority. My parents were not partners or peers in the health decisions.
>
> This kind of behavior is not uncommon for individuals with low health literacy (Yin et al., 2012). (The problematic nature of this dynamic would not be completely clear to me until I was closer to adulthood.) Whether intentionally or not, my parents would place physicians in very high regards, placing them in high status. It was from this upbringing that I developed my understanding of physicians as exceptional, as being different from the people I knew. From my naivety, I assumed that they were unaffected by the same issues as their patients: How else could they do what they did? I assumed that they could see problems from an objective lens and derive solutions from their vast knowledge. I began viewing them as heroes. As I got older, my perception of physicians was challenged. The more I learned about physicians' work and interacted with them, in what felt like a peer level or in a non-medical context, the more I saw them not just as ordinary people but as people in need of support.

In 2019, through a collaborative project with colleagues at Dell Medical School at the University of Texas Austin and the University of California San Francisco School of Medicine, we began shadowing primary care physicians at a local clinic. The focus of that study is to understand the relationship between the objective times as stipulated in physicians' schedules, their subjective experiences of time, and how it relates to burnout. The initial driver for our interest came from a decades-long trend of high levels of burnout among physicians (Passalacqua, 2017) and extensive data showing that issues surrounding time and timing are key stressors that begin with medical training (Klitzman, 2007; Linzer et al., 2000; Özbilgin et al., 2011; Westbrook et al., 2008).

The seriousness of physician burnout and mental illness is reflected in statistics showing that physician suicide rates in the United States (U.S.) are currently the highest of any profession and twice that of the general population (Anderson, 2018). Additionally, the Association of American Medical Colleges estimates that, by 2032, the United States will have a deficit of physicians (from 46,900 to 122,000) across all specialties. Prior to COVID-19, this was driven by a rapidly aging population, a stagnant rate of new physicians, and an alarming rate of turnover. Problems with burnout have been compounded in light of COVID-19, which has led many doctors to retire early or change professions (Abelson, 2020). During the early days of the pandemic, the public witnessed stark deficiencies in resources (e.g., a lack of personal protective equipment [PPE] and ventilators) and practices (e.g., overwhelmed emergency rooms and long hours). Rather than the tools needed to carry out their work, physicians were largely offered symbolic (rather than material or policy-based) support.

In this chapter, we interrogate the public celebrations of their sacrifice and active framing of physicians as "heroes" in light of ongoing threats to their work quality and personal wellbeing. Rather than supernatural beings (as is suggested by the hero frame), physicians are employees who—under normal circumstances—attempt to carry out their work despite limited resources, rigid schedules, and recurring trauma. We address the interrelationships among burnout, trauma, recovery, and resilience offering examples of how—during the pandemic—healthcare institutions and the general public placed additional, moral-based expectations on a system already teetering on failure. In the following section, we first describe the research setting that we found ourselves in during the weeks and months leading up to the global shutdown caused by COVID-19. We then examine the related literature on trauma, burnout, and recovery—which together make up the larger process of resilience, the focus of our conclusion.

Our Ongoing Fieldwork

The initial phase of our study began with observational data collected in the form of time shadowing, to understand the relationship between time and burnout in primary care medicine. We took an engaged research approach (Barbour et al., 2017) in our interactions with the doctors that began with the process of coordinating with doctors (over email or in person) which shifts to observe in advance. The process of time shadowing then involved three aspects. First, throughout a full shift (averaging five hours) we recorded each physician's time spent in various locations (e.g., patient rooms, at their desk charting, talking to medical assistants, etc.). Because of the challenges in capturing such information in a physically dynamic environment where individuals were constantly moving, we typically had two to three team members on site observing the same setting for reliability (as well as practical needs like bathroom breaks). We compared these time observations to what our colleague and collaborator, Urmimala Sarkar, Professor of Medicine at the University of California San Francisco, calls their *fictive schedule*, or the official schedule as determined by the clinic management. From these activities, we gain insight into the differences between what they "should be" doing and the work they actually perform. We stayed with each physician until the end of their shift, which often extended beyond the scheduled time.

A second aspect of the time shadowing included taking ethnographic notes based on salient observations throughout the shift. Depending upon the pace of work or unusual events, sometimes we held conversations with physicians and their team during their shift, including interns, medical assistants, nurses, administrators, and social workers to understand more about what we were observing. Because of the collaborative approach we took to the fieldwork, doctors sometimes asked to see how they were doing, and we showed them the times we were observing and asked any clarifying questions. A third aspect of the shadowing included a brief four-item semi-structured debriefing interview at the end of the completed shift where we asked how typical the shift was, how they felt about it, and whether they felt like they got enough time with patients.

Each physician was observed at least twice to capture a "typical" day. It was during these debriefing sessions that the remaining veil of heroism and imperviousness that the first author had placed on people in the medical profession as a child began to dissipate. During these debriefing sessions, the complexity of each physician's life and the personal and professional challenges they faced came into focus. In addition to the discrepancies they faced between their fictive schedule and their actual, emergent workday, they described a range of emotions. They experienced guilt in their limitation to help patients, pressure and stress from organizational structures to operate in a particular way, delays from inefficient technology, and the challenges everyone faces in just being human. Just like every other profession and every other person, their challenges and issues did not stop when they walked into work or stepped into a room with a patient.

In one debriefing interview, a physician began to cry when describing the exhaustion and frustration associated with the structural conditions she faced in practicing medicine. This mid-career, energetic, well-liked doctor specializing in internal medicine talked about wanting to help patients while not having the organizational resources to do so. Contrary to what the resilience literature suggests, she described how mindfulness classes had not helped as a buffer against the stressors of the job. Neither had the things she did outside of work to bring more joy to her life helped her ability to cope. Despite her best countermeasures, coming to work still created a feeling of dread associated with facing the same insurmountable challenges day after day associated with inadequate institutional resources.

Thus, the issue of burnout in physicians—the focus of this chapter—was not created by the pandemic, it was exacerbated by it. COVID-19 contributed unique compounding issues to physicians and their work. A few weeks after the debriefing session described above, shelter-in-place mandates were issued across the country in hopes to assuage the spread of COVID-19. Our data collection efforts had to cease and we awaited some return to normalcy, a year later, before contacting our participants again. Nonetheless, we heard stories from and about other physicians about their experiences. We watched in horror as healthcare and government institutions continually failed them, offering platitudes and symbolic gestures in place of material resources.

Not All Superheroes Wear Capes

In much the same way that the first author placed the concept of hero on physicians, the global conversation around physicians and healthcare workers during the pandemic took the same heroic stance. The intentions of everyday citizens were wholesome. They felt helpless knowing the sacrifices being made by these individuals without adequate protection and resources. As Fig. 17.1 shows, in March a hashtag surfaced called #Solidarityat8 that was used to encourage people to go outside every night at 8 pm and cheer, shout, clap, honk their horns, ring bells, or turn on lights to show support for frontline healthcare workers and other essential workers. The Twitter feed for #Solidarityat8 shows people dancing for them, singing for them, showing their appreciation with words, photos, and video. By April, #Solidarityat8 had even given birth to howling as a way to honor doctors and other first responders. Scheier (2020) wrote for the *Los Angeles Times*:

> It began with Italians singing from their balconies. In Spain, people banged pots and pans.

Fig. 17.1 #Solidarityat8 hashtag

But residents of this leafy hamlet north of the Golden Gate Bridge have come up with their own unique way of expressing their gratitude for doctors and nurses on the front lines of the fight against the COVID-19 pandemic. It also gives them some release from their worries and frustrations about the current plight of the planet.

They howl.

The "Mill Valley Howl," as it's come to be known, was started by a retired renewable energy consultant named Huge Kuhn. He was inspired by the social media campaign #SolidarityAt8, which encourages people from New Delhi to New York to go outside at the same time every night and cheer on medical workers fighting the coronavirus.

While this movement had wonderful intentions, and certainly served a cathartic function for the people at home howling or singing or banging their pots and pans together, it did little to help the physicians that we were studying just days before the shutdown.

More helpful were individual and community efforts to donate personal protective equipment (PPE) to healthcare workers (Diaz & Taylor, 2020). There was even a viral story of a farmer in Kansas who sent an N95 mask to Governor Andrew Cuomo to help protect a nurse or doctor (Spector, 2020). Along with the masks he sent, he wrote a letter with his request (see Fig. 17.2). Yet, despite the material and valuable resources offered by many, the impact was modest at best in addressing the preexisting, underlying working conditions that physicians faced before COVID-19. While hospitals and other organizations were erecting billboards and signs to salute the heroism of doctors and other healthcare workers, such as in Fig. 17.3, their already dysfunctional working conditions had deteriorated to intolerable by many (Abelson, 2020). The American Medical Association acknowledged this severity of the problem and underscored how physicians' basic needs were not being met (Berg, 2020):

> In times of crisis and stress, sometimes basic needs go out the window, including food, water, safety and sleep. For example, when physicians work 14- or 16-hour days they may not think about these basic needs....

Additionally, Dr. Linzer explained:

> There is a common fear of acquiring COVID-19 and giving it to family members, loved ones or colleagues...a lot of physicians are unsure about "what is required and doing things that are not easy to understand, and the consequences of not getting it right feel pretty severe."

Among the suggestions made by Dr. Linzer for addressing these stressors was to watch the number of hours worked and to focus on mental health resources: "People need to know about the effects of acute and chronic stress and how to alleviate it, whether it's pushing resilience, meditation or counseling." Therefore, below we address the interrelationships among trauma, burnout, and recovery within a larger process of continually achieving (or failing to achieve) resilience.

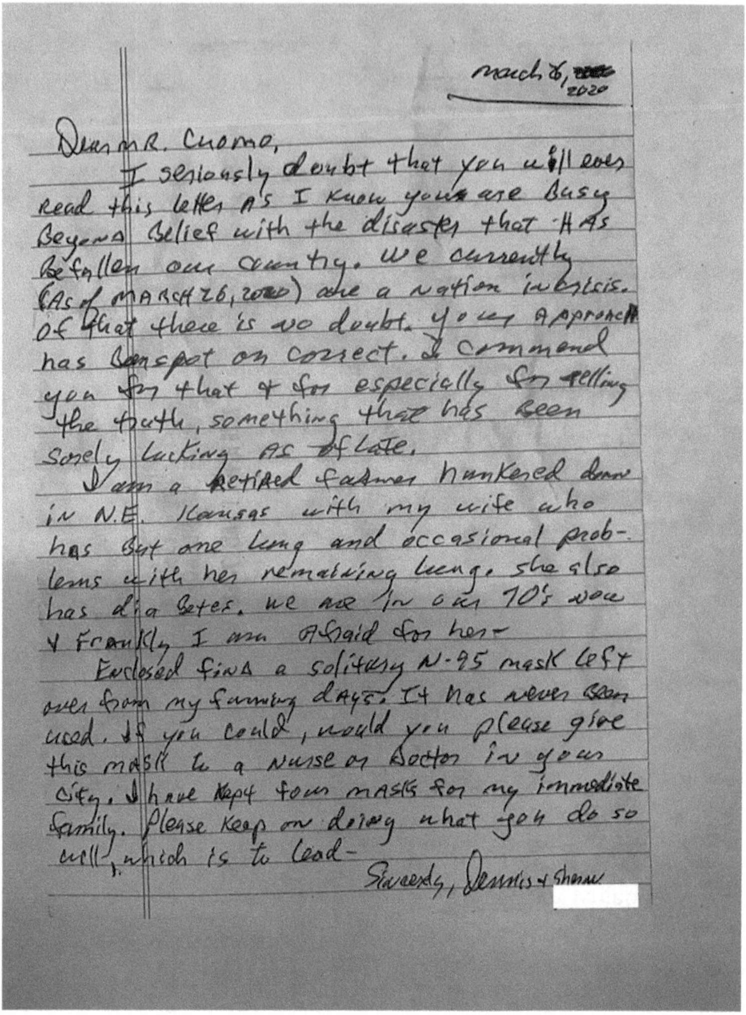

March 26, 2020

Dear MR. Cuomo,

I seriously doubt that you will ever read this letter AS I know you are busy beyond belief with the disaster that HAS befallen our country. We currently (As of MARCH 26, 2020) are a nation in crisis. Of that there is no doubt. Your Approach has been spot on correct. I commend you for that & for especially for telling the truth, something that has been sorely lacking AS of Late.

I am a retired farmer hunkered down in N.E. Kansas with my wife who has but one lung and occasional problems with her remaining lung. She also has diabetes. We are in our 70's now & Frankly I am Afraid for her.

Enclosed find a solitary N-95 mask left over from my farming days. It has never been used. If you could, would you please give this mask to a nurse or Doctor in your city. I have kept four masks for my immediate family. Please keep on doing what you do so well, which is to lead.

Sincerely, Dennis & Shana

Fig. 17.2 Letter from Kansas farmer donating an N-95 mask to a nurse or doctor in New York

Fig. 17.3 Not all superheroes wear capes billboard

Trauma in the Time of COVID-19

The location where we spent months shadowing physicians and their patients suddenly became one of the central locations in Austin caring for COVID-19 patients. Around the country, and world, other similar sites with doctors already struggling to keep up with the demands of their work while coping with symptoms of burnout suddenly found a new *trauma* unlike anything they faced in the past: treating a deadly respiratory virus without adequate supplies of PPE to protect themselves and ventilators needed to treat patients. Trauma refers to "internal and external life prompts, stressors, adversity, opportunities, and other forms of change. The sources may originate externally with resultant perceptions of seriousness or internally from thoughts and feelings. The stimuli can be new bits of information, new experiences, or recurring thoughts or feelings" (Richardson, 2002, p. 311). Trauma is the spark that ignites the resilience process.

An especially useful way to conceptualize trauma[1] before, during, and after the pandemic is by understanding that trauma can be either *cumulative* or *acute* (Winwood et al., 2006). Winwood et al. (2006) describe cumulative trauma as reflected in mental, physical, and emotional components (including a depressive element) caused by persistent fatigue. Acute trauma reflects an "'incapacitation'; an inability and/or unwillingness to engage with normal nonwork activities (including self-chosen pleasure activities) as a direct consequence of previous activity" (Winwood et al., 2006, p. 382). Cumulative trauma is experienced as a constant state and is the result of unaddressed and prolonged acute trauma. It develops over time and recovery from it is more complicated than what is required to mitigate acute trauma from one shift.

The challenge associated with treating the trauma experienced by certain physician specialties during COVID-19, such as the internal medicine and family medicine doctors we shadowed, stemmed from the extended and continually expanding period of time that COVID-19 cases were on the rise. The initial estimates of a 15-day time window needed for a worldwide shutdown to, could, contain the virus, soon grew from days to months to the unknown. Therefore, whether a doctor had previously experienced cumulative trauma or not, the likelihood of experiencing both acute and, ultimately, cumulative trauma as the pandemic continued was high. While most experienced the horror of the pandemic from a personal perspective, the millions of deaths lost worldwide were part of both the personal and professional landscape faced by these physicians.

For instance, *The New York Times* featured a story from an emergency room physician, Dr. Colleen Smith, in Elmhurst, Queens, who was explicit and candid about what hospital staff faced in New York (Stein & Kim, 2020). She made a video to expose the conditions in March 2020 and described:

> [Machine beeping] "Today is kind of getting worse and worse. We had to get a refrigerated truck to store the bodies of patients who are dying. We are, right now, scrambling to try to get a few additional ventilators or even CPAP machines.... Leaders in various offices, from the president to the head of Health and Hospitals, saying things like, 'We're going to be fine. Everything's

> fine.' And from our perspective, everything is not fine. I don't have the support that I need, and even just the materials that I need, physically, to take care of my patients....On a regular day, my emergency department's volume is pretty high. It's about 200 people a day. Now we're seeing 400 or more people a day. At first, we were trying to isolate patients with cough and fever and be more careful around them, but we weren't necessarily being extra careful around all the other patients. And then we started to realize that patients who were coming in with no fever but abdominal pain actually had findings on their X-rays and chest CTs that were consistent with this coronavirus, COVID-19.... Ten residents and also many, many of our nurses and a few of the attending physicians got sick. The anxiety of this situation is really overwhelming...We're exposed over and over again. We don't have the protective equipment that we should have. I put on one N95 mask in the morning. I need to have that N95 mask on for every patient I see. I don't take it off all day. The N95 mask I wore today is also the N95 mask I wore on Friday. We're always worried that we'll be out of N95 masks. What's a little bit scary now is the patients that we're getting are much sicker. Many of the young people who are getting sick don't smoke, they're healthy, they have no co-morbidities....I don't really care if I get in trouble for speaking to the media. I want people to know that this is bad. People are dying...."

Similarly, even for healthcare workers not at the epicenter of the pandemic in large densely populated cities like New York, the basic problem of inadequate resources was the same. A local Austin news station (KVUE) ran a story featuring Dr. Natasha Kathuria who likened her experience to a war and explained that the lack of PPE was untenable: "If we can't protect ourselves, there's no way we can (treat patients)—it's like sending our army out to fight with no guns and saying 'Good luck!'" (Marut, 2020). Both Dr. Smith in New York and Dr. Kathuria in Austin gave video recorded interviews showing them visibly distraught and begging for help to do their jobs. Their poor working conditions contributed to acute trauma (because of the daily fear for their lives they described) as well as cumulative trauma (given how long the pandemic lasted). If left untreated this leads to burnout, a topic described next.

Physician Burnout and Recovery During COVID-19

According to Maslach and Jackson (1981), "Burnout is a syndrome of emotional exhaustion and cynicism that occurs frequently among individuals who do 'people-work' of some kind" (p. 99). The concept of burnout consists of three dimensions: *emotional exhaustion, depersonalization*, and *reduced personal accomplishment* (Maslach & Jackson, 1984). The first dimension, *emotional exhaustion*, refers to being emotionally depleted by contact with other people. The second dimension, *depersonalization*, refers to apathetic and callous responses toward people at work, commonly those who should be the recipients of care or service as well as other organizational members. The last dimension, *reduced personal accomplishment*, refers to a decline in a person's feelings of competence and achievement in their work.

Burnout has been identified as a significant issue in healthcare workers, particularly in physicians. National studies have indicated that both physicians-in-training and practicing physicians report higher levels in all dimensions of burnout when compared to their non-physician counterparts (Dyrbye et al., 2014), with specialties such as emergency medicine, general internal medicine, and neurology reporting the highest frequency of burnout (West et al., 2018). In addition to increasing the likelihood of voluntary departure, burnout has been associated with reduction in patient satisfaction, greater likelihood of malpractice lawsuits, longer patient recovery times, mental and physical health issues for physicians, and reduced work satisfaction among various other issues (Hamidi et al., 2018; West et al., 2018). Results of a survey conducted on behalf of The Physicians Foundation in 2018 found that 78% of the 8774 physicians who responded indicated that they sometimes, often, or always experience feelings of burnout (The Physicians Foundation, 2018).

Abedini et al. (2018) describe two types of burnout: *circumstantial* and *existential.* Circumstantial burnout comes from "self-limited circumstances and environmental triggers" (p. 26). It can be addressed through practices such as nurturing their personal lives, resolving workplaces challenges, and taking time off work. Among the three means of resolving circumstantial burnout, none were available during the early days of the pandemic. First, the human toll and fear associated with COVID-19 as well as shelter-in-place mandates and closures of many public spaces (i.e., restaurants, bars, movie theaters, and recreational facilities) made it challenging for physicians to nurture their personal lives. Second, the lack of PPE and ventilators made it difficult to resolve workplace challenges. Third, taking time off work was not easy because of the rise in patients needing to be seen (as Dr. Colleen Smith described in Elmhurst, Queens).

Existential burnout comes from a loss of meaning in medicine and an uncertain professional role. It requires other methods of resolution including recognition of burnout, forming connections with others in their workplace, finding meaning in medicine, feeling validated, forming a professional identity, clarifying professional roles, and focusing on career development. It would be comforting to imagine that the hero narrative allowed doctors to find the validation, meaning, and identity formation they needed to resolve existential burnout caused by the COVID crisis. However, the toll of the trauma and the lack of recovery were more highly documented than any stories of how being called a hero helped them to cope. To the contrary, Dr. Lorna M. Breen, the medical director of New York Presbyterian Allen, one of Manhattan's hardest hit hospitals, died by suicide while home recuperating from COVID-19 because of the work conditions she faced (Watkins et al., 2020).

> The elder Dr. Breen said his daughter had contracted the coronavirus but had gone back to work after recuperating for about a week and a half. The hospital sent her home again, before her family intervened to bring her to Charlottesville, he said...
>
> Dr. Breen, 49, did not have a history of mental illness, her father said. But he said that when he last spoke with her, she seemed detached, and he could tell something was wrong. She had described to him an onslaught of patients who were dying before they could even be taken out of ambulances.
>
> "She was truly in the trenches of the front line," he said.
>
> He added: "Make sure she's praised as a hero, because she was. She's a casualty just as much as anyone else who has died."
>
> In a statement, NewYork-Presbyterian/Columbia used that language to describe her. "Dr. Breen is a hero who brought the highest ideals of medicine to the challenging front lines of the emergency department," the statement said.

Note that the war metaphor resurfaced in this story and the hero metaphor was prominent and embraced. Our argument is not that their work was not heroic, but that sometimes this metaphor is invoked by institutions to sidestep the issue of personal safety and recovery. Key to war metaphors is a short-term time frame wherein individuals must continue, without relief, until the enemy retreats.

Reports of Dr. Breen's life suggest that she had done everything right to reduce symptoms of burnout prior to the pandemic. The story continues:

> Aside from work, Dr. Breen filled her time with friends, hobbies and sports, friends said. She was an avid member of a New York ski club and traveled regularly out west to ski and snowboard. She was also a deeply religious

> Christian who volunteered at a home for older people once a week, friends said.
>
> Once a year, she threw a large party on the roof deck of her Manhattan home.
>
> She was very close with her sisters and mother, who lived in Virginia.
>
> One colleague said he had spent dozens of hours talking to Dr. Breen not only about medicine but about their lives and the hobbies she enjoyed, which also included salsa dancing. She was a lively presence, outgoing and extroverted, at work events, the colleague said.

Thus, by all accounts she was engaged in the routine recovery behaviors touted as solutions in the resilience literature. Dr. Breen's story was heartbreaking. We appreciated that the story of her death made it clear to anyone who was paying attention that she had all the personal and social tools to thrive in her chosen profession, but that the insurmountable institutional structures she faced were too high. Her resilience was broken, stretched too far. Many commentaries were written during the months to follow warning of a rise in physician suicide unless countermeasures were taken to protect their lives (Gulati & Kelly, 2020; Kingston, 2020). Thus, we conclude this chapter with our shared vista on the issue of physician resilience.

A Shared Vista on Physician Resilience Before, During, and After COVID-19

In one of our early conversations with a psychiatrist, an expert in resilience, responsible for supporting the mental health and wellness of physicians, we learned that there are no easy or fast answers. She told us that all the resilience interventions described in the literature—such as going for a walk, mindfulness mediation, or journaling—required that doctors actually had time to regularly practice them. She confessed feeling frustrated at the fact that she regularly counsels doctors to adopt practices that the larger institution of medicine will make nearly impossible. This was two years before COVID-19 emerged. In light of what unfolded during the early days of the pandemic, the situation felt hopeless to us as researchers reflecting on how our participants would likely fare during and after this colossal assault on their work and their bodies. We talked about how they were doing, worried about them, knowing that they would be asked to cultivate resilience, without any structural support to do so.

The concept of *resilience*, believed to originate in ecology (Batabyal, 1998), has been applied in a variety of social science disciplines, including communication studies (Buzzanell, 2010). Early psychological research on resilience focused on traits that prevented "at risk" children from developing psychopathological disorders (Garmezy, 1993; Masten et al., 1999). The idea of resilience as a trait soon lost its popularity for a more complex understanding of resilience as a process (Richardson, 2002). It was no longer understood as something someone possessed or lacked but was something in which an entity engaged. The construct of resilience has moved far beyond its original focus of children and expanded to studying adults, teams, organizations, communities, and even nations (Afifi, 2018; Buzzanell & Houston, 2018; Doerfel & Haseki, 2015).

Based on an extensive review of the literature, Krause et al. (2001) found that psychosocial job characteristics predicted the resilience process. Factors including time pressure, physically demanding work, low control over work-rest schedule, and long work hours predicted prolonged work disability. In contrast, improvements in these stressors led to greater resilience. Recent work by Shakir et al. (2020) extended these findings. In a study of neurosurgical residents in the U.S., the number of personal and social stressors faced by respondents was associated with reduced resilience and increased burnout. Similarly, when personal and social stressors were minimized their resilience improved.

None of the findings about resilience, recovery, and burnout are surprising. The COVID-19 pandemic would certainly qualify as a personal and social stressor as Shakir et al. (2020) describe. No one was responsible for its occurrence and, fortunately, it has already improved. We hope that it will continue to do so. However, many psychosocial job characteristics are under the control of key decision makers. These factors can be addressed and the data suggests these changes will minimize burnout, improve resilience, and decrease turnout. The vista we consider in conclusion is whether these issues will ever be addressed. Below are ten important professional events of our past and ten important professional events in the future that reflect our shared vista. We project an optimistic future because we are both optimists by nature. Nonetheless, the scatterplot for this chapter suggests that if we are too optimistic in our vista, the hero trope for physicians and other healthcare workers will continue, and doctors will trade adequate working conditions for electronic billboards that celebrate their heroism (Fig. 17.4).

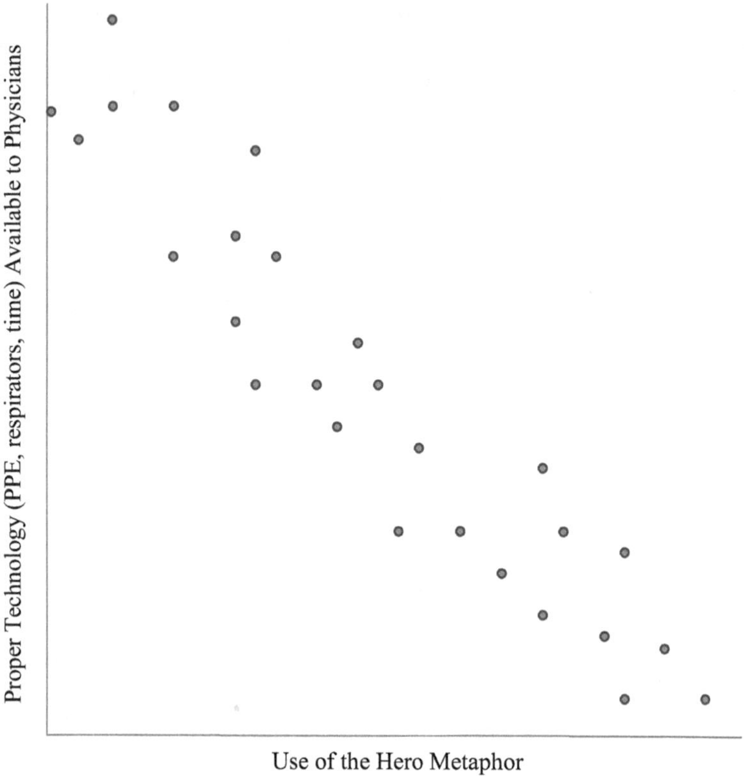

Fig. 17.4 Scatterplot depicting the relationship between the needed technology afforded to physicians and the use of the superhero metaphor

1994–2007:	Ana works as a translator, accompanying her parents to the medical appointments in a rural part of Northern California. It was then that she began to see doctors as heroes.
March 2016:	Dawna gives a talk about time in work at the South by Southwest conference in Austin Texas and meets Dr. Urmimala Sakar who introduces herself and invites Dawna to give a talk at the University of California, San Francisco (UCSF) Medical School.
September 2016:	Dawna travels to UCSF, and during small talk between meetings, Dawna asks about a typical day for her and

Urmimala mentions the fictive physician schedule. Dawna is fascinated and they jointly decide to study the relationship between time and burnout in primary care medicine.

August 2017: Ana and Dawna begin to study resilience and meet with Dr. Carrie Barron, the Director of Creativity for Resilience at Dell Medical School.

2017–2018: The study gets underway and the research team (comprised both UT and UCSB members) begins to meet and iron out details needed for approval from their Institutional Review Boards. The initial team includes Ana, Urmimala, Dawna, Dr. Mike Pignone, Dr. Liz Jacobs, Kate Sebastian, R.N., and Dr. Deepak Maharaj.

April 2019: The UT Austin arm of the research team receives IRB approval and begins shadowing local physicians at a CommUnity Care Clinic.

March 2020: All research at CommUnity Care Clinic shuts down because of the COVID-19 pandemic.

March 2020: All the local healthcare organizations in Austin and around the U.S. begin erecting signs saying things like, "Heroes Work Here." Physicians and frontline workers beg for help from the U.S. government and receive mostly platitudes.

August 2020: Ana moves back to Northern California in order to complete her dissertation.

April 2021: Ana defends her dissertation prospectus "Time in Trauma: Burnout and Recovery of Physicians' Work" and advances to candidacy.

May 2021: Ana begins interviews with physicians at CommUnity Care and Zuckerberg San Francisco General Hospital.

June 2021: Dawna continues to work with Dr. Victor Montori at Mayo Clinic (and the co-founder of the Patient Revolution) to learn how to redesign time to create a model for careful and kind care.

July 2021: Ana completes remaining data analysis and dissertation write-up.

August 2021:	Ana files her dissertation and earns a doctorate in organizational communication and technology from UT Austin.
August 2021:	Ana begins her position studying time and resilience in healthcare.
September 2021:	Dawna completes her book, *Time by Design*, published with MIT Press.
2022:	Dawna's work with Victor goes live in the field at Mayo Clinic.
2026:	Ana becomes a leading advocate for healthcare reform.
2028:	Structural changes are made in healthcare delivery that increases the resilience of physicians and other healthcare workers.
2032:	Retention rates of physicians are on the rise, and more people go into the profession of medicine because important changes being made in medical training and healthcare delivery.

Note

1. In this chapter, we have opted to use the term of trauma, but it should be noted that the term is closely related and will be used interchangeably with the terms *stressors*, *disruption*, and *fatigue* to reflect the original language used in their respective fields (Huibers et al., 2003; Leone et al., 2011). All the terms are used to indicate the same construct within a larger process of resilience.

References

Abedini, Nauzley, Stack, Shobha W., Goodman, Jessie L., & Steinberg, Kenneth P. (2018). "It's Not Just Time Off": A framework for understanding factors promoting recovery from burnout among internal medicine residents. *Journal of Graduate Medical Education, 10*(1), 26–32. https://doi.org/10.4300/JGME-D-17-00440.1

Abelson, Reed. (2020, November 15). Doctors are calling it quits under stress of the pandemic. *The New York Times*. https://www.nytimes.com/2020/11/15/health/Covid-doctors-nurses-quitting.html

Afifi, Tamara D. (2018). Individual/relational resilience. *Journal of Applied Communication Research, 46*(1), 5–9. https://doi.org/10.1080/00909882.2018.1426707

Anderson, P. (2018, May 7). Physicians Experience Highest Suicide Rate of Any Profession. *Medscape*. https://www.medscape.com/viewarticle/896257?reg=1

Barbour, Joshua B., Ballard, Dawna I., Barge, J. Kevin, & Gill, Rebecca. (2017). Making time/making temporality for engaged scholarship. *Journal of Applied Communication Research, 45*(4), 365–380. https://doi.org/10.1080/00909882.2017.1355556

Batabyal, Amitrajeet A. (1998). The concept of resilience: Retrospect and prospect. *Environment and Development Economics, 3*(2), 221–262.

Berg, Sara. (2020, March 20). *6 ways to address physician stress during COVID-19 pandemic*. American Medical Association. Retrieved from https://www.ama-assn.org/delivering-care/public-health/6-ways-address-physician-stress-during-covid-19-pandemic

Buzzanell, Patrice M. (2010). Resilience: Talking, resisting, and imagining new normalcies into being. *Journal of Communication, 60*(1), 1–14.

Buzzanell, Patrice M., & Houston, J. Brian. (2018). Communication and resilience: Multilevel applications and insights–A Journal of Applied Communication Research forum. *Journal of Applied Communication Research, 46*(1), 1–4. https://doi.org/10.1080/00909882.2017.1412086

Diaz, Johnny, & Taylor, Derek Bryson. (2020, April 1). How to donate your N95 masks to New York doctors. *The New York Times*. https://www.nytimes.com/2020/04/01/nyregion/donate-masks-coronavirus.html

Doerfel, Marya L., & Haseki, M. (2015). Networks, disrupted: Media use as an organizing mechanism for rebuilding. *New Media & Society, 17*(3), 432–452.

Dyrbye, Liselotte N., West, Colin P., Satele, Daniel, Boone, Sonja, Tan, Litjen, Sloan, Jeff, & Shanafelt, Tait D. (2014). Burnout among US medical students, residents, and early career physicians relative to the general US population. *Academic Medicine, 89*(3), 443–451.

Garmezy, Norman. (1993). Children in poverty: Resilience despite risk. *Psychiatry, 56*(1), 127–136. https://doi.org/10.1080/00332747.1993.11024627

Gulati, Guatam, & Kelly, Brendan D. (2020). Physician suicide and the COVID-19 pandemic. *Occupational Medicine, 70*(7), 514–514. https://doi.org/10.1093/occmed/kqaa104

Hamidi, Maryam S., Bohman, Bryan, Sandborg, Christy, Smith-Coggins, Rebecca, de Vries, Patty, Albert, Marisa S., Murphy, Mary Lou, Welle, Dana, & Trockel, Mickey T. (2018). Estimating institutional physician turnover attributable to self-reported burnout and associated financial burden: A case study. *BMC Health Services Research, 18*, 1–8. https://doi.org/10.1186/s12913-018-3663-z

Huibers, M. J. H. (2003). Fatigue burnout and chronic fatigue syndrome among employees on sick leave: Do attributions make the difference? *Occupational and Environmental Medicine*. https://doi.org/10.1136/oem.60.suppl_1.i26

Kingston, Amanda M. (2020). Break the silence: Physician suicide in the time of COVID-19. *Missouri Medicine, 117*(5), 426–429.

Klitzman, R. (2007). "Patient-time" "doctor-time" and "institution-time": Perceptions and definitions of time among doctors who become patients. *Patient Education and Counseling, 66*(2), 147–155. https://doi.org/10.1016/j.pec.2006.10.005

Krause, Niklas, Frank, John W., Dasinger, Lisa K., Sullivan, Terry J., & Sinclair, Sandra J. (2001). Determinants of duration of disability and return-to-work after work-related injury and illness: Challenges for future research. *American Journal of Industrial Medicine, 40*(4), 464–484. https://doi.org/10.1002/ajim.1116

Leone, Stephanie S., Wessely, Simon, Huibers, Marcus J., Knottnerus, J. André, & Kant, Ijmert. (2011). Two sides of the same coin? On the history and phenomenology of chronic fatigue and burnout. *Psychology and Health, 26*(4), 449–464.

Linzer, M., Konrad, T. R., Douglas, J., McMurray, J. E., Pathman, D. E., Williams, E. S., Schwartz, M. D., Gerrity, M., Scheckler, W., Bigby, J., & Rhodes, E. (2000). Managed care time pressure and physician job satisfaction: Results from the physician worklife study. *Journal of General Internal Medicine, 15*(7), 441–450. https://doi.org/10.1046/j.1525-1497.2000.05239.x

Marut, Mike. (2020, March 20). *"We are in a war": Austin doctors running out of protective equipment to treat coronavirus patients.* KVUE. https://www.kvue.com/article/news/health/coronavirus/coronavirus-doctors-masks-austin-protective-equipment-goggles/269-a803b7ac-1ab0-4a6a-bfb8-af8b08d72028

Maslach, Christina, & Jackson, Susan E. (1981). The measurement of experienced burnout. *Journal of Occupational Behavior, 2*(1), 99–113. https://www.jstor.org/stable/3000281

Maslach, Christina, & Jackson, Susan E. (1984). Burnout in organizational settings. *Applied Social Psychology Annual, 5*, 133–153.

Masten, Ann S., Hubbard, Jon J., Gest, Scott D., Tellegen, Auke, Garmezy, Norman, & Ramirez, Marylouise. (1999). Competence in the context of adversity: Pathways to resilience and maladaptation from childhood to late adolescence. *Development and Psychopathology, 11*(1), 143–169.

Özbilgin, M., Beauregard, T. A., Tatli, A., & Bell, M. P. (2011). Work–Life Diversity and Intersectionality: A Critical Review and Research Agenda. *International Journal of Management Reviews, 13*(2), 177–198. https://doi.org/10.1111/j.1468-2370.2010.00291.x

Passalacqua, Stacey A. (2017). Occupational burnout and the case study of physicians. In D. I. Ballard & M. S. McGlone (Eds.), *Work pressures: New agendas in communication.* Routledge.

Richardson, Glenn E. (2002). The metatheory of resilience and resiliency. *Journal of Clinical Psychology, 58*(3), 307–321. https://doi.org/10.1002/jclp.10020

Scheier, R. (2020, April 4). Coronavirus has people howling at the moon. *Los Angeles Times.* https://www.latimes.com/california/story/2020-04-04/coronavirus-has-people-howling-at-the-moon

Shakir, Hakeem J., Cappuzzo, Justin M., Shallwani, Hussain, Kwasnicki, Amanda, Bullis, Carli, Wang, Jiefei, Hess, Ryan M., & Levy, Elad I. (2020). Relationship of grit and resilience to burnout among U.S. neurosurgery residents. *World Neurosurgery, 134*, e224–e236. https://doi.org/10.1016/j.wneu.2019.10.043

Spector, Joseph. (2020, May 6). *Kansas farmer who donated mask to Gov. Cuomo gets college degree.* https://www.usatoday.com/story/news/nation/2020/05/06/kansas-farmer-who-donated-mask-gov-cuomo-gets-college-degree/5174679002/

Stein, Robin, & Kim, Caroline. (2020, March 25). Video: 'People are dying': 72 hours inside a N.Y.C. hospital battling Coronavirus. *The New York Times.* https://www.nytimes.com/video/nyregion/100000007052136/coronavirus-elmhurst-hospital-queens.html

The Physicians Foundation. (2018). *2018 survey of America's physicians: Practice patterns and perspectives.* R https://physiciansfoundation.org/wp-content/uploads/2018/09/physicians-survey-results-final-2018.pdf

Watkins, All, Rothfeld, Michael, Rashbaum, William K., & Rosenthal, Brian M. (2020, April 27). Top E.R. doctor who treated Coronavirus patients dies by suicide. *The New York Times.* https://www.nytimes.com/2020/04/27/nyregion/new-york-city-doctor-suicide-coronavirus.html

West, Colin P., Dyrbye, Liselotte N., & Shanafelt, Talt D. (2018). Physician burnout: Contributors, consequences and solutions. *Journal of Internal Medicine, 283*, 516–529. https://doi.org/10.1111/joim.12752

Westbrook, J. I., Ampt, A., Kearney, L., & Rob, M. I. (2008). All in a day's work: An observational study to quantify how and with whom doctors on hospital wards spend their time. *Medical Journal of Australia, 188*(9), 506–509. https://doi.org/10.5694/j.1326-5377.2008.tb01762.x

Winwood, Peter C., Lushington, Kurt, & Winefield, Anthony H. (2006). Further development and validation of the occupational fatigue exhaustion recovery (OFER) scale. *Journal of Occupational and Environmental Medicine, 48*(4), 381–389. https://doi.org/10.1097/01.jom.0000194164.14081.06

Yin, H. Shonna, Dreyer, Benard P., Vivar, Karina L., MacFarland, Suzanne, van Schaick, Linda, & Mendelsohn, Alan L. (2012). Perceived barriers to care and attitudes towards shared decision-making among low socioeconomic status parents: Role of health literacy. *Academic Pediatrics, 12*(2), 117–124.

CHAPTER 18

Applied Scholarship in Extreme Contexts: Emotion, Meaning, and Risk in Pandemic Response

Rebecca M. Rice

Becoming a Volunteer Ethnographer

March 2020 as an organizational communication scholar who studies crisis was horrifying and fascinating, in that order. I started the month holding my breath, waiting to see if the International Crisis and Risk Conference would be canceled like so many other conferences. It was not. We ate from a buffet and greeted each other with "elbow bumps." I used a Clorox wipe on my plane tray table. As I flew back to Las Vegas I felt like the entire country was enveloped in a shadow, starting at the coasts and narrowing in as more and more cities announced stay-at-home orders. I sat in a crowded Italian restaurant with my parents on March 20th. As I looked

R. M. Rice (✉)
Department of Communication Studies, University of Nevada, Las Vegas, Las Vegas, NV, USA
e-mail: rebecca.rice@UNLV.edu

L. D. Browning et al. (eds.), *Organizational Communication and Technology in the Time of Coronavirus*,
https://doi.org/10.1007/978-3-030-94814-6_18

around at the smiling faces sharing garlic bread I felt a deep sense that this would be the last time I felt normal for a long time.

As the days ticked past, I also felt like I was waiting. I research emergency management, and I knew that those organizations were probably busy. I thought often about a fieldsite I had already studied, CET. CET was a community emergency management office that typically responded to natural disasters, but I imagined that they were busy preparing for the pandemic as it spread. I pictured their previously crowded meeting room filled once again with people I had interviewed for my dissertation, sitting behind their assigned computers, ordering emergency supplies, and quieting down once every few hours to go "around the room" sharing what each person had been working on. I wondered how involved I could be if I was no longer in the same city. Part of me was just trying to survive, put my classes online, get enough groceries. But as the days ticked past, I couldn't wait on the sidelines any longer. I emailed the CET deputy director, Nick, on March 18th. I didn't expect to hear anything back, but within 15 minutes we were on the phone. "Rebecca Rice, how the heck are you?" he said. Nick sounded happy, energized, the greeting felt like we had just run into each other at a high school reunion. I said I was okay and asked how he was. "I'm good," he said, "you know, living the dream." We both laughed as I remembered exactly what I admire about emergency managers—they're doers. They thrive on the adrenaline and stress of unfolding situations. And I, by extension, have picked up the attitude. I was jittery on the phone call, wondering what would happen. Nick didn't seem to notice. "So, we're setting up for tomorrow," he explained, "you want in?"

Of course, I said yes. Starting on March 19th I was on a twice-daily Zoom call with all of the CET personnel. The COVID pandemic created a unique opportunity to do fieldwork without a field—all the meetings would be virtual to keep the emergency management personnel from infecting each other. Instead of the bustling office, typically staffed with upwards of 60 people and twice as many cell phones and radios ringing, we would stay home and check in on Zoom. During my initial fieldwork with CET in 2017 and 2018, I had gone through volunteer training as a way to learn the emergency management practices. This time, I reasoned, I owed them some hours back. I was hesitant to get "too involved" at first, but I was quickly assigned to the role of "situational awareness" on the daily briefing video calls. My job was to take notes on what everyone on the call said, to be posted online for those who missed the meeting or needed resources or wanted to know who to contact. The job was a perfect fit for an ethnographer and I quickly learned that ethnographers are often the people paying the most attention in any given room anyway.

March was my first foray into volunteer ethnography. Volunteering creates the opportunity to experience day-to-day life in an organization alongside members, while also giving back to the organization that is granting research access (Hill O'Connor & Baker, 2017). Being a volunteer creates opportunities and drawbacks. In my case, volunteering took up a great deal of time, yet positioned me as a peripheral member of the organization. Volunteers often feel tension in their level of commitment and identification, in contrast to paid organizational members (McNamee & Peterson, 2014). This is further complicated by emergency response cultures, which can involve strong hierarchies among members (Jahn & Black, 2017; Rice, 2021). Tinney (2008) warned volunteer ethnographers to maintain boundaries around their work, a warning that I quickly abandoned. Being a volunteer and a researcher controlled my presence in multiple ways. Unlike a regular volunteer, who might work with emergency management offices to give back or feel a sense of involvement and purpose, I also felt pressure to collect data. Ethnography requires deep immersion in the field (Geertz, 2000), and as demand to publish quickly on the tenure track builds (Taylor et al., 2021), I found it impossible to walk away from the chance to observe meetings. CET met on Zoom twice a day, Monday-Friday, from March through mid-May. I missed two meetings in that time, and only because my volunteer supervisor told me I had to take a day off to rest. Interactions with professional colleagues reinforced this drive, with many fellow professors telling me that it was amazing that I was getting "such good data."

Volunteering did create advantages for fieldwork, including the experience of embodiment. In previous emergency management trainings, emergency managers expressed to me that exercises can prepare you, but there is nothing like "the real thing." Even though I had *observed* real-time emergencies in the past, the experience of responding to an emergency was completely different. I felt firsthand the momentary "freeze" that new people get when they are asked to spring into action as members of the emergency management team and spent several days simply wondering if I was doing anything right. I second-guessed every note I wrote down and checked in with my supervisor constantly.

I also struggled to separate research participants as friends and colleagues and as subjects of my research analysis (Garthwaite, 2016). The fieldwork was particularly intense, and I quickly felt that everyone on the call was bonded by the circumstances—we were "in the trenches" together, exhausted. Ethnography became my secondary task, with my first priority being my volunteer job. Ethnographers have considered a spectrum of levels of participation from complete observer to complete participant (Lindlof & Taylor, 2019), however, there is a common emphasis on being a researcher first and foremost, and using distance to ensure rigorous research and analysis (Hill O'Connor & Baker, 2017; Tinney, 2008). In the moment, and given the circumstances of research during a crisis, I found this boundary difficult, if not impossible, to defend. While there are growing calls for research in crisis organizations, the intensity of experiences in these organizations can pose a challenge to researchers, both in terms of safety and access (Bean & Rice, 2019; Hällgren et al., 2017). An additional challenge here was that the emergency was not neatly bound within the site of observation. COVID was everywhere—in the field and out, in the Zoom meetings and on my news app, in my meetings as a professor and my after-work social calls with friends. I wish I could say I tried to be an ethnographer first, but my field notes from March are often copied and pasted meeting notes and a few added interpretations from my perspective. The act of volunteering and simply surviving the current situation took most of my energy and the pace of observations did not allow any time to pause. Worse, I didn't want to pause for fear of acknowledging my own feelings about the situation.

Technology and Emotional Burnout

April was, I thought, the strangest month of my life. I was laying on the floor in my office after an 8 AM meeting, avoiding student emails. The transitions between emergency management volunteer ethnographer and just plain professor were the most difficult. I felt like I was drifting out to sea on an iceberg. I knew April was weird for everyone, but I didn't have the words. Friends around me seemed to treat it like a snow day: We don't have to commute! Let's play board games over Zoom and drink hot toddies! We have so much time! I didn't know how to explain just how little time I suddenly had. Emergency management took over my life. I woke up, grabbed coffee, kept my video off, jumped on the 8 AM Zoom call, and typed, furiously, for 30–45 minutes. I learned who was on the daily meetings: a public health staff member, a sheriff's deputy, someone from housing and human services, county transportation, donation management, resource management. I learned new acronyms and terms: PPE, "epi", 5-day rolling case count. The public health representative rattled off the same numbers every day: number of people testing positive, number hospitalized, deaths, ICU capacity, percentage testing positive. I knew that Taylor, a sheriff's deputy, would give the weather report every morning like he was running a radio talk show; that Angelica, from human services, loved to remind us to fill out our census. I knew everyone's first and last names even if they didn't know me.

In early May, I was sitting on the floor in my office (I spent a lot of time on the floor), propping a laptop up to compile "the numbers" for a daily situational awareness report. This report went out to county stakeholders at the end of each workday to give them a broad overview of the pandemic and actions taken by county personnel that day to manage it. I went to the CDC website to get the national COVID case count, which was updated daily in the report. Sometime in early April, I had made a decision to stop reading the news. I, like everyone else I knew, was spending hours on news apps every day, scrolling in fear, trying to understand what COVID-19 even was. It felt like a negotiation—what's safe? Do I have to disinfect groceries? Can I order takeout? By May I had completely shut myself off from anything that wasn't my fieldwork—I got my news from morning and evening briefings. So as the CDC site loaded that day I experienced the complete shock of seeing the US case numbers. If someone asked me how many cases the US had I might have guessed 600,000. As of May 4th, it was 1.1 million. I didn't realize how hard I had put my head down until that moment. The best thing about emergency management, I told friends, is that "there's no time for despair." With two calls a day, notes to email, reports to compile, all I could do was put one foot in front of the other. But I hadn't looked up in a long, long time.

Charting my relationship to technology during the pandemic, I saw a contradiction. In my relationship to fieldwork, the amount of time spent on Zoom meant I felt incredibly close to my participants, even though we weren't in the same state (see Fig. 18.1). By this logic, it makes sense that I felt more distance from my university. I didn't see most of my students or colleagues on Zoom at all in the spring. Ethnographers effectively "leave" their academic positions to join the field, learning new organizational norms and ways of being while continuing to occupy their old posts (Gilmore & Kenny, 2015). Because of technology practices in place early in the pandemic, I spent two or more hours a day on video calls with CET, while never seeing my entire university department. This experience was

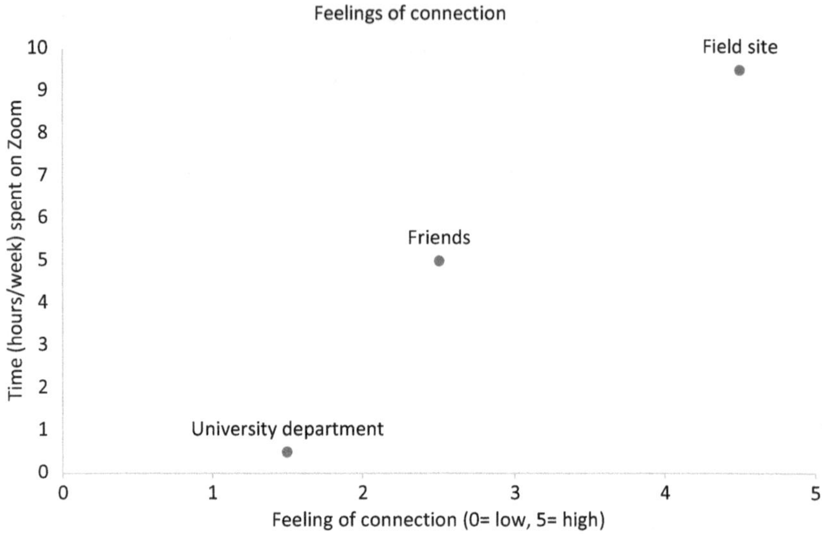

Fig. 18.1 Feelings of connection to various groups throughout the pandemic, as correlated to the amount of time spent on Zoom with each group

made even stranger by being a first-year faculty member—as time stretched on I had taught online for longer than I had ever taught in-person at the university. I jokingly called my spring semester my "postdoc" because I felt like I only did research, even with students enrolled in my online classes.

The closeness felt via Zoom created advantages and disadvantages as a researcher. On the one hand, I was able to see more interactions than I likely would see in person. It was clear throughout 2020 that virtual spaces were no longer "not real life," and instead were an essential part of the social world that researchers should be observing (Hallett & Barber, 2014). Online fieldwork also allowed me to easily record fieldnotes without participants noticing or becoming distracted by my writing. Simultaneously, this posed an ethical dilemma as participants may have forgotten my role as a researcher when speaking on calls. I addressed this by introducing myself as a researcher on calls where introductions occurred, and by reminding people of my researcher role in emails. Despite my feeling of connection, some offline conversations did impact the daily meetings as a few key employees did go into the emergency management office, which led to feelings of missing some information, especially when big decisions were made without any explanation. In interviews, other online-only participants expressed the same limitations.

In my personal relationships, the time spent with friends and family online had an inverse effect: I felt more distant from people even if we spent more time on Zoom. This tracks with early research findings about technology use during the pandemic, where use for work is more satisfying than use for personal connections (Pennington et al., in press). As I spent more time online connecting with family and friends, I felt less of a connection to these people, in part because our relationship was based on so much in-person interaction before 2020. However, I also believe the decreasing feeling of closeness came from fieldwork as the fieldwork changed my thoughts and my identity.

Exiting the Field and Losing Identity

On May 8th, Gabriel, the emergency manager, announced that this would be the last briefing call. I knew that things were slowing down—the stay-at-home order for the county had been lifted as cases decreased—but I was still surprised, and surprised to find myself tearing up (camera off, unfortunately). I was in the middle of grading final exam papers, I had just forgotten my best friend's birthday, I was ducking another friend's calls because I didn't know if I could stand another minute of my day on the phone or computer. I was completely overwhelmed but my tears were not from relief. I realized that if the calls ended, it would be like facing COVID alone. Others on the call seemed unsettled, too. Someone asked why we were shutting down the meetings if COVID was still an issue. Gabriel replied that our goal had been to preserve the capacity of the county medical system, and, because the system was holding steady, now would be a good time to take a break. If cases surged, he said, we could always "get the band back together."

I felt myself relax at this promise and it seemed that others did, too. Then I felt bad: was I upset that the pandemic was getting better? No, but I was afraid of what it would be like to return to my normal life during abnormal circumstances. Everything was completely out of order, for all of us, but I had survived the first 3 months of staying inside with my extra purpose. Fieldwork was like looking at coronavirus without ever making eye contact with it—I could handle it because at least I knew people who were doing things about it. I was not ready to return to reading the news instead of hearing straight from public health officials. I didn't know how to talk to my summer term students. I owed a lot of friends and family phone calls that I was still not ready to make. As I did fieldwork, I allowed the rest of my life to stop, and now I would have to get back to it.

Knowing when to leave the field is a challenge in ethnography (Lindlof & Taylor, 2019), and in this case, doing event-centered fieldwork dictated when data collection started and stopped. Leaving the field was challenging in several ways: first, the field was virtual, so the exit was not physical. I did not turn in my badge, I deleted events off my Google Calendar. It felt strange to be in my house after fieldwork ended so my partner and I decided to go to a family cabin for a weekend. I felt like every emotion I had suppressed for three months came back both abruptly and unevenly. For the first week, I felt on the verge of tears at all times. For several months afterward, I was most startled by my anger. I was angry at everything. Angry when I saw someone with their facemask under their nose, angry when someone stepped too close to me at Trader Joe's, angry when I saw a friend post a picture at a bar. I didn't understand my anger until I conducted participant interviews, which became a shared sensemaking experience. Jessica, a CET volunteer I had worked closely with, told me that for the first month after we stopped having meetings, she felt angry all the time, too. She said that she felt like she had worked over 40 hours a week to stop COVID and she didn't do all that work just for people to "blow it" by going out without a mask on. Hearing someone else name my feelings during interviews was extremely helpful.

Despite the emotional components of ethnography, there is very little training or discussion of how researchers should deal with emotions in the field (Vincett, 2018). While ethnographers are often told to describe the scene, including the emotions within it, ethnography can instead be thought of as emotional interactions *among* the researcher and participants (Brannan, 2011; Rivera, 2015). Ethnographers experience liminality between their home organization and observed organization and liminality between emotional states (Lindlof & Taylor, 2019). In a crisis situation like the pandemic, it was impossible not to experience shared emotions with participants. Indeed, the experience of these emotions was an important part of understanding the embodied aspects of crisis work. The emotions I felt certainly increased my humility as a researcher as well. I was not an outsider looking in to produce omniscient knowledge, I was also a participant stumbling through my confusion, anger, and incomplete understanding of the situation.

Returning to the Field and Embracing New Technology Practices

The rest of the summer felt like easing back into the new normal. I relaxed into my role as an online professor. I realized that I had ended my first year as an assistant professor without even a thought. While my impostor syndrome had felt ever-present during my first semester, by March I simply didn't have time for it. I was excited as colleagues and students alike asked me about my COVID research, but also committed to not giving definitive answers about best practices, when the vaccine would be available, or when we would return to normal life. Still, I sensed that everyone was optimistic as cases evened out. Gabriel had told the CET that we expected this wouldn't hold and there would be a second surge, so as cases ticked up in September, I thought about what CET might be doing. I was in the middle of a student newspaper interview about COVID when my phone lit up with a notification. It was Trey, my volunteer supervisor. The email had no greeting, it just said "We're getting the band back together. You in?" I was momentarily speechless and apologized to the student reporter. Was it wrong that my heart was pounding, that I rushed through the interview questions so that I could reply "I'm in!?"

March through May was about saving the medical system. September and October were about college students, who had partied enough (so said university administrators) to drive a huge case spike. I felt conflict as a professor. Did I believe students were partying? Yes. Did I think it was their fault they had been brought back to campus, invited to pay to live on campus, and then told that they should not get near each other? Anyone who has ever handed out a syllabus could anticipate how these directions would go over. This response involved, again, two virtual meetings a day, plus a third on Thursday. And some Fridays. And a quick check-in on Monday. Some of my friends started to ask me why I wasn't being paid for all this work, which made me angry and defensive. That's not how research works, I said, this is great data.

Still, I was exhausted by mid-October. Students in my graduate seminar seemed to check in on my research weekly. They were interested, but I also think they sensed my distraction. I met with a student dealing with mental health challenges, who assured me she was "fine" and would finish a midterm paper soon. "You're not fine. I'm not fine. How could we be fine?" I asked her, tearing up at a thought I hadn't allowed myself to think for six months. I realized that I had spent the whole year forgetting myself—forgetting my feelings, then forgetting how tired I was, forgetting how challenging the fieldwork had been. Now I was back and I couldn't forget anymore. I had been subconsciously writing myself out of field notes. Everything was about what others said and seemed to be thinking, while I was a voiceless observer whose hands hurt from typing meeting notes. I turned to the tool we had all become too familiar with, Zoom, for help. At the end of each fieldwork day, I opened a Zoom room and started recording my own observations. It felt embarrassing, vulnerable, and cheesy at first, but talking was far easier than writing, and I found myself saying more and more about how I felt about that day or week. I kept my camera on because I didn't want to let myself forget what I had looked like (my face really says it all during the height of the response in October). I sometimes see pictures of myself from early 2020 and realize I felt and looked like a completely different person, definitely lighter despite what seemed like real worries at the time. I still feel like a completely different person.

It would be false to end this story in the Fall because the CET work continued and is continuing into 2021. It feels significant to be writing this chapter during the week of my first vaccine appointment, even though I know that won't be the ending I'm looking for either, not for a while. When we've made it through, I will wonder what this fieldwork did to me, even as I know I would do it all over again if invited. I feel incredibly sappy about the research participants, who I hope to have a beer with one day. I hope the edges of my anger about people disobeying public health orders soften. But I'm not "fine" yet. How could any of us be?

The second phase of fieldwork marked my transition to more conscious practices of autoethnography. I started to welcome the "messiness" of my fieldwork, and that my emotions were entangled with both the situation at hand and my participants' sensemaking (Bochner & Ellis, 2016). Autoethnography also allowed me the space to make sense of and track my own interpretations. COVID was, in Weick's terms, a cosmology event that caused uncertainty around my professional identity (Stephens et al., 2020). The transition in and out of fieldwork shifted which part of my identity was at the foreground, though there were days where I struggled to remember that my fieldwork was my "real work" and that I had done something productive toward my research agenda. Additionally, I felt that ethnographic training prepared me to *observe* emotion, just not *my* emotion. I felt the call to be "professional" and therefore removed, calm and collected—outside of the scene. It was not until late in fieldwork, when I did start to write myself back into the story, that I realized that research participants were likely dealing with the same tension between being "in" the emergency and being outsiders who managed the emergency (Mastracci et al., 2012). Embracing autoethnography helped me to understand this tension as productive to my own reflections.

This break in normalcy also caused a break in my typical field methods. I learned to adapt to online observation, before eventually finding that technology could do more than adapt my methods, it could also facilitate new processes for reflecting and creating knowledge. As such, I feel optimistic that this study helped me to create new practices of resilience that I can carry forward in my career. I felt that technology became a tool for observation and for observing myself. It facilitated access to a high-risk and stressful research environment that I may not have otherwise received. I do wonder, as I submit this research for publication, if there will be any resistance to this new way of doing ethnography. The common thought is that the richness of our social worlds gets lost online, but I am optimistic that 2020 forced us all to see and maintain those connections—to understand that online is and will continue to be a contributor to "real life."

As I look at my "professional vistas," I believe this research project is and will continue to be one of them. This project changed my relationship with research organizations and I now feel more welcome, but also more understanding, of the challenges caused by crisis collaboration. I feel like I have more of an insider perspective on emergency organizations, but I also believe that each organization dealt with the pandemic differently, and try not to overgeneralize my knowledge from this one experience. COVID felt like a loss of innocence around crisis communication, for me. Before 2020, I thought that if practitioners just used good crisis communication tactics, the public would listen and comply and the crisis response would be successful. 2020 tested all of that, with different organizations sending out very different messages and public resistance growing throughout the year. This research made me feel more aligned with organizational and crisis communication as parts of my identity, even when that was painful and created strained relationships, especially with friends and family who did not exercise caution to stop the spread of COVID.

This year also opened up possibilities to view virtual ethnography and autoethnography as tools for my future research and I hope we will see more research using these methods in the future. However, it also stretched my limits and taught me the necessity of boundary work in order to continue researching difficult topics without becoming burnt out. I do not have the ending to this story yet, but if I get to write it, I hope we can become open to more hybrid methods of participation in research projects. I believe technology is not the only avenue forward for organizational communication, but technology did create opportunities to observe an organization that faced an extreme situation.

This month, almost a year after fieldwork began, I finally feel a bit of distance, like maybe I can start to reflect and analyze instead of just surviving the data. I have started looking through my interviews with CET members, recorded between May and September of 2020. I find myself laughing at moments in our conversations or feeling that their observations are especially poignant to my own understanding as I step back. As one CET staff member explained to me, "It's thankless. This is why you gotta enjoy the moment. It's a special moment you get to live for. A moment where no one knows you did it, but you achieved your full human potential during a disaster." I stop and stare at the transcript and understand that resonance doesn't just flow from researcher to participants, it also moves from participants to researcher.

Professional Vistas

2012 A professor stopped me after a communication class to ask if I had ever considered graduate school

2013 Graduated with BS in Communication Studies, decided to pursue MA in Communication

2015 A professor asked me if I had ever considered getting a PhD, decided to pursue a PhD

2016 Received access to a university emergency management organization for research—personnel with this organization introduced me to city and county emergency management organizations that later became the site for this COVID study

2018 Began research with CET for dissertation study on emergency management and collaboration

2019 Graduated with PhD in Communication from CU-Boulder, accepted a position at UNLV

2020 Began work on a book about interorganizational collaboration and authority, signed a book contract

2020 Transitioned my classes online in a week, wondered what CET was doing during the COVID-19 outbreak, agreed to volunteer and conduct new research virtually

References

Bean, Hamilton, & Rice, Rebecca M. (2019). Organizational communication and security. In Bryan C. Taylor & Hamilton Bean (Eds.), *The handbook of communication and security* (pp. 136–152). Routledge.

Bochner, Arthur, & Ellis, Carolyn. (2016). *Evocative autoethnography: Writing lives and telling stories.* Routledge.

Brannan, Matthew J. (2011). Researching emotions and the emotions of researching: The strange case of Alexithymia in reflexive research. *International Journal of Work Organisation and Emotion, 4*(3–4), 322–339. https://doi.org/10.1504/IJWOE.2011.045969

Garthwaite, Kayleigh. (2016). The perfect fit? Being both volunteer and ethnographer in a UK foodbank. *Journal of Organizational Ethnography, 5*(1), 60–71. https://doi.org/10.1108/JOE-01-2015-0009

Geertz, Clifford. (2000). *The interpretation of cultures: Selected essays* (2000 ed). Basic Books.

Gilmore, Sarah, & Kenny, Kate. (2015). Work-worlds colliding: Self-reflexivity, power and emotion in organizational ethnography. *Human Relations, 68*(1), 55–78. https://doi.org/10.1177/0018726714531998

Hallett, Ronald E., & Barber, Kristen. (2014). Ethnographic research in a cyber era. *Journal of Contemporary Ethnography, 43*(3). https://journals.sagepub.com/doi/abs/10.1177/0891241613497749

Hällgren, Markus, Rouleau, Linda, & de Rond, Mark. (2017). A matter of life or death: How extreme context research matters for management and organization studies. *Academy of Management Annals, 12*(1), 111–153. https://doi.org/10.5465/annals.2016.0017

Hill O'Connor, Clementine, & Baker, Rachel. (2017). Working with and for social enterprises: The role of the volunteer ethnographer. *Social Enterprise Journal, 13*(02), 180–193. https://doi.org/10.1108/SEJ-07-2016-0033

Jahn, Jody L. S., & Black, Anne E. (2017). A model of communicative and hierarchical foundations of high reliability organizing in wildland firefighting teams. *Management Communication Quarterly, 31*(3), 356–379. https://doi.org/10.1177/0893318917691358

Lindlof, Thomas R., & Taylor, Bryan C. (2019). *Qualitative communication research methods* (4th ed.). SAGE Publications.

Mastracci, Sharon H., Guy, Mary E., & Newman, Meredith A. (2012). *Emotional labor and crisis response working on the razor's edge.* MESharpe.

McNamee, Lacey G., & Peterson, Brittany L. (2014). Reconciling "third space/place": Toward a complementary dialectical understanding of volunteer management. *Management Communication Quarterly, 28*(2), 214–243. https://doi.org/10.1177/0893318914525472

Pennington, Natalie, Holmstrom, Amanda J., & Hall, Jeffrey A. (in press). The toll of technology while working from home during COVID-19. *Communication Reports*. https://doi.org/10.1080/08934215.2021.1993947

Rice, Rebecca M. (2021). High reliability collaborations: Theorizing interorganizational reliability as constituted through translation. *Management Communication Quarterly*. https://doi.org/10.1177/08933189211006390

Rivera, Kendra D. (2015). Emotional taint: Making sense of emotional dirty work at the US Border Patrol. *Management Communication Quarterly, 29*(2), 198–228.

Stephens, Keri K., Jahn, Jody L. S., Fox, Stephanie, Charoensap-Kelly, Piyawan, Mitra, Rahul, Sutton, Jeanette, Waters, Eric D., Xie, Bo, & Meisenbach, Rebecca J. (2020). Collective sensemaking around COVID-19: Experiences, concerns, and agendas for our rapidly changing organizational lives. *Management Communication Quarterly*, 0893318920934890. https://doi.org/10.1177/0893318920934890

Taylor, Bryan C., Barley, William C., Brummans, Boris H. J. M., Ellingson, Laura L., Ganesh, Shiv, Herrmann, Andrew F., Rice, Rebecca M., & Tracy, Sarah J. (2021). Revisiting ethnography in organizational communication studies. *Management Communication Quarterly*. https://doi.org/10.1177/08933189211026700

Tinney, Jean. (2008). Negotiating boundaries and roles: Challenges faced by the nursing home ethnographer. *Journal of Contemporary Ethnography, 37*(2), 202–225. https://doi.org/10.1177/0891241607312487

Vincett, Joanne. (2018). Researcher self-care in organizational ethnography: Lessons from overcoming compassion fatigue. *Journal of Organizational Ethnography, 7*(1), 44–58. https://doi.org/10.1108/JOE-09-2017-0041

CHAPTER 19

Identity Interruptions: Organizational and Occupational Identification During a Global Health Pandemic

Luke A. Dye and Stephanie L. Dailey

> *The great thing, if one can, is to stop regarding all the unpleasant things as interruptions of one's "own", or "real" life. The truth is of course that what one calls the interruptions are precisely one's "real life"* .... (Lewis, 2008, p. 97)

When COVID-19 paralyzed our personal and professional lives, Luke (the first author of this chapter) felt useless as a graduate student in organizational communication. Just five years earlier, he was in the US Navy and returning from a deployment in the Middle East. Now, he was just another student complaining about participating in online classes. Meanwhile, the lives of everyone around him were in a freefall, with no end in sight.

L. A. Dye (✉)
Department of Communication, Cornell University, Ithaca, NY, USA
e-mail: lad268@cornell.edu

S. L. Dailey
Department of Communication, Texas State University, San Marcos, TX, USA
e-mail: dailey@txstate.edu

L. D. Browning et al. (eds.), *Organizational Communication and Technology in the Time of Coronavirus*,
https://doi.org/10.1007/978-3-030-94814-6_19

Although he had a comfortable assistantship with little fear of termination, his friends and family faced uncertainty and interruption in nearly every domain of their careers. Despite Luke's desire to make a difference in the lives of his friends and family, he felt guilty and isolated—like an academic who locked himself away in a guarded ivory tower.

At the time, Luke was taking a research methods class with Dr. Stephanie Dailey (the second author of this chapter). Luke approached her about his dilemma and desire to investigate the pandemic's role in workers' personal and professional lives outside of academia. How was their life impacted? What did it feel like for employees labeled as "essential" versus "non-essential?" At the start of the pandemic, we wrote a research proposal to interview employees about how their work changed due to COVID-19.

We were specifically interested in how changes in the workplace impacted participants' sense of organizational and occupational identification. Rooted in social identity theory, identification involves "the perception of oneness or belongingness to a group" (Ashforth & Mael, 1989, p. 34), whether that be one's employer or their work role. Communication is an important part of identification, because it is through interaction with others that people come to experience identification (as a process), and individuals express their identification with (or against) a group through communication (as a product or outcome) (Cheney et al., 2014). Although many scholars understand identification as fluid and changing, most investigations of identification have focused on singular internal activities, like orientation programs (Stephens & Dailey, 2012) or strategic planning meetings (Scott et al., 1998), suggesting that identifications change by "activity" or social context. The pandemic was a different kind of external activity that shook personal, organizational, and occupational identities more than a simple change in context. Due to the mass interruption in the lives of workers across the globe, we were interested in how the pandemic shifted workers' identifications.

We hoped to gather stories from a number of industries and work experiences to get a broader picture of how organizational changes impacted identification. Despite our best efforts, we struggled finding participants, which led us to interview the people that were closest to us: our best friends, old roommates, and war-buddies. Thus, unlike many conventional research studies, the stories we share are not the stories of strangers, students, or paid participants found online; they are the stories of the people that we care about dearly. They are our friends, family, and neighbors, and the following five ethnographic accounts tell of interruptions to their organizational and occupational identities as a result of COVID-19.

Stories from the Field

Troy

For anyone who knew Troy prior to the start of the pandemic, they would describe him as a happy and optimistic person with four major loves in his life: his cats, God, dancing, and the Dallas Cowboys. For Troy, work is something that people do to support the things and people they love in life. As such, work never played into his sense of self very much—at least before the pandemic.

For the past nine years, Troy has worked at a regional corporate center for a global aerospace company, where he procures military parts and other equipment for third-party contractors. He spends most days corresponding and sending quotes to clients. He never imagined himself doing this job; nonetheless, Troy had worked for nearly a decade at this company with no intention of leaving soon. Although he despised parts of his job, like preparing weekly and monthly reports, in general, he looked forward to interacting and building relationships with his clients.

When COVID-19 shut down most of the country, it was extremely uncertain whether Troy's company would be switching to remote work. During the period leading up to the announcement that the entire office would be switching to remote work, rumors spread like wildfire, including talks of whether the company would keep their work site altogether. As a whole, the communication between Troy and the decision makers in the company was, as Troy described, "stressful."

As Troy's work went remote, he noticed a shift in communication within his team. For one, tasks that would normally require minimal effort now took much longer because of frustrating technology lapses. Troy observed an uptick in task-related communication, while relational communication waned. Normally, Troy's team would have morning "touch base" meetings. During these gatherings, the team lead ensured employees had clocked-in, shared announcements, and answered questions. However, after the shift to remote work, those meetings plummeted, happening only a few times a week as opposed to every day.

Despite this fluctuation in team communication, Troy enjoyed working remotely. As he explained, the situation "worked" because the move to remote work transpired globally, impacting both he and his clients in similar ways. For Troy, the fact that everyone in his network was working remotely brought everyone closer together. Troy's experience strongly aligns with early theorizing about relationships in computer-mediated contexts—specifically, the hyperpersonal perspective, which suggests that mediated communication can foster interactions that surpass traditional face-to-face relationship development (Walther, 1996). Troy began experiencing friendlier and deeper conversations with his suppliers, where messages were exchanged about concerns for each other's safety. Troy had already loved the relationship building aspect of his job, and COVID-19 seemed, to Troy at least, a way to cultivate new relational bonds with his clients.

Another difficult part about Troy's shift to remote work was dealing with distractions at home. Troy lived in a one-bedroom apartment without a set place to work, aside from his living room. This caused a major disruption in his productivity, because Troy had grown accustomed to having "segmented" roles with clear boundaries between work and home (Ashforth et al., 2000, p. 476). Because his work and home roles were more integrated than before, Troy spent an entire afternoon completing tasks that would have normally taken him 15–30 minutes. Troy's reduced productivity prompted uncertainty about his job security, something that he had taken for granted for the previous nine years. Major projects within Troy's company began disappearing, and he watched as layoffs followed. Instantly, Troy conceived his job as much more important than he previously considered. His commitment to his organization, and work in general, grew because of the pandemic. As Troy explained, "all of a sudden I am thinking that the job is just that much more important. So I guess I cherish it more because I have seen so many people losing their job."

Troy's experience demonstrates that despite how an organization may have communicated changes in the workplace, workers' sense of belonging may increase from fearing (and surviving) job loss. Particularly at organizations where layoffs occurred, employees who were spared during the pandemic may have felt an increased sense of attachment because they maintained their jobs. Research shows that when workers feel high levels of perceived organizational support—when employees think their employers value staff contributions and care about workers' personal well-being—they are more likely to identify with the organization (Lam et al., 2016). Other important takeaways from Troy's experience are the challenges of productivity and team communication for remote workers. As we will see in our next story, some of these challenges have persisted long before COVID-19, yet organizational leaders are just now becoming aware that remote work creates stress on employees in ways that working at a traditional office setting does not.

Dani

Sometimes it is still difficult for Dani to think about how she arrived to her current position. After all, her college degree is in nutrition—a field completely unrelated to her job as a social media specialist for a technology retail company. She began working for the organization as a part-time worker at one of the company's corporate call centers three years earlier. When she started, it was a side-gig to make extra money while finishing school. After graduation, she transitioned to full-time work while sorting out her next steps. When a social media role in her company came open, she saw the position as an opportunity for growth and exposure to a different part of the organization. She was not sure if this role was a lifelong career, but it was a welcome change of pace from the fast-moving and exhausting call center work.

In 2019, Dani joined a social media team comprising both remote and stationary workers. Most of the group worked out of the main corporate headquarters located in another state, while a handful of team members worked remotely. Because Dani did not live near the corporate campus, the organization provided all the requisite technology for Dani to work from home. At first, Dani found the experience liberating. No more having to spend hours getting ready for work or having to fight the traffic heading into the office—now she could simply log off, and she was already home! Yet, Dani quickly discovered that although she was working from home, she was also living where she worked, making the task of separating work from home all the more challenging than before (Ashforth et al., 2000). Furthermore, because she was new to the team, she did not know many other workers. As Dani explained, "I really don't have anyone that is here locally; it feels that I am in my own little world away from everything else." In short, Dani felt isolated from her coworkers even before the start of the COVID-19 pandemic.

Dani sought solace in joining her city's roller derby team. Derby was her chance to escape from everything and everyone. Dani was insecure at work because of her educational background, where she was from, and her tenure at the company, but when she was playing roller derby, none of that mattered. Derby was without question one of the most important parts of Dani's identity until everything changed in March 2020. COVID-19 shut down the roller derby season, and social distancing regulations halted team practices. What little social interactions Dani had outside of work evaporated, leaving her isolated and alone. Because her social outlet was gone, Dani felt as if she was living in an office, rather than working in an apartment. In addition, because the company's retail storefronts were closed, the team's work was labeled "essential" and increased exponentially due to customers' increased use of social media. Dani felt like she was back at the call center.

Worse yet, the corporate campus shut down altogether, forcing all of Dani's team to work remotely. With this shift came, unsurprisingly, a series of complaints over the teams' challenged work-life balance in working from home. Such gripes prompted the team's leadership to make changes, affording more time for non-task activities, like a book club and town hall discussions. For the members of the team that had shifted from work on the corporate campus to remote work, it felt like the company was looking out for their employees, but Dani felt differently, as she had never perceived such organizational support like this in the past (Lam et al., 2016). She had tried to bring up her struggles in working remotely to her team prior to COVID-19, but because she missed out on a traditional, face-to-face socialization experience in joining her team (due to her remote status), she left conversations with coworkers feeling ignored and unimportant.

Nearly two years later, the company is still trying to figure out what work looks like moving forward for Dani's team. Her peers expect to return to the corporate campus soon, causing Dani to wonder what will happen to all of the initiatives that made life easier for remote workers. Most likely they will disappear, she imagines, leaving those few remaining remote team members fighting the same struggle of isolation and loneliness. Dani tries not to think about what life will be like when things get back to normal, because for her, nothing will really change, except that she will hopefully be playing roller derby once again.

Dani's experiences illustrate that the "new" issues employees faced in working remotely during the pandemic will still exist for workers who will remain working from home long after the pandemic has ended. Particularly for new employees who will not get traditional, immersive socialization experiences that foster identification (Ashforth & Mael, 1989), establishing remote-team identity may continue to pose a challenge for Dani's team. Altogether, Dani and Troy's mirrored story shows us that not all remote work is created equal, and although these experiences are fresh in our minds now, many workers will not have the pleasure of returning to the office. Furthermore, these stories underscore the fragility of organizational and occupational identification, which can be affected by factors outside the organization's purview or control.

Anthony

Anthony's professional career had been built around one robust desire: to help others. One would think that 20 years of military service would satisfy that desire, but not for Anthony. Even after his retirement from the US Navy, Anthony felt he had more to give, so at age 45, he began working as an emergency room technician. Anthony already had comfortable pension from his years of service, but he still wanted to help people like he did in the military. As an Independent Duty Hospital Corpsman, Anthony spent his time with both Navy ships and United States Marine Corps battalions saving people's lives, so working in an emergency room came natural to Anthony:

> When I am in the room with you as a patient and I am helping you, whether it's wiping your ass or putting an IV in or whatever it is, I am helping you in your need and what you're here for. I am into that…. well, I don't enjoy wiping people's asses, but I enjoy my job at its core.

Whether in a foxhole, on a warship, or in the ER, helping people is at the core of Anthony's personal identity.

When Anthony has been able to help people, he has loved his job. Unfortunately, a big part of Anthony's job was communicating with hospital management, which he found incredibly frustrating. As a retired Navy chief with experience running *entire* medical departments, Anthony became frustrated when he saw hospital management making poor decisions without any foresight. Nonetheless, Anthony gladly traded his joy from interacting with patients for the headaches that ensued after interacting with management. At least that was the case until COVID-19 changed everything.

As one can imagine, COVID-19 interrupted Anthony's mission of helping others. At the outset of the pandemic, Anthony's hospital furloughed him for two weeks in an effort to cut expenses. When Anthony returned to work, everything had changed. Anthony learned new rules on how, when, and where to wear masks and other essential PPE. To complicate matters, those rules seemed to evolve daily, and many of the shifting guidelines did not make sense to Anthony, because they still placed both staff and patients at risk for exposure to COVID-19.

Despite his complaints, nobody seemed to listen. In addition to the changes themselves, management's lack of a consistent communication channel for information maddened Anthony. Previously, the emergency room team would have a morning huddle where important information was disseminated; however, because of how busy the hospital got during COVID-19, those meetings ceased, and Anthony often found out about new protocols in the middle of treating a patient. He summed up his thoughts by saying that "they [hospital management] should be able to think multiple steps ahead. If this retired chief can do it, somebody where it is there fundamental job should be able to do that, but it seems that they are either not using it, or that person is grossly ineffective." Like Dani, Anthony felt unheard and unsupported (Lam et al., 2016).

Did his organization have the pandemic under control? Were they doing what was best for hospital staff and patients? Anthony's uncertainty grew, fueled by concerns for his asthmatic wife at home. Every night, Anthony would strip down on his porch prior to entering his home so that he would not bring in any traces of the virus inside. The frustrations Anthony felt combined with the tenuous measures he was taking to ensure the safety of his family began taking toll on Anthony's motivation to keep working. Anthony finally said, "I hate it. I fuckin' hate my job now. It is exhausting."

Despite his feelings for his job, which may be understood more as frustrations with his organization, Anthony still loved what he did. The pandemic could not shake his personal identity—helping others—and his occupational identification. In fact, despite his terrible experience with management, Anthony's identification as a healthcare worker could not be stronger: "I identify as a healthcare worker but not as a [hospital's name] employee. I could not give a shit about that organization. I'll work anywhere. I am a healthcare worker first." Sadly, Anthony paid the price for this dedication to his role as a healthcare worker. Anthony was diagnosed with COVID-19 a week after our interview with him.

Anthony's story displays the power that organizational communication, specifically information dissemination, can have on an employee's organizational identification (Cheney et al., 2014). Moreover, Anthony's experience demonstrates how the pandemic may have affected workers' organizational and occupational identification in different ways. Specifically, in times of job insecurity, workers may fiercely cling to their occupational identity. This attachment could be as a result of instability with the organization, or as in the case of Anthony, displeasure with managerial communication. Nonetheless, Anthony's experience demonstrates that one's occupation may have just as large an impact on their personal identity than the specific organization where they work. We observed a similar finding in Oliver's experience, which we share next.

Oliver

At the start of the pandemic, Oliver was climbing the corporate ladder of a mid-sized financial firm. As a banker, Oliver built his success by fostering and sustaining financial relationships with mid-sized local businesses. Oliver worked in one of the 57 branch offices of the statewide corporation, headquartered in a different city. Oliver always felt a bond with his local team, who worked together to serve clients in their community. Despite his eight-year career at the bank, Oliver had never developed a strong sense of attachment to the large organization. To Oliver, the greedy big-city executives were interested, much too often, in protecting their stacked retirement nests rather than taking calculated risks to grow the bank and cultivate employees' well-being.

The company leaders' early reaction to the pandemic followed this entrenched pattern of behavior that had bothered Oliver. "There was very little action," Oliver lamented. "They put shareholders' interests first, then employees, and *then* customers," Oliver explained, emphasizing his disapproval of the firm's last priority. In Oliver's eyes, the company should have reacted in the opposite order, with customers top-of-mind, followed by employees, and then shareholders. Another misstep, according to Oliver, occurred with the corporation's broad-brush approach to COVID-19 health policies. The firm bureaucratically prescribed the same protocol (e.g., self-screening, social distancing) for all branches across the state, rather than tailoring procedures for each local office, where the virus was wreaking havoc in unique ways across different populations.

In his local branch, Oliver had advocated that employees work from home, which many could do quite easily. Schools and restaurants were closed, and the open roadways on his commute assured Oliver he was one of the few "essential" employees going into work. Yet Oliver's suggestion faced resistance—why would they need to stay home for a virus "like the flu?" In mid-March, an employee reported to work in Oliver's office with a fever and infected another employee. After two positive COVID-19 test results, the bank found themselves living a human resources nightmare, with rumors of a lawsuit.

"That was the change that finally prompted management to allow us to work from home," Oliver remembered. Overnight, the entire financial firm pivoted to working remotely, which had previously been limited, least of all encouraged. Alongside this relocation of work, the nature of Oliver's team shifted unexpectedly, too. Oliver's autonomous tasks became micromanaged, and the flexibility he had enjoyed in-person was replaced with daily phone check-ins.

Recalling that first month of the pandemic, Oliver painted a stressful picture of his job. He guided his clients through the government's new "Paycheck Protection Program" process, helping to keep their small businesses afloat. Oliver had always called his clients the "lifeblood" of his career. The customer was his primary responsibility, evidenced by a full pre-pandemic social calendar and ever-present discussions of meeting clients' financial needs. But now Oliver was literally saving his customers from bankruptcy, and he was worried about the demise of the local business community that fueled the work that supported his family.

Working from home added stress to Oliver's work-life. His two young children ran throughout the house, while his kids' preschool (and even playgrounds) remained closed. Oliver hijacked the guest room of his house for his makeshift office—a common practice for home-based workers seeking segmentation (Ashforth et al., 2000). However, the room did not lock, and it was inconveniently close to the home's boisterous kitchen, which made Oliver's work prone to physical and mental distractions. With much of his work communication taking place over the phone, Oliver found himself pacing the backyard on calls with clients, uplifting devastated customers through the most uncertain of times they had seen, while inside the house, his kids squabbled over toy trains.

To make difficult matters worse, most of Oliver's colleagues did not have kids and could not empathize with his situation. Moreover, his coworkers had less workload, because Oliver shouldered one of the largest client portfolios in the region. Prior to the pandemic, Oliver had felt a sense of team identification—a sense of belonging with the colleagues in his branch. Before COVID-19 was a concern, "We would collaborate… I'd ask [name] and [name] for their advice or opinion on how to structure transactions." But with the COVID-19 crisis, all Oliver's attention, and that of his coworkers, shifted to customers. Oliver's experience during the pandemic weakened this workgroup attachment, as his work felt micromanaged, and his focus rested upon his clients' well-being.

The pandemic reinforced Oliver's connection with his clients, what we coin here as "client identification." Oliver found purpose and meaning in his work by helping his customers. Communication and organization studies scholars contend that social identities are multifaceted and that workers attach themselves to many identities or "targets," including the organization, their workgroup, and vocation (Scott et al., 1998). Oliver's case shows that employees might also feel attached or identified with their clients, an additional identification target. Indeed, six months after the start of the pandemic, Oliver left his organization, taking many of his clients with him, to a different bank. Beyond an example of client identification, Oliver's story (like Anthony's) also tells us how events can affect different identification targets in unique ways. Oliver, for example, did not identify with his organization before the pandemic, and the corporation's actions during the pandemic reinforced his ambivalent attachment. Oliver had perceived a strong sense of identification with his team before the pandemic, which was shaken amidst the crisis.

Doug

Growing up in a broken home, all Doug ever wanted was a family—to such an extent that he dropped out of school to move in with his high-school sweetheart. Doug's dream of a family became reality; yet, living in a rural area without a high school degree limited his employment options. Finding steady work was a constant challenge for Doug. Finally, four years ago, Doug found a fulfilling career working at an industrial paint company, a job for which he felt extremely grateful.

The pay was poor, but Doug's job paid his bucolic home rent and fed his growing family. While Doug was working a grueling 12-hour shift, his expecting wife cared for their young children, aged two and five, until Doug returned home to play wrestle with his boys. Doug loved his family—the core of his personal identity—and he was motivated to work hard so that he could offer his kids a better childhood than his own.

Doug's rural community saw few changes at the start of the pandemic, but because his wife was pregnant, Doug avoided any risks of having him or his family infected. In March 2020, Doug used ten paid vacation days to quarantine with his family to avoid risk of getting the virus at work. At the time, Doug felt that everything would be back to normal after a week or two, but after ten days, the world remained at a standstill. The physical nature of his work left him no choice but to return. Doug's first day back at work after his ten days of vacation was one of the worst days of his life. Shortly after clocking-in for the day, Doug's supervisor laid him off, effective immediately. The company had seen a decrease in work orders because of the shutdown, so in an effort to save money, cuts had to be made. Doug was now unemployed.

Doug's geographic constraints meant that reemployment as an industrial painter at another organization was unlikely, because he was limited to the jobs available in his rural community. Doug eventually found work at a gas station, but he had trouble letting go of the parts of himself that loved being an industrial painter. His wife delivered a healthy baby boy, and now the five of them brace for an uncertain future. Doug does not know what he will do for work five years from now, because he cannot really think that far ahead. He would love to work as an industrial painter again, but that may not be an option. For now, he is thankful that he has a job at the gas station, a lovely wife, and three beautiful children. "That is enough to keep anyone happy," Doug said with a twinkle in his eye.

Doug's story is important, especially for scholars who often ignore the plight of the working poor in both urban and rural communities. To begin, the physical nature of Doug's role prohibited him from working remotely—a luxury that many other workers took to protect themselves and their families from the virus. Furthermore, Doug had a career and a strong identification with both his organization and vocation. However, none of that mattered when he lost his job. Doug faced both a resource crisis (i.e., "How will I make money and provide for my family?") and an identity crisis (i.e., "What will I do for work?") when looking for a new job. Traditionally, identification researchers have largely focused on organizational factors (e.g., socialization strategies) that affect workers' attachments (Cheney et al., 2014). Exploring experiences like Doug's have the potential to extend the literature, demonstrating how communication and one's identity outside the workplace (and the organization's control) may impact organizational and occupational identification.

Making Sense of Identity Interruptions

Theoretical Implications

Conceptually, these narratives demonstrate that communication within an organization is not the only factor that influences one's organizational and occupational identification. In their summary of identification scholarship,

Cheney et al. (2014) acknowledge that "organizations intentionally provide a significant part of the discursive material through which individuals accomplish their life projects and recognize themselves as carriers of specific identities" (p. 707). Indeed, Troy and Oliver's experience shows how communication at work impacts organizational and occupational identification (Ashforth & Mael, 1989). Yet to some extent, COVID-19 exposed what little control organizations actually have over employee identities, as several of the stories highlight a number of personal, non-work-related factors that may influence employees' work attachments. For example, Dani's feelings of isolation impacted her feelings of belongingness within her team, causing her stress and anxiety and impacting her performance. In addition, Doug's communication with his family *outside* of work directly influenced his feelings of identity *inside* the workplace. Given that many workers may have experienced blurred roles during the pandemic due to having their work-life and home-life interconnected (Ashforth et al., 2000), our findings open the door for researchers to further investigate factors outside of management's purview, which may impact workers' identifications.

Methodological Implications

As previously mentioned, our sample was a convenient sample, composed of close acquaintances for which we care deeply. Scholars commonly fault studies using convenient sampling, which can be biased. However, our chapter displays the power of close-network convenient sampling in interpretive research. Telling the stories of those who are most dear to us can be a powerful tool in outlying the experiences of a specific group of people, especially considering that the researcher may be more familiar with the context surrounding the stories of a close friend rather than a stranger.

Even more, our chapter issues a challenge for scholars to rethink the way we approach convenient sampling. Especially for scholars that come from marginalized and underrepresented communities, recruiting people in one's inner circle is an effective way to present unheard voices in the literature. Blue-collar workers and trade laborers like Anthony and Doug are unique and underreported in scholarship. We were able to include these diverse perspectives because of our close-network convenient sampling of friends and families, and we encourage other communication researchers to consider expanding the scope of their samples in this way, too.

Conclusion

The narratives provided in this chapter reveal how COVID-19 interrupted the identities of workers across the United States. Altogether, our stories demonstrate that identification is influenced by numerous factors outside organizational leaders' control. Additionally, the salience of occupational and client identification in our narratives represents promising opportunities for future identity research to explore. Though the threats of COVID-19 will eventually pass, the interruptions experienced therein remain "real life" (Lewis, 2008, p. 97) for the people in all of our communities. Our ability as academics to make a difference in the world hinges upon understanding the real lives of the people around us, including their multifaceted identities amidst the "unpleasant things" (Lewis, 2008, p. 97) of the pandemic.

References

Ashforth, Blake, & Mael, Fred. (1989). Social identity theory and the organization. *Academy of Management Review, 14*(1), 20–39. https://doi.org/10.2307/258189

Ashforth, Blake, Kreiner, Glen, & Fugate, Mel. (2000). All in a day's work: Boundaries and micro role transitions. *Academy of Management Review, 25*(3), 472–491. https://doi.org/10.2307/259305

Cheney, George, Christensen, Lars Thøger, & Dailey, Stephanie. (2014). Communicating identity and identification in and around organizations. In L. L. Putnam & D. K. Mumby (Eds.), *The SAGE handbook of organizational communication: Advances in theory, research, and methods* (pp. 695–716). SAGE.

Lam, Long Wai, Liu, Yan, & Loi, Raymond. (2016). Looking intra-organizationally for identity cues: Whether perceived organizational support shapes employees' organizational identification. *Human Relations, 69*(2), 345–367. https://doi.org/10.1177/0018726715584689

Lewis, Clive Staples. (2008). *Yours, Jack: Spiritual direction from C.S. Lewis.* Harper Collins.

Scott, Craig, Corman, Scott, & Cheney, George. (1998). Development of a structurational model of identification in the organization. *Communication Theory, 8*(3), 298–336. https://doi.org/10.1111/j.1468-2885.1998.tb00223.x

Stephens, Keri, & Dailey, Stephanie. (2012). Situated organizational identification in newcomers: Impacts of preentry organizational exposure. *Management Communication Quarterly, 26*(3), 404–422. https://doi.org/10.1177/0893318912440179

Walther, Joseph. (1996). Computer-mediated communication: Impersonal, interpersonal, and hyperpersonal interaction. *Communication Research, 23*(1), 3–43. https://doi.org/10.1177/009365096023001001

CHAPTER 20

The Perpetually Conditional Citizens

Kerk Fong Kee

The Perpetually Conditional Citizens

On March 11, 2020, the World Health Organization declared the Novel Coronavirus Disease, COVID-19, a global pandemic. All 50 of the US states and the District of Columbia declared a state of emergency (as early as February 29, 2020, in Washington State) and issued stay at home orders (as early as March 19, 2020, in California). The pandemic created major disruptions across industries and various workplaces for months, and it affected the US for the rest of 2020 and 2021.

The origin of COVID-19 was introduced in the media as linked to Wuhan, a city in Central China. Due to this association, Chinese, Chinese Americans, Asians, and Asian-Americans, in general, became concerned about the possibility (which did materialize quickly) of facing a backlash. Similar backlashes were experienced by the Muslim and Muslim Americans following the 9/11 terrorist attack (Peek, 2011). The first victim of backlash and revenge killing following 9/11 was a Sikh man mistaken as

K. F. Kee (✉)
Department of Professional Communication, Texas Tech University, Lubbock, TX, USA
e-mail: kerk.kee@ttu.edu

L. D. Browning et al. (eds.), *Organizational Communication and Technology in the Time of Coronavirus*,
https://doi.org/10.1007/978-3-030-94814-6_20

Muslim on September 15, 2001, in Mesa, Arizona, because he wore a turban (Basu, 2016).

On March 14, 2020, Jose Gomez, a 19-year-old man approached a Burmese American family of four at a Sam's Club in Midland, Texas, and stabbed the father, and his 2-year-old and 6-year-old sons (Wallace, 2020). Zack Owen, a store employee, tackled Gomez to the ground, suffering a cut to his leg and hand while struggling for the knife. Bernie Ramirez, an off-duty Border Patrol Agent, who happened to be shopping at the store, detained Gomez before the police arrived. Upon arrest, Gomez admitted that he thought the Burmese family was Chinese, and they were infecting other Americans with the coronavirus. That was his reason for trying to kill the Burmese family. Gomez was charged with one count of aggravated assault with a deadly weapon and three counts of attempted capital murder. The Federal Bureau of Investigation (FBI) listed the incident as a hate crime, and as early as in March 2020, predicted a surge in anti-Asian hate crimes across the US (Reporter-Telegram, 2020).

Upon learning about the hate crime in Midland, the Chinese Faculty and Staff Association (CFSA) at Texas Tech University (TTU) became concerned. As Midland is about 120 miles from TTU's location in Lubbock, slightly under two hours by car, the Chinese and Asian communities in Lubbock were shaken by the incident. It hit home because of the proximity and cultural similarity between Midland and Lubbock. The false assumption that a Burmese family was Chinese alerted the Asian community in Lubbock that everyone who looks Asian could be at risk of being a victim of anti-Asian hate crimes. The history of backlash faced by Muslims and Muslim Americans following the 9/11 terrorist attack twenty years ago could repeat itself among Asians and Asian Americans following the outbreak of COVID-19.

In this chapter, I reflexively documented an ethnographic account of how CFSA responded to the incident in Midland and a series of hate crimes across the US from approximately March 2020 to March 2021. This account reveals how Chinese and Chinese Americans experienced the pandemic as both a public health crisis and an anti-Asian threat of violence. I explored how communication technologies play a role in community organizing among this group. The stories told here do not represent all CFSA members nor do they claim any truth about all CFSA members' lived experiences, but the stories shed light on how their ethnic and cultural identities created a complicated narrative during the pandemic.

To achieve the stated goals, I first provide a brief history of anti-Chinese and Chinese Americans in the US, which undergirded CFSA's (sub)conscious responses to the resurgence of anti-Asian hate. Second, I recount the CFSA LOVE projects, which demonstrated how CFSA engaged in impression management, alliance building, self-reliance, and ongoing conversations regarding their immediate responses to the emerging threats of anti-Asian violence. Third, I provide an analysis and interpretation of CFSA's story, from the perspectives of organizational communication and communication technologies. Finally, I reflect on what the ethnographic account may mean for the future of work for Chinese, Chinese American, other Asian, and Asian American academic workers in the US, with some implications beyond the academic workplace.

The Historical Context of Anti-Chinese Sentiment in the US

Anti-Chinese sentiments were not new in the US during the 2020 COVID-19 pandemic. On May 6, 1882, President Chester Arthur signed into law the Chinese Exclusion Act, prohibiting the immigration of all Chinese laborers into the US (Soennichsen, 2011). Further, under this act, Chinese workers already in the US were prohibited from becoming US citizens. This law was preceded by the Burlingame Treaty of 1868 and the Angell Treaty of 1880 that suspended Chinese immigration to the US. It was further strengthened by the Geary Act of 1892, which was made permanent in 1902. As the anti-Asian sentiment grew, the National Origins Act of 1924 further banned all immigration from East Asian countries. Chinese and then Asian immigration was federally banned for many years; it was not abolished until the Immigration and National Act of 1952 and the Immigration and National Act of 1965. However, the history of treating Chinese (and all Asians) as unwelcome immigrants left a strong imprint on American history. This history gave rise to what later became known as the 'Yellow Peril' (Kil, 2012).

Another historical incident of anti-Asian hate was the murder of Vincent Chin in 1982 (Kurashige, 2002). By the 1980s American auto industries faced tremendous competition from Japanese auto makers. As a result, many American autoworkers lost their jobs. Chin, a 27-year-old Chinese American man from Highland Park, Michigan, was beaten to death with a baseball bat by two white men, Ronald Ebens, a plant supervisor at

Chrysler, and Michael Nitz, Ebens' stepson who was also an autoworker who had lost his job. The incident followed a brawl at a strip club in Detroit, where Ebens and Nitz had mistaken Chin as Japanese. Ebens reportedly said, "It's because of you little mother fuckers that we're out of work" (Zia, 2010). Although Ebens and Nitz were convicted of manslaughter, they were only given a fine of $3000 and paid $780 for court costs; they served no jail time and only three years of probation. Judge Charles Kaufman who gave the lenient sentence reportedly said, "These weren't the kind of men you send to jail... You don't make the punishment fit the crime; you make the punishment fit the criminal" (Kuo, 2017; Zia, 2000). This unjust sentence marked another critical moment in the history of anti-Asian hate crimes, telling Asians that the US will not protect them.

Fast forward to more recent history, and more specifically the context of the academic workplace, the introduction of the Department of Justice's China Initiative on November 1, 2018 (Lewis, 2020). The China Initiative is a systematic criminal investigation of Chinese researchers and professors in the US for espionage and intellectual property thefts. While economic espionage by the Chinese government is a real threat, the implementation of the China Initiative led to some wrongful profiling of Chinese and Chinese Americans in science and research. For example, Gang Chen, Carl Richard Soderberg Professor of Power Engineering and former chair of the Department of Mechanical Engineering at the Massachusetts Institute of Technology (MIT), was arrested on January 14, 2021, by the FBI for several charges, including receiving $19 million from a Chinese university (Barry, 2021). However, following the arrest, MIT president released a statement explaining that the funds went to MIT to support a Chinese-US research collaboration, not Chen personally.

While the initiative was launched in 2018, it built on years of wrongful accusations and investigations of Chinese American scientists, such as Xiaoxing Xi, Laura H. Carnell Professor and former chair of the Department of Physics at Temple University (Watanabe, 2019). Xi's case in May 2015 and other similar cases were additional examples of wrongful cases, which were dropped abruptly after FBI investigations. Although these Chinese scientists were not found guilty in the end, their reputations and careers were tarnished or destroyed. These cases led to fear among Chinese faculty and researchers, and since 2018, some left the US because of the racially charged climate (Silver, 2020). Many Chinese faculty and researchers in the US are fearful of being the next victims of anti-Chinese hate and bigotry.

There is a parallel in sentiment between the Chinese immigrants in the nineteenth century and some Chinese faculty and staff in the larger US society today. Chinese immigrants came to the US in the 1850s in response to the California Gold Rush and subsequently contributed to the building of the First Transcontinental Railroad, but their contributions to American economy—rather than being honored—were met by the Chinese Exclusion Act of 1882 (Lai, 2004). Today, Chinese American professors and researchers contributed to scientific advancements and STEM education for decades in the US, yet their contributions to the American scientific competitiveness in the world were met with wrongful accusations enabled by the China Initiative of 2018 and prior anti-Chinese suspicions (Lewis, 2020). Many Chinese and Chinese American academics, including CFSA members, suddenly became reminded of their 'perpetual foreigner' status in the US, regardless of their contributions to their disciplines and universities. Hence, their acceptance in the US could be framed as *perpetually conditional*, despite any valuable contributions they may have made.[1]

I was born to ethnic Chinese parents on the East Malaysian side of Borneo, one of the largest islands and oldest rainforests in the world. During my childhood, Borneo was, and still is today, a developing economy. Although Chinese migration to West Malaysia took place as early as the early 1400s (Brezina, 2016), the largest Chinese migration to East Malaysian side of Borneo did not take place until almost 500 years later during British colonization due to the Medhurst's Scheme of 1882 (D. Wong, 1999), the same year as the Chinese Exclusion Act in the US. Growing up as ethnic Chinese, I watched and experienced the Chinese community's political struggles for equality in Malaysia. I listened to Voice of America Chinese broadcast (https://www.voachinese.com/) through shortwave radio, and dreamed of living the stories of Chinese in America I listened to on the radio, although I did not know about the history of anti-Asian sentiments described above. The dream came true 25 years ago. Then about six months before the pandemic, I joined TTU as a faculty and moved to Lubbock from Southern California. It is with this personal history that I ethnographically documented the story of CFSA.

The CFSA Community Organizing and the LOVE Projects

As the largest Asian cultural group of faculty and staff at TTU, CFSA is a public organization representing a group of about 100 members. While majority of the members are immigrants from China, CFSA welcomes members who are not native Chinese, including me. Around the time of the emergence of COVID-19 and before its escalation to a pandemic, CFSA held its 2020 Chinese Spring Festival celebration on campus in February. Just a month later, CFSA found itself organizing community activities in response to the dual crises of the pandemic and the rise in anti-Asian hate crimes. Their response included impression management, alliance building, self-reliance, and ongoing conversations.

Impression Management

Within a month of the COVID-19 shutdown in the US, CFSA launched the LOVE (Lubbock cOVid-19 rElief) Project. The LOVE project had three components and sub-projects. First, the LOVE-Medical/PPE project raised about $3672 from members, and CFSA used the fund toward purchasing 2040 masks and donated them to the TTU Health Sciences Center (HSC) between April 6 and April 17, 2020. Furthermore, a portion of the funds was used to purchase meals delivered to medical professionals at the TTU University Medical Center (UMC) between April 15 and May 7, 2020.

Second, the LOVE-Community project involved networking efforts with the Lubbock Police Department (LPD) and Meals on Wheels (MOW). With $854.59 raised from members for this project, CFSA donated 300 face masks to LPD on April 17, 2020, and collaborated with a local Chinese restaurant to provide Chinese lunch for 80 police officers on May 6, 2020. Around the same time, CFSA raised another $3440 to donate meals to senior citizens in Lubbock via MOW. I became a volunteer in the planning of the meal donations to LPD and UMC, after I learned about the LOVE projects during the webinar on March 28 (discussed in next section). I was happy to help because Spring 2020 was my second semester at TTU, and I was eager to make new friends beyond my immediate department and college; CFSA welcomed me as a new member of the association.

Third, the Love-Education project was an attempted community service collaboration with the Lubbock Independent School District. Since CFSA members are university professors and staff, they volunteered their time to provide free tutoring for local high school students. Due to certain logistical challenges, this last project did not fully materialize.

In addition to carrying out these LOVE projects, CFSA was strategic in promoting visibility and publicity. For example, CFSA designed eye-catching flyers and put them on all four sides of the boxes containing PPE and food donations. The flyers with CFSA's name and logo ensured that beneficiaries of the PPE and food donations down the chain will see where the donations came from. Second, CFSA members who delivered the donations to UMC, HSC, and LPD took pictures with receiving officials and the boxes, prominently displaying the flyers in the pictures. They then posted the pictures on the association's Facebook page, and collaborated with receiving organizations to post the same pictures on their respective social media accounts as well. Some receiving organizations posted additional pictures of their organizational members enjoying the food, and the prominent flyers continued to be visible in these additional pictures beyond the points of delivery. Finally, CFSA's LOVE projects were featured in the local news, KCBD (Davis, 2020). All these efforts helped create positive impression management via external communication.

Alliance Building

On March 28, 2020, CFSA organized a Zoom webinar with a sergeant from the Community Engagement Unit of the Lubbock Police Department (LPD) to discuss hate crimes in Lubbock. CFSA advertised the event, and many attended, including non-CFSA members. I was one of the non-members who attended the event, when a Chinese faculty member in my college told me about it. During the webinar, the sergeant talked about a case of vandalism at a local mosque in 2004, describing it as an example of an anti-Muslim hate crime in Lubbock. The exchange between the sergeant and the attendees focused on multiple aspects of hate crimes, including what qualifies as a hate crime, a hate crime versus hate speech, the use of video evidence following a hate crime, de-escalation strategies during a hate incident, and the legality/consequences of using firearms. It was at this event that I came to know CFSA.

During the Zoom webinar, the sergeant expressed an interest in community partnerships. He encouraged members to reach out with questions after the Zoom meeting, and he left his email address with the organizer of the webinar. This conversation became CFSA's first effort to build an alliance with LPD. Such an alliance helps CFSA increase its readiness to confront a hate crime incident. The CFSA then president seized the opportunity to mention the CFSA LOVE projects (discussed earlier) to the sergeant. Given the conversation, CFSA further pursued the opportunity to build alliances with LPD beyond the initial webinar. The activities described above serve both the function of alliance building and impression management.

Self-Reliance

In response to the rising anti-Asian hate crimes, preparation and readiness for self-defense became an important step. Some CFSA members formed the 'Lubbock Chinese Friends of Guns' group on WeChat, a Chinese social media platform. WeChat is the most popular Chinese communication technology, one that is widely adopted across generations and age groups in China and among immigrant Chinese in the US (Montag et al., 2018). Given that many CFSA members came from China, they continue to use WeChat in order to stay in touch with friends and family in China and other Chinese in the US. CFSA already had a general WeChat group with all its 100 plus members, where members share information with each other. However, in this new WeChat group, a smaller group of members share news, information, and ideas about Chinese buying guns for self-defense, how to select guns, neighborhood watch, self-organized patrols with guns in Chinatowns across the US, gun laws, and so on. A few members who joined this new group also self-organized to purchase guns from a local gun shop in Lubbock, trying out guns together and comparing their choices. While not every member ended up buying a gun, the group provided a space where members could legitimately and openly discuss guns.

Members in this sub-group engaged in discussions on WeChat, often in Chinese on English materials, such as the castle doctrine (i.e., Texas law that permits someone to use deadly force to defend their 'castle' or residence under the right circumstances) (Boots et al., 2009) or the defense of habitation law in Texas, while members unpacked the Texas gun laws (Library, n.d.) and deepened their understanding of laws that allow everyone to exercise self-defense without getting into trouble with the laws. The discussion was oriented toward protecting themselves should they be attacked first and how to fight back. They shared information about membership packages offered by USCCA (US Concealed Carry Association, http://www.usconcealedcarry.com/). USCCA tiered membership packages offer members different levels of access to self-defense education, online/onsite training, and liability insurance, should an incident escalate to the use of firearms.

On WeChat, members shared videos of how self-organized volunteers patrol businesses in the Chicago Chinatown. In a discussion in April 2020, a member also shared the YouTube Channel by Jun Wang (https://www.youtube.com/channel/UCqTjBKy2rOyd4tewLN3VARw/featured), the president of the 'Chicago Chinese Friends of Guns' club. In Wang's videos, he teaches viewers about different aspects of guns in Mandarin. His topics include basic and practical knowledge, federal laws and state regulations, and how to apply for a gun license. Another popular Chinese gun expert with a YouTube Channel in Mandarin is TK Xu (see https://www.youtube.com/channel/UC8jFI9Ffdl_DgKPqlAl_XhQ). Xu's YouTube channel gained popularity across the US among Mandarin-speaking viewers because his videos are both informative and entertaining. His message focuses on self-defense during the rise in anti-Asian hate crimes. These activities increased members' internal readiness to face a hate crime incident and demonstrated self-reliance.

Ongoing Conversations

The fourth and final activity CFSA organized what they called the 'CFSA Weekend Square' to maintain an active informal network. Metaphorically named after the physical public square where an open space at the intersection of two or more streets, which provides a place for assembly for people to meet, CFSA hosted an open space on Zoom for 30 minutes on Friday nights at 7 pm to meet informally and discuss topics of members' choices, while ushering in the weekend. I participated in more than half of the meetings held during this time.

CFSA recognized the need to have an open space for members to engage in informal and internal communication with each other on a regular basis. This kept the community active but flexible enough for conversations to adapt to the interests of participants, and to respond to emerging needs of the community. For example, several topics proposed for the 'Weekend Square' included growing a victory garden, parenting, and home security; but conversations were often improvised based on who

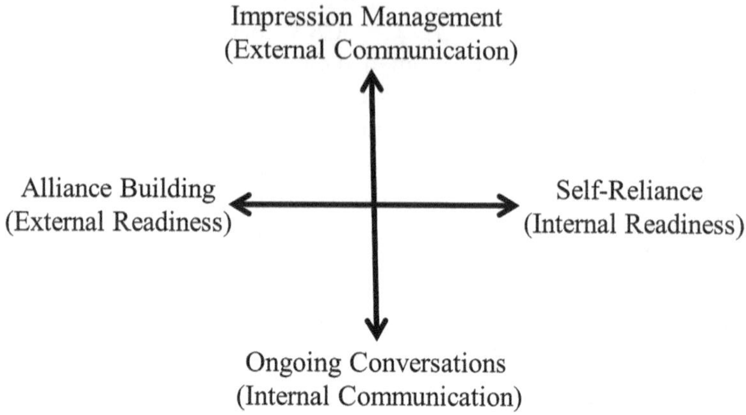

Fig. 20.1 The organizational communication and readiness matrix

attended that day. It was an informal meeting that some members dropped in and brought their dinner to eat while chatting on Zoom or stopped by and said "hi" to other CFSA members. However, this online space was especially important because it allowed members to stay connected with each other while physical meetings were not possible due to COVID-19 social distancing.

Given the description above, these four organizing activities can be further re-arranged into an organizational communication matrix made up by two axes (communication and readiness), contrasted with their internal and external focus. See Fig. 20.1.

Community Organizing by the Invisible and Perpetual Foreigners

So, what can we learn from this ethnographic account of CFSA community organizing? As I reflected on my participations in many of CFSA's events and activities, I noted the following points. First, CFSA members instinctively understood that they were already perceived as 'perpetual foreigners' (Lee et al., 2009), but COVID-19 pushed them further into the margins and away from the centrality of being American. Because the perception that Asians are non-American or 'not from America' is already entrenched in the US culture, COVID-19 further reinforced the perception that they are the outgroup. Once perceived further as an outgroup, it could be justified in the minds of the attackers that Asians are indeed responsible for COVID-19.

Second, CFSA members felt the need to share information about COVID-19 and anti-Asian hate crimes to support each other as a community. Following the previous point that Asians are a permanent outgroup in American society, there was a sense that they needed to support each other during the dual crises. In some way, why would the 'real Americans' protect the 'perpetual foreigners'? This doubt is further confirmed on March 29, 2021, in the case of a 65-year-old Asian woman being knocked down and repeatedly kicked in the head on the street outside a luxury apartment building in New York City, while witnesses in the lobby simply watched the attack as it unfolded, and worse, the security guard closed the lobby door further isolating the woman as she laid on the ground (W. Wong, 2021). Self-reliance was strengthened by informal conversations, so information could travel effectively throughout the social networks.

Third, as COVID-19 forced visibility on Asians, they can no longer remain 'invisible'. Perhaps due to cultural differences and/or language preferences for some, Asians tend not to be active in local, regional, and national communities and politics. In mainstream media and Hollywood entertainment, Asian representation is also limited. Furthermore, the Asian cultures de-emphasize individualism, but promote collectivism, therefore, individual members often do not speak up and speak out to stand out from the crowd. As a result, Asians are often 'invisible' in American society. This cultural tendency solidified Asians' outgroup status. However, COVID-19 heightened public awareness of them. In response, CFSA engaged in community service activities in an attempt to brand themselves as 'good citizens' in the local community.

Fourth, they were savvy with using mass media and social media to disseminate stories of their community service. They also intentionally engaged with the local police and medical professionals, as these two groups can have an impact on their very survival and safety. They further engaged with seniors, perhaps due to their cultural orientation to respect the elderly. Overall, the effort of impression management could be argued as born out of being forced into the spotlight. In fact, I have argued that behind the public messages and community service was the fear of becoming the victims of anti-Asian hate crimes.

Communication Technologies

What is the role of communication technologies in CFSA's community organizing? First, Zoom helped facilitate synchronous communication. For example, the LPD webinar and ongoing Weekend Square meetings were facilitated on Zoom. During the same period, CFSA hosted a few other Zoom meetings, including a welcome event for new Chinese faculty and staff joining TTU in Fall 2020, webinars on real estate and financial investments, and the 2021 Chinese Spring Festival Celebration in February. Members were able to see and/or hear each other during Zoom interactions, which created mediated social presence.

Second, WeChat allowed asynchronous communication and information sharing. Social media with information, news, stories, and so on about COVID-19 and anti-Asian hate crimes were circulated among members in the general WeChat group to support asynchronous ongoing conversations, and the smaller WeChat Group facilitated discussions specific to self-defense and guns for self-reliance. I also become an active WeChat user during this time, and I now check for messages from CFSA members on a daily basis. Zoom and WeChat each supported two types of activities as shown in Fig. 20.2.

Fig. 20.2 Communication technologies in the organizational communication and readiness matrix

Third, traditional and social media (e.g., Facebook) as well as printed flyers on their donations supported external communication for impression management. Moreover, social media (e.g., YouTube) supported knowledge about guns and self-defense among members of the smaller WeChat group. Additionally, CFSA also maintained an email list of all members. Finally, while not digital in nature, food donations to UMC, HSC, and LPD are symbolic messages for alliance building. A range of communication technologies created an ecosystem for CFSA members to maintain a sense of community to support each other. While not every CSFA member was active and/or active across all platforms at all times, many benefited from passively receiving information. See Fig. 20.2.

Similar to all other faculty and staff at the university, everyone was thrown into the whirlwind of COVID-19 and rapid transitions to working and teaching online. On top of that, CFSA members and other Asians within and beyond the academy had to prepare for the possibility of anti-Asian hate crimes. During this time, many community organizations across the US spread news about 'Stop Asian Hate' rallies and protests, hosted webinars on self-defense and Q&A with Asian police officers and detectives, and so on. The images and videos of Asians, especially the elderly, being brutally beaten, injured, and/or killed circulated on social media and in mainstream TV news. While such media consumption appears to be virtual, mental health experts believe that the Asian communities are suffering and/or have suffered from 'collective trauma' (Huang, 2021).

According to Russell Jeung (Relations, 2021), a professor at San Francisco State University, three out of five Asian Americans have experienced racism. Many Asians were bullied at some point in their lives, especially those who grew up in the US. For example, Andrew Yang, who ran in the 2020 Democratic presidential primaries and currently the frontrunner to be mayor of New York City in 2021 at the time of this writing, admitted that he was bullied as an Asian boy in Somers in Westchester County, New York (Admin, 2021). Watching and re-watching the videos and imageries of anti-Asian violence could trigger adverse childhood memories (Reja, 2021), further amplifying the collective trauma Asians experience by watching victims who resemble them in these videos and images.

Conclusion

I wrote this chapter in March/April 2021, during the height of anti-Asian hate crimes in the US. According to StopAAPIHate.org, between March 2020 to March 2021, there were almost 4000 anti-Asian hate crimes documented by their website. In August 2020, the New York Police Department (NYPD) established the first Anti-Asian Hate Crimes Task Force in the US (Romine, 2020). On January 28, 2021, an 84-year-old Thai American man was violently pushed to the ground in San Francisco by a 19-year-old attacker, and the man died as the result of brain damage (Lah & Kravarik, 2021). Although it was not confirmed as a hate crime at the time of this writing, following the mass shooting by a 21-year-old man who killed eight victims, six of whom are Asian women, at three Asian businesses in the Atlanta area, Georgia on March 16, 2021 (Cohen, 2021), rallies and protests under the slogan 'Stop Asian Hate' started around March 18, 2021, in Milwaukee, Wisconsin, and March 19, 2021, in San Diego, California, West Hartford, Connecticut, Cincinnati, Ohio, Knoxville, Memphis, and Nashville, Tennessee, San Antonio, Texas, and Madison, Wisconsin.

Learning about the anti-Chinese history in America during the pandemic, I started to re-ask many questions I asked as a teenager in Borneo, but this time about Asians in the US: Are Asians and Asian Americans perpetually conditional citizens? What can Asians do if the anti-Asian sentiment is a permanent condition? What logical actions should be taken? If Asians will continue to be perpetual foreigners, perhaps Asian researchers should consider finding a new home as soon as possible, where they will be fully accepted as full-fledged members of the country (Silver, 2020). Another possibility is to continue their research work in the US for the short term, but begin planning to seek a new home country for the long term. A third possibility is to change the condition from perpetual foreigner to one that is permanent member of society. Regardless of which possibility to take, the matrix in Figs. 20.1 and 20.2 shows organizational communication strategies that Asians in the US could employ to increase their community organizing and readiness to combat hate crimes. Perhaps the complicated CFSA narrative documented can raise awareness of the unsettled belonging and permanent alienation experienced by Asians in the US, and lead to actions and advocacy toward social justice.

According to Frey (2020) at the Brookings Institution, the 2020 US Census reveals that the national population is diversifying more rapidly than previously anticipated. Furthermore, Budiman and Ruiz (2021a) of the Pew Research Center explain that Asian Americans are actually the fastest-growing ethnic group in this diversifying trend of the national population between the years 2000 and 2019. They note that this growth in the Asian American ethnic group continues despite the reported anti-Asian hate crimes since the pandemic. In another article, Budiman and Ruiz (2021b) trace the growth of the Asian American population and report that this ethic group grew about 95%, nearly doubling in numbers, from 2000 to 2019. They also projected that by 2060, this ethic group will nearly quadruple its 2020 population size, surpassing 46 million in number 40 years later. Finally, perhaps over the next four decades, anti-Asian sentiments will slowly subside as the Asian population grows.

Another possibility for changing the perception of 'perpetual foreigner' and the anti-Asian sentiment is by strategically dismantling the ideologies behind them. According to Vedantam and Mesler (2021), engaging in angry debates will not work, as haters with strong anti-Asian ideologies will rationalize any facts and arguments as further evidence that their position is confirmed and true. Instead, dialogues could be facilitated to tactfully question the assumptions and bases from which anti-Asian ideologies and hate emerge. In fact, such dialogues will be productive for counteracting all hate ideologies, beyond the Asian case. It will be a collective effort from all ethnic and social groups, as haters exist in all groups, and all groups have members who embrace diversity, equity, and inclusion (DEI).

The COVID-19 pandemic is a complex event. It was not simply a public health crisis in the US, Asians are also fighting the threat of racist violence at the same time. Would they need to worry about their safety and the safety of their loved ones constantly, and never really live the lives that they are entitled to given human rights and civil rights? Would their suffering be known to others, or they would once again silently and 'invisibly' endure the hardship? A year after the attack, the father of the Burmese family of four in Midland, Texas, shared "I can forgive him (Gomez), but we cannot accept racism or that kind of terrorist attack" (CBSDFW.com, 2021). Will anti-Asian racism and hate go away after COVID-19 is fully resolved?

Racial tensions are complicated, and there are no easy solutions. Given the changing demographics in the decades to come, it is important to keep in mind that diversity is the perpetual condition in our lives, today and in our future. Intergroup conflicts do not help any of us and will only hurt us in the long run. Perhaps we should heed the wisdom in Atlanta Mayor

Keisha Lance Bottoms when she said in response to the March 16 mass shooting in her city, "A crime against any community is a crime against us all" (Pagones, 2021).

The future of academic workers, and arguably all workers across all industries, would benefit from effective leadership that can guide us through negotiating differences that reduce or eliminate the practice of 'Othering' (Eko, 2010). No other group is fully good or bad, and so DEI help to make room for everyone. While it is not an easy condition to manage, if left unmanaged, DEI can be hijacked by evil doers to do harm against us all. However, if we take the time and effort to learn to harness it, DEI can make our world a more beautiful place for all.

Note

1. Given that Chinese can be mistaken as Japanese in the case of Vincent Chin in Michigan, and the Burmese family in Texas was mistaken as Chinese, I note that much of what I wrote in this chapter affect the diverse community of Asian Americans and Pacific Islanders. In order to be inclusive of all, unless I am referring to a specific group (e.g., Chinese in CFSA), I use 'Asians' to refer to individuals who are concerned about and/or are affected by anti-Asian hate crimes during the pandemic. I also use 'Asians' to refer to both non-immigrants, naturalized citizens, and Asian Americans born and raised in the US.

References

Admin. (2021, April 4). Andrew Yang's Asian American Superpower. *The Patriot Wire*. https://thepatriotwire.org/?p=3279

Barry, Ellen. (2021, January 26). A scientist is arrested, and academics push back. *The New York Times*. https://www.nytimes.com/2021/01/26/us/mit-scientist-charges.html

Basu, Moni. (2016). 15 years after 9/11, Sikhs still victims of anti-Muslim hate crimes. *CNN*. https://www.cnn.com/2016/09/15/us/sikh-hate-crime-victims/index.html

Boots, Denise P., Bihari, Jayshree, & Elliott, Euel. (2009). The state of the castle: An overview of recent trends in state castle doctrine legislation and public policy. *Criminal Justice Review, 34*, 515.

Brezina, Corona. (2016). *Zheng He: China's greatest explorer, mariner, and navigator*. The Rosen Publishing Group, Inc.

Budiman, Abby, & Ruiz, Neil G. (2021a). Asian Americans are the fastest-growing racial or ethnic group in the U.S. https://www.pewresearch.org/fact-tank/2021/04/09/asian-americans-are-the-fastest-growing-racial-or-ethnic-group-in-the-u-s/

Budiman, Abby, & Ruiz, Neil G. (2021b, April 29). Key facts about Asian Americans, a diverse and growing population. https://www.pewresearch.org/fact-tank/2021/04/29/key-facts-about-asian-americans/

CBSDFW.com. (2021, March 2). *Victims of Asian hate crimes in Texas & across US reflect 1 year Into COVID pandemic.* https://dfw.cbslocal.com/2021/03/02/victims-asian-hate-crimes-texas-us-reflect-1-year-pandemic/

Cohen, Li. (2021, March 17). "An unspeakable tragedy": Asian American community reacts to deadly spa shootings in Georgia. *CBSNews.* https://www.cbsnews.com/news/atlanta-shooting-asian-american-pacific-islander-community-reaction/

Davis, Kasie. (2020). LPD encourages kindness as local association spreads 'LOVE'. *KCBD.* Retrieved from https://www.kcbd.com/2020/03/27/lpd-encourages-kindness-local-association-spreads-love/

Eko, Lyombe. (2010). New technologies, ancient archetypes: The Boston Globe's discursive construction of internet connectivity in Africa. *Howard Journal of Communications, 21*(2), 182–198.

Frey, William H. (2020, July 1). The nation is diversifying even faster than predicted, according to new census data. https://www.brookings.edu/research/new-census-data-shows-the-nation-is-diversifying-even-faster-than-predicted/

Huang, Josie. (2021, April 1). The collective trauma of anti-Asian hate: We talk to 5 mental health experts. *LAist.* https://laist.com/2021/04/01/collective_trauma_anti-asian_hate_mental_health_experts.php

Kil, Sang H. (2012). Fearing yellow, imagining white: Media analysis of the Chinese exclusion act of 1882. *Social Identities, 18*(6), 663–677.

Kuo, Michelle. (2017). *Reading with Patrick: A teacher, a student, and a life-changing friendship.* Random House.

Kurashige, Scott. (2002). Detroit and the legacy of Vincent Chin. *Amerasia Journal, 28*(3), 51–55.

Lah, Kyung, & Kravarik, Jason. (2021, February 16). Family of Thai immigrant, 84, says fatal attack 'was driven by hate'. *CNN.* https://edition.cnn.com/2021/02/16/us/san-francisco-vicha-ratanapakdee-asian-american-attacks/index.html

Lai, Him M. (2004). *Becoming Chinese American: A history of communities and institutions* (Vol. 13). Rowman Altamira.

Lee, Stacey J., Wong, Nga-Wing A., & Alvarez, Alvin N. (2009). The model minority and the perpetual foreigner: Stereotypes of Asian Americans. In N. Tewari & A. N. Alvarez (Eds.), *Asian American psychology: Current perspectives* (pp. 69–84). Routledge/Taylor & Francis Group.

Lewis, Margeret K. (2020). Criminalizing China. *Journal of Criminal Law and Criminology, 111*(1).

Midland Reporter-Telegram. (2020). Report: FBI lists stabbing at Sam's as hate crime. https://www.mrt.com/news/crime/article/Report-FBI-lists-stabbing-at-Sam-s-as-hate-15166683.php

Montag, Christian, Becker, Benjamin, & Gan, Chunmei. (2018). The multipurpose application WeChat: A review on recent research. *Frontiers in Psychology, 9*, 2247.

National Committee on U.S.-China Relations. (2021, April 1). https://www.youtube.com/watch?v=JrtdWlWcB5M

Pagones, Stephanie. (2021, March 17). Atlanta mayor speaks out after mass shooting, calls attacks 'a crime against us all'. *Fox News*. https://www.foxnews.com/us/atlanta-mayor-keisha-lance-bottoms-shootings-attack-crime-against-us-all

Peek, Lori. (2011). *Behind the backlash: Muslim Americans after 9/11*. Temple University Press.

Reja, Mishal. (2021, March 7). Rise in anti-Asian American hate crimes may lead to mental health crisis. *ABCNews*. https://abcnews.go.com/Health/rise-anti-asian-american-hate-crimes-lead-mental/story?id=76211964

Romine, Taylor. (2020, August 18). NYPD creates Asian hate crime task force after spike in anti-Asian attacks during Covid-19 pandemic. *CNN*. https://www.cnn.com/2020/08/18/us/nypd-asian-hate-crime-task-force/index.html

Silver, Andrew. (2020, September 8). US political crackdown spurs fears of Chinese brain-drain. *Daily Science News*.

Soennichsen, John. (2011). *The Chinese Exclusion Act of 1882*. ABC-CLIO.

Texas State Law Library. (n.d.). Gun Laws. https://guides.sll.texas.gov/gun-laws

Vedantam, Shankar, & Mesler, Bill. (2021). *Useful delusions: The power and paradox of the self-deceiving brain*. W. W. Norton & Company.

Wallace, Danielle. (2020). Texas man accused of stabbing Asian family over coronavirus could face FBI hate crime charge. *Fox News*. https://www.foxnews.com/us/texas-man-stabbing-asian-family-coronavirus-fbi-hate-crime

Watanabe, Teresa. (2019, July 22). Is it police work or racial profiling? U.S. crackdown puts Chinese scholars on edge. *Los Angeles Times*. https://www.latimes.com/california/story/2019-07-21/trump-china-racial-profiling-university-fbi-spy

Wong, Danny T.-K. (1999). Chinese migration to Sabah before the second world war. *Archipel, 58*(3), 131–158. https://www.persee.fr/doc/arch_0044-8613_1999_num_58_3_3538

Wong, Wilson. (2021, March 30). Asian woman, 65, knocked down, repeatedly kicked as witnesses appear to watch. *ABCNews*. https://www.nbcnews.com/news/asian-america/asian-woman-65-knocked-down-repeatedly-kicked-witnesses-appear-watch-n1262431

Zia, Helen. (2000). *Asian American dreams: The emergence of an American people*. Farrar, Straus and Giroux.

Zia, Helen. (2010). 3. Detroit blues: Because of you motherfuckers. In *Asian American studies now* (pp. 35–54). Rutgers University Press.

CHAPTER 21

Review: A Grounded Theory of Organizational Communication and Technology (OCT) of COVID-19 Before Delta and the Vaccine

Larry D. Browning, Jan-Oddvar Sørnes, and Peer Jacob Svenkerud

How do the preceding chapters illustrate the concept of *emergent complexity* that we invoked in our Introduction (Mitchell, 2003)? Well, here we see a fairly disparate group of scholar-researchers setting off with exactly the same set of research questions and producing a pleasingly varied—and pleasingly complex—set of answers. Yet the chapters also illustrate another

L. D. Browning (✉) • J.-O. Sørnes
Business School, Nord University, Bodø, Norway
e-mail: lbrowning@austin.utexas.edu; lbrowning@mail.utexas.edu; Jan-Oddvar.Sornes@nord.no

P. J. Svenkerud
Inland Norway University of Applied Science, Elverum, Norway
e-mail: peer.svenkerud@inn.no

L. D. Browning et al. (eds.), *Organizational Communication and Technology in the Time of Coronavirus*,
https://doi.org/10.1007/978-3-030-94814-6_21

handy concept: ***equifinality***—namely, they all eventually arrive at pretty much the same place, since each documents yet another very human reaction to the virus (Gresov & Drazin, 1997). Important for our purposes here, they have ***integrative complexity***, in which complexity can be represented by the number of different positions created to represent them and the order necessary to integrate them (Park & DeShon, 2018).

In this final chapter we argue that organizational-communication technology is the integrator of that differentiation.

But in what ways are the chapters different despite originating from the very same questions? To nail down the answer to this question, we performed a grounded-theory analysis. We eventually identified 18 categories that summarize them, or major parts of them. And then we grouped them accordingly. The core element of grounded theory is a focus on the emergence of theory from the data (here, the data are chapters) while remaining open to all possible meanings and interpretations of data (Treem & Browning, 2017). We looked for likenesses among the 19 content chapters and linked them to one or more of the 18 categories listed below.

Our goal in this final chapter was to make as many ties as possible among the 19 content chapters by searching for, and highlighting, the commonalities among them. The outcome of this analysis produces ***modularity***, which "refers to the property of a system where the system can be divided into different numbers of chunks called modules (categories), which have strong intra-connections within individual modules and weak interconnections between modules" (Sinha et al., 2017, p. 2). This sorting highlights different components of value within chapters by showing to how many different categories any single chapter might get assigned.

Here's an overview of the 18 categories emerging from our 19 content chapters:

1. **Constrained. Organizations give directions.**
2. **Ventriloqual. People give themselves directions.**
3. **Utilitarian. People act toward desirable goals.**
4. **Rhetorical. People use language with style.**
5. **Protective. People are reticent to talk on the record about the crisis.**
6. **Autonomous. People speak for themselves.**
7. **Ante-narratological. People speak up in "act one" of the story.**
8. **Theoretical. People use concepts to draw attention to ideas.**

9. **Synergetic. Writers double up and address the crisis in this and other venues.**
10. **Chaotic. It is not difficult to find things falling apart in the crisis.**
11. **Strategic. Communication toward others is planned and sequenced.**
12. **Multiple Identities. There are multiple voices within and across chapters.**
13. **Sequential. The stories are sequential and self-aware of their phases.**
14. **Adaptive. People make changes based on data.**
15. **Procedural. People follow steps and are rewarded when they do so.**
16. **Pedagogical. Teachers adapt to the requirements of the crisis.**
17. **Communitarian. People look to reaffirm and develop community in the crisis.**
18. **Vulnerable. People are at risk and feel it.**

Now we'll elaborate on these 18 categories, providing examples of each from the 19 content chapters.

1. **Constrained. Organizations give directions.** This category refers to the external constraints that our chapter writers had to deal with. In Chap. 2, for example, Czarniawska, Pallas, and Raviola note one such constraint: "Swedish National Agency for Education, saying that all pupils who are at home must return to school; otherwise, their absence would be reported to the Compulsory School Unit." Similar organizational constraints are evident in most of the chapters. In Chap. 6, for example, Westerberg recalls hearing a particularly scary announcement: "Six short weeks into my career as a cyber academic we had to return to Norway. When Norway closed down and the Norwegian government stated that they were to implement the 'most invasive measures in peace time' I didn't know what to do. What was this? Were we at war?" In Chap. 14, Storhaug-Hole and Bakken are controlled by a special team given the power to set standards for action for their university: "Our students and employees got little preparation time and we were ordered to leave campus and our offices at 1800 on that day, and to take our computers, head-

sets, devices, and books with us." In Chap. 12, Szmania notes: "On March 19, the Jordanian government imposed a state of emergency in the Kingdom due to the COVID-19 pandemic. All international borders closed, workplaces shut down, group gatherings of more than ten limited, and citizens could not leave their homes." Szmania's chapter identified some constrained personal practices that were particularly rare. Fortunately, none of our other writers had to satisfy any of the three requirements to participate in writing that she faced, including (1) getting pre-certification to participate in an online US State Department conversation before entering the meeting, (2) getting advanced permission from authorities to compose a chapter for this book, and (3) once her chapter was completed, getting organizational approval before it was submitted for publication. As Szmania's account shows, she was able to meet her three requirements seamlessly, and her description of the approval steps becomes part of her analysis of the organizational-communication protocols she had witnessed in the US State Department. Its requirements, though seemingly authoritarian, were actually reasonable. When an organization is tasked with representing and protecting national interests, we want no loose cannons on the deck or technical errors in the representation; the State Department's organizational-communication technology requirements suggest it runs a tight ship indeed.

In contrast, other chapter writers report being free to respond to their own interpretation of the technology they used to deal with their COVID constraints (see our sixth category, "Autonomous," below). An exception is Parker's Chap. 7, where she describes the controls she was obliged to follow, unlike all the other chapter writers, who operated virtually on their own. The context of their freedom of speech will be addressed in the "Autonomous" section below.

2. **Ventriloqual. People speak to themselves.** We invoke the concept of *ventriloquism* (Cooren & Sandler, 2014; Cooren, 2012) because ventriloquality beautifully captures the movement, the locomotion, of the self-speech of many of the writers. Ventriloquism is a subset of organizational-communication theory. It emphasizes how communication is not only *in* the organization, but, more than that, it actually *constructs or constitutes* the

organization. Cooren and Sandler (2014) say, "The communicative constitution of organization (CCO) is a stream of research that represents the power to enact organizational structure via communication practices as *literally* and *figuratively* expressing themselves in any given form of communication (a text, an utterance, a dialogue, an icon, a gesture, etc.), and can thus be acknowledged as *constituting* a given situation" (p. 226). One version of CCO can be captured with a single question: What do we say to ourselves to induce action? To illustrate this point, the Montreal School of Communication—with its continental flair—uses the image of a hand puppet at the end of our arm, speaking directly back to our human face, giving us directions, commanding us to follow its lead and to act on any direction it gives us. The ventriloquist "is able to speak in such a way that his or her voice seems to come from the dummy or figure he or she is manipulating" (Cooren & Sandler, 2014, p. 228). In other words, we convince ourselves.

The ventriloqual chapters are set apart by the self-direction of writers who are activated by the direction they have set for themselves during the pandemic. Of the chapters in this book that demonstrate this self-direction, none demonstrates it more directly than Bartunek's in Chap. 9. She observes to herself about emotions: "I have several notes to myself in past months commenting 'Feeling overwhelmed with work stuff. ... I'm aware of how over committed I am. I have a ton more stuff to do.'" Like many of us, she questions her own judgment: "Why did I decide to edit a book? I must be nuts." She responds to multiple overlapping challenges that demand from her a prominent online and in-person leadership role among her peers. Hers is a classic ventriloqual story: she has no external obligation for any of the action she takes. Bartunek could've easily and justifiably settled into a legitimate role with half of the work demands she places on herself. She says: "I am aware that working on this book has been in addition to my other full-time work load, and has made me extra busy. I have several notes to myself in past months commenting 'Feeling overwhelmed with work stuff.'" Managerial models like the idea of ventriloqual speech are fond of self-control strategies because external controls are typically expensive, awkward, and broad-band, being dependent upon how sensibly they are administered. When self-controls operate effectively, actors *satisfice* (March, 1981) and do an acceptable job even though they are unmonitored. Take the conscientious Tracy, ever mindful of her colleagues, who in Chap. 11 asserts: "If I want to be responsible to the collective, I've got to have some restraint when it comes to my own self-soothing habits of overwork. Further, I can mindfully develop some side roads of new self-soothing habits that would not have the same type of harmful effect on others even when I must flex them for my own personal well-being." Stephens, in Chap. 5, marvels to herself: "I was in complete disbelief. I even watched the video interview I had recorded through Zoom to hear them shout at me in the background. They were not exaggerating! I was so focused on conducting the interview, I had completely missed the accident, and since my make-shift COVID-19 home office had no doors, and I never wear a headset, the emergency had happened right behind me." Actually, all of the chapters here tend to be ventriloqual because they are self-accounts even while composed for a larger audience.

3. **Utilitarian. People act toward desirable goals.** In economic terms, organizational-communication technology has utility when it "assumes that when people choose from among various behavioral alternatives, they always try to select the course of action whose *consequences* will give them the greatest *utility*" (Lynch & Cohen, 1978, p. 1138). In these chapters, organizational-communication technology's utility is emphasized, and its costs minimized, because control is minimized. "More often than not we do not have control over the factors determining the consequences of our choices. Those consequences are determined by the way the world unfolds, by what turns out to be the true state of the world" (Sahlin, 2019, p. 108). But in these chapters the writers do have control over the technology. The true state of the world is a challenge: How do we use OCT to solve a problem like the coronavirus crisis? Given what we face, organizational communication has value when it allows us to live our lives even with our hands on the keyboard—isolated, yes, but still alive and contributing. Chapter writers' effect on the lives of others can be gauged through the exchanges of costs in relation to rewards. In economic terms, technology has utility when it "assumes that when people choose from among various behavioral alternatives,

they always try to select the course of action whose *consequences* will give them the greatest *utility*" (Lynch & Cohen, 1978, p. 1138). The estimation of consequences as a basis for action necessarily leads to an estimation and interpretation of results.

The examples of utility in the chapters are both large and small. For example, in Chap. 5 Stephens says: "I decided to cut my nails short, something that had not happened for over 25 years. I needed to be sure I could keep my hands as clean as possible." In Chap. 8, Szmania explains utility to her pre-school daughters about a life of carefulness and caution in Amman, Jordan: "I found myself trying to objectively explain to my daughters why air-raid sirens blared each night and why they needed to be inside the apartment immediately after they heard the alarm. I tried to reassure them about safety when they saw armed police on the sidewalk outside our apartment building. 'They are here to make sure we follow the rules,' I told them, omitting the fact that we could be fined or jailed for not adhering to the lockdown measures." In Chap. 7, Parker observes the opposite of utility: "What employees *did* see interim leadership investing in during the pandemic was expensive consulting firms and messaging workshops that often created frustration within teams rather than forward progress. In one example, over $1 million was allocated for a consulting firm to turn around what amounted to 1% of the business." The general tone of the chapters shows the predominance of utility. In Chap. 2, Czarniawska, Pallas, and Raviola offer this data piece from their interviews: "Overall, I think that [digital meetings] work very well. No matter if it is two people who meet, like now, or if they are larger meetings. We had a meeting with 100 people. In the beginning, it was awkward: People forgot to unmute and there was a hassle, but everybody has become great at this now. And these meetings are much more efficient, though shorter." In his summary, Brummett notes that the technology allowed people to be effective: "It was to Zoom that users across the world turned to stay in touch during the lockdown effected to stop the spread of the virus."

4. **Rhetorical. People use language with style.** This rhetorical category applies to both chapter writers and to the data from within chapters. The dimension of rhetorical style is evident in the artful language in the chapters. Czarniawska, Pallas, and Raviola in

Chap. 2 offer this self-reflection from an interviewee: "I have become a Zombie, this living-dead creature who, with hollow eyes, sits cowardly, hour after hour staring at the screen—at other living-dead screen workers." As this example shows, the Rhetorical category represents those chapters distinguished by their artfulness, beauty, and style (Brummett, 2008). Ashcraft's Chap. 4 exemplifies this aesthetic as she traverses pressure at her university: "We had been charged to 'do more with less!' for so many years that the ever-constricting belt became a badge on the uniform. So we kept right on going—sprinting, wheezing, and medicating, whetting our cynical tongues—through individualized workloads that spiraled out of control. Here and there, we'd check out for a spell, or check in with a colleague: 'You too?'" The Ashcraft chapter is stylish as she remains elusive, composed, sophisticated, careful, and mindful. Rhetorical style connects personal selves to grand and expansive imaginations. For Brummett in Chap. 3, Zoom is an iconic feature. Brummett's description of Zoom meeting software has participants looking at and listening to each other through mysterious little squares on the computer screen that are both specific and direct and simultaneously confusing and hidden, thus mysterious. He says: "The way that Zoom works is precisely to remake the real, the immediate, the physically experienced into something mediated. That does not mean these become unimportant, but I think we can understand how Zoom works by thinking in terms of how icons work. Anyone on Zoom becomes an icon, leaders especially so. We all of us are icons, and gaze at the faithful from within our little frames, and they at us."

5. **Protective. People are reticent to talk on the record about the crisis.** The protective category is made up of chapter writers' early difficulties enrolling interviewees for the data-collection process. Tracy and her colleagues in Chap. 12, Czarniawska, Pallas, and Raviola in Chap. 2, and Dyle and Dailey in Chap. 19 showed research teams that struggled to enroll participants for their field-research project. Category 5 is about individual caution in talking about their actions and beliefs in early-COVID. Because the crisis is inherently uncertain, there are ample chances of being wrong about any given comment or prediction. Because they failed to gain externally selected field-research participants, our

chapter writers often turned to convenience sampling and asked friends, close colleagues, and family members to provide data as subjects on how they responded to the constraints and demands during the early months of COVID. This category is about the reluctance to participate in research. It highlights the caution and risk associated with the topic of the COVID crisis and reaffirms why ethnographic writing that makes up many of our chapters is a convenient way to interpret the crisis when caution abides.

To be interviewed allows for the possibility that one's practices might be viewed as wrong-headed, so staying off record for an interview exemplifies Goffman's notion of impression management (Goffman, 1959; Dillard et al., 2000). The friendship networks of the chapter writers provided convenience samples of data for this book. While category 5 is coded as a methodological issue, protectiveness is noteworthy because it raises the classic research problem: How much do you trust the data and interpretations?

6. **Autonomous. People speak for themselves.** The autonomous voices of the chapter writers are coded in this category. *Ethnographic autonomy* typically refers to the autonomy of field-research participants—the individuals being studied, not the autonomy of the ethnographers themselves. For example, Botti et al. (2009) employ interviews to analyze the autonomy of research subjects with dire medical conditions on whether they choose their own fate (pull the plug) or leave it to the doctor to decide it for them. But in our book, "autonomy" refers to the autonomy of the researcher, which is the standard presumption of ethnography because the writing experience is typically freely chosen and independent. The organization structure asserts less control in our autonomous chapters. In Chap. 14, Storhaug-Hole and Bakken even ask, "Is our autonomy being usurped by the crisis?" "Autonomous" is a category here because it is set apart from the constraints and control conditions found in category #1 above. While the writers we categorize as "autonomous" didn't choose the virus emergency, they chose to write about it and to account for themselves as independent actors.

   They are answering to no authoritative figure. They are anti-Oedipal; they smooth out rather than break down during crises; there's no point of a showdown or breakdown where one person's authority overrides another (Deleuze & Guattari, 1983). In Chap. 13, we hear Ndlela and Madsbu observe: "Concerns from the older employees were slightly different. Most of the employees at the department John leads are between 50 and 60 years old, and this group is accustomed to a large degree of autonomy." In Chap. 5, Stephens notes, "I hope I openly communicated my own struggles in ways that help you make sense around your [own] COVID-19 pandemic experiences." Stephens assumes that she's allowed here to speak from experience. Czarniawska, Pallas, and Raviola in Chap. 2 note, "The professional response to the pandemic has built on previously acquired expertise, and the professionals' abilities and autonomy of judgment are based on that expertise."

7. **Ante-narratological. People speak up in "act one" of the story.** Ante-narrative theory is the source of our Category 7 because the actions and feelings expressed in this book are necessarily incomplete and play into a story for which we have no ending (Boje, 2011). For example, Czarniawska, Pallas, and Raviola in Chap. 2 note, "Just like you, we know nothing. This is completely new to us, too. We haven't a clue what is to come." Because they cannot be completed, chapters in Category 7 call to mind a poker player, in mid-game, wagering against an uncertain outcome; the dealing isn't done. They act out Bakhtin's philosophical position: "Nothing conclusive has yet taken place in the world, the ultimate word of the world and about the world has not yet been spoken, the world is open and free, everything is still in the future and will always be in the future" (Bakhtin, 1984, p. 166). The focus on ante-narrative in the chapters demonstrates the category's integration with organization theories of uncertainty (Weick & Sutcliffe, 2011; Lomi & Harrison, 2012). The chapters' mimicry of ante-narratology is demonstrated by how incomplete the stories are. The writers are as interested as we readers are in how the coronavirus crisis ends. The ante-narratology category returns us to a theme of this book: What is the story of organizational-communication technology during this pandemic? The answer here: ongoing and emergent. It would be an error to conclude the story. The chapters that emphasize uncertainty are coded in this category. For example, in Chap. 7, Parker says: "Teams were wary of any changes being made by interim

leadership, knowing entire systems and modes of communication were simply likely to change *again* as the expected permanent leadership was brought in over the next weeks and months." The next example shows the extent of people's reaction to what is happening next. Again, from Czarniawska, Pallas, and Raviola in Chap. 2, we step into an uncertain story: "You definitely become more thick-skinned. My changing room is next to the cold storage where the bodies end up. I'm starting an evening shift, and on the way to my dressing room there is a bed, and I see that a bit of a bumpy surface outlining a face. It's a body lying underneath, but you think, 'Oh, I'll just go by and get changed!' And then you think, 'What or who did I just pass by? Should I just continue my day?' It feels unreal." Finally, in Chap. 6, Westerberg is more philosophical about the next chapter in the story: "We are not done with corona yet, and what happens next nobody knows. We have to be prepared for the unexpected. Through everyday life and its social activities both we, as individuals and the societies, are wholly constructed, constituted, and reproduced. Entering into the new, not yet established, everyday life opens up for reflection about what kind of working life one wants."

8. **Theoretical. People use concepts to draw attention to ideas.** The "Theoretical" chapters tend to make a theoretical statement or invoke theory to support the point of their story. For example, what began as an introductory concept offered by Czarniawska, Pallas, and Raviola in Chap. 2, "pandemicracy," is an original theoretical formulation that could be applied in general to COVID organization. Szmania, in Chap. 12, organizes her story around improvisation theory. She says, "I also returned to some of the readings that had most impacted me during my graduate studies. Above all, Bateson's (1993) essay, 'Joint performance across cultures: Improvisation in a Persian garden,' made a deep impression on me when I read it for the first time in a graduate seminar on interaction analysis. In the essay, the author, an anthropologist, describes her experience of attending a religious ceremony involving the sacrifice of a sheep in Tehran. In this new and unfamiliar situation, Bateson discusses how she tries to explain the events to her young daughter, taking on the roles of 'a learner, as an observer, [and] as an outsider'" (Bateson, 1993, p. 115). The techno-ethnographies in Section Four are steeped in theory. They

all set out to establish a theoretical relationship between data collection and findings. For example, Ndlela and Jens Petter Madsbu in Chap. 13 elaborate the literature on crisis communication as it relates to the appropriation and domestication of new communication technologies. Storhaug-Hole and Bakken in Chap. 14 offer a complete theoretical review of crisis communication and crisis management. In Chap. 15, Kwei-Narh and Rydstedt review the role of communication, institutional trust, and reputation as it relates to health-advice adherence. The effect of the careful literature reviews in these Norwegian chapters is to make the findings applicable to global research literatures.

9. **Synergistic. Chapter writers accomplishing more than one goal with the same research project**. This is a methodological category; it shows that our chapter writers view their work in this book as one of several research projects. Rebecca Rice's Chap. 18, for example, performs dual duty. It is about her talent and passion for field research, but it is also about the work she does on an emergency team. Bartunek, in Chap. 9, comments about her overlapping projects: "Editing the book resulted from 'hovering' over several different elements—including a desire to respond to the coronavirus in some unspecified way, rereading a book by Camus, Ed Schein's rant, and my co-editorship of a book series—in a way that led to joining academic and consultant voices on, essentially, the same side of the tension, while leaving each free to contribute their own insights." Aguilar and Ballard in Chap. 17 use Aguilar's dissertation data for their chapter. Czarniawska, Pallas, and Raviolas' Chap. 2 is a subset of a larger research project.
10. **Chaotic. It is not difficult to find things falling apart in the crisis.** There is an unclear link between means and ends. Westerberg in Chap. 6 addresses the chaos in shipping: "Worldwide, some 400,000 seafarers are unable to disembark, leaving them stranded onboard for very long periods. Some have been onboard for close to two years now. This means that others are left unemployed waiting to embark." Soelberg in Chap. 8 analyzes the distribution and logistics of personal protection equipment (PPE). His focus is on the layered and chaotic backstory of prices, production, shipping, and allocation of PPP in Norway. Parker's chapter is also chaotic; she relates in Chap. 7: "Communication between teams was often a further challenge

even when not deliberately siloed, as cultures from previous companies made through various acquisitions butted up against one another. For example, without strong leadership, our hybrid teams often failed to create new sustainable and global methods of communication, further compounded by stand-alone brands using different tech. The negative effect on morale, drive, and expected career progression cannot be overstated." Stephens in Chap. 5 relates, "I imagine my own work-from-home innovations happened because I was forced to exist in a zone of emergent complexity ... Living in this zone almost constantly for a year, I feel like I have been continuously bouncing back and forth between these edges, and sometimes slipping, even if briefly, into full chaos." As Parker in Chap. 7 similarly comments, "As a manager I tried my best to communicate everything I knew with my team, but I knew very little."

11. **Strategic. Communication toward others is planned and sequenced.** Strategic communication is "broadly defined as the purposeful use of symbols to achieve individual, organizational, and/or political goals" (Conrad & Poole, 2010, 2012). Yet this category includes the subset of ideas that urge not being totally dependent on plans (Garcia Contreras et al. 2020; Wildavsky, 1973). A theme of the Norwegian chapters (13, 14, and 15) on the purpose of this book was to take action by providing the research on organizational change to respond to the crisis in Norway. Their commitment, rather than personally ethnographic, was to look for communication solutions to the problem of the coronavirus. Their goal was to develop a trustworthy communication climate so that people have faith in the directions from their government. In addition to these examples, Kee's Chap. 20 focuses on the strategic actions he took to protect himself from anti-Asian threats in his culture. Kee offers four strategies for himself and the Asian community at his university, including these: organizing community service events to brand Chinese as good citizens, building relationships with the local police department, creating a "Lubbock Chinese Friends of Guns Group," and meeting weekly on Zoom for social support. Tracy and her colleagues' strategy in Chap. 11 threaded the needle between personal disclosure of emotions experienced during the crisis and building a community of support using the same philosophy.

12. **Multiple identities. There are multiple voices within and across chapters.** Multiple identities thread through most of the chapters—especially in the one by Tracy (11) and Mitra (16) and their coauthors. The chapters with multiple authors can overtly be labeled as multiple-identity chapters. The value of team research in qualitative data collection and analysis is long established because multiple perspectives can result from different observations. Of note are the chapters that showcase multiple identities within a single person. Here, the best example is offered by Soelberg in Chap. 8. Soelberg relates the story of a man whose family was from China but who himself was born and raised in Norway with natural citizenship and who speaks perfect Chinese in dialect. This person was the front man for purchasing PPE from China and was able to monitor conversations, listen for slang, and in effect complete the job of purchase with local information. His multiple identities were a huge asset there. Bartunek in Chap. 9 comments on the identities that get blurred: "I never even imagined a dualism/duality between practitioner and academic work in carrying out these tasks. My experience was completely either/or. In fact, I found it hard to do academic work while I was focusing on collecting dues and making videos about people being celebrated for their scholarly achievements. The purely academic side of me would never have had purple hair in an 'I'm glad this is over' video." In another chapter, multiplicity is represented in Ashcraft's contrasting account of the two Karens—first, the Karen in temporary popular culture who represents the flakey woman who is presumptuous about her privilege enough to call the police when she encounters a man of color nearby in the park and, alarmed, feels entitled to immediately phone 911 for protection from him. The real Karen is the professor in the university system whose positional role is to represent gender and ethnic minorities in university policy and decision-making. Ashcraft contrasts the two Karens and articulates how she is wedged between the stereotype and the policy actor.
13. **Sequential. The stories are sequential and self-aware of their phases** (Browning & Morris, 2012). Narratives "are not mere snapshot photographic images, but require sequencing" (Gabriel, 2004, p. 5). The examples in this category exemplify Polster's (1987) claim of sequential ordering. Kwei-Narh and Rydstedt in

Chap. 15 note the movement from creeping crisis to recognition. Czarniawska, Pallas, and Raviola in Chap. 2 obtain reports from participants in the Swedish state bureaucracy during the first eight months of COVID-19; their chapter summarizes those reports by making different phases of the early development: "The pandemicratic practices were transformed between March and October 2020 from an anxiety-generating emergency to a new normal, with a debated projection of the future ... and the unimaginable possibility to get back to a pre-COVID-19 world." Organizational communication technology reduces uncertainty in the crisis by enabling continuous communication. The chapters show communication responsiveness (cycle time) of actors in relation to the situations they faced in the first eight months of the crisis.

14. **Adaption. People make changes in structure.** DeSanctis and Poole (1994) term this process *Adaptive Structuration Theory* (AST), which "provides a model that describes the interplay between advanced information technologies, social structures, and human interaction. Consistent with structuration theory, AST focuses on social structures, rules and resources provided by technologies and institutions as the basis for human activity" (p. 125). In these chapters individuals are continually adapting to the technology, and that is taken as a given. The adaptive process can be separated into two features: preplanning and adapting to the situation. The old plan is matched with new circumstances (Alterman, 1988). For example, in Chap. 3, Brummett notes how his university adapted like the flip of a switch: "I was struck by how quickly my university went from strict prohibitions against staff working from home to strict prohibitions against staff coming in to work. We went from decades of 'this work cannot be done from home' to 'this work must be done from home.'" In her administrative role, Doornich in Chap. 10 is careful to keep abreast of information: "In between the meetings, I needed to update myself on the virus's behavior and regulations that affected our activities at the university. I would search national and international news media and journals to gain a greater understanding of the virus—how it spreads and how to fight it. I watched every press conference from the national and local government with deep concentration and concern for how my organization was

affected and what we needed to act upon." Szmania in Chap. 12 shows how quickly an organization can adapt: "The pandemic has shown that an institution's ability to allow some work online—both internally and externally—provides employees with new tools to experiment and improvise with new approaches and organizational patterns to complete work requirements. In a time of crisis, this flexibility has brought expended opportunity and has not, in most cases, negatively impacted work relationships." The change in interpersonal practices switched without a hitch. For example in Chap. 2, Czarniawska, Pallas, and Raviola note: "Yes, you can work normally without shaking people's hands. It is possible to make people feel welcomed anyway, just in a different way. You look people in the eye. You look a little kinder and so on. Everyone knows how to reach out."

15. **Procedural. People follow steps and are rewarded when they do so.** Procedures are lists and routines that can be enacted as processes (Browning, 1992; Pentland et al., 2010). Meeting the requirements of the COVID crisis took simple discipline but required no protection beyond vaccines, masks, distance, and sanitation. Szmania's work in Chap. 12 is consummately procedural as she plans meetings, fulfills tasks, travels to conferences, and manages contracts at the US embassy in Jordan. Doornich's Chap. 10 emphasizes a different conception of a leader than her organizations' culture. Her efforts are data-driven and procedural. Late in her chapter she worries that her vigilance for procedure has faltered. The chapters in the section on techno-ethnographies that emphasize the data-collection process are procedural, including Chap. 13, where Ndlela and Madsbu summarize the wholesale changes in procedure required during the crisis: "This rapid transformation of routines required a full redeployment of organizational communication." In Chap. 15, Kwei-Narh and Rydstedt survey the Norwegian Institute of Public Health's trustworthiness and the impact of that trust on Norwegian rule-following during the early stages of the crisis. Stephens in Chap. 5 observes her own organizational procedures: "When beginning to work on a project, I ritualistically open that specific binder, and when I complete my work for the day, I close the binder and place it back on the shelf. I have a clean desk at the end of the day."

16. **Pedagogical. Teachers adapt to the requirements of the crisis.** In this category we offer examples of the challenges of teaching during a pandemic. In Chap. 6, Westerberg comments on what the classroom means to her: "In my experience I love the feeling in the classroom. The classroom is my stage where I get to use language, humor, pictures, cartoons, graphs, videos, and texts to teach my students about maritime management and leadership, maritime offshore technology, and the bigger picture of the maritime industry. My goal is to make students fall in love with the ocean and the maritime industry the way I have." In Chap. 13, Ndlela and Madsbu analyze the teaching conditions that a manager supports when teachers are unsure of what is going on: "For a majority of lecturers, completing the teaching digitally was a completely new and unknown experience, and John, as the immediate manager, received a number of inquiries regarding teaching. Most inquiries concerned practical information about how the connections should be done, how the tools and applications for the digital teaching worked, and how the teaching itself should be carried out with displays of PowerPoint presentations." In Chap. 5, Stephens reviews the administration around teaching as she comments about university meetings: "While there was hand sanitizer at every event, I found myself trying to sit a few seats away from others, a practice that made me worry I was being overly paranoid. I took a photo of my graduate students, happily collaborating during class on Tuesday, March 10th, in our Communication Studies building. I told them then at that meeting that I was concerned this might be our last time physically together for the semester. It was. I made the decision that Wednesday would be my last day on campus before Spring Break; I just felt unsafe around other people. I phoned into a meeting on Friday, and learned three days later that the Dean who led that meeting had tested positive for COVID-19. He was the second person on our campus diagnosed." In Chap. 10, Doornich, then Vice Dean of Education at the Business School at Nord University in Bodø, Norway, and manager of a teaching faculty, worries about the controls she needed to exert concerning campus visitors—some arriving masked, others not—and what controls were necessary to protect students and faculty.

17. **Communitarian. People look to reaffirm and develop community in the crisis.** The communitarian category is especially evident when contributions emphasize membership growth and development (Etzioni, 1996; Selznick, 1987). In Chap. 9, Bartunek shows her communitarian orientation when she asks this question: "Will we recognize that we need to use or invent methods of collaboration on a global level to deal with the global environment as a finite resource that we are currently depleting by encouraging at least sanctioning competition among countries, industries, and political parties?" Tracy in Chap. 11 relates the interpersonal practices she models in the name of community: "In every research meeting, we checked in with one another and honestly shared how we were coping with the pandemic and social distancing. During these discussions, we disclosed the sicknesses in our families, our difficulties in keeping up with work and school, and the upset in having to cancel plans or do without. We laughed. We cried. We talked over each other and didn't mute ourselves. We were authentically curious about each other's everyday lives." Many of these meetings took place in May, 2020—after the academic semester was complete and during a period when many of us were facing an expanse of unscheduled time due to canceled summer plans. In Chap. 5, Stephens ponders what she sees in an airport: "During our three-hour layover in the San Francisco, California, airport, I sat in the food court and watched as many people walked by with masks covering their faces. I remember thinking, 'Are this many people sick?' While I had seen pictures of people in China wearing masks to protect their lungs from pollution, and I'd read about their cultural, collective values of protecting others when they go into public while they are sick, I still felt very uncomfortable and confused. These seemingly healthy people were scurrying past us donning face masks." In Chap. 12, Szmania comments on how recognition for performance that is typically done with public recognition is now only completed on line, and something is lost: "Typically, high-level leaders like a government minister or an ambassador speak to a seated audience to congratulate participants on their achievements. Press may attend formal ceremonies in which participants receive official certificates. Now, in lieu of bringing several hundred people together in a room, these events turn into a virtual

'talking heads' platform, and much of the individual recognition of achievement is lost." Parker, in Chap. 7, laments the lack of a communitarian spirit: "People get meaning and community from the experience of doing a job with people—not having it showed just how important work life is. It is entirely possible to build this meaning and connection remotely, but that requires skill and intentional practice which wasn't being modeled or supported by the new interim leadership."

18. **Vulnerable.** This category identifies people who are liable to exposure (Couser, 2018), which in this instance is literal. The chapters here describe people living in fear. Accordingly, "vulnerability" refers to the potential for harm, not to actual harm that has occurred. The concept of vulnerability is an encouraging and different way of addressing inequities present in modern life (Malgieri & Niklas, 2020). Examples of vulnerability using the inequity definition include Rahul Mitra and his co-authors in Chap. 16 and also Kee in Chap. 20, who fears that his best professional and intellectual effort will be met with racism against his yellow skin. Vulnerability from exposure includes Stephens in Chap. 5. She recalls: "As soon as my daughter returned to Chicago her classes were converted to being online. More people were dying every day, and I was scared to death she would get COVID-19 and I could not travel to be with her if she needed help recovering. I was working as many hours as I could to keep my mind off my concern for my daughter. She started calling regularly and I could hear in her voice that she was literally scared for her life and for the lives of those around her." Westerberg, in Chap. 6, comments: "When Norway closed down and the Norwegian government stated that they were to implement the 'most invasive measures in peace time' I didn't know what to do. What was this? Were we at war? I felt like I was running right in front of a tsunami that was about to swallow us all." Aguilar and Ballard in Chap. 17 comment about their uncertainty: "The information flow was overwhelming, yet the knowledge about what was happening seemed limited." These examples of being at risk, of not knowing the conditions we were in, permeate the chapters.

Conclusion

Our chapter writers accepted the invitation to write as they pleased in responding to the questions in Chap. 1. Some chapter writers decided to answer all of the questions; others were selective and drilled down on a few key features of the coronavirus story. Still others analyzed organizational-communication technology exclusively. We employed a wide latitude of acceptance for what counted as a contribution to ethnography. Some writers joined the project because the queries in the prospectus were compelling; some saw the breadth of the invitation to self-organize their response—knowing they'd have more to say in their later publications (see Synergy category). Still others took the queries as a chance to do strategic narrative planning, to set a course for a personal narrative. The chapters show that operating from the same instructions produced a varied response; we demonstrate this by noting their integrated complexity—the features that make them different in this analysis. "Integrative complexity" denotes the number of identifiable differences within the data and the uncertainty of the meaning of each of them. Integration amounts to the links that can be drawn among the data set. Where are the ties that bind the complexities? Our answer here: organizational-communication technology.

Our strategy for summarizing the chapters of the book was to identify a prominent feature, then assign to it chapters with features like that. This iteration of the 18 categories includes a prime example of how the chapter fits the category. The 18-category analysis differs from the five sections of the introduction to the book. Chapter listings in the introduction are necessarily mutually exclusive. In this post-analysis, the sorting is based on the resulting chapter contents. Additional examples within the category showed how the category is evident in three to five other chapters in the book, which is the number grounded theory used for category density. The 18 categories are pervasive among the chapters of the book. The assignment of chapters to categories shows how examples fit in different contexts. Even though the grounded-theory categories are dense, with several examples in each category, they are not mutually exclusive. The same example from a chapter can fit in more than one category. The value of the examples of our overlapping data in codes allows us to thread single chapters through and across categories. The overlapping categories create a blurred distinction, another prism, through which to view the data. Categorical abstraction increases the overlap among the chapters in the analysis. For example, the techno-ethnographies are completely different from the ethnography chapters, yet the techno-ethnography chapters appear across a majority of the categories. The final step of the grounded-theory process is to complete another condensing of the data by organizing the 18 categories in a tighter set of codes called *axial codes,* which are "more abstract conceptual categories" (Scott & Medaugh, 2017, np). Here they are:

UNCERTAINTY. The axial uncertainty codes include *multiplicity* (different authors and different identities expressed by single authors are evident), i*dentity* (chapter writers locate who they are in relation to the perspective they are taking), *rhetoric* (chapter writers express stylistic differences within their texts), *autonomy* (the chapter writers speak for themselves without restrictions), chaos (the future is unpredictable and uncontrollable), utility (is rationality about what is anticipated?), and ventriloquism (who really is the puppet at the end of your arm?), and *vulnerability* (what might happen under these conditions of risk?).

STRUCTURE. The axial structural codes include: *constraints* (the limits placed on individuals as special requirements during the crisis), *autonomy* (taking local control is its own kind of structure), *adaptation* (responding to information establishes a pattern), *pedagogy* (teaching a class involves creating a particular kind of order), *procedure* (the platforms and steps taken comprise the procedure), *strategy* (the plans and practices used in response to the crisis), *sequence* (there is an order to the phases of response to the crisis), *communitarian* (acting in behalf of a future set of conditions), and *utility* (utility is about structured actions).

THE FUTURE. The future axial codes include: *autonomy* (the best response to uncertainty in the future depends on many independent actors organizing and enacting personal, individualistic responses), *procedures* (lists are the base of stability and provide the platforms for moving forward), *strategy* (what we do in the future depends on what they do), *chaotic* (the uncertainty we face in the crisis), *ante-narratological* (we are the players who toss in a bet on a future outcome), adaptable (we communicate remotely, apart, and electronically), *utility* is subjective (it is what is expected, what is hoped for, what is planned for; we can only know utility in the future), *communitarian* (it is about acting toward an outcome that we want to create; it is a desire to create a future memory).

To summarize the axial code analysis, showcasing uncertainty verifies the 70-year phase of organizational theory from 1950 to 2020. The central purpose of an organization is to reduce uncertainty—causing us to continually ask: What information do we have at hand and what does it mean? Our key concept, organizational-communication technology, exemplifies uncertainty even though, ironically, we depend on it for solutions. Organizational-communication technology is uncertain because it performs double duty. As Fulk (2017) notes, "organization structure and the communication of it is a cause and consequence" (p. 923). Organizational-communication technology is reflexive; its order is uncertain, thus it can be interpreted in different, even oppositional, ways, across organizational settings. Organizational-communication technology covers so much territory it risks being too definitionally pliable. It scales up from the individual, to the culture of a work group, to an organization (Orlikowski et al., 1995). It can be as local as a fist bump and as global as a common communication software.

Our options for uncertainty are either to live with the doubt it produces or to import structures to wrestle with uncertainty, which are exemplified by the axial categories of structure we offer here. By applying different communication structures—software, hardware, personal norms, and organizational rules through such convenient technologies as the laptop and the phone—we insert ourselves into our environments by defining them and acting upon them. If and when COVID is the problem, organizational-communication technology is the solution. The presumption is that meaning comes from action, and our chapter writers universally pursue action through structures, asking "What organizational-communication technologies can I apply?"

If these 18 categorical differences are examples of complexity, what is the integrator? The answer: organizational-communication technology—the organizational structures that we interface with technology. We do it with organizational-communication technology when we log in, email, or communicate, in some technical way, a specific message to a limited community, and then monitor and evaluate the responses we receive. This cycle continuously repeats itself.

References

Alterman, Richard. (1988). Adaptive planning. *Cognitive Science, 12*(3), 393–421.

Bakhtin, Mikel M. (1984). *Problems of Dostoevsky's poetics.* (Ed. and trans. Caryl Emerson). University of Minnesota Press.

Bateson, M. C. (1993). *Joint performance across cultures: Improvisation in a Persian garden.* London: Taylor and Francis.

Boje, David M. (Ed.). (2011). *Storytelling and the future of organizations: An antenarrative handbook* (Vol. 11). Routledge.

Botti, Simona, Orfali, Kristina, & Iyengar, Sheena Sethi. (2009). Tragic choices: Autonomy and emotional responses to medical decisions. *Journal of Consumer Research, 36*(3), 337–352.

Browning, L. D. (1992). Lists and stories as organizational communication. *Communication Theory, 2*, 281–302.

Browning, L. D., & Morris, G. H. (2012). *Stories Of life in the workplace: An open architecture for organizational narratology.* New York: Routledge.

Brummett, Barry. (2008). *A rhetoric of style.* Southern Illinois University Press.

Conrad, Charles, & Poole, Marshall Scott. (2010). *Strategic organizational communication in a global economy* (7th ed.). Wiley-Blackwell.

Conrad, Charles, & Poole, Marshall Scott. (2012). *Strategic organizational communication: In a global economy.* John Wiley & Sons.

Cooren, François. (2012). Communication theory at the center: Ventriloquism and the communicative constitution of reality. *Journal of Communication, 62*(1), 1–20.

Cooren, François, & Sandler, Sergeiy. (2014). Polyphony, ventriloquism, and constitution: In dialogue with Bakhtin. *Communication Theory, 24*(3), 225–244.

Couser, G. Thomas. (2018). *Vulnerable subjects: Ethics and life writing.* Cornell University Press.

Deleuze, Gilles, & Guattari, Felix. (1983). *Anti-oedipus: Capitalism and schizophrenia.* University of Minnesota Press.

DeSanctis, Gerardine, & Poole, Marshall Scott. (1994). Capturing the complexity in advanced technology use: Adaptive structuration theory. *Organization Science, 5*(2), 121–147.

Dillard, C., Browning, L. D., Sitkin, S., & Sutcliffe, K. (2000). Impression management and the use of procedures at the Ritz-Carlton: Moral standards and dramaturgical discipline. *Communication Studies, 51*, 404–414.

Etzioni, Amital. (1996). The responsive community: A communitarian perspective. *American Sociological Review*, 1–11.

Fulk, J. (2017). Social construction of communication technology. *Academy of Management Journal, 36*(5), 921–950.

Gabriel, Yiannis. (2004). Narratives, stories, texts. In D. Grant, C. Hardy, C. Oswick, & L. L. Putnam (Eds.), *The Sage handbook of organizational discourse* (pp. 61–79). Sage.

Garcia Contreras, Angel F., Ceberio, Matine, & Kreinovich, Vladik. (2020). Plans are worthless but planning is everything: A theoretical explanation of Eisenhower's observation. In *Decision making under constraints* (pp. 93–98). Springer.

Goffman, E. (1959). *The presentation of self in everyday life*. Garden City, NY, Anchor books.

Gresov, Chistopher, & Drazin, Robert. (1997). Equifinality: Functional equivalence in organization design. *Academy of Management Review, 22*(2), 403–428.

Lomi, A., & Harrison, J. R. (2012). *The garbage can model of organizational choice: Looking forward at forty*. Emerald Group Publishing Limited.

Lynch Jr., John G., & Cohen, Jerry L. (1978). The use of subjective expected utility theory as an aid to understanding variables that influence helping behavior. *Journal of Personality and Social Psychology, 36*(10), 1138–1161.

Malgieri, Gianclaudio, & Niklas, Jędrzej. (2020). Vulnerable data subjects. *Computer Law & Security Review, 37*, 105415.

March, James G. (1981). Footnotes to organizational change. *Administrative Science Quarterly, 26*(4), 563–577.

Mitchell, Sandra D. (2003). *Biological complexity and integrative pluralism*. University Press.

Orlikowski, Wanda J., Yates, Jo Anne, Okamura, Kazou, & Fujimoto, Masayo. (1995). Shaping electronic communication: The metastructuring of technology in the context of use. *Organization Science, 6*(4), 423–444.

Park, Guihyun, & DeShon, Rirchard P. (2018). Effects of group-discussion integrative complexity on intergroup relations in a social dilemma. *Organizational Behavior and Human Decision Processes, 146*, 62–75.

Pentland, Brian T. B. T., Hærem, Thorvald, & Hillison, Derek. (2010). Comparing organizational routines as recurrent patterns of action. *Organization Studies, 31*(7), 917–940.

Polster, Erving. (1987). *Every person's life is worth a novel*. WW Norton.

Sahlin, Nils-Eric. (2019). The ontology of decision-making. In Tobias Hansson Wahlberg & Robin Stenwall (Eds.), *Maurinian truths: Essays in honour of Anna-Sofia Maurin on her 50th birthday*. https://lup.lub.lu.se/record/35448559-6bf9-4974-8663-ee04ff83a679

Scott, Craig, & Medaugh, Melissa. (2017). Axial coding. *The international encyclopedia of communication research methods*.

Selznick, Philip. (1987). The idea of a communitarian morality. *California Law Review, 75*, 445–463.

Sinha, K., Suh, E. S., & de Weck, O. (2017). Correlating integrative complexity with system modularity. In *International design engineering technical confer-*

ences and computers and information in engineering conference. American Society of Mechanical Engineers.
Treem, J., & Browning, L. (2017). Grounded theory. In C. Scott & L. Lewis (Eds.), *The international encyclopedia of organizational communication*. Wiley.
Weick, K. E., & Sutcliffe, K. M. (2011). *Managing the unexpected: Resilient performance in an age of uncertainty* (Vol. 8). John Wiley & Sons.
Wildavsky, Aaron. (1973). If planning is everything, maybe it's nothing. *Policy Sciences, 4*, 127–153.

Index[1]

[1] Note: Page numbers followed by 'n' refer to notes.

L. D. Browning et al. (eds.), *Organizational Communication and Technology in the Time of Coronavirus*,
https://doi.org/10.1007/978-3-030-94814-6

F

M

N

Z

FSC
www.fsc.org
MIX
Papier | Fördert gute Waldnutzung
FSC® C083411

Kolibri 360 GmbH
Ferdinand-Jühlke-Straße 7
99095 Erfurt, Deutschland
produktsicherheit@kolibri360.de